ENGELMANN'S DIRECT INSTRUCTION: SELECTED WRITINGS FROM THE PAST HALF CENTURY

Edited by Timothy W. Wood

Design and Marketing Editor: Christina Cox

Design: Beth Wood Design

Engelmann's Direct Instruction: Selected Writings from the Past Half Century

Edited by Timothy W. Wood

Copyright © 2014 by NIFDI Press
   A division of the National Institute for Direct Instruction
   805 Lincoln Street
   Eugene, Oregon 97401-2810
   USA

All rights reserved. No part of the work covered by this copyright hereon may be reproduced or used in any form or by any means – graphic, electronic, or mechanical, including photocopying, recording, taping, or information storage and retrieval systems – without the written permission of the publisher.

Printed in the United States of America

1 2 3 4 5 6

Library of Congress
Cataloging-in-Publication Data
Wood, Timothy W.
   Engelmann's Direct Instruction: Selected Writings from the Past Half Century
   Includes bibliographical references and index.
ISBN 978-1-939851-03-1

CONTENTS

    Page

Introduction   1
Timothy W. Wood

Section I: Theoretical Understandings of Learning and Instruction   7

1. The Structuring of Language Processes as a Tool for Thought (1966)
   Siegfried Engelmann   11

2. Teaching Reading to Children with Low Mental Ages (1967)
   Siegfried Engelmann   27

3. Does the Piagetian Approach Imply Instruction? (1971)
   Siegfried E. Engelmann   43

4. Diagnosing Instruction (1979)
   Siegfried Engelmann, Alex Granzin, & Herbert Severson   57

5. Student-Program Alignment and Teaching to Mastery (1999)
   Siegfried Engelmann   73

Section II: Developing Effective Curricular Material   111

6. An Academically Oriented Pre-school for Culturally Deprived Children (1966)
   Carl Bereiter, Siegfried Engelmann, Jean Osborn, & Philip A. Reidford   115

7. Tactual Hearing Experiment with Deaf and Hearing Subjects (1975)
   Siegfried Engelmann & Robert Rosov   145

8. Direct Instruction Outcomes with Middle-Class Second Graders (1982)
   Siegfried Engelmann & Doug Carnine   167

9. DI for Severely Handicapped Learners (1983)
   George Singer, Dan Close, Geoff Colvin, & Siegfried Engelmann   177

10. Video Disk Instruction (1984-1985)
    Douglas Carnine, Siegfried Engelmann, & Alan Hofmeister   187

11. Teaching Absolute Pitch (1989)
    Paul Williams & Siegfried Engelmann   195

12. Sponsor Findings from Project Follow Through (1996)
    Wesley C. Becker & Siegfried Engelmann   207

Section III: Promoting Reform and Change in Education   225

13. A Study of 4th – 6th Grade Basal Reading Series: How Much Do They Teach? (1982)
    Ziggy Engelmann   231

14. Engelmann Compares Traditional Basals with SRA's New *Reading Mastery 3 & 4* (1983)
    Siegfried Engelmann   249

15. The Logic and Facts of Effective Supervision (1988)
    Siegfried Engelmann   273

16. Change Schools Through Revolution, Not Evolution (1991)
    Siegfried Engelmann   293

17. Socrates on Teacher Training (2009)
    Siegfried Engelmann   307

18. Socrates on Program Adoptions (2012)
    Siegfried Engelmann   325

19. Socrates on Gold Standard Experiments (2013)
    Siegfried Engelmann   337

Section IV: Responding to Criticisms and Roadblocks   353

20. Response to "The High/Scope Preschool Curriculum Comparison Study Through Age 23" (1999)
    Siegfried Engelmann   357

21. The Dalmatian and Its Spots: Why Research-Based Recommendations Fail Logic 101 (2004)
    Siegfried Engelmann   371

22. Chapter One, *Data Be Damned* (2004)
    Siegfried Engelmann   379

23. Professional Standards in Education (2004)
    Siegfried Engelmann   397

24. The Dreaded Standards (2010)
    Siegfried Engelmann   413

Appendices
Timothy W. Wood

    A. Direct Instruction Programs Authored by Engelmann, 1969 to 2014   423

B. Articles, Chapters, and Books Authored by Engelmann,
   1966 to mid-2014   435

C. Trends in Engelmann's Writing Career, 1966 to 2014   445

D. A Chronology of Engelmann's Career Highlights   449

Author Biographies   453

Acknowledgments   456

Subject Index   457

Name Index   464

INTRODUCTION
Timothy W. Wood

Siegfried "Zig" Engelmann is a maverick in the field of education who has dedicated his life to helping all children succeed. Beginning in the 1960s, Engelmann conducted research on learning and the most effective and efficient methods of teaching. From this work, he developed the philosophy that if a child fails to learn, it is not the fault of the student, but rather the instruction. The highly successful Direct Instruction model that he developed—and for which he is best known—is based on this tenet. He has shown that *all* children can have academic success and become self-confident learners if they are properly taught. Engelmann has become a significant influence on the world of education over the past 50 years. His influence can be seen in the vast number of his publications over that time, and this book contains some of those works.

The publications in this book were chosen to represent his entire career, the varying topics he has covered, and his unique insight into the problems that have plagued the world of education. This collection of writings demonstrates Engelmann's wide ranging influence and effect on the field of education. In selecting the articles for this book, special consideration was given to publications that have not previously been widely distributed, but are crucial to understanding the development and evolution of Engelmann's career. They demonstrate Engelmann's wide ranging influence on the field of education. They were selected from a total of 142 publications completed between 1966 and 2014 and which originally appeared in journals, in books, and on Engelmann's website zigsite.com. Each article was specifically chosen to represent the breadth of Engelmann's career by showcasing four key themes of his writing over the years: his theoretical understandings of learning and instruction, the development of the highly effective Direct Instruction (DI) curricular material, promoting reform and change in education, and responding to criticism and roadblocks.

Engelmann's educational career began with the creation of the Bereiter-Engelmann preschool in 1964. In this setting, he refined his understandings of how children learn and the importance of carefully designed, explicit, and efficient instruction – instruction that involved only clear and unambiguous communications. This work also led to the development of the DISTAR curricular programs. (DISTAR is an acronym for Direct Instruction System for Teaching and Remediation.)

Over the next five decades, the Direct Instruction corpus of curricula expanded as Engelmann designed dozens of instructional programs that embodied the principles of his philosophy of learning. He developed programs in reading, language, math, writing, social studies, history, and science. Engelmann continued to revise these programs to improve their effectiveness and efficiency and in response to new state standards and requirements.

Engelmann developed his understanding of how children learn by applying a scientific approach to his pursuit. He analyzed every aspect of the process of learning a given subject and how all variables involved in the process were interrelated and needed to be accounted for and controlled in order for the child to succeed. He furthered his understanding of the critical relationship between how he instructed children in terms of wording, set of examples, sequencing of examples, and what they learned. He also learned the importance of appropriate placement of students, assigning them within a given program based on their level of skill, preventing them from being presented information they were not adequately prepared to comprehend and to master or material that would be too easy and a waste of time. Engelmann determined, as no one had before, that the placement of the student, the assignment of an appropriate program, and the communication between teacher and student were all essential to the success of the student. No single element could succeed without the careful coordination and execution of the others.

The first section of this book includes articles related to Engelmann's theoretical understanding of learning and instruction and his core belief that all children can learn when given proper instruction. Most of these articles were written in the earlier part of his career as he was formulating his understandings of learning and instruction. The articles included examine areas as diverse as the importance of teaching language skills to at-risk students (Chapter 1); the role of mastery learning in supporting student success and self-confidence (Chapter 5); focusing on problems with instruction, rather than with students, when diagnosing learning problems (Chapter 4); and why the often cited theories of Jean Piaget are not supported by empirical evidence (Chapter 3).

Articles in the second section of the book demonstrate the power of Engelmann's approach. They summarize the extraordinary accomplishments of students in the Engelmann-Bereiter preschool in the 1960s (Chapter 6), those in Project Follow Through in the 1970s (Chapter 12), middle class students (Chapter 8), and the severely handicapped (Chapter 9). They also describe the application of DI principles to less traditional modes of instruction with the use of video-disks (Chapter 10), tactual vocoders (Chapter 7), and to rarely studied subject matter with the teaching of absolute pitch (Chapter 11). Thus, these articles provide a glimpse of the power, strength, and versatility of Engelmann's understandings and the Direct Instruction programs.

As Engelmann worked with schools throughout the country, he realized that students' success is not only affected by the actions and decisions made within the classroom. Instead, the entire world of education, the entire system within which children learn, influences their education. Beginning with his work at the Bereiter-Engelmann preschool, Engelmann determined that preschools needed to be academically oriented in order to better prepare the children for their entrance into primary education and future success. In later years, he investigated the influence of the organization of schools, the policies and standards they operate under, colleges of education, and education researchers. All of these entities play important roles in the education of children. Engelmann concluded that the educational system and the actions of powerful decision makers from the national to the local level were holding students back and preventing the realization of high student success that could be attained. The education of children could be improved by changing the educational system.

The third section of this book gives selections of Engelmann's writings related to this area. Some of the articles analyze the problems with traditional curricular approaches and describe how schools could improve supervision of teachers (Chapters 13, 14, and 15). Others take a broader view, urging large scale changes in the organization of schools and critiquing teacher training, publishing policies, and educational research (Chapters 16, 17, 18, and 19).

Engelmann's research and theories on instruction were often not well received in the academic circles of education and psychology, despite their demonstrated success. Throughout his career, Engelmann has faced criticisms and backlash from the educational establishment. His response to these criticisms has been as systematic and thorough as his development of the Direct Instruction programs. The fourth section of this book includes examples of these works. They range from a response to a flawed analysis of the impact of Direct Instruction (Chapter 20) to critiques of educational research (Chapter 21) to analyses of the problems in educational policies (Chapters 22, 23, and 24).

Appendix A lists all of the programs he has developed from 1969 to 2014. Appendix B lists all of Engelmann's published articles and books through mid-2014. Appendix C provides a series of graphs that summarize the trajectory of his publications throughout his career. This analysis illustrates the significant amount of work created over time, as well as trends in the topics addressed. Appendix D provides a brief chronology of Engelmann's career.

Of course, no collection of articles can capture the entirety of a publication record such as Engelmann's. For instance, none of the selections address the vast corpus of curricular material that Engelmann has developed throughout his career. In addition, none of the selections involves Engelmann's highly technical theoretical writings such as the widely acclaimed *Theory of Instruction*. Given the vast scope of Engelmann's career, scholars will no doubt be examining his writings for decades to come.

Engelmann's broad understanding of learning and the world of education, coupled with his passion to help all children succeed, has led to the development of highly effective curricular programs, a well-developed and insightful philosophy of learning and instruction, extensive proposals to transform the structure of schools and the policies that govern them, and well developed defenses of Direct Instruction against unfounded criticisms. His dedication and passion for education, the work he has produced, and his determination to improve the world of education is unmatched.

Engelmann has been a significant influence on education over the past half century. The world and lives of millions of students are no doubt much more greatly enriched as a result of his efforts than they would otherwise have been. Conducting research on how children learn for 50 years, Engelmann has created an extraordinary collection of instructional programs, research, analyses, and musings on the world of education. Engelmann's unique understanding of learning and ability to analyze, synthesize, and communicate this information is unmatched. His analyses of problems with schools and the failures of the educational system reflect unparalleled insights as well as an undying passion for helping children succeed. The publications selected for this book provide a glimpse into the wealth of knowledge he has accrued and shared over his career.

SECTION I

THEORETICAL UNDERSTANDINGS OF LEARNING AND INSTRUCTION

Engelmann's initial exposure to learning and instruction was not in the classroom as a teacher, but rather while working as a marketing director for an advertising agency in the 1960s. He was given the task of determining how many exposures it would take for children to recognize or remember slogans presented on TV. Engelmann researched techniques for marketing to children in order to determine what type of input was necessary to induce retention, but found no answers. This discovery led him to begin studying different approaches to instructing children, eventually using his three sons as participants. Through these experiments, he developed his own techniques for teaching children and the basis for what would become the Direct Instruction programs. Perhaps most importantly, through these experiments, Engelmann realized the relationship between what his sons learned and how he instructed them. This realization and the recognition of the lack of published research on the theoretical understanding of learning and instruction inspired him to pursue a career in education.

Engelmann's involvement in the field of education began with the creation of the Bereiter-Engelmann preschool in 1964 and the development of instructional programs for its at-risk students. Engelmann's work at the preschool strengthened his theoretical and practical understanding of how to effectively present instruction. The gains made by the preschoolers in reading, language, and math were extraordinary and brought Engelmann's ideas to the attention of the world of education. As the preschool program progressed, Engelmann became more convinced that a child's acquisition of knowledge and development of skills depends on the clarity of instruction. With this understanding of how children learn, Engelmann conducted studies to demonstrate the validity of his philosophy and techniques. He explained the inherent challenges of instruction and described his personal experiences in designing instructional programs and administering them.

Engelmann's earliest publications, in the mid-1960s, discuss his philosophy of instruction, its application in effective instructional programs, and the difficulties in implementing these programs. His philosophy of learning was unmatched at the time and stood on the frontier of a new field of study. Engelmann believed it was necessary to justify the rationale behind the philosophy, but equally important was to demonstrate its effectiveness. To do so, he discussed his experiments of teaching techniques for at-risk children and his first-hand observations of how they received and interpreted instruction. In these experiments, he specifically sought to determine how children learn, how to instruct them most effectively and efficiently, and how appropriate instruction differs for children of different backgrounds and skills. Engelmann utilized scientific methods to analyze each variable of instruction to determine the most effective and efficient approach for each student.

Through his experiences of working directly with children, Engelmann determined that, in comparison to their more affluent peers, at-risk students had a deficit in language skills, which hindered their learning rate. This lack of language skills made the acquisition of reading skills more difficult, so Engelmann began focusing on developing language and reading skills in tandem. This research solidified Engelmann's theory that students' acquisition of knowledge and development of skills depends on the teacher's appropriate instruction, which needs to be adjusted based on the child's skill level. A teacher must recognize and understand the students' skills and what type of instruction they need to progress and acquire new skills in the most effective and efficient manner. This would allow them to become confident and successful students. He concluded that the success of students depends on the use of appropriate academic curriculum, the proper placement of students into classrooms in terms of their skill level, and adequate instruction from teachers.

The publications in this section were selected to cover the development of Engelmann's philosophy of learning, how it evolved, and how it served as the inspiration and basis for the design of his instructional programs. They also demonstrate the broad application of the principles behind his philosophy. The chapters that follow focus on topics ranging from the importance of specific instruction in language (Chapter 1) and teaching reading to children with intellectual disabilities (Chapter 2), to flaws in the theories of Piaget (Chapter 3), how teachers should diagnose learning problems by focusing on problems with instruction rather than the student (Chapter 4), and the importance of teaching to mastery (Chapter 5). Engelmann's publications not only promote the theories and the programs he developed, but also demonstrate the flaws in other academic programs and how they are not as effective and efficient as the programs he designed. By comparing the varying techniques and approaches to instruction, Engelmann shows why his techniques succeed when others fail. This in-depth analysis of instruction legitimized Engelmann's theories, but it also helped bring light to a new area of study, to increase attention on the world of education, and to propose scientifically sound ideas on how it could be improved.

CHAPTER 1

Through his work with at-risk students at the Bereiter-Engelmann preschool, Engelmann identified how children's instruction should be based on their skill level, not necessarily their age or grade level. His experiences at the preschool revealed how traditional instruction did not produce the same results for at-risk students as their more affluent peers, precisely because they entered preschool with very different skills levels, especially in language development. Avoiding placing blame on the students' abilities, Engelmann determined the instruction for at-risk students had failed. These at-risk students required instruction based on their already established skills and building upon this pre-existing knowledge.

Through his interactions with these students, Engelmann realized the importance of language skills in the process of a child's learning, and how teachers must adapt teaching strategies to fit students' particular language skills in order to improve communication and retention of information. He stressed that a language instruction program must be more than a vocal-auditory program. Instead, it needed to be a conceptual program, because basic language must be taught simultaneously with its content. Communication and mastery of content is essential for students to understand concepts and be able to build upon those concepts and skills.

With this understanding of how at-risk students needed instruction tailor fitted for their skill set, Engelmann developed an approach to communicate more effectively and help at-risk students achieve the same level of success as their more affluent peers. Attempting to create greater equality among all students, Engelmann established a blueprint for structuring language as a tool of thought, giving teachers clearer guidelines for instruction. This blueprint would help teachers recognize their students' skills and how to properly remediate skill deficits. This early publication marked the beginning of Engelmann's exploration and promotion of understanding learning and instruction. The ideas and concepts in this article resonate through his future publications.

THE STRUCTURING OF LANGUAGE PROCESSES AS A TOOL FOR THOUGHT (1966)*

Siegfried Engelmann

The teacher needs a standard that will tell her what to teach the child who does not exhibit adequate language skills. The teacher needs a standard that will serve as a criterion for selecting tasks, for rejecting them, for teaching something one way and not another. Unfortunately, the different explanations of language that are currently in favor in psychology and education do not provide the needed standard. They tell the teacher about language as a system as "process," as a mediator, but she is concerned with language as content. She deals only in content. The only possible way she can alter the behavior of a child is by controlling the content of his experiences. Her contact with processes and mediators must occur through content—and only through content.

To derive the kind of standard the teacher needs, we must adopt a strategy that is theoretically consistent, which involves forgetting about linguistics, psycholinguistics, verbal mediators and the other standards that are obviously incapable of generating specific content. Before we can do a comprehensive job of structuring language as a tool for thought, we must proceed very carefully from the very obvious to the less obvious, taking the following steps:

1. We begin by treating language as a *behavior*, as something that children use; no prejudgment is made about the kind of behavior that should be considered. The judgment is based on our observations of the consistency and range of the language behavior children actually exhibit.

2. We then draw inferences about the cognitive structure the language-knowledgeable child must have, basing these inferences on the child's consistency and range of language

---

* Engelmann, S. (1966). The structuring of language processes as a tool for thought. In D. Kestel (Ed.), *National Catholic Educational Association bulletin: Curriculum for renewal, 63*(1), 459–468. Reprinted with permission of the publisher.

behavior and on the behavioral requirements imposed by the conventional concepts he has mastered.

3. We demonstrate the relationship between language and non-language behavior, with the emphasis on how language is related to other forms of behavior and ultimately to observations of reality.
4. Finally we clarify the role of diagnosis and remediation, in a way that is consistent with the characteristics of language and in a way that will give the teacher the guidelines she needs.

LANGUAGE AS A BEHAVIOR

This is our first step, and probably the most difficult one we will have to take. We must map the territory occupied by language. The big danger is that of following the trails indicated on old maps instead of putting down what we actually see. If language consists of nothing more than grammar, we would teach language accordingly. But are language and grammar coextensive? Is language somehow divorced from reality? Do we expect a child to use language only as grammar? Do we expect him to use language as a tool of thought?

To help evaluate the role of language in behavior, we can draw inferences from the language-wise child's *behavioral consistency*. The child is consistent when he uses the same response in different situations. But if the same response is to be produced consistently, there must be something that is the same about the presentations to which he responds. If there is nothing that is the same, there is no possibility that he can consistently treat them as if they are the same. We can vary the presentations to which he responds, isolate the objective sameness to which he is reacting, and infer the nature of the behavior rule he is using when he responds to a given word or statement. For example, we can ask the language-wise child to tell us whether each of the objects we present is a chair. We can then present various objects, and we can systematically determine which characteristics of chair must be present before he indicates that an object is a chair. We can vary the size of the objects, the features, the color, and so on.

All of the objects he calls *chair* must have something in common. Since he uses the same response (*chair*) for each, each must be the same as the others in some respect. But the only sameness shared by all of the objects he identifies as *chair* is that: (1) all have backs; (2) all are designed to accommodate one person; (3) all are designed to accommodate the person in a conventional sitting position.

These are the characteristics to which the child is reacting. He is not simply reacting to retinal stimuli. He is not simply associating the word *chair* with some concrete thing, nor does his image of the word *chair* have anything to do with color, texture, fabric, number of legs, presence of arms, or position. The rule that he uses for identifying chairs according to his behavioral consistency is that chair equals back, plus conventional sitting position, plus one-person limit.

Just as the child learns a behavioral "definition" of *chair*, he learns similar definitions for all of the concepts with which he deals. He learns that *red* is something that can attach to any physical object, that *red* is independent of the kind of object, the shape, the texture, the position, and so on. He learns the behavioral definition of *red*. He learns that *bigger* can be used to describe any physical object, that it is independent of shape, color, position, and so on, but that it involves some kind of spatial comparison with at least one other object (which is smaller). Again he learns the rules, and again we can demonstrate that the language-wise child has learned the rules.

Unless a child learns the basic definitional meaning of a concept, he will not be able to perform in the manner that is expected of him. The child will confuse couches with chairs if his behavioral rule does not alert him to the one-person limit placed on chairs. He will confuse chairs with beds if his rule does not contain a "sitting position" clause. He will confuse chairs with hassocks and stools if his rule does not contain a note about the back. Similarly, he will make terrible mistakes in identifying colors if his rule does not make it clear that color is independent of balls, or blocks or teddy bears.

The idea that the language-wise child is running around with a number of definitions in his head certainly runs contrary to traditional explanations. These rules are theoretically necessary, however, because we present tasks that are insoluble unless the child is capable of learning the appropriate rules. For example, we indicate that a certain object is to be called by the following names: *boy, child, human, Caucasian*. We expect the child to use these words correctly, a task which is impossible if he simply associates the words with objects, because the object is the same in all cases. Criteria of usage are therefore needed to resolve the ambiguity. The child must discover the appropriate characteristics that go with the various words. What are the shared characteristics that come into play when the word *boy* is used? What is the same about all situations in which the word *child* is used? What is the common characteristic of all *human* situations? Unless the child learns the appropriate defining characteristics for each word, he is in trouble, and his trouble will most certainly be reflected in his behavior. Conversely, if he learns to use the words properly—understanding that all boys are children, but not all children are boys, and that all children are humans, but not all humans are children—we can infer that somehow he has incorporated the appropriate definitional rules.

THE BEHAVIORAL REQUIREMENTS ON CONVENTIONAL CONCEPTS

A task imposes certain behavioral requirements on the child's performance. It presents a kind of "find the rule" game. This rule is always objective. It is observable as a critical sameness that is shared by some situations and not by others. Since we require all children to learn the same basic vocabulary and same basic language skills, we impose the same conventional rules on all children. This point is extremely important. The sub-realistic approach adopted by some educators treats concept acquisition as a matter of individual preference, a matter of "style." But obviously we impose many universal standards of behavior on all children, and we demand absolute conformity in the form of conventional responses. All children are required to learn such concepts as *red, on, chair,* and so on. There is a great deal to be learned about each of these concepts, but all children *must* learn—in addition to whatever else they learn—the basic rule about the defining characteristics. For many basic concepts, the defining characteristics represent the only shared sameness, the only possible basis of behavioral consistency. If the child has not learned to attend to these, he has not learned the concept at all—regardless of the amount of specific concrete information he has acquired. He has the frosting without the cake.

The mentally retarded child as well as the gifted child must respond the same way when asked to "Hand me all of the balls." We do not have one set of standards for the gifted child and another set for the retarded child. We do not indicate that the mentally retarded child is correct if he hands us all of the blue objects instead of all of the balls or if he hands us only some of the balls. We impose the same behavioral standards on both children.

The child's ability to learn language is sometimes explained in terms of a supposed language generalizing mechanism. This explanation palpably begs the question. Generalization is the act of using the same response in situations that are the same in some conceptual dimension. The child's consistent generalizations are based on the objective sameness of these situations and on the child's awareness of this sameness. Generalization is a part of initial learning. The child must know when to use the word *chair* and when not to. If he generalizes the verbal response *chair* to objects that are not chairs, couches, beds, stools, and so on—he uses the word in a way that is unacceptable. To use the word to refer to a certain segment of objects that should be called *chair* is to use the word in a way that is unacceptable. We say that the child has learned the word only when he exhibits the ability to generalize it in a manner that is consistent with the concept.

If the same response is called for in more than one situation, something has to be generalized.

THE SCOPE OF WHAT THE CHILD LEARNS ABOUT LANGUAGE

We present a child with a variety of simple objects, some of which are balls. We ask him to "Hand me all of the balls."

The task imposes certain minimum behavioral requirements on the child that can be seen as minimum essential steps:

1. He must consider all of the objects presented to him. If he considers only some of them, he may omit an object that is a ball.

2. He must apply the same criterion to each of the objects presented. The criterion must be the precise equivalent of the question, "Is this thing a ball?" If he uses one criterion for some of the objects and another criterion for other objects, his behavior will most likely be inconsistent. For example, if in the middle of the selection process he introduces the new criterion "Is this thing red?," he may hand the investigator things that are red that are not balls.

3. He must inspect the objects and answer the criterion question, "Is this thing a ball?," basing his answer on whether or not he detects the defining characteristics of ball in the object. He must conduct an exchange that is equivalent to this one: "Is this a ball? Does this thing have the characteristics of ballness? Yes, this thing does have the characteristics of ballness. So this thing is a ball." He must exclude those things that are not balls by using a variation of the same exchange: "Is this a ball? Does this thing have the characteristics of ballness? No, this thing does not have the characteristics of ballness. So this thing is not a ball." If he does not conduct such an exchange, he will not be assured of success. He must select on the basis of the concept *ball* as it is conventionally understood.

4. He must then treat those objects that are balls in one way and those things that are not balls in another. He must translate his "yes" response into one kind of behavior and his "no" response into another. If his inspection discloses that a candidate is a ball, he is to hand it to the investigator. The entire procedure: "Is this a ball? Does this thing have the characteristics of ballness? Yes, this thing does have the characteristics of ballness. So this thing is a ball. If it is a ball, I hand it to him. It is a ball, so I hand it to him."

All objects that are not balls receive a different treatment. "Is this thing a ball? Does this thing have the characteristics of ballness? No, this thing does not have the characteristics of ballness. So this thing is not a ball. If it is not a ball, I do not hand it to him. This is not a ball, so I will not hand it to him."

This simple language task demonstrates the role of language in thought. The language was given, and the child was forced to do something with it. He had to break the code, transform it into action, use it as a standard for evaluating the objects, use it as premise for drawing deductions about what he should do. The simple language task demonstrates that language is certainly not merely grammatical behavior, or vocabulary behavior, or psycholinguistic behavior. It is all of these plus action behavior that is consistent.

LANGUAGE TRUTH AND REALITY TRUTH

Since the content of what the child learns about language must have been learned from the experiences he has had, we are obligated to recognize that the normal child learns his complex language skills—all of them—through the experiences he has had. This point is very important. Specific content must come from the environment. But how are his experiences capable of teaching him the broad language skills he exhibits? In addition to his understanding of words, he understands the rules of statements. He understands that statements have parts, that the parts can be transplanted into other statements without losing their identity, that the meaning of the statement changes as the parts change, that declarative statements are somehow related to questions and to imperatives. Just as he understands the definitions imposed by individual words, he has somehow learned the meaning of statements.

Part of the conventional behavior demanded of the child by the "normal" environment is statement behavior. The child is required to learn how to use statements, which means he must learn the rules governing statement usage. For example, part of the behavior that is associated with the concept *in* has to do with *in* statements and how they are to be used. A child does not actually understand *in* unless he understands these statement conventions. If, for example, he does not know that when the ball is in the bucket, one cannot say, "The bucket is in the ball," he will make some serious mistakes. Children who do not learn adequate statement rules (the deaf and mentally retarded) sometimes make errors of this kind.

The child's experiences teach him about the statement rules by demonstrating that statements are based on familiar "truths" of physical reality. The child's experiences demonstrate that statements are basically tools that allow the child to express much of what he already knows. He will learn to use statements properly if their relation to what he observes is defined—which is usually done in the household of the normal child. In the household of the deaf and culturally disadvantaged child, the relations between reality and statement are not defined well, and the child often fails to handle statements in an acceptable manner.

The normal child learns that statements about reality direct his observation of reality. He learns that a statement of the type "That's a ..." tells him something about what is observable on the level of physical reality, and he learns that all statements of this type are analogous. He learns that statements of the form "No, that's not a ..." tell him that he has misclassified something, that he should attend to another observable dimension of reality. A series of conclusions follows from this rule:

1. If statements about reality direct observation of reality, the statement and the reality are the same in terms of the truth they convey. Therefore, statements can be treated as if they represent reality, as if they are true.

2. A statement can be used more efficiently than a reality presentation, because the statement is more precise and contains less extraneous cues. A presentation that corresponds to the statement "The ball is on the table" contains many extraneous relations and things which are pruned from the statement.

3. When all instances of a statement type that have been experienced direct observation of reality in the same way, instances that have not been experienced will direct it in the same way. For example, all instances of the statement type "The ... is on the ..." that have ever been experienced direct observation of reality in the same way: The ball is on the table; the cat is on the roof, the block is on the floor. All contain the same directions. Therefore, instances of this statement type that have not been experienced direct observation in the same way. "The cow is on the moon"—obviously, we have

never experienced this reality, yet we know what kind of relationship would be observed. The child learns how to generalize statement types when they direct the same observation of reality. When asked questions about the statement "The glerb is on the splim" (Where is the glerb? Is the glerb under the splim?), he answers in the same way he would answer questions asked about the statement "The ball is on the table." Since his responses are analogous, we can infer that he appreciates the manner in which the presentations are analogous.

4. When a given action leads to a certain reality presentation, the statement that expresses the action can be linked with a statement about the reality presentation. Both statements are part of the same experience. The action of putting the ball on the table always leads to the presentation of a ball on a table. The action can be put into words, "Put the ball on the table," and the reality presentation can be put into words, "The ball is on the table." These statements are related because the observations to which they refer are related. They are not arbitrary grammatical transformations. Grammar is not something that is divorced from reality. A child would not learn grammar unless the rules governing grammar were clearly defined in his experiences. They are. The child learns transformations from imperatives to declaratives to questions only because these transformations are observably related.

The fact that reality determines the nature of the transformation can be demonstrated by presenting the child with a problem of creating a presentation that can be achieved through more than one action. If reality determines the child's use of grammar, we would expect him to be able to produce more than one imperative. This is what happens. When the child is given the task of operating on a balance board to create the declarative "The left side is down," we find that he is capable of producing two imperatives: "Push down on the left side" and "Push up on the right side." When we give the child the task of creating the presentation that satisfies the declarative "The ball is over the chair," we find that he can create the presentation in two different ways and that he can express these ways with the two imperatives: "Put the ball over the chair" and "Put the chair under the ball."

The child learns a grammar that is consistent with his understanding of reality.

DIAGNOSIS AND REMEDIATION

We cannot hope to do a careful job of diagnosing difficulties related to language and of providing remedies if we do not understand what language is. If we suppose that language performance is somehow necessarily related to the properties of sound (as many educators of the deaf suppose), we will most certainly provide inadequate language remedies. If we suppose that the best way to teach language to the language-deficient child is to replicate those conditions under which the normal child learns language, we will not recognize that this child has an educational deficiency that is not shared by the normal child. If we do not acknowledge the ways in which the language-wise child uses language as a substitute for reality, we will run the risk of reducing language to mere vocabulary or of reducing it to some kind of linguistic "fit-fat-fut" exercise. If we do not recognize that the child learns content—rules—we may get caught up in aimless process training, when such training represents a theoretical ambiguity of the first order (since it is impossible to teach a process without introducing specific content and teaching specific rules).

We must limit any diagnoses of language difficulties that are to be used by the teacher to content considerations. These diagnoses must not go beyond a statement of what the child knows and what he does not know about language. Any other diagnosis (at this time) is presumptuous. (The diagnostician may base his diagnosis and prognosis of one child on "similar" cases, but this diagnosis is presumptuous if the similar cases have been treated in a traditional manner. The diagnosis suffers from a misuse of normative data. It is not based on studies in which concerted attempts were made to teach similar children what they must learn about language. To this extent, his diagnosis is presumptuous).

The usual language diagnosis is far less plausible than it actually seems. The diagnosis may indicate that the child is brain damaged, culturally deprived, or neurologically immature. These classifications seem reasonable. The diagnostician may then suggest a treatment that appears to be based on his diagnosis—give the child a more structured environment, more drill on basic skills of one kind or another. The trouble with this diagnostic procedure is that the remedy does not follow from the diagnosis. Before we can manipulate the environment, we must make the monumentally important acknowledgement that the environment to which the child has been exposed is inadequate. The environment, after all, is solely responsible for specific content. And unless we acknowledge that the environment is responsible for whatever specific content the child has learned, we are not justified in changing the environment.

The environmental assumption is necessary, but the rest of the diagnosis is not. In fact, it is pure conceptual noise. So long as we acknowledge the relative failure of the child's previous experiences to teach him conventionally defined rules, we can say anything we wish about the child. We can say, for instance, that he is a potential genius, that he is suffering from cerebral anoxia, that he has the "X" syndrome, or that he suffers from birth trauma. So long as we make the environmental assumption, we can do something for the child. But without this assumption we can do nothing. After we say that the child is brain damaged, we can nod intelligently and consider the matter closed. After we say that the child's psycholinguistic processes are inadequate, again the issue is closed. Nothing follows—no action, no remediation, no education. One must acknowledge that the environment has failed to teach these processes—whatever they may be—before any action follows.

When the environmental assumption is stated in a slightly different manner, it goes something like this: Regardless of what else is done for the child through so-called remediation programs, an attempt must be made to overcome the child's content deficit. Even after the child learns to creep, he must learn the various conventional concepts in which he is deficient. Even after he receives process training, he must learn about language and how to use it.

The diagnosis that goes beyond a statement of the child's educational deficiency (and the assumption that the child's environment is responsible for what the child has learned) is irrelevant to the educator. After the diagnosis has been offered, we can ask, "So what? Has the educational problem facing the child been changed by the diagnosis? No. Can we now alter our approaches in teaching him those skills in which he is deficient? No."

The diagnosis of the child's adequacy is not only irrelevant, but it distracts from the more central issues, which are: How do we structure the child's environment so that he learns the skills in which he is deficient? What is the most effective approach for teaching those skills that the child's previous experiences failed to teach him?

THE REMEDIATION PROGRAM

The language-structuring program that follows this general diagnosis-remediation orientation begins with an appraisal of the child's language behavior, not merely in terms of grammar, or syntax, but as much as possible in terms of the child's understanding of what language is, how the words function, how statements function as a substitute for reality presentations, how language is used in thinking.

We appraise his performance in various ways. Can he repeat simple statements? Can he answer questions that are inferred by simple statements? Can he carry out the actions that are implied by simple commands? Can he translate commands into actions? Can he classify objects according to the criteria that are provided by simple commands? Can he extract salient details from a reality presentation and express them in a way that will lead to conclusions? Does he have basic language knowledge that is necessary for him to learn more sophisticated concepts?

If the child's basic language behavior is inadequate, the child's previous environment is blamed. If our investigation tells us that the child failed to learn necessary content rules, we conclude that the only source of specific content is the environment; therefore, regardless of what we say about the child, the environment is inadequate and should be replaced by one that does the job.

1. The remedial environment attempts to teach the fewest possible elements so that the rote learning burden placed on the child is reduced. Accordingly, the program concentrates on teaching

a *basic presentational language*, which is adequate for the introduction of virtually any concept but contains a limited number of statement patterns and elements.

2. The program addresses itself to teaching the behavior implied by this basic presentational language. Tasks impose rules of behavior. The nature of these rules is made as obvious as possible. The steps are articulated. The child is shown precisely what he must do when asked to "Hand me the balls." He is shown that he must ask about each of the candidates, "Is this a ball?" He is shown how to go about answering the questions, "Look at it." Every behavioral step that is imposed by the task is spelled out. Non-verbal performance is carefully translated into verbal statements, and the child is required to produce these verbal statements whenever possible.

3. The program presents concepts so that appropriate generalization is encouraged. Concepts that are analogous are presented in a manner that articulates the area of analogy. All opposites are analogous in that all allow for certain conclusions. If something is not wet, it is dry. If it is not bigger, it is smaller. If it is not dirty, it is clean. The program articulates this analogous structure by teaching the various opposites as a unit, so that the child sees that analogous presentations and analogous statements apply to all opposites. Similarly, all classes of things that contain more than two elements are presented as a unit, so that the area of analogy is dramatized. Exceptions are ruled out during the initial presentation of any concept because these obscure the structure of the general rules the child must learn. Exceptions often help to reinforce the over-concrete orientation to language and corresponding reality.

4. The child's learning is systematically programmed according to the complexity of the concepts involved.

   a) The simplest language behavior is the point-and-say act of naming objects: Point–"Ball." To make this behavior completely formalized in the framework of language, the act of pointing must be verbalized, thereby creating basic statements: "This is a ball." The truth of this statement is clarified through the use of questions that are associated with the statement: "Is this a ball? ... This is a what?"

b) The next step up the conceptual ladder involves concepts that are related to the concepts that are learned through the point-and-say labeling process. The familiar object, ball, is now treated as big, round, red, rolling, and so on. The presentation of these second-order concepts is potentially confusing because the new concepts "reside" in objects that have already been named. Unless the teaching presentation clarifies the relationship between the familiar name and the new concept, great confusion may result. The most economical way to reduce ambiguity is through the introduction of a new statement form: "This ball is ...."

In this statement form, the identity of the familiar object is acknowledged; the relationship between the new concept and the familiar concept is therefore articulated. Note that the statement pattern is not introduced for any linguistic reasons but solely for pedagogical reasons. If there is a simpler way to teach the relationship, it definitely should be introduced.

c) Next, compound language tasks are introduced. These are tasks that involve two statements: "If I let go of it, it will fall." These tasks are more difficult because they involve behavior that is more complicated. The child who is given an *if-then* must understand how both parts translate into behavior.

The aim of the program is to teach the child as much as possible in the allotted time. Tasks are selected accordingly and judged accordingly. When it is possible to simplify a complex task, it is simplified. When it is possible to show the continuity of various concepts by pruning a few exceptions, the exceptions are pruned. When it is possible to teach one rule instead of three or four, the more economical approach is selected. When a task is an essential prerequisite to those that follow, however, the task is taught. It is presented in the simplest manner possible, but no attempt is made to reduce it beyond its conceptual limits. Basic skills—basic rules—must be learned through brute force, through rote learning, through many repetitions. These must be taught because other concepts rest on them.

The program that is designed to teach language is not simply a vocal-auditory program; it is a conceptual program, because basic language cannot be divorced from its content. The language behavior that is expected of the child is behavior that is generated from an understanding of what words and statements mean, of how they function as an extension of reality experiences. Nothing less than this is language behavior; therefore, the remediation program should aim at teaching nothing less.

CHAPTER 2

If a child fails to learn, it is not the fault of the child, but rather the failure of instruction. Based on this theory, Engelmann used a scientific approach to examine instruction, determine all of the relevant variables, and create the ideal conditions for maximizing the effectiveness and efficiency of instruction. In this article, Engelmann builds on his previous research to show how to help an underserved population succeed. He explores the reasons why traditional academic programs and instruction have failed students with what was then called "students with low mental ages" and what they need to succeed. Engelmann uses task analysis to break down all the different elements involved in learning to read and determine problem areas and procedures for solving them. He discusses the program used at the Bereiter-Engelmann preschool, its design and goals, and contrasts it to traditional programs. As with many of his other writings, Engelmann not only identifies problems in the world of education, he determines their cause, and provides a solution.

TEACHING READING TO CHILDREN WITH LOW MENTAL AGES (1967)*

Siegfried Engelmann

Little progress has been made in developing effective reading instruction for children with low mental ages, i.e., below six and one-half years. In fact, little progress has been made in developing effective approaches for school age children with average mental ages (MA's). Although the average child learns to read, he does not usually learn very quickly; some average children have extreme difficulties, although they are intelligent and seem to have the mental equipment necessary to read.

Why does this situation exist? The answer seems to be that the authors of reading programs have typically approached in an awkward way the problem of teaching children to read. They have worked with average children of about six and one-half years. These children are relatively sophisticated. They have a pretty good idea of what reading is and they know what they are supposed to do in a new learning situation. They know how to treat words as sounds and not merely as signals that convey content. They play word games; they rhyme and alliterate. They probably know letter names and have a fair idea of some letter sounds. These children are able to learn to read from a variety of approaches, so they are thus able to compensate for gaps in an instructional program. They often learn in spite of the program. If the program does not provide adequate instruction for a particular subskill such as rhyming or blending, the children usually learn anyhow.

When the author of a beginning reading approach works with such children, he cannot clearly see the relationship between the effectiveness of his program and the children's reading performance. He cannot clearly see which skills he has successfully taught, which

---

* Engelmann, S. (1967). Teaching reading to children with low mental ages. In F. E. McDowell (Ed.), *Education and training of the mentally retarded* (pp. 193-201). Washington, DC: Council for Exceptional Children. Reprinted with permission of the publisher.

skills were taught before the child began the program, and which were obliquely induced through instruction. In other words, the author cannot refer to the performance of the children after they have received the instruction and specify how much of it he is responsible for and how much of it is accounted for by home and previous training. Typically, he presumes that he is responsible for a great deal more than he deserves credit for. But since most of the children learn to read, it is difficult to discredit his presumption. For example, he may introduce exercises that are supposed to teach comprehension. He can refer to most of the children in the class who have received the instruction and note that they do comprehend. He may then conclude that his exercises were a success. But it is quite possible that these children would have comprehended well without the instruction he provided; it may be that their performance is not clearly a function of the instruction they have received. The author may justify readiness exercises in a similar manner, noting that the children who received the instruction are ready to read. However, much of the readiness training may be quite irrelevant to the problems associated with learning to read. If one provides a broad enough scope of tasks, one will undoubtedly hit upon some tasks that actually do prepare the child. In the process, however, one may provide many tasks that accomplish little.

When the author works with children who may have mastered skills that are necessary to read, there are relatively few checks on his imagination. He may identify skills that are basically irrelevant to the act of translating those clusters of squiggles on the printed page into word sounds, and he may fail to identify subskills that are crucial to the translation process. It might be difficult for us to demonstrate possible weaknesses in his problem for the simple reason that most of the children who receive instruction perform well. It can be pointed out that a certain number of children who receive the instruction do not perform well, but the author is not usually compelled to take responsibility for these children. These children can be viewed in two ways: as children who fail because they have not received adequate instruction, or as children who fail because they lack aptitude, readiness, or intelligence. By attributing their failure to a lack of aptitude rather than a lack of appropriate instruction, the author can write them off, maintaining that his program is designed for "average" children. There is a certain appeal to this argument. Children do vary in aptitude, as any teacher knows, and it seems reasonable that not all can learn from a given approach. The danger in this argument, however, is that it leaves the author unbridled. He is provided with a floating standard. If the children succeed, the program is responsible; if they fail, the children are responsible. The instruction is exonerated from all responsibility for failure. Obviously, this situation is not healthy and does not promote better instruction. Rather, it encourages post hoc justification of what happened, with no fixed standard against which to measure the effectiveness of various approaches.

There have been comparisons of different reading approaches, but such comparisons do not tell us precisely in what areas a given program is strong or weak, and they do not effectively discredit the approach that is relatively poor in comparison to others. The author of an approach that does not do well in comparative studies may contend that his program achieves objectives that are not measured or taken into consideration in the comparison, such as an appreciation of reading. The act of reading is so broad and involved that it may be difficult to demonstrate that he is mistaken.

SOLVING THE PROBLEM

To solve the problem of providing better reading instruction for children who may have trouble with traditional approaches (including preschool and mentally retarded children), we must identify the various trouble spots encountered by those children in learning to read. Obviously, we cannot do this by working with children who are more sophisticated than those with reading trouble, because more sophisticated children often do not encounter the severe difficulties that the children with less reading aptitude encounter. Therefore, children that are more sophisticated don't provide the kind of feedback that is necessary to identify the primary problems in learning to read. An analysis of the reading code provides important information about what is involved in reading, but it doesn't tell which skills are relatively difficult to learn and which are easy. The only way one discovers what the central problems are is to work with children who have low MA's. These children are ideal subjects for developing solid instructional approaches for these reasons: (a) they learn slowly, which means that the method developer can observe the problems they encounter in some detail; and (b) they probably have not learned or even partially learned the key subskills in reading outside of the instructional setting, which means that if they learn to handle a particular subskill, we can credit the instruction with their learning.

The method developer working with low MA children is less likely to use a floating standard, less likely to say that those children who fail lack aptitude. All of his subjects lack aptitude: therefore, he is in a better position to accept the idea that if the children fail, the instruction has failed, and if they learn, the instruction has succeeded. This attitude is potentially productive because it allows the method developer to look at each segment of reading behavior and see whether or not he can teach it. It is difficult to evaluate an approach by looking at it as a whole. An approach is more productively viewed as a series of components, each of which can be separately evaluated and subsequently improved. This kind of evaluation assumes that we clearly understand what the components are. The best way to find out is to work with the children who will tell us through their performance. The slow learning child does this. When he comes to a gap in instruction, he doesn't merely pause before working through the gap. He stops and he may remain stopped for weeks. His performance tells the curriculum designer when a technique works and when it doesn't work. The performance of the more sophisticated child does not.

A NEW READING PROGRAM

The reading program that we are currently using in the Bereiter-Engelmann preschool certainly does not represent the ultimate in reading instruction, but it is a good start. The program was developed by working with preschool children. Some were culturally deprived (with entering Stanford-Binet IQ scores of about 91); others were middle class children (with entering IQ scores of about 113); all four years old. After 48 hours of classroom instruction the culturally disadvantaged children read on the 1.25 grade level (Wide Range Achievement scores) and the middle class children read on the 2.3 grade level. Another group of disadvantaged children who received instruction for two school years read on the 2.6 grade level at the end of their kindergarten year. Not one child read below the 1.6 grade level, although some of these children wouldn't have been expected to read by the second or third grade if they had received traditional instruction.

While our work has been primarily focused on culturally disadvantaged children, it has implications for teaching reading to mentally retarded children for the following reasons:

1. Over one-third of the disadvantaged children we work with have entering IQ scores in the 80's, which place them on the fringe of the mentally handicapped.

2. Typically, IQ scores of four and five year old children who have IQ scores in the 80's will drop as the children get older, which means that these children are potentially mentally handicapped at age four.

3. The mental ages of these children are as low as many children in special classes. An eight year old child who has an IQ score of 75 has a mental age of six years. The initial mental age of the disadvantaged children we work with is less than four years. This means that many of the children we have taught to read have less knowledge of the world and fewer skills than children who do not learn to read in special classes.

4. The younger child is often more difficult to teach than the older child with the same mental age because the younger child is generally more difficult to motivate, has a shorter interest span, and knows less about the type of classroom behavior that is expected of him.

Thus the approach that we use should work with all children who have MA's of four and above, whether they are classified as mentally retarded, culturally deprived, or gifted children.

The method– Our motto in trying to work out a successful reading approach was simply to "keep the baloney out of the program." We did not analyze the reading code as the linguist or the educator typically analyzes it. We tried to determine what kind of behavior is demanded of the children, asking ourselves, "What must they be able to do?" Next, we tried to develop tasks to teach them the appropriate behavior. And finally, we tried to remain sensitive to the children's reaction to the presentations. If they stalled and failed to learn a skill such as blending, we tried to make the rule for blending more obvious so that the children could see more clearly what they were expected to do. If various approaches seemed to make little difference in the children's progress, we used the approach that seemed most economical and manageable, but we did not close the book on the issue. We recognized that it may be possible to supplant the drill with an approach that is far superior.

The children were taught in small groups, averaging about five children each. They were grouped homogeneously, according to performance in the classroom. The method of instruction demanded a great many responses from the children, so that the teacher received maximum feedback and the children received maximum corrected practice. Each daily reading period lasted from 15 to 20 minutes. The goal of instruction was to pack as much learning into these periods as possible.

We were particularly interested in identifying the places at which the children encountered difficulties. The first stumbling block encountered by our low MA children was in learning that the letters in a word stand for sounds that are sequenced in time. When a person says the word "Batman," some of the parts occur before other parts, and the order of the parts (or sound elements) is fixed. The word "manbat" or "tabman" are not the same as "Batman," because in these words, the order of parts has been violated. The instruction must therefore teach the naïve child (a) that the spoken word is composed of parts, (b) that the parts occur in a fixed order of time, and (c) that the reading code represents the passage of time through a left to right progression of symbols.

To teach the child to focus on parts of words, the teacher introduces rhyming and alliteration tasks. In rhyming, the child must hold part of the word constant –the ending–and vary the other part. "Okay, I want to hear some words that rhyme with superman.... Here's one: boo–perman. Here's another: foo–perman. And another: moo–..." To teach alliteration (in which the beginning part stays the same and the ending changes) the teacher says, "I want some words that start out the same way as SSSS-uper. Here's one: SSSS-ister. Another: SSSS-ee. Another SSSS-..."

If the child has not mastered rhyming and alliteration skills, he will probably have an extremely difficult time reading. Specifically, he'll have difficulty understanding how similar words are similar. Similar words are similar because part of one word is the same (makes the same sound) as a part of the others. If the child cannot hear the way in which "car" is the same as "far," he is not in a very good position to look for the sameness in the orthography of the two words.

To teach the children the rule for mapping the passing of time from left to right, the teacher begins by demonstrating how to sequence events from left to right. The teacher claps her hands together and follows this action by tapping herself on the head with one hand. "I'm doing it the right way," she says, and invites the children to do it with her, pausing between each trial. After the children have produced the pair of actions a number of items, the teacher says, "My turn. Watch me and tell me if I'm doing it the right way." She then produces the action either in the correct or the reverse order. "Did I do it the right way?" Not all the children will be able to see the difference. Some will insist that the sequence head tap-hand is the right way.

After the teacher has made the children aware of the right way using a variety of examples, she symbolizes the actions and presents them on the chalkboard from left to right. For the hand clap she uses this symbol: "----" (demonstrating how it is formed by holding her hands at the ends of the line and bringing them together in a clap); for the head tap, she introduces this symbol: "O." She draws an arrow on the board pointing from left to right. She claps her hands and makes the corresponding symbol at the tail of the arrow. "I'm drawing a picture of what I did." She then follows with the head tap, and makes the symbol for it near the head of the arrow. She asks the children to read what happened. "Start here and go with the arrow." After demonstrating how the code works, she presents a series of examples in which the children are asked to do what the symbols tell them to do. For example, she may present the following series and have the children read it and do what it says.

Figure 1 Sample Code Series

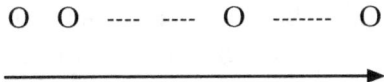

As the children become increasingly proficient in working with the code, she can introduce other symbols and introduce more difficult tasks, such as having a child symbolize a series of events that is produced either by the teacher or by another child.

As the children learn the rules for translating events that occur in time onto space, they are also introduced to the conventional sound symbols used in reading. Initially, the following sounds are presented: "ă," "ŏ," "e," "m," "f," "r," "s," and "n." There is no particular difficulty involved in teaching these. Young disadvantaged and retarded children learn the symbol slowly, but they succeed in time. The teacher should be careful not to overload the children by presenting too many examples. She must also be careful not to present the same objects unless she wants to induce mislearning. She must present many different examples of each letter, as it appears on cards and on the chalkboard in different colors and different sizes. All letters are presented as sounds; "a" is identified as the short "a" sound ("and"); "f" is the unvoiced sound that occurs at the beginning of words such as "fan."

These initial letters are selected not on the basis of frequency of occurrence or on the basis of linguistic considerations, but on the basis of specific difficulties the low MA child has in learning to read. Stated differently, they are selected because they allow for the most precise demonstration of the relationship between the unblended word and the blended word. Typically, the disadvantaged and the retarded child have trouble learning to blend. One can walk into virtually any third grade class for disadvantaged children and note many children making the same type of error. They can sound out a word such as "cat," saying "cu-ah-tu." But they cannot put the pieces together to form a word. When asked, "What word is that?" they either shrug or repeat, "ch-at-tu." Their failure to see the similarity between "cu-ah-tu," and "cat" is not without cause. The relationship between "cu-ah-tu," and "cat" is not particularly obvious. The parts of the unblended word are separated by pauses in time; the parts of the blended word are not. There are sounds in the unblended word that do not appear in the blended word. The relationship between blended and unblended words can be made more obvious by the following method:

First, the teacher introduces only those words that begin with a continuous sound, not a stop sound. Such words as "cat" are not introduced. Such words as "fan" and "ran" are introduced. Next, the teacher teaches the children to blend without pausing between letters. The child is taught the convention that one sound is held until the next one is produced. When the child attempts to sound out the word "ran," he says "rrraaannn." In this unblended word there are no pauses; there are no extra sounds. Its relationship to "ran" is therefore quite obvious.

After the child has learned to process simple two and three letter words composed of continuous sound letters, he is introduced to words that contain stop sounds. The stop sounds are first introduced at the end of three sound words—"rat," "rag," and "rab."

The stop sounds are then moved to the beginning. To demonstrate how they work, the teacher begins a series of familiar endings, such as: "an," "an," and "an." She introduces familiar continuous sound beginnings: "fan," "ran," and "man." She then erases these beginnings and introduces stop sound beginnings: "can," "gan," and "tan." Before attacking a word she calls attention to the vowel. "What does this say? Yes: ă. So this word is că –n." By calling attention to the vowel, the teacher allows the child to produce the sounds of the first and second letter together—"că" –thereby eliminating some of the difficulties associated with stop sounds.

The conventions introduced to demonstrate blending make a significant difference in the performance of the children.

The teacher next introduces a long vowel convention. A long line drawn over a vowel changes the sound to the letter names, "a," "e," "i," "o," and "u." The teacher proceeds quickly to exercises in which the children first sound out and identify a familiar word, such as "rat." The teacher then draws a line over the vowel, "rat," and the children sound out the new word, "rate."

The children now have a large enough repertoire of sounds to begin reading small stories. Initially, the teacher avoids any of the vowel sounds that have not been introduced (such as the vowel sounds in the words "all," "foil," etc.) and she avoids such combinations as "th" and "ch."

She limits herself to those sounds the child has learned and she spells all words phonetically. For example, she spells the word, "said" as "sed," and the word "have," hav." The following is an example of the kind of story the teacher might introduce:

A cat līks mēt.

Hē ēts mēt and he runs.

Hē has fun.

These stories familiarize the children with the conventions involved in moving from one line of text to the next.

The teacher then introduces new sound combinations—"th," "ch," "oo," "ee," "oi," and "oy"— and expands the scope of her stories.

The final step, which is actually taken in gradual stages starting when the children begin reading stories, is to introduce irregularly spelled words. These are presented as "funny words," that is, words that are spelled a sound at a time, the way any other word is spelled, but that are pronounced as if they were spelled differently. Handling irregulars in this way is extremely important. The child must learn that the spelling of words is not arbitrary. The word "have" is always spelled the same way; however, it is pronounced as if it were spelled differently, without the final "e." "It looks like 'hav-ĕ, but we don't say 'hav-ĕ,' we say, hav.'" Unless irregulars are handled this way, a certain number of children will abandon any kind of phonetic attack, trying to remember individual words and making wild guesses such as calling the word "have," "got."

Some irregular words are introduced early so that the child doesn't get the idea that the reading code is perfectly regular. The initial irregular words the teacher introduces are: "he," "she," "we," "me," "go," "so," and "no." These are presented by erasing the diacritical marks over the vowel. To prompt the children on how to sound out these words, the teacher simply indicates with her finger (drawing an imaginary line over the vowel) that the vowel should be treated as a long vowel.

After the children have become reasonably familiar with the initial set of irregulars, the teacher introduces other common words that are not as neat as the originals: "to," "want," "like," "was," "were," etc. These are carefully programmed so that the child receives sufficient exposure on one or two of them every day until these are mastered. Then, the next pair is introduced while the previous pair is continued as a fairly regular schedule.

IMPLICATIONS

The major implication of our work seems to be that children with relatively low mental ages (initially less than four years) can learn to read if the instruction is adequately geared to give them instruction on all of the subskills demanded by the complex behavior we call reading. Furthermore, virtually all children with mental ages of four or over can learn to read. Their progress is relatively slow, but all can progress from one subskill to the next until they are reading. With the emphasis on subskills, the teacher is in a position to know precisely what skills a child has not learned. She therefore knows which skills to work on. When a child masters a given skill, the teacher can proceed to the next one.

If a child has a mental age of four to six years, the chances are overwhelming that he can learn to read, if the instructional program is adequate. Such programs are not commercially available, however, and the teacher of the mentally retarded child is therefore faced with a dilemma. Should she continue to use material that has been proven to be inadequate to teach mentally retarded children to read, or should she wait until programs are commercially available? She should not wait, because the children she is teaching cannot wait. They cannot place themselves in a state of suspended animation for several years, at which time adequate programs will probably be on the market. She must do the best she can. Specifically, this means:

1. She should recognize that the most difficult skills the child must learn are not gross comprehension or experiential skills, but skills in learning how to translate a written word into a series of sounds and putting these sounds together to form a spoken word.

2. She should be extremely skeptical of published materials that do not concentrate on these skills; she should not use a given method merely because it works on normal children; she should not introduce whole words.

3. She should be cautious about assuming that different children "learn in a different way" and must be treated differently. If the criterion of performance is the same for all children, the steps they must take to arrive at that criterion must be the same; therefore, the instruction should be basically the same, in that it should concentrate on the skills that the children must learn in order to achieve the desired criterion of performance (which is to be able to translate clusters of symbols into words).

4. She should work with i.t.a. if possible, recognizing that the program as published is inadequate, but also recognizing that it provides the children with clear demonstrations of the relationship between sounds and symbols, since one symbol stands for one and only one sound.

5. She should not try to teach all of the symbols, but merely enough of them to allow for word building; she should not initially program stop sound consonants ("b," "d," "c," "g," "h," "k," "p," and "t") but only those consonants which can be blended continuously ("f," "j," "l," "m," "n," "r," "s").

6. She should introduce word blends early with the continuous sound convention.

7. She should simultaneously teach the children the verbal skills of saying words fast, saying words slowly, rhyming, and alliterating. Saying words fast is a blending task; the teacher says a words such as "ta–ble" and asks the children to "Say it fast–'table.'" Saying words slowly is an unblending task in which the teacher says words and asks children to say it slowly, a sound at a time. ("Listen: 'man.' Say it slowly–mmmaaannn.'"). The focus of rhyming should be a task in which the children are assigned an ending, the teacher says various beginnings, and the children say the ending and identify the word. ("Here are some words that rhyme with table: 'table,' 'ra-ble,' 'ma–,' 'ca–,' 'sta–.'") The focus of alliteration should be a task in which the children are assigned a beginning to which the teacher attaches various endings; the children must then identify the word. (Children say "sss." Teacher follows with "'and' –What word is that?" Children say, "ssss." The teacher follows with "'eee'–What word is that?"

8. She should introduce stop sounds only after the children have learned to handle continuous sound blends.

9. She should introduce irregulars very cautiously (but relatively early); she should treat these as "funny words," pointing out that they are sounded out in the same way other words are, but aren't pronounced that way.

Teaching reading to children with low mental ages is not easy because these children must learn a great deal before they can hope to read. Their progress is much slower than that of children with higher mental ages. But they can and should be taught if the aim of education is to educate. There is nothing unique about the problems encountered by mentally handicapped children. The problems are the same as those encountered by any child with a relatively low mental age. To read, all children must learn the set of skills. The child with a higher mental age has already been taught many of these before he steps into a classroom. By focusing on these skills and forgetting about such empty labels as "dyslexia" and "perceptually handicapped," a teacher can succeed with children who have mental ages of four or over. The secret of success is simply to provide the children with adequate instruction.

CHAPTER 3

To support the principles of Direct Instruction, Engelmann's writings had to demonstrate why other programs failed and that his theories were valid. Apart from criticizing traditional programs, Engelmann had to combat existing theories on instruction and child development that were well-accepted, although not supported by empirical evidence. Beginning in the mid-1960s and continuing into the 1980s, Engelmann wrote a series of articles on Jean Piaget's theories of child development. Piaget's theories were well-accepted in education, but Engelmann felt that they misrepresented children's capabilities and were detrimental to children learning all that they could. Piaget claimed that children could be taught skills and concepts such as analytic induction and the conservation of water only after reaching a certain age. Demonstrating that a child could learn these skills before this age would disprove his universal theories and support Engelmann's view that all children could learn when given proper instruction.

In this article, Engelmann directly confronts Piaget's theory of development and education by questioning the validity of Piaget's theory in terms of instruction. He provides examples of flaws in Piaget's theory by showing how learning is not subordinated to development as Piaget claims. He also describes his own experiments with young children that disproved key components of Piaget's theories. Thus, Engelmann demonstrates how Piaget's theories are nothing more than a series of accurate descriptions about the performance of children at different ages, not a theory that clearly implies instruction, lack of instruction, or evaluation of instruction. Engelmann was able to disprove Piaget's universal theories while simultaneously providing support for the principles of Direct Instruction.

DOES THE PIAGETIAN APPROACH IMPLY INSTRUCTION? (1971)*

Siegfried E. Engelmann

The key issue associated with Piaget's theory of development and learning has to do with the mechanism by which a child progresses from one stage of development to the next. The Piagetian observations about what children can and cannot normally do at different ages are generally accurate. But what do they mean? How are they explained? Does the explanation imply instruction, and does it account for the facts that can be observed not only under what we might call "normal circumstances," but also under exceptional circumstances?

It is always possible to find a number of tasks that children at different ages typically fail. And it is possible to order these tasks so that we are provided with a typical "developmental profile" of children on the selected tasks. But for this type of endeavor, we do not need a theory. A theory must tell us how and why. It must specify the ways in which these tasks are related. Studies, such as those by Tuddenham (1971), cast serious doubt on whether the various Piagetian tasks are linked together in the manner suggested by the Piagetian theory, or whether they simply represent a collection of tasks that children typically fail before the age of 6. Tuddenham obtained low intercorrelations on pass-fail performance for a variety of concrete-operational tasks. Décalage phenomena are inexplicable in the Piagetian scheme. Yet these phenomena cannot be shrugged off very easily. The Piagetian theory is supposed to be more than an account of normative data. It is supposed to tell us about necessary conditions, not statistical tendencies. If a child passes the conservation-of-substance test with plasticine balls and fails the conservation-of-substance test with liquids, his performance is not consistent with the Piagetian theory. Each of these problems supposedly requires the same cognitive "structure" for its solution. Does the child have the structure or not?

---

* Engelmann, S. E. (1971). Does the Piagetian approach imply instruction? In D. R. Green, M. P. Ford, & G. B. Flamer (Eds.), *Measurement and Piaget* (pp. 118–126). New York: McGraw-Hill. Reprinted with permission of the publisher.

Chapter 3: Does the Piagetian Approach Imply Instruction? (1971)

One of the problems associated with trying to either substantiate or discredit the Piagetian interpretation of development is that there are often alternative ways of explaining behavior within the Piagetian scheme. It is quite easy to find conservation tasks that sophisticated adults generally fail. In other words, the cognitive processes of these adults do not seem to operate within a structured whole. (One problem that usually stumps adults is this: We have a glass of oil and a glass of water. Both are identical; both are filled to the same level. We remove precisely one spoonful of water from the water glass. We put the spoonful of water into the oil glass, and mix the contents thoroughly. Now we remove precisely one spoonful of the oil-water mixture from the second glass and return it to the water glass. The questions: Is there more oil in the water glass than there is water in the oil glass? Is there more water in the oil glass than there is oil in the water glass? Or are the amounts the same? Answer: They are the same.)

The problem of the mechanism by which changes in behavior are induced, however, remains critical to the Piagetian theory. We can observe in many ways that a 14-year-old child is different from a 5-year-old child. The older child uses more sophisticated language. He knows more words and understands more about the properties of different types of objects. He exhibits gross differences in the type of arithmetic problems he can handle, in the types of inferences he can draw from statements that are presented to him, in his general knowledge, and so forth. But what is the mechanism that has changed the older child? To say that he has matured is to beg the question. We base our judgment of maturity upon his behavior, upon the things that he is able to do. It is very difficult to judge whether or not a child who is sitting in a chair with his hands folded is mature or immature. We base judgment on performance. If he performs well on a number of problems, if he measures up to specified criteria, we conclude that he is mature. If not, we judge that he is immature.

When dealing with "developmental theories," there seems to be a temptation to treat every difference between a 6-year-old and a 14-year-old as a critical difference. There is a tendency to note that "older children generally respond in such and such a way." The response, however, may simply be different, not more accurate or appropriate for the task. The response may be no more revealing about the presence of a cognitive structure than the response of the younger child. If we treat such differences as a critical difference, simply because older children who are more sophisticated in other ways tend to respond in this way, any difference becomes "proof" of our theory, regardless of how preposterous it is. For example, we could postulate a radiational theory of growth. Invisible, undetectable rays are being projected from outer space. The longer one is exposed to these rays, the more he learns. We would predict that older children would know more than younger children because of the increased exposure to the "learning-producing" ray. We could produce a number of tests that happily substantiate our theory.

The argument that a child's maturation or development can be inferred from his improved performance over the years is to beg the question. We are using the words *maturation* or *development* as catchalls that are synonymous with our observations. What do we mean by development? We mean that the child has progress in A, B, C, etc. What do we mean when we say that he has progressed in A, B, C, etc.? We mean that he has developed or matured. We still have not identified the mechanism by which the change has been induced. We have merely constructed something of a circular definition.

Although there are other mechanisms suggested by the Piagetian theory, there seem to be five primary principles that describe development:

1. "Learning is subordinated to development and not vice versa" (Piaget, 1964a, p.17).

2. Learning is associated with developmental stages, and these stages occur in an invariant succession. Stage B must always follow Stage A.

3. Only one type of learning can be accelerated through the use of "external reinforcement." "The logical structure is not the result of physical experience. It cannot be obtained by external reinforcement. The logical structure is reached only through internal equilibration, by self-regulation" (Piaget, 1964a, p.16).

4. It follows that the only way to "teach" logical structures is through the process of internal equilibration and self-regulation. Conversely, if we observe a child who has acquired "logical structure" in connection with a specific test, we could conclude that the child had acquired his skills through an internal process of self-regulation.

5. The structures that are induced through equilibration last a lifetime.

We could certainly add to the list above, but for the sake of this paper, let's limit ourselves to these five points. If they represent valid principles, a great deal is implied both for assessment of a child's "development" and for curricular development. (We could not introduce tasks into a curriculum if it is impossible for the children to learn to handle these tasks.) If the Piagetian principles are not valid, however, then they are of questionable value for either assessment or curricular development. If, for example, operational learning (or logical structures) can be induced through the use of external reinforcement, the implications both for assessment and curricular development would be drastically altered.

I have conducted several experiments that question the Piagetian theory. In one (Engelmann, 1967a, pp. 25-51), I taught a group of kindergarten children the principles of compensation. During the instruction, the children never observed water transfer and never saw even a diagram of water transfer. They had no opportunity to "equilibrate" or observe what happens when water is transferred. On the test of conservation after 54 minutes of instruction, distributed over a 5-day period, 10 of the 15 experimental subjects conserved, according to the criteria established for the experiment. None of the comparison subjects, who were nearly a year older than the experimental subjects, conserved on the posttest.

In another experiment (Engelmann, 1967b, pp. 193-207), I taught a small group of disadvantaged and another small group of advantaged 4- and 5-year-old children how to handle different applications of a particular formal operation. I then tested them on a new application that had not been presented during instruction. Four of the five advantaged children and three of the five disadvantaged children successfully solved the new problem. Yet all but one of the children who solved the problem failed a test of conservation of substance (liquid transfer).

When I was invited to this conference, I decided to perform another, more elaborate experiment. The object of the experiment was to accelerate children's operational knowledge or "logical structures" without seriously accelerating their experiential learning. The objective, in other words, was to accelerate only that aspect of development that the Piagetian theory assumes cannot be accelerated.

Before describing the experiment, I would like to make two points:

1. I would not normally teach the skills in the way I did if I were interested in teaching the children in the most interesting, most reinforcing manner. The method of presentation I used was not designed for most efficient learning; it was designed to provide maximum inferences about the five principles above. Also, because of time limitations, I did not check out the children at each step of the program before proceeding to the next.

2. I discovered that there was some "coaching" of the children in the experiment by one of the assistants in our program. The coaching was minimal and had no real effect on the outcome.

I worked with seven kindergarten children on the logical structure of conservation problems, including specific gravity problems. The instruction was designed so that the children had no opportunity to handle physical objects, to observe transformation, to equilibrate. At only two points in the program did the children observe demonstrations other than static diagrams. One time was when I introduced two cups that were identical in size and shape. One was filled with cotton, the other with a rock covered by cotton. I had the children hold both of the objects and note whether one of the objects was bigger than the other and whether one of the objects was heavier than the other.

The other time that they had an experience with real objects was when I demonstrated with two pieces of chalk that objects could move at different speeds during a specified duration of time. I abandoned the demonstration when it became apparent that I could not teach conservation of speed without using real objects.

Aside from these two instances, the children worked on the logic of conservation. The training was designed to prepare them for a range of possible tests, not for any given specific test. The total instructional time was about 3 hours, distributed over a 2-week period. I did not bring the children to specific criteria of performance. If I had had more time, I would have.

Four of the children were then tested primarily on conservation of substance, weight, volume, specific gravity, and speed. (These were not the four best performers in the instruction sessions.) By chance all of these children were 6.0 or 6.1 in age. Since the children were taught only certain logical operations, they would not be expected to perform any differently than other children their age on problems other than those for which instruction prepared them. In other words, the 3 hours of instruction were not designed to change these children into older children. Their verbal behavior, their spontaneity, their ability to extract the meaning from complex statements, and their general knowledge about things—all would remain unchanged. As noted earlier, we can find many differences between these and older children, but if we allow these to form the basis for our conclusions about development, then any test that will allow us to discriminate between younger and older children becomes a critical test.

One child, a disadvantaged black girl (Ann)[1] did not conserve on problems of liquid amount. However, her performance was generally very good on problems of conservation of weight, volume, and specific gravity. There was some question about her performance on several items, but she was quite consistent both on the problems that involved transitivity and problems involving transformation of identical objects. Her performance on the problem of specific gravity was quite interesting. Before putting the objects in the water, she classified them in a typical preoperational way. Again, no assumption

---

1. The fictitious children's names have been inserted here to correspond to those in Kamii's paper which follows. (See citation in reference section.)

should be made about how the children will perform in this type of situation, because they were taught nothing about the behavior of specific objects. They were not taught, for example, that wood floats and iron sinks. They were taught only the logical structure or the rules about floating or sinking. They weren't even taught that if an object sinks one time, it will sink the next which I realized later was a rather obvious oversight on my part. After the child had placed the objects in the water and observed their behavior, her explanations were anything but preoperational; they were formal and correct. She seemed to use the information yielded by her experiment quite well. Throughout the test, however, there was some problem of phrasing questions so that she could respond to them.

The critical issue associated with this child's performance was the discrepancy between her ability to handle the specific gravity problem (a formal operational problem) and her inability to conserve on the test of liquid amount. Although she failed the test of conservation of substance with water, she passed the conservation test with plasticine balls.

The second child (Dan) was a bright kindergarten-age boy, the son of a mathematician. He did very well on the tests of conservation of substance, weight, volume, and specific gravity. His answers were spontaneous and given with certainty. To test his ability to generalize his "logical structure" of floating or sinking, he was presented with a container filled with mercury and two steel balls, one large and one small. The boy indicated, "Both of those balls will float in the mercury." When asked whether the mercury is heavier than the water or vice versa, the child indicated that the mercury is heavier.

This child failed the test of class inclusion, again implying something of a contradiction about the invariant succession of stages.

There was some doubt about whether the children in the experiment understood that objects made of the same material were actually made of the same material. A test was introduced in which the investigator asked whether or not a candle would float. The investigator then proceeded to cut the candle into a large piece and a small piece—a more obvious instance in which the objects to be tested were made of the same material. The children were asked whether the large piece would float and whether the small piece would float. Any inconsistency in responses to this test would clearly be taken as evidence that the child did not have the concept of ratio as it relates to floating and sinking of objects. When the black girl was presented with the test, she suddenly changed her mind, indicating that the candle would float and that either part of the candle would float. When asked why she had changed her mind, she pointed to a flake of the candle that had dropped into the water. She said something to the effect, "That piece is floating, so the whole candle will float."

A third boy (Bill), who did relatively poorly on a number of the substance, volume, and weight problems, did surprisingly well on the test of specific gravity. He generally accounted for the behavior of the objects tested (although his remarks were not spontaneous, and additional questions were often required to clarify his response). When he was presented with the problem of the steel balls and the mercury, he correctly concluded that if the small ball floated, the other ball would float. When asked which of the media, water or mercury, was heavier, he studied the problem for perhaps 10 seconds. He then asserted that the mercury was heavier.

A fourth kindergarten-age boy (Carl, a fraternal twin) performed solidly on all tests, including the test of class inclusion. However, he (and all of the other children) missed items in the conservation-of-speed test.

These children did exhibit the ability to generalize. For example, they had never seen during the instruction that a plasticine ball could be transformed into a ring. They hadn't seen transformations with any three-dimensional objects. The children handled these problems very well. The black girl indicated at one point that the object could be returned to its original shape. She even reached for the object, saying, "Here, let me show you." The fraternal twin drew a series of imaginary lines from the center to the perimeter of the ring and indicated, "It's longer this way." He then held his hand palm down, making a downward pushing motion and said, "But it's shorter this way."

The children generally did well on the test of specific gravity. They used the information they received from the experience of floating an object to classify it. They understood that if the whole object sinks, any part of the object will sink. They could indicate why the objects floated or sank, and they could generalize to another medium which they had not seen before, mercury.

Before returning to the Piagetian assumption about development and learning, let me make several points quite clear. I selected the examples above because they relate to the question of mechanism. Not all of the children performed with 100 percent accuracy on all tests. One of the children actually did rather poorly on some. However, I have no doubt that this child could be brought to the desired criterion of performance with additional training, using only external reinforcement and not physical experiences. And remember, these changes in behavior noted above were the product of about 3 hours of instruction. If it is desirable for children to perform well on these and similar tests, 6 or even 10 hours of instruction would represent a modest investment. Children normally require years to learn what the children in the experiment mastered in a few hours.

Let's take a look at the Piagetian assumptions about learning in relationship to the performance of the children in the experiment.

1. Is learning subordinated to development? These children seemed to have learned, and learned a great deal. Furthermore, they learned from presentations that did not allow for internal self-regulation. They learned very little about things and about how they would behave. They did not perform differently than other children their age on classifying objects before putting them in water. What they had learned was the logical structure that would allow them to handle a variety of floating and sinking problems, a variety of displacement and substance problems, not merely those presented in the test. Generally, they would have been able to draw conclusions about the relative weight of any two media—helium and neon for example—given the facts that a particular object "sinks" in neon and "floats" in helium. Generally, they would have been able to work a variety of conservation-of-volume problems. For example, they would have been able to indicate

how one goes about getting a volume of water equal to a volume of clay. They had learned the logical structure, and it is not at all obvious how this learning was subordinated to their "development."

2. Does development of learning occur in an invariant succession of stages? If so, how do we explain the performance of some of our experimental children? The black girl did not seem to be building structures on existing structures. She seemed to have a very solid fix on weight, volume, and substance as it relates to plasticine balls. Yet she failed the water transfer test. The second boy, the most solid and spontaneous performer, failed the test of class inclusion (as did all but the fraternal twin). All of the children failed the conservation-of-speed test. Some of these children "developed" in a rather unusual fashion, according to Piagetian principles.

3. Can learning of logical structures be induced through the use of external reinforcement? I think the answer is clearly yes. The children in the experiment were not taught items. They were taught rules. In general they used these rules appropriately in response to presentations they had not observed during instruction.

4. Can we clearly infer from the child's performance whether or not he has gone through the equilibration process? I think not. We can certainly find "differences" in performance, but for these differences to be relevant they must be related to the child's demonstrable ability to handle "logical-structure" problems.

5. Do the structures that are induced through equilibration last a lifetime, and do they differ generally from structures induced through "external reinforcement"? I doubt whether they are different. This is not to say that "externally reinforced behavior" will not extinguish if it is not continually reinforced. It is to say that there is probably no difference between this behavior and "self-regulated behavior." This is strictly my opinion, but I find nothing in the literature to contradict it (including the extinction experiments in which the important

53

variable of duration since time of acquisition is not controlled). Certainly, we can write off the experiment I have described by saying that the learning will not last. And I certainly cannot present data that it will last a lifetime. However, I believe that these children will retain what they have learned. I'll find out next year.

In many respects, the experiment I have described is as sloppy as my description. There was no control group. The children were not given pretests. (However, it was apparent from the children's responses during instruction that initially none of them could conserve substance, weight, or volume; nor could they perform on tests of specific gravity.) However, the experiment is useful and worth reporting, I believe, because it gives some insight into the mechanism by which children are transported to higher stages of development. Changes occurred, and these changes were a function of specific experiences that these children had. The experiences were not "normal" for most 6-year-old children, and the resulting performance was not "normal."

The main point of confusion associated with Piagetian theory has to do with the relationship between the observations of what children normally do and the theoretical principles that account for these observations. It is quite possible for one to acknowledge that the Piagetian observations are generally quite accurate and for one to totally reject the theory. This is the position that I take. Children at a given age cannot generally handle conservation of weight problems. But if you want them to be able to handle such problems, you can teach them. If you want them to be able to handle a class of similar problems (or deal with a class of objects or events that have the same characteristics as conservation of weight problems), you can teach them. The mechanism is actually quite simple. Children are taught. They may be taught through physical experiences. They may be taught through other types of experiences.

It is possible to teach children a wide variety of discriminations, including those that involve logical structure. All red objects share a certain characteristic. This characteristic can be taught. It can be demonstrated in such a way that a child can generalize it. So it is with other rules, and to learn "red" is to learn a rule. All instances of compensating changes share a set of characteristics. These characteristics can be taught in quite the same way red is taught. The child is presented with instances of the concept and is taught the relationship between the characteristics and the language used to describe these. Unfortunately, I cannot go into great detail on the nature of concept analysis and the procedures by which generalization is induced, but I would like to stress that the most efficient way to teach is rarely the way suggested by the Piagetian model. Although a child must be exposed to instances of a particular concept before he can learn the concept, the physical experience often represents a noisy instance, one that is not well designed to teach what the salient characteristics of the concept are, or which aspects of the objects or events should be attended to. Many more instances of the noisy physical experience may have to be presented before the child learns the rule.

So far as I am able to determine, the Piagetian theory provides us with nothing more than a set of accurate descriptions about the performance of children at different ages. It does not provide us with the theory that clearly implies instruction, lack of instruction, or evaluation of instruction. An ordinal scale of developmental stages would, I'm sure, provide a great deal of interesting data that is not easily extracted from present IQ tests or other developmental instruments. But of what particular value would it be? Would it actually tell us what we can or cannot teach a given child? Would it actually imply the procedure that we should use to teach? Would it help describe that mechanism that transports a child from one stage of development to another? Or would it tend to give stature and credence to a theoretical framework that is not only highly suspect but equally irrelevant to instruction? If the Piagetian theory specified the mechanism that causes change, the children in the experiment I have described would not have been able to learn the logical structure they learned. They would not have been able to violate the supposed invariant succession of stages. They would not have responded to a presentation that did not allow for equilibration. And if the Piagetian model did provide a tight, theoretical framework, we would have been able to specify, for example, why the black girl failed to conserve on the liquid-amount test. The reason is appallingly simple, but it is not to be found in the Piagetian theory. The girl was not taught the rules needed to handle liquid-transfer problems. She was absent during 2 days of instruction that focused upon the compensating changes of rectangular objects.

REFERENCES

Engelmann, S. (1967). Cognitive structures related to the principle of conservation. In D. W. Brison & E. V. Sullivan (Eds.), *Recent research on the acquisition of conservation of substance* (pp. 25–51). Toronto, Ontario, Canada: Ontario Institute for Studies in Education.

Engelmann, S. (1967). Teaching formal operations to preschool advantaged and disadvantaged children. *Ontario Journal of Educational Research, 9* (3), 193–207.

Kamii, C., & Derman, L. (1971). Comments on Engelmann's paper: The Engelmann approach to teaching logical thinking: Findings from the administration of some Piagetian Tasks. In D. R. Green, M. P. Ford, & G. B. Flamer (Eds.), *Measurement and Piaget* (127-145). New York: McGraw-Hill.

Tuddenham, R. D. (1971). Theoretical regularities and individual idiosyncrasies. In D. R. Green, M. P. Ford, & G. B. Flamer (Eds.), *Measurement and Piaget* (64-74). New York: McGraw-Hill.

CHAPTER 4

The promotion and development of Direct Instruction, as well as the principles behind it, was a continuous and relentless process. Engelmann and his colleagues had to repeatedly demonstrate the effectiveness of Direct Instruction, how it was designed, and why it succeeded when traditional programs failed or were less effective. This promotion coincided with a continued effort to better understand the process of learning and how instruction could become more effective and efficient. To reiterate and elaborate on previous articles that discussed Engelmann's theoretical understanding of learning and instruction, this article emphasizes the importance of evaluating the instructional context and not just the student when trying to understand school failure. At the time (and often today), teachers were accurately identifying students who were demonstrating problems with learning, but the teachers were not successfully adjusting their instructional approaches to ensure the students understood and mastered the content. Traditional diagnostic approaches inform teachers that if the students fail, it is the result of some basic flaw in the learner. However, these diagnoses do not specify the extent to which the learner's problems are related to poor instruction and precisely what the teachers could do to remedy an observed problem.

Utilizing a scientific approach, the authors argue the teacher can only achieve behavioral change by manipulating environmental events—by changing instruction. Teachers need to be clearly informed of how to manipulate the environment to resolve the issues through their behaviors. Effective diagnosis must focus both on the learner and the teacher in order to determine the solution. Procedures for determining adequate instruction are presented to show educators why instruction needs to be designed for the student. Instructional diagnosis is important for understanding which aspects of instruction are inadequate, how they are inadequate, and to determine how to correct the inadequacies. By not examining the role of instruction, the chances for student success are limited.

DIAGNOSING INSTRUCTION (1979)[*]

Siegfried Engelmann, Alex Granzin, & Herbert Severson

Traditional diagnostic approaches usually occur outside the instructional context and focus on the learner. Accurate conclusions about the learner, however, can only be reached after an adequate diagnosis of instruction. Failure to consider instruction as a variable results in diagnoses that lack specific implications for teaching. Assumptions and procedures critical to an adequate diagnosis of instruction are discussed and applied to a variety of examples. The process of derivation of remedies and its relationship to the diagnostic process is illustrated with examples. Implications for the diagnostician and the consequences of failing to provide adequate instructional diagnoses are discussed.

VARIABLES OF DIAGNOSIS

Traditional procedures used to diagnose the learner are extremely weak because they do not assess the instruction the learner receives; they only assess the learner. Typically, a diagnosis is called for when there is trouble, generally because whatever the teacher is doing is not working. The learner is not "growing," "developing," "interacting," or "behaving" in an appropriate manner. A diagnosis is achieved by removing such learners from the instructional setting and giving them a series of tests that provide a sample of the learner's behavior. The assumption is that the sample provided by tests is somehow better than other samples. While the interpretation of the sample ostensibly tells something about the learner, the diagnostician never draws conclusions about persons or factors other than the child, e.g., "The child's performance on the Bender Gestalt clearly indicates that the teacher is very poor at classroom management." On the contrary, interpretation always tells about the learners—their predisposition, mental abilities, skills, personality, intelligence, sensorimotor performance, and so on.

---

[*] Engelmann, S., Granzin, A., & Severson, H. (1979). Diagnosing instruction. *The Journal of Special Education, 13*(4), 355–363. Reprinted with permission of the publisher.

There is no severe problem with the diagnosis until a remedy is drawn from it. For while the sample of behavior may be useful for classifying the learner, it fails to suggest adequate remedial action. Every special educator who has played the remedy game recognizes the problems encountered at this juncture. "It seems," the psychologist says thoughtfully to the teacher, "that you should work on auditory sequencing."

"Like what?"

"Well, counting."

"We do it."

"Well, what about completing words in a sentence?"

"Like what kind of sentence?"

" 'We find cows in the ….' "

"He can't do it."

"That's probably what you have to work on."

"How?"

At this point, diagnosticians are so far beyond the information provided by the test, and so far from the realities of the teaching situation, that if they're smart they'll retreat from the concrete details that teachers need to the more comfortable generalities that characterize staffings. Actually, the diagnostic procedure is a perfect charade if the goal of diagnosis is to lead to a remedy. For a remedy to follow from the diagnosis, the remedy must provide teachers with information that they don't have. It must tell them what, if anything, they can do to improve learner performance. It should not tell them what they already know, that the learner has some sort of deficiency. Teachers know precisely how the deficiency manifests itself, what the learner has trouble learning, and how the learner responds to different situations. Teachers, however, are not usually insulted by a diagnosis that may tell them far less than they already know if that diagnosis assures them that (a) the instructions they have provided are adequate and (b) the learner's failure is the result of some basic flaw in the learner. Traditional diagnoses are designed to provide these assurances. Unfortunately, they carry very limited remedial implications because they do not specify (a) the extent to which the learner's failure is caused by poor instruction and (b) precisely what the teachers could do to remedy an observed problem.

The traditional diagnosis is incapable of expressing remedies in the basic units the teacher manipulates when teaching. The teacher achieves teaching (or changing behavior) *not* by manipulating neurons, the learner's past history, or internal processes of any sort. Rather, the teacher achieves behavioral change only by manipulating environmental events. This point is extremely important. It follows that the remedy must clearly imply manipulation of those environmental events. It must tell teachers what they are doing wrong and what types of different teaching behaviors they should implement. The remedy must be specific and concrete because teaching always involves specific, concrete acts. The instruction "Teach seriation" does not tell the teacher what to do, when to do it, how to respond to specific errors, how to sequence examples, how to review, or how to reinforce. Yet, in order to "teach seriation," the teacher has to present examples in sequence, say specific words, and respond in some way to the learner's attempts.

Traditional diagnosis assumes that all relevant information comes from a study of the learner. An equally tenable position is that all relevant information comes from a study of the instruction the learner receives, not from the learner. Neither position is reasonable. The learner's behavior is influenced by two major factors: (a) the innate capacity or predisposition of the learner and (b) the instruction the learner receives. In other words:

$$B \text{ (Behavior)} = P \text{ (Predisposition)} + I \text{ (Instruction)}.$$

In this formula, *Predisposition* would include all factors that remain unaffected by instruction. (If the learner exhibits the same problem regardless of instructional approach, the problem is controlled by predisposition.) *Instruction* refers to the effects of teaching – intentional or unintentional. (If the problem can be eliminated through instruction, the problem is controlled by instruction.)

When we observe a given behavior, we cannot specify the extent to which it is controlled by predisposition or by instruction. We may assert that it is controlled primarily by one factor or another, but our assertion is based on ignorance, not on fact. We might conclude that the learner has a perceptual problem when in fact the observed behavior has been caused by poor instruction and can be eliminated through instruction.

One way to extricate ourselves from this diagnostic dilemma would be to rule out one of the two variables (P or I). If we could eliminate the learner's predisposition from the observed behavior, we could use the formula: $I = B - P$. If we could rule out the instructional influence and look only at the learner's predisposition, we could use the formula: $P = B - I$. Unfortunately, we cannot remove the learners from the effects of the instruction they receive or from their innate predispositions. We must therefore try to control the variables P and I in some other way, and the control must be designed so that it doesn't require removing a variable (or pretending that we remove it).

There is no obvious way to control P by improving it, maximizing it, or redesigning it so that we know precisely how it works. We can, however, control I. To do this, we maximize I, which means that we design it so that it works across a wide range of learners. When we design I so that it is basically faultless and incapable of contributing to the learner's behavior problem, we can draw conclusions about both P and I. If B changes greatly with I controlled, we conclude that I is the primary factor in determining B. If B does not change greatly, we conclude that P is primarily responsible for the status of B.

We have now gone full circle and have come to the central diagnostic problem. We wish to control I. First, we must determine what type of control is needed and to what extent I is in need of maximization. In other words, we must diagnose instruction. The diagnosis perforce must be of instruction, not of the learner. The instructional diagnosis involves two steps: (a) interpreting instruction the learner receives according to the minimum-knowledge assumption, and

(b) testing the minimum-knowledge assumption by providing a maximum-knowledge test.

The minimum-knowledge assumption

When we view instruction, we see the learner responding to different things the teacher does. The teacher presents tasks, and the learner responds. The minimum-knowledge assumption holds that the learner uses the least possible knowledge required to produce the various behaviors we observe. For example, the teacher says, "Open the door, Henry," and points to the door. If Henry opens the door, we cannot assume that Henry understands the command, "Open the door," because Henry was not required to respond only to the words. He could have responded only to the teacher's pointing. The minimum-knowledge assumption holds that Henry did just that – responded to the point, not to the words.

The maximum-knowledge test

The minimum-knowledge assumption is perfectly consistent with the observed behavior. Further, it carries implications for instructional control. That is, we can design a test that eliminates the teacher's point and presents only words. This test requires knowledge of the words – the maximum-knowledge test. The minimum knowledge assumption identifies the simplest mechanism that accounts for what the learner does. The test of maximum-knowledge restructures the situation so that the learner cannot use the simplest mechanism.

Failure to make the minimum-knowledge assumption results in failure to test the possibility that the learner is responding to messages other than the ones the teacher intends. Let's say the teacher hands a learner a piece of candy and says, "Eat this." The traditional interpretation assumes that if the learner ate the candy, the learner understood the directions (maximum- knowledge). The minimum-knowledge assumption holds that the learner is responding to the candy in the hand, not to the words; in other words, the learner would eat it no matter what the teacher said. Then the minimum-knowledge assumption can be tested (perhaps by handing the learner candy and telling him/her, "Don't eat it," or "Shut the door.") The minimum-knowledge assumption implies the maximum-knowledge test. If the minimum-knowledge assumption is not made, however, the role of the instruction in the learner's performance is not tested.

Two points about the diagnosis of instruction should be noted:

1. The minimum-knowledge assumption is just that – an assumption, not a fact. The assumption should be tested, and the test will clearly determine the extent to which it is confirmed.

2. The minimum-knowledge assumption can be made about written descriptions, but the use of these descriptions in formulating diagnoses is not efficient because they do not provide sufficient detail about what happens during instruction. Written descriptions only tell about those details of which the writer is aware. If the writer is unaware of such details as sequencing items, the written instruction obviously will not mention these. Also, written descriptions are often useless because teachers do not follow them.

APPLICATIONS

Below are three applications of the diagnostic procedure, relatively elementary examples. The same basic procedure can be used in more complex situations, however. The first two examples involve situations in which a problem has been identified. Situation 1 involves a learner whose behavior is not changing in the expected way. Situation 2 concerns a learner who seems to have trouble following instructions. Situation 3, however, involves a learner who is performing acceptably but who exhibits a problem when the procedure used in the previous examples is applied. The minimum-knowledge assumption identifies possible misinterpretations that are conveyed through instruction. The maximum-knowledge test confirms that the deficiency in instructional procedures has resulted in a deficiency in the learner's understanding. The point is that the diagnostic procedures can be applied before the problem is identified and that preventive measures can be designed to obviate the instructional deficiency.

Situation 1

The teacher is trying to teach or reinforce number skills of low-language children by playing a game with oversized dominoes. After placing a domino in the middle of the table, the teacher says the number shown by his/her domino. If a child has a domino with a matching number of dots, the child is to place that domino in the middle of the table.

The problem child in the group throws out a domino every time the teacher places one on the table. The teacher's response is simply to ignore the inappropriate responses by pushing the domino back to the child and continuing the task. When the child's response is appropriate, the teacher reinforces it. The teacher's attempts to "shape" the child's behavior have not worked.

Minimum-knowledge assumption. To formulate the assumption we ask, "What is the least amount of knowledge learners could possess and perform in the observed way?" They would not have to count the dots on the dominoes and would not have to understand that they are supposed to throw out a domino only if it matches. They could perform in the observed manner if they operated from the principle: "Throw out your domino each time the teacher presents one. From time to time, you'll be reinforced."

We assume, therefore, that the learner operates from this behavioral rule and that the learner has no knowledge of numbers, matching, or the rules of the game.

Maximum-knowledge test. A number of maximum-knowledge tests are possible here. The requirement for each is that it must test the child's knowledge of whether the number of dots match. For instance, we could provide the learner with a row of dominoes and hand him/her one domino, which the child must place next to the domino with the same number of dots.

Situation 2

Jenny performs successfully when the following tasks are presented in random order: "Touch your head…touch your nose…stand up…pick up the fork…pick up the pencil."

Jenny has difficulty with tasks such as, "Put the pencil under the chair," and "Touch the pencil." (She puts the object handed to her on the chair, and she picks up the pencil.)

Minimum-knowledge assumption. Jenny performs by cueing on the last word in the command. She cannot perform on preposition tasks because words other than the last word provide instruction about what to do. She cannot perform on "Touch the fork" because she ignores the word touch.

Maximum-knowledge test. The maximum-knowledge test must first determine whether Jenny could follow two different commands involving the same object. Could Jenny, for instance, "touch the fork" as well as "pick up the fork?" The test would involve random trials of these commands. If the minimum-knowledge assumption is correct, Jenny would pick up the fork on every trial, even after the correct response to touch had been modeled and emphasized in the commands.

Situation 3

Ann, a junior-high student, performs well on a variety of arithmetic tasks. She works simple algebra problems; however, the program that she uses requires application of laws, such as associative and distributive, and always requires problems to be solved for X or A (not for 2x or ½A).

Minimum-knowledge assumption. Ann has learned strategies for solving problems that would not permit her to solve a problem such as: $4X = 7$; $3X =$ ___. This minimum-knowledge assumption is based solely on the program, not an observed behavioral deficiency. The assumption is that if Ann is "normal," it is quite probable that she developed a strategy that would not work well in solving for values other than X.

Maximum-knowledge test. The most direct test would be to require Ann to solve the same problem for different values:

$4X = 7$	$4X = 7$	$4X = 7$	$4X = 7$
$3X =$ ___	$\tfrac{2}{3}X =$ ___	$7X =$ ___	$\tfrac{1}{2}X =$ ___

Remedies

Remedies follow logically from learners' performance on the maximum-knowledge test. If learners fail the test, they must work on tasks or activities that can account for passing the test.

If the domino player did not pass the test that required matching a domino with the appropriate one in the teacher's display, the task would be simplified (reducing the number of dominoes displayed by the teacher), and the preskill of counting the dots would be taught and then applied to the matching procedure. Initially, the structure of the task would involve steps such as: "Count the dots on your domino…How many dots on your domino?…Show me the other domino that has four dots…Put your domino next to the domino that has four dots…Good job." Later, the steps would be "faded" and the learner would be required to perform without prompting. Once he/she had demonstrated proficiency required to pass the maximum-knowledge test (in which he/she would be given different dominoes to be placed next to those that match), the original domino game could be reintroduced, perhaps with new rules: "If you put out a domino that does not match, I get one of your points."

Again, if Jenny failed the maximum-knowledge test, the implied remedy is to teach the skills required to pass the test. To achieve this, we might first teach her single word commands, such as "touch." We would initially present unfamiliar objects or those that are not easily picked up. The teacher would say the word "touch" and then demonstrate or model the response. Jenny would next be tested. After performing acceptably on these objects, objects such as forks and candy would be introduced. Next, she would be taught to discriminate between the command "touch" and the command "pick up." Both commands would be given for the same object. For instance, a fork would be presented, and Jenny would be given these commands: "Touch…touch…pick up…touch…pick up…pick up…pick up…touch" etc. After Jenny performed acceptably on this type of task, tasks that name both the object and the action would be introduced: "Touch the ball…Pick up the book…Touch the fork…Touch the candy." When Jenny can perform these tasks, she passed the maximum-knowledge test. To respond correctly, she must attend to and understand the meaning of the commands, which means that she must have maximum-knowledge.

The remedy for the poor arithmetic sequence would be to teach Ann a strategy that would permit her to solve problems that require solutions for values other than X. A possible strategy is to show Ann that a problem of this type:

$$4X = 7$$

$$3X = \underline{}$$

is simply a ratio word problem with equivalent fractions on either side of the equal sign:

$$\frac{4}{3} = \frac{7}{\boxed{}}$$

The game involved in solving the problem is to find the number that 4 must be multiplied by to change it into 7. We must multiply 3 by the same value to get the answer.

Once Ann has applied this analysis to various problems (both ratios and those involving letters), she should have no trouble with the maximum-knowledge test.

ASSUMPTIONS, TESTS, AND REMEDIES

The procedures outlined show the relationship between the minimum-knowledge assumption, the maximum-knowledge test, and the remedy. The examples of remedies are based on situations in which the learner fails the maximum-knowledge test. If the learner passes the test, of course, no remedy is implied; we simply conclude that our assumption of minimum-knowledge was not confirmed by the test. Possibly, the test will provide only a partial confirmation of the assumption, which means that the learner will fail only part of it or only some types of items. Performance will imply what we must teach before the learner performs adequately on the missed part or items.

DIAGNOSIS AND REMEDY

The purpose of instructional diagnosis is to determine aspects of instruction that are inadequate, to find out precisely how they are inadequate, and to imply what must be done to correct their inadequacy. The assumption of minimum-knowledge is central to the diagnosis. If it is not made, the instruction is automatically exonerated, and the fault for poor performance is automatically placed on the learner. If we fail to recognize that instruction permits and reinforces domino players for throwing out their domino on every trial, we may conclude that they are slow learners, that they do not respond to the "punishment" of teachers ignoring their inappropriate responses. The teacher's procedures, although faulty, become exonerated, and the diagnosis shifts to questions of why the learner tends to respond in such a strange way.

By failing to make the minimum-knowledge assumption about Jenny's performance, we are left with the uncomfortable conclusion that she is apparently capable of responding to commands; however, this is not always so. Unless we note that her performance is perfectly consistent with what she has been reinforced for doing (responding to commands in which the last word conveys all the important information), we must try to account for her erratic behavior. Our attention moves from the instruction to Jenny's personality, learning style, developmental pattern, or whatever.

Similarly, failure to apply the minimum-knowledge assumption to Ann prevents us from further tests of the program's adequacy. Instead, when she develops serious problems in arithmetic, we conclude that her problems are caused by an internal mechanism, not by the program: "Ann lacks aptitude."

In every case, our conclusions are premature and unfounded. They represent a *possible* interpretation; the other, and equally possible, interpretation is that the learner responds in a way consistent with the instruction presented.

When instructional deficiencies are not identified, the teacher may understandably become frustrated. Even though the teacher works harder on following directions, Jenny persists in making the same mistakes. Playing the domino game more frequently does not seem to improve the learner's performance. Reviewing simpler problems does not seem to help Ann work the more difficult ones.

In short, the teacher draws dangerous conclusions about the learners; instruction apparently does not seem to change their responses; therefore, the problem must be with their predispositions.

DIAGNOSING THE LEARNER

The only valid way to draw conclusions about deficiencies involves first determining the degree to which the learner's performance is controlled by instruction. We must go through the following steps:

1. Diagnose the instruction the learner receives (observing instruction using the minimum-knowledge assumption and then providing the maximum-knowledge test.)

2. Provide instructional remedies that account for the skills required by the maximum-knowledge test.

3. Observe discrepancies between the learner's performance and that of a normal learner.

The first two steps factor out instruction and identify the extent to which it is reasonable for the observed behavior. We can then indicate the extent to which performance is caused by the learner's basic makeup—the third step. If the learner's performance does not improve in response to instruction designed to teach maximum-knowledge skills, we can conclude that the performance deficiency is caused primarily by predisposition. If the learner learns in a so-called normal way, however, we can conclude that predisposition plays a minor role.

We must temper our conclusions with an understanding of learning. For example, when a remedy requires the learner to abandon behaviors that have been reinforced for years, we would expect learning to proceed slowly, even if the learner is normal. Relearning requires much more practice than initial learning. Moreover, learning unfamiliar discriminations requires considerably more practice than does learning familiar discriminations (Engelmann & Granzin, in press). In the case of a learner who has never attended to verbal utterances, we can assume that initial learning (even for a normal learner) would be quite slow (requiring hundreds of trials to master only a few discriminations). When our goal is to assess normality, we can use any deficiency as the basis for concluding that the learner is below normal. If we wish to find out the extent to which this behavior implies a persistent and irreversible deficiency, we must first *teach* the learner and observe responses.

IMPLICATIONS FOR THE DIAGNOSTICIAN

Traditionally, the diagnostician's role has been to provide the teacher with a fine-grained classification of the learner's problems. As noted, the instruments focus solely on the learner in an attempt to tell what type of deficiency he/she has, to relate to the norm, and to convert the teacher's casual observation of the problem into more scientific language.

The diagnostician must recognize that this orientation is faulty. The purpose of diagnosis is not primarily to provide a refined statement of what the teacher already knows, nor is it to sanction the idea that merely because the learners possess a deficiency, they are automatically the cause of the deficiency. The diagnostician can perform a useful role only by recognizing that the goal of instructional diagnosis (as opposed to a demographic statement about the child's deficiency) is to imply an instructional remedy.

Accepting this orientation is to accept the fact that *teachers need help*. Not all problem children are abnormal. Not all the procedures teachers use to correct these children are well conceived. And certainly not all the instructional sequences they use are faultless—or even adequate. This being so, the remedial focus must move to the teachers. For the children to receive effective remedies, their teachers must behave in different ways. Teachers probably will not change their behavior, however, unless they are taught to do so. If they are not taught, new behavior problems and learning problems among children may be created at an expected rate.

REFERENCE

Engelmann, S., & Granzin, A. Unfamiliar learning. In J. Pickett & A. Risberg (Eds.), *Proceedings of the Gallaudet Conference on Speech Processing Aids for the Deaf,* in press.

CHAPTER 5

The ability to maximize the effectiveness and efficiency of instruction depends on recognizing every variable in the instructional process. Through his previous publications, Engelmann had demonstrated the importance and interconnectedness of the design of a program, the proper placement of a student in a program that matches his/her skills, appropriate instruction, and teaching to mastery. This article, written in 1999 for a presentation to teachers of DI programs, summarizes the importance of teaching to mastery for student success.

By teaching to mastery, students have a firm understanding of the information taught and are prepared to progress in their program. Teaching to mastery increases effectiveness and efficiency because it ensures all students have the necessary skills to advance and they will not need additional review to progress. Furthermore, if students learn to mastery they develop confidence in their ability to learn, making them more likely to continue their educational pursuits and to succeed. Engelmann has promoted teaching to mastery as a key principle of Direct Instruction throughout his career.

In this article, he demonstrates the importance of teaching to mastery and how it is essential for the development of academic programs and the success of students. Engelmann explains the key features of the Direct Instruction model, from the basic properties of mastery to the procedures and criteria for measuring student mastery performance. Building upon decades of analysis and research, Engelmann demonstrates how teaching to mastery not only increases the effectiveness and efficiency of instruction, but also results in students learning how to learn, a cornerstone for success in any field of study.

STUDENT-PROGRAM ALIGNMENT AND TEACHING TO MASTERY (1999)[*]

Siegfried Engelmann

When students are taught to mastery, they become smarter, acquire information faster, and develop efficient strategies for learning. Teachers must have an understanding of what mastery is and how to achieve it in their students. However, teachers cannot teach to mastery without referencing the performance of their students. In addition, teachers cannot teach to mastery without a program design that supports the approach. Teaching to mastery is built upon effective student/program alignment. This paper discusses the features of a program design that supports mastery, properties of mastery, criteria and procedures for measuring mastery, procedures for aligning program placement with student performance and the benefits of mastery.

FEATURES OF A PROGRAM DESIGN THAT SUPPORTS MASTERY

A program design that supports mastery does not present great amounts of new information and skill training in each lesson. Rather, work is distributed so new parts in a lesson account for only 10-15 percent of the total lesson. The rest of the lesson firms and reviews material and skills presented earlier in the program. The program assumes that nothing is taught in one lesson. Instead, new concepts and skills are presented in two or three consecutive lessons to provide students with enough exposure to new material that they are able to use it in applications. So, a lesson presents material that is new today; material that is being firmed, having been presented in the last two or three lessons; and material that was presented even earlier in the sequence and is assumed to be thoroughly mastered.

---

[*] Engelmann, S. (1999). Student-program alignment and teaching to mastery. Paper presented at the 25th National Direct Instruction Conference, Eugene, OR. (Reprinted in 2007 in the *Journal of Direct Instruction*, 7(1), 45–66.) Reprinted with the permission of the author.

This material often takes the form of problems or applications that require earlier-taught knowledge.

The amount of new material is relatively small because most students are not capable of assimilating more. This design provides for some "overlearning," but having the program err in the direction of providing too much practice is better than providing too little practice. Work on material presented in the preceding few lessons is needed to ensure that students are "automatic" with information or operations that were previously taught.

The review of earlier material assures that students use and apply what they have learned. Reviews also prompt students toward an understanding that they are expected to retain and use material learned—not just learn it for the moment. Basically, most things are taught in the program so they can be used in applications or problem-solving settings. Therefore, the program is constructed so students review and use what they have learned according to a systematic schedule. Because reviews are a regular feature of every lesson, the program design provides daily prompting that material presented will appear again. Also, applications that involve earlier-taught skills provide the kind of practice that students need to keep from mixing up different things they are learning. If students partially learn things, new learning is easily confused with things that are similar. If students learn material well, less confusion results.

Mastering a Step at a Time

A program designed with small amounts of new material in each lesson is something like a stairway. Like a stairway, it needs strong support. That support is in the form of the previously taught skills and knowledge that are logical underpinnings for what is to come next in the program. Also, for the stairway to work well, the "steps" in this series should be about the same size. Certainly, they can't be fashioned with the accuracy of a physical stairway, but they can be designed so they are close to each other in size.

If we conceive of the program as being like a stairway that transports students to increasingly complex performance, we recognize the supreme importance of mastery, what it is, and how it relates to the curriculum. The following six points clarify the relationship between mastery and the stairway.

1. The program will function as a stairway if the student reaches every stair on schedule. If students are firmly on the fifth stair (which is analogous to the fifth lesson), the new learning that students must achieve to reach the sixth stair is manageable. The students' position on the fifth stair represents a foundation that places the sixth lesson within stepping distance. Because the foundation is in place, the sixth lesson does not overwhelm students with too much new vocabulary, unfamiliar or unpracticed operations, too much information, or too many unknown or unexplained details.

2. The steps are levelers of individual differences. Not all students who stand on the fifth stair are the same age, learn at precisely the same rate, have equal intelligence, or exhibit the same "style" of learning. However, every student who is firmly on the fifth step is the same with respect to the program sequence. Each has the skill repertoire and knowledge needed to take the next step and reach that step within 30-45 minutes of instruction. Because students could not reach the fifth step without specific skill and knowledge, the stairway structure of a well-designed program serves as a leveler. All students with a particular skill profile are placed on the same stair. Certainly, the program design does not guarantee that all students will progress at exactly the same rate; however, the greatest individual differences occur on the very beginning levels. On higher levels, after students have mastered a battery of skills and knowledge, the difference in rate of ascent for appropriately placed students is far less because all students tend to have enough skill to master the new material at around the same rate.

3. The benefits of the design of the program are obliterated if a student falls below the level of a stair. This fact holds for students who are "smart" as well as those who have a history of failure. If a student is below the fifth stair and tries to reach the sixth stair with one step (which means thoroughly mastering the sixth lesson in one period), the student must learn substantially more than students who are firmly on the fifth stair. Furthermore, the students must learn this material during the same amount of time allotted for students who

are firmly on the fifth stair. Therefore, the student who is below the fifth stair must learn the material at a faster rate. The student on the fourth stair must learn material at twice the rate of students who are correctly placed. The student who is on the third stair must learn at three times the rate. For the typical student, a step that requires three times the amount of new learning is too great. Even if the student is able to perform acceptably on lesson 6 after some repetition, the retention rate of the student on the subsequent lessons drops dramatically.

4. Just as the design of the program "guarantees" a successful future for students who are firmly based on a stair, the design suggests an unsuccessful future for a student who is greatly below that stair. The systematic stairway design does not provide relief because skills and knowledge do not go away. Once introduced, they are used throughout the rest of the program, either as elements that are used regularly (such as a word type that is learned), as details that are embedded in problems and applications (such as the math operation of carrying), or as items that are frequently reviewed (such as identifying the verb in sentences). Because of this program design, once a student falls behind, the student will tend not to catch up. If the student is initially 3 steps below the lesson, the student will probably end up a little more than 3 steps below the next lesson, a little further below the following lesson, and so forth until the student is not 3, but 4, steps below the level of the lesson, then 5 steps below, and so forth.

5. This student is not able to benefit from the design of the program, because although the program presents small increments of learning, this student must master large increments of learning to catch up. For this student, the program presents a poorly designed sequence. It requires too much new learning and does not provide adequate reviews.

Because the program's design benefits are transmitted only to students who are on the lesson stairs, student performance must match the level of performance assumed by each stair. This goal is achieved if teachers teach to mastery. Mastery assures that everything that is supposed to be taught is taught thoroughly and at the time it is introduced in the program (not 20 or 30 lessons later).

Note, however, that DI programs are designed with enough redundancy that a student who is absent for two or three days will not be perfectly lost for the rest of the year. Also, if students do not master a new skill on the first day it is introduced, the following lessons provide at least one—possibly two—reviews of the introduction so that students will have sufficient opportunity to learn the skill before it is assumed to be in their skill repertoire and begins to appear in applications.

The problem occurs when students are not brought to mastery on skills that will be used later. For instance, students in Level 1 of *Reading Mastery* are supposed to be taught to follow the teacher's directions about "touching words" before lesson 30. The tasks that the teacher presents require students to follow directions to "touch the first word. ... Touch the next word. ... Touch the next word. ..."

Often students are not brought to mastery when this series of tasks is introduced. These students have problems in the lesson range of the 40s [in *Reading Mastery* 1] because now they are expected to first "touch the next word..." and then "sound it out." If they are not firm on touching the next word on signal, the activity becomes very sloppy and students often become confused about what they are supposed to do. If students are taught on time, however, they have far less difficulty mastering the mechanical steps of touching the next word and then touching the individual letters as they sound it out. The program design provides for enough practice; however, that practice must not be mere exposure or practice with a very low standard of performance. The practice must lead to mastery.

6. Most programs do not require teaching to mastery. Teaching to mastery is a foreign practice to many experienced teachers because most programs do not require mastery. Instead of providing continuous skill development, these programs present topical or thematic units. Students will work on a particular unit for a few days and then it will be replaced by another unit that is not closely related to the first and that does not require application of the same skills and knowledge. This design, referred to as a "spiral curriculum," is

more comfortable for the program designers, teacher, and students; however, it is inferior for teaching skills and knowledge.

It is comfortable for the designers because the design does not have to be careful. The designers do not have to document that everything that is presented is "teachable"; the amount of new learning does not have to be carefully measured. The amount of time required for a "lesson" does not have to correspond precisely to a period, because the design assumes that different teachers will take different amounts of time to get through a particular "lesson" and "unit." The amount of new material is not controlled. The expectations for student performance are low because teachers understand that students actually will not master the material. They simply will be exposed.

The accountability of the teacher is therefore more "comfortable" because the teacher is not expected to get through the material in a specified period of time or bring students to mastery. The spiral curriculum is more comfortable for students because they are not required to learn, use, or apply the skills from one unit to the next unit. They quickly learn that even though they do not understand the details of a particular unit, the unit will soon disappear and be replaced by another that does not require application of skills and knowledge from the previous unit. The design clearly reinforces students for not learning or for learning often vague and inappropriate associations of vocabulary with a particular topic.

If the systematic program is like a stairway, the spiral curriculum is like a series of random platforms suspended on different levels. Students are mysteriously transported from one platform to another, where they remain for a few days as they are exposed to information that is not greatly prioritized. Mastery is impractical with a spiral curriculum design because many students lack the background knowledge they need to stand on a particular "platform." The poor design relieves the program designer of assuring that earlier-taught skills and knowledge are mastered and used. The poor design also relieves students of the responsibility of learning to mastery and it relieves the teacher of teaching to mastery. It therefore promotes poor teaching and poor learning.

In summary, a program that teaches to mastery is like a stairway. Mastery is the guarantee that students are able to reach each stair without falling.

PROPERTIES OF MASTERY

Clearly, mastery is the handmaiden of a systematic program. Mastery is effective for a number of reasons. The most important reason is that mastery permits teachers to achieve steady, reliable progress in student learning. When teachers teach to mastery, we can make predictions about student performance. We can very accurately project where students will be 100 school days from now or 200 school days from now.

Such projections are very powerful, but very foreign to traditional orientations about learning, which view the students' performance as a function of their ability to learn and motivation to learn. Therefore, to predict that student X will be accurately reading 30 words per minute by the end of the kindergarten year would be something of a contradiction because it assumes that the teaching somehow controls the student's learning.

The traditionalist hopes to reach and motivate the student and hopes that the student does not have some type of mysterious "learning disability" that interferes with learning to read. The traditionalist, however, is unable to predict who will read and who won't. Readiness tests are tools that are supposed to predict performance according to what the student brings to school. Because they don't take into account the kind of reading instruction the student will receive, readiness tests fail to predict accurately. In fact, the traditional orientation to reading has a classification for students who are predicted by readiness tests to succeed but who fail to learn to read on schedule—specific learning disabilities. Note that this label holds fast to the assumption that the student's failure to learn to read has to do with a flaw in the student, not a flaw in the instruction. The school or teacher does not have a "disability." The student does. In other words, for the traditionalist, the performance of the student is not clearly linked to teaching. The more scientific orientation to teaching that DI espouses assumes that the student who meets the entrance requirements for the program and who is taught appropriately (to mastery and on schedule) will respond in perfectly lawful ways and will be reading at a predicted skill level by the end of the kindergarten year.

Individualization must occur from the beginning. Projections are keyed to the performance of a student. Not all children entering kindergarten have the same projections because not all of them start at the same place. Those who enter with more skills have a headstart and are expected to be farther after nine months of instruction than the child who enters with a lower skill level. However, even if children begin as low performers, the prediction is that they will master beginning reading skills in kindergarten and will be reading by the end of kindergarten. For the child who enters with a low skill level, the projected end-of-K-year performance may be lesson 120 [in *Reading Mastery* 1]. The projection for the higher performer may be double that number.

The fact that projections are met means that the DI orientation to teaching and mastery is correct. Students will learn if the teaching is appropriate. If they fail to learn, the reason lies not with their inability to learn but with the delivery system's inability to teach.

The concept of individualization is closely related to the issue of mastery and to projections about students' performance. The teacher cannot teach to mastery without referring to the performance of the students being taught. The teacher bases decisions about what to do next on samples of each student's behavior. This sample may come from tasks presented to the group, tasks presented to individual students, or worksheets and similar work samples. DI is designed so students' thinking is made overt. The teacher therefore receives samples of behavior at a high rate on everything that is being taught. The teacher uses this information to judge what rate of presentation is appropriate. If students already have learned the skill or concept, the teacher is to move on. If the teacher determines that some students have not mastered what is being taught, the teacher corrects the mistakes and possibly repeats parts of the exercise. If quite a few students missed the item, the teacher may repeat the entire exercise with the whole group, which is more efficient than presenting it to some students individually.

In summary, teaching to mastery is possible only if the teacher keys the amount and type of practice students receive to the performance of these children.

CRITERIA AND PROCEDURES FOR MEASURING MASTERY

Teaching to mastery is a difficult procedure for teachers to learn. They must learn to reference what to do next according to the student's performance. They must learn high, but realistic, expectations for their students. They must also learn to coordinate mastery with fast pacing so that the lesson is neither a chore for students nor busy work. The teacher uses efficient means of checking students' work, of providing additional practice and firm-ups for students who do not achieve mastery on skills that were taught, and of providing reinforcement for trying hard and for succeeding.

First-time-correct Procedures

An important key to teaching to mastery is the use of first-time-correct procedures. Procedures for inducing mastery require the teacher to interpret students' performance. The primary indicator of mastery is how well students perform the first time a particular task or exercise is presented in the lesson. Each time a task is presented, the group either responds correctly (all students correct) or incorrectly (some students giving the wrong response or no response). First-time correct means all students are correct the first time a task is presented in a lesson.

Also important is how well students perform on the task or exercise if the teacher presents it more than once. If the teacher corrects and repeats the task or exercise, it is important for students to perform correctly the second time. However, for diagnostic purposes, students' responses to the first time the task or exercise is presented provide the most critical information about where students are positioned on the stairway and whether they are appropriately placed in the program. For instance, the first time the teacher asks a question such as, "Do we multiply or divide to solve this problem?" or the first time students read a particular word list, their responses reveal information about the mastery level the students bring to the lesson.

The students' pattern of correct responses also provides important mastery information. If they are making too many mistakes, or if they are not firm on material that had been taught earlier and that is assumed to be firm, they are placed too far in the program and should be moved back. If students give solid indications that they already know what the lesson is teaching, the students may not be placed as far in the program as they might be, and the rate of lesson presentation should increase. Finally, the "correct-response" patterns of a group indicate whether all students belong in the group or whether some should be placed in other groups.

Four criteria permit precise interpretation of the correct-response performance for groups and individuals:

Criterion 1. Students should be at least 70% correct on anything that is being introduced for the first time.

Criterion 2. Students should be at least 90% correct on the parts of the lesson that deal with skills and information introduced earlier in the program sequence.

Criterion 3. At the end of the lesson, all students should be virtually 100% firm on all tasks and activities.

Criterion 4. The rate of student errors should be low enough that the teacher is able to complete the lesson in the allotted time.

Again, all the percentages are based on how students perform the first time a particular task is presented in the lesson. For material that is assumed to be mastered, the group should respond perfectly at least 9 out of 10 times.

As noted above, students' first-time performance shows what they have brought with them to the lesson. That is the material that is in their memory and skill repertoire. The performance of students after the teacher repeats the material indicates only what the students may retain for possibly less than 10 minutes. That time span does not measure mastery. When students master a skill they know it "as well as they know their own name."

All four criteria should be considered in evaluating the mastery of the group. If students meet the first three criteria but can't seem to get through lessons in the allotted time, something is wrong. The following sections examine the four criteria in more detail.

Criterion 1

Students should be at least 70% correct on anything that is being introduced for the first time. This percentage is based on the understanding that even the new skills or procedures that are being introduced are not composed entirely of material that is new. Much of it will be familiar. Therefore, the initial rate of correct responses should not drop below 70%. If students are at mastery on the preceding lessons, this outcome will occur in almost all cases.

If students perform much below 70%, they are not learning the material. If they are only 50% correct, they may be at a chance level—guessing at the answers or the steps in the operation. Their responses are not generated by an overall understanding of what they are learning. At 70% correct, their responses show that they are much closer to understanding the new material than they are to taking blind stabs at responding, and therefore should be able to master the new material during the lesson.

Criterion 2

Students should be at least 90% correct on the parts of the lesson that deal with skills and information introduced earlier in the program sequence. Criterion 2 is based on the fact that students must be completely at mastery on earlier-taught material. When earlier-taught material occurs in later lessons, no reteaching should be required. If substantial reteaching is needed, the amount of new learning that students must achieve to master the lesson becomes too great. If students are not consistently at the 90% correct level on material that had been taught earlier in the program, students need more extensive firming and more delayed tests. Possibly, the teacher should use a game format in which she asks students different questions at the end of the lesson. Students who respond correctly receive points. When virtually all students consistently earn points, they have learned good techniques for learning and retaining information presented in the lesson.

Criterion 3

At the end of the lesson, all students should be virtually 100% firm on all tasks and activities.

Criterion 4

The rate of student errors should be low enough that the teacher is able to complete the lesson in the allotted time. Criteria 3 and 4 go together. When the rate of errors for the overall lesson is low, the teacher does not need to spend great amounts of time firming students, and the teacher should be able to complete the lesson in the allotted time. If students enter the lesson with skills that permit them to attain 70% correct on new material and 90% correct on material taught earlier, students should be able to achieve virtually 100% on all exercises presented in the lesson. Achieving this performance level may require a little additional firming, but it should not be necessary or excessive lesson after lesson. Therefore, if Criteria 1 and 2 are met, students should easily achieve Criterion 3 and the teacher should be able to complete the lesson during the allotted time.

Calculating Percentages

Several different procedures are effective for teachers to learn how to "estimate" or calculate the percentage of first-time-correct responses. One way is to place sticky tabs in the teacher presentation book after each task, or affix a sheet of paper to the page so the teacher can mark whether the group (or individual) correctly responded to each task. After the children have responded to 10 tasks, the teacher simply counts the number of tasks that were correct. If seven were correct, the percentage is 70%. (Note: If the teacher repeats a task, she would not mark the second-time performance the same way she would mark the first-time performance. She could circle the second-time performance, note the performance in a second column, or use another way to separate the first-time performance from performance on tasks or exercises that are repeated.)

After using a procedure of actually counting the responses within each exercise, the teacher should try to make estimates in her head. One way is to "ball park" patterns in terms of whether students are performing closer to 50% or 100%. If they seem closer to 50% (missing a little less than half of what the teacher presents) their first-time percentage is too low. If they clearly are closer to 100% than 50%, their performance tends to be high and in the ball park.

For some tasks, such as reading a passage, the percentage should be high, even on the first reading, because virtually all the words should be familiar. Students should not fall below 90% correct on the first reading of a passage. On the second reading, students should perform close to 100%.

Once the teacher becomes facile at estimating the percentage of correct responses, she has learned to respond sensitively to students' progress and problems. The teacher would apply this skill. If only some of students in the group consistently make mistakes, they probably should be placed in another group.

Decisions about mastery do not derive only from the percentages of first-time-correct performance. The teacher also has information about in-program test performance and independent work performance. The value of identifying the first-time-correct performance is that it affords the teacher the opportunity to correct problems of mastery when they first appear. This opportunity results in greater efficiency in teaching to mastery.

Assessing Mastery Through Delayed Tests

Delayed tests are simply selected tasks from the lesson that are presented again later in the lesson. Because of the "delay" between the time students worked the task and when they work it again, the teacher is provided with a good indication of whether students have the information in their memory.

Presenting delayed tests, either to the group or to individuals, is the best way to shape or improve students' ability to remember new information and to learn how to organize it mentally so that they are able to recall and use it. The tests work best when there is a contingency attached to them. If students know that they will be tested later on any exercise, skill, or problem type presented in the lesson, students will tend to learn the material far better than when no contingency exists. For instance, at the beginning of a reading lesson, the teacher indicates that at the end of the reading lesson, "I'll call on individuals to read some of the harder words in the lesson. Let's see if we can get a perfect score."

After the word attack, the teacher says, "Now you're going to read some of those harder words. Remember, if you read all the words correctly when I call on you, you earn five bonus points. If everybody reads the hard words, everybody receives another three bonus points." This procedure could be repeated at the end of the story before students begin independent work. Similar routines are effective for math and language lessons as well.

To further assure that students are at mastery, the teacher could present delayed tests at different times of the day. A good rule is that whenever students are lined up in the classroom, ask them questions about the newly taught material. Praise students who do well. Remember, the more students understand that they will use the information that they are learning, the more they will develop strategies that permit them to master new material quickly and efficiently. More importantly, by providing delayed tests, the teacher shows students what is important. If the teacher shows that their learning and retention of material are important—not simply within the time frame of the period during which the material is taught—the teacher models what they are to think about, mentally rehearse, and use. This message goes a long way to help students prioritize their thoughts and goals.

PROCEDURES FOR TEACHING TO MASTERY

One of the most obvious questions about teaching to mastery is: If mastery teaching has so many benefits, why haven't we seen the effects of mastery teaching on lower performers? The reason is simply that schools typically (and historically) have not been designed to provide for teaching to mastery. The schools have not been organized either to recognize mastery teaching as important or to address the technical details of achieving it, particularly with lower performers.

Three basic components must be in place if a school is to achieve the transformations that are possible by teaching to mastery: (a) programs in various subject areas that are designed to accommodate mastery teaching; (b) teachers who scrupulously teach everything to mastery; and (c) a system that provides for the grouping of students and the coordination that is required to achieve maximum acceleration of student performance.

Until very recently, no schools have incorporated these three components into a systematic plan that involves all the teachers and all the instruction. The following sections examine these three components in detail.

Programs for Teaching to Mastery

The requirements for instructional sequences are very different from the requirements that states and districts use to adopt instructional material. All instructional programs must have two primary features to make teaching to mastery uniformly possible:

1. The programs must be designed to present instruction for each skill and concept in a way that permits the teacher to teach it to mastery (given that the teacher follows program specifications).

2. The program must be coordinated from level to level so they are continuous and so the later level builds efficiently on what was taught in the earlier level.

Program design—A slogan for a well-designed program is that it teaches everything that students will need for later applications, and it doesn't teach anything that is not needed for future applications. This feature sets the stage for mastery. Students who are at mastery in the program know at least 70% of any new skill or operation that will be taught in the program. Therefore, their first-time percentage on new material will be in the acceptable range. Traditional programs do not have this structure and therefore do not permit application of the rules about first-time correct. Although traditional programs may work adequately with higher performers, they tend to be very ineffective with the lower end of the student population (those students for whom the material is unfamiliar).

The small-step program has a "track" structure, which means that more than one separate skill is taught during each lesson. What had been taught earlier is reviewed. Traditional lessons often are organized around single topics, rather than around a series of continuing tracks. Also, traditional programs are frequently based on loose associations of ideas, such as the various meanings of a vocabulary word like fine. Except in limited cases, the well-designed program would present only the meaning that will be used in upcoming applications.

Traditional programs also do not provide the review students need. Advanced material presented in the traditional textbook is not actually designed to teach content. Rather, the text is a reference book—something like an encyclopedia organized around different topics. The teacher is expected to transfer this information to the students, but the manner in which this transfer is supposed to occur is not clear. What is clear is the fact that it doesn't happen with many students.

A key element of the effective program is that it is designed so that it does not generate possible misrules. For instance, if students are actually taught to guess at the word by figuring out the beginning sound and the general shape of the word, teaching students to mastery will simply guarantee later failure. This is a false rule. If applied, students will certainly confuse words like *slop, shop,* and *stop.* A program with spurious teaching may work when there is a small range of examples (only the word *shop* appearing in what students read). Later, however, the program will fail (when *stop* also appears in what they read).

Also, the program cannot have false or spurious clues that permit students to give the right answer for the wrong reason. If students always recite number facts in the same order, they could learn a serious misrule, which is that the answers always follow the counting order. What's 1+1? What's 2+1? What's 3+1? What's 18+1? Students who have always recited the facts in the counting order will respond to the last question by saying, "Five." The sequence is seriously flawed and introduces a serious misrule.

Unless the program is well designed for teaching to mastery, it often will not produce gains, but frustration, both for students and the teacher. The program must provide both for the rapid teaching of new skills and for a high rate of student responses. These responses let the teacher know whether or not students are at mastery.

Level-to-level coordination—For mastery teaching to be possible, programs must be thoroughly coordinated from level to level. Different levels of traditional instructional programs present the same topics and the same examples. For instance, over 75% of a sixth-grade math program may be presented in the corresponding fifth-grade program. Obviously, this sequence makes no assumption that students have mastered anything that was taught in the fifth grade. In fact, math assessments regularly disclose that students have not mastered any of the content that is new to the current level of the program. Rather, students know only what had been taught one to two levels earlier. This relationship confirms that students have not received consistent experiences in learning what the teachers and textbooks teach. They tend to learn the material much later, through experimentation and trial and error.

Teachers Who Teach Everything to Mastery

This criterion is necessary, but very difficult to attain. Teaching to mastery is the most difficult skill for teachers to learn. One problem is that teachers have a strong tradition of simply exposing students to material, rather than assuring that they master it. What often occurs, even in schools that are supposed to be full-immersion DI schools and that do well with the DI subjects, is that teachers tend to have split teaching philosophies. When presenting DI lessons, they teach to mastery, but when they present other instruction—social studies units, art, vocabulary information—they don't. Instead of constructing variations of routines that they have used in DI sequences, they simply expose students and don't consider the effects of their instruction on student's knowledge base and attitudes.

For example, we recently observed a good DI teacher presenting a "unit" on Sweden to children in the third grade. These children had completed *Reading Mastery 3*; yet, when the teacher presented the unit, she did not refer to anything they had learned in *Reading 3*, did not present the information about Sweden in a systematic way, and did not provide any tests to determine whether the students had mastered the new information about Sweden. Instead, she passed out a worksheet that contained a map of Sweden, some facts, and some questions. She read the facts, briefly discussed some of the customs, told the students about several other things that characterize Sweden, and then directed the students to write answers to the questions and color the map.

At this point, we asked students a series of questions to determine whether they knew the new information and knew how to fit it into what they already knew about the world. Here are some of the questions.

"It says that Sweden is a country in Europe. Do you live in that country? ... What's the name of the country you live in? ... Can you find Sweden on the globe? ... Can you show me where Europe is on the globe? ... Have you read about any other countries in Europe? ..." We then asked about several of the vocabulary words that appeared on the worksheet. The students failed nearly all of these items.

It would not have taken the teacher more than five minutes to teach students to mastery on all the information they would have needed to fit the worksheet material into the framework of knowledge they already possessed. They had read about Herman the fly, who flew around the world, landing in Italy. Students were able to locate Italy on the map. This is a good reference point for going north to Sweden. Once they saw Sweden on the globe and saw its distance from Italy and from the United States, they would have had a good schema of its size and its relation to places they already knew. That was the purpose of teaching the global information in *Reading*

3–to provide them with "stepping stones" upon which to build new facts and operations.

The teacher, however, did not know how easy it was to teach to mastery on things that were not in the DI curriculum, or how important it was. Her approach was very ill advised because it promoted compartmentalization of information and discontinuous learning strategies. When doing the social studies, the students had a dabbling attitude. Some of the material was so strange to the students that they apparently didn't even know what sort of questions they should ask to make sense of it. They didn't even try to understand it. In the case of Sweden, they didn't know clearly where it was, what it was, or how it related in any way to the things they had learned.

During the direct-instruction periods, in contrast, the students had strategies that permitted them to learn to mastery. The net result of the unit on Sweden was that the teacher lost lots of opportunities to build on what students already knew. Furthermore, she lost opportunities to help accelerate the intellectual growth of her students.

To make sure that they really learned the information on Sweden, the teacher would have to add several items to part of her daily routine—the openers—which consist of a series of questions the children are to answer. The new items would relate to Sweden. What's the name of the country you live in? ... Is that country in Europe? ... Name some countries in Europe. ... Is Sweden as big as the United States? ... I'll touch places on the globe. Tell me the name of the country I touch. ..."

"Compartmentalized" teaching is far more common than teaching designed to build on what students already know. The general guideline for a teacher who wants to accelerate intellectual growth is: If you teach anything, teach it to mastery.

To do that, the teacher figures out how the new material is related to what students already know and makes this relationship explicit and part of the mastery teaching. Before teachers are able to teach everything to mastery, they must be trained and they must receive extensive models about how to do it.

A System That Supports Mastery and Acceleration

Because students will not be seriously accelerated unless they receive possibly three or more years of undiluted immersion in mastery teaching, the school must have a system that requires teaching to mastery. A system is necessary because immersing students in mastery instruction involves more than one teacher. In fact, if mastery-teaching immersion is to occur for all students, it must involve all teachers, all subjects, and virtually all aspects of the school day.

This system meets seven primary requirements:

1. All students must be appropriately placed in each instructional program. All placements are based on first-time-correct performance. Mastery is not possible unless students are placed according to the criteria for first-time-correct performance.

2. All groups must be homogeneous with respect to the performance level of all students in the group. This requirement is an extension of the first-time-correct requirements. Unless all students in the group are appropriately placed, the teacher will not be able to bring the group to mastery in a reasonable amount of time. The teacher will have to spend time providing additional practice to students who should not be in the group. This additional practice tends not to serve students who need it nor the other students, who waste time while the teacher works on firming skills that they have already mastered.

3. There are actually three critical scheduling issues. The first is that adequate time must be scheduled on a daily basis for teaching each group each subject. The second is that the schedules must be coordinated to permit relatively easy movement of students from one instructional group to another, based on their performance. If two students should be in a math group that is 55 lessons earlier in the program, the transfer is relatively easy if the group that is to receive these students is teaching math at the same time as the group in which the students are currently placed. The third issue is that movement of students from one instructional group to another should occur frequently throughout the year. A general rule for grades K-3 is that major regrouping should occur at least three times during

the year. This regrouping assures that instructional groups remain homogeneous in performance. Note that regrouping is generally not required as frequently in the upper grades after the implementation is stabilized. However, periodic changes may have to occur in math and language. All schedules must be coordinated across classrooms and grades so that cross-class grouping and regrouping is possible. This need is met only if specified classrooms teach the same subjects at the same time.

4. Schedules must provide adequate time for each subject and each instructional group, and teachers must faithfully follow schedules. The schedules must include time for worksheets, so that students receive timely feedback on any mistakes they made, and so teachers receive information about any skills or items that need additional firming. The worksheets and possible firming periods are particularly important during the first several years of the implementation.

Many problems of scheduling periods occur in the beginning grades. Sometimes, schedules provide adequate time for two of three groups in a subject, but not for the third. Sometimes, the schedule is different on different days, which means that students may not receive instruction in some subjects on some days. Sometimes, the time allotted for the teaching of a subject is not adequate. All these problems must be corrected if adequate mastery is to be attained.

5. A group's progress in mastering new material must be continuous throughout the year. If the group completes level 3 reading in the middle of February, students must begin level 4 within no more than two or three school days. Level 4 should not be delayed until the beginning of the next school year.

6. All teachers must enforce the same set of schoolwide management rules and practices for celebrating academic achievements. There should be rules for how students are to behave in the class, so that if students misbehave, they understand both the rule that they broke and the consequence. The system of rules should be designed so students receive reinforcement for complying with rules. The schoolwide celebration of students' achievement should be the centerpiece of the school's ceremonies. Students who achieve

well should be recognized in a way that leaves no doubt about how important the school feels mastery accomplishments are.

7. The performance of students must be regularly monitored. The school must have systems for regularly monitoring students' progress. The monitoring information may consist of weekly summaries of progress in each subject, summaries of student performance on in-program tests, and reports on daily independent work. The purpose of the monitoring is to guarantee that no students fall through the cracks and that all receive the best instruction that the school is able to deliver.

This full set of seven requirements is rarely met. Each, however, is necessary if the school is to achieve maximum acceleration of student performance.

Four Rules for Teaching to Mastery

One of the reasons that mastery instruction is difficult for teachers to learn is that facts about mastery soundly contradict beliefs that teachers have about individual differences and how children learn. Note, however, that the teachers' misconceptions are perfectly consistent with their experiences. The teachers' beliefs are based on exactly what they have observed. The problem is that they have usually never observed students who have received extensive mastery instruction. To engage in mastery instruction, teachers must adhere to four basic rules that contradict conventional wisdom and the beliefs that many teachers hold.

Rule 1: Hold the same standard for high performers and low performers— This rule is based on the fact that students of all performance levels exhibit the same learning patterns if they have the same foundation in information and skills. The false belief that characterizes the conventional wisdom about teaching is that lower performers learn in generically different ways from higher performers and should be held to a lower or looser standard. Evidence of this belief is that teachers frequently have different "expectations" for higher and lower performers. They expect higher performers to learn the material; they excuse lower performers from achieving the same standard of performance. Many teachers believe that lower performers are something like crippled children. They can walk the same route that the higher performers walk, but they need more help in walking.

These teachers often drag students through the lesson and provide a lot of additional prompting. They have to drag students because the students are making a very high percentage of first-time errors. In fact, the students make so many mistakes that it is very clear that they are not placed appropriately in the sequence and could not achieve mastery on the material in a reasonable amount of time. The teachers may correct the mistakes, and may even repeat some parts that had errors; however, at the end of the exercise, the students are clearly not near 100% on anything. Furthermore, the teacher most probably does not provide delayed tests to assess the extent to which these students have retained what had been presented earlier.

The information these teachers receive about low performers is that they do not retain information, that they need lots and lots of practice, and that they don't seem to have strategies for learning new material. Ironically, however, all these outcomes are predictable for students who receive the kind of instruction these students have received. High performers receiving instruction of the same relative difficulty or unfamiliarity would perform the same way. Let's say the lower performers typically have a first-time-correct percentage of 40%. If higher performers were placed in material that resulted in a 40% first-time-correct performance, their behavior would be like that of lower performers. They would fail to retain the material, rely on the teacher for help, not exhibit self-confidence, and continue to make the same sorts of mistakes again.

If students are placed according to their first-time-correct percentages, they tend to learn and behave the same way, whether they are "lower performers" or "higher performers." In Project Follow Through, we mapped the progress of students of different IQ ranges. The results showed that regardless of students' entering IQ, the rate of progress was quite similar across all children and across different subjects. Lower performers learned as fast as higher performers. They simply started at a different place, with material that higher performers had long since mastered. Note that this conclusion may be somewhat biased because we paid particular attention to the instruction for the lower performers. They tended to have better teachers and their instruction tended to be monitored very closely. In any case, they learned at a very healthy rate, one that paralleled that of students with IQs 40 points higher.

The typical practices of placing and teaching students are completely opposed to appropriate placement and teaching procedures. At the University of Oregon, we place teaching-practice students in special-ed classrooms that use direct-instruction programs. During the years that we first offered these practica, we typically worked with teachers who were teaching DI but had not generally received much training. Before we arranged for a placement with a new supervising teacher, therefore, we made sure that the classroom was "appropriate" for our students, which means that the children the practicum students were to work with were placed appropriately and that the teacher was using and modeling appropriate practices. As part of the review of the new classrooms that were candidates for receiving practicum students, we checked the program placement of the students and changed their placement if necessary.

Our estimate is that in the first 40 or more classrooms we used, the children were moved back in DI reading programs an average of 100 lessons—sometimes 120 lessons. The children, in other words, were placed about three fourths of a school year or more beyond the optimum first-time-correct percentages. Nearly all teachers had children that were seriously misplaced. Furthermore, I don't recall a single classroom in which children's percentages required us to move children ahead in the programs. Children were always "over their heads."

Coincidental with the inappropriate placement was inappropriate expectations. Often, teachers were good technicians—acting positively, exhibiting good pacing and other mechanical skills, and correcting mistakes in a timely and apparently appropriate manner. They often had noble motives for placing the students where they were, so that students would be closer to the appropriate placement for their age. Their error, however, was that this placement made mastery impossible. Without achieving steady and predictable mastery, children could not gain at a healthy rate.

An almost inevitable conclusion that teachers derive from observations based on inappropriate placement of children is that these children are different. For many teachers the difference suggests that the children need a "different approach." We have seen many teachers who have asserted that "that group has been through the program two times, and it just doesn't work with them." The teacher is not actually blaming the children for not learning, but rather suggesting that they may be able to learn more easily with some kind of approach that matches their different way of learning.

In about 12 cases, we were able to test the children who, according to the teachers' reports, had gone through the program and not mastered the material. In every case, it was very apparent that they had never been through the program at anything approximating mastery. In some cases, the appropriate placement (based on first-time-correct percentages) was the beginning of a lower level of the series—about 300 lessons from the end of the level the teachers said the children had completed two times. Furthermore, when children were placed appropriately and actually taught to a high standard of performance, they learned at a predictable rate, and they indeed mastered the material.

Rule 2: At the beginning of the school year; place continuing students who have been taught to mastery no more than five lessons from their last lesson of the preceding year—If something is thoroughly learned and applied, it will be retained by lower performers as well as by higher performers.

The conventional wisdom, in contrast, holds that lower performers "have it one day and forget it the next." And whatever they have, "they completely lose over the summer." Again, this expectation results largely from the kind of instruction students have received. Even after teachers have learned to teach students to mastery, however, they often retain their expectations about how much lower performers will retain. In the first ASAP schools we worked with in Utah, teachers routinely placed continuing students at the beginning of the school year 80 to 100 lessons behind the last lesson they had completed the preceding spring.

Teachers had been told the ASAP policy for placing students at the beginning of the school year: Go back no more than five lessons in the program sequence and bring students to a high level of mastery on the material. This firming is to take no more than five school days. After the review, students should be well prepared to pick up in the program where they had finished in the spring.

The teachers were openly skeptical about this procedure, and they ignored it. They argued that, over the summer, students forget much of what they had learned. We told them that learning didn't work that way. We pointed out that there is a lot of literature on learning and retention that shows that even if something had been thoroughly learned and had not been practiced for years, there would be great "savings" in the amount of time needed to reteach this material to mastery. Therefore, if appropriate placement for students in the fall (based on error performance) is 80 lessons behind where they finished in the spring, the only possible conclusion is that they had never learned the material in the spring.

For several years, the teachers resisted following the fall placement rules and continued to use their traditional practices. To correct this situation, we documented the mastery of all students several weeks before the end of the school year. We staged "show off" lessons that were observed. The observations confirmed what students did know, and in some cases, identified some things they had not adequately mastered. Before the end of the school year, students were placed according to the rules about first-time-correct percentages so they were firm in everything that had been presented in the program sequence.

At the beginning of the next school year, we controlled the placement of students to make sure that teachers were placing students no more than five lessons behind where they had left off in the spring. Students performed as predicted. After possibly one or two lessons, they clearly performed as well as they had in the spring.

The response of the teachers was overwhelmingly one of disbelief and revelation. Most of them said something like, "I'm amazed. They actually retained what they had learned."

The magnitude of their surprise suggests how strong the belief was that students could not possibly retain the information over the summer. This strong belief had been supported by what they had observed in the past, which was based on spring placements that were far beyond what students had actually mastered.

Rule 3: Always place students appropriately for more rapid mastery progress—This fact contradicts the belief that students are placed appropriately in a sequence if they have to struggle—scratch their head, make false starts, sigh, frown, gut it out. According to one version of this belief, if there are no signs of hard work there is no evidence of learning. This belief does not place emphasis on the program and the teacher to make learning manageable but on the grit of the student to meet the "challenge." In the traditional interpretation, much of the "homework" assigned to students (and their families) is motivated by this belief. The assumption seems to be that students will be strengthened if they are "challenged."

This belief is flatly wrong. If students are placed appropriately, the work is relatively easy. Students tend to learn it without as much "struggle." They tend to retain it better and they tend to apply it better, if they learn it with fewer mistakes.

The prevalence of this misconception about "effort" was illustrated by the field tryouts of the *Spelling Mastery* programs. Over half of the tryout teachers who field-tested the first and second levels of *Spelling Mastery* with lower performers indicated on their summary forms that they thought the program was too easy for the children. Note that most of these teachers were not DI teachers and had never taught DI programs before. When asked about whether they had ever used a program that induced more skills in the same amount of time, all responded, "No." Nearly all agreed that the lower performers had learned substantially more than similar children had in the past. When asked if students were bored with the program, all responded, "No."

What led the teachers to believe that the programs were too easy? All cited the same evidence: students didn't have to struggle. For them, it wasn't appropriate instruction if it wasn't difficult for the lower performers.

Often, good DI teachers place students who are behind as close as possible to their age-appropriate placement. Their rationale is that if students can make good progress at this placement, they will be farther ahead. Placing students at the edge of their ability to perform, however, means placing them where the students are "working very hard" and where they will make a high percentage of mistakes. This placement effectively negates good teaching.

One teacher we observed would have scored a 10 on the teaching behaviors that good teachers are supposed to exhibit. She was working with fourth graders who were placed far beyond where they should have been placed in the *Corrective Reading* program. In trying to read one of the longer sentences, the students missed five words. The teacher corrected each mistake with alacrity. The teacher faithfully returned to the beginning of the sentence and directed the reading again. At last, the students read the sentence without error, and the teacher praised them. They smiled and apparently felt good about their achievement. Later, we tested the students individually on the sentence. No student made less than three errors in reading the sentence. The teacher's expectations for these students were simply unrealistic, and although the teacher had superior teaching skills, all were effectively negated by the placement of the students. When asked why she placed the students where she did, she expressed her concern with their future if they didn't catch up to grade level. She wanted them to learn as much as possible in the available time, and she assumed that the closer they were to working on fourth-grade material, the greater their chances of achieving this goal sooner.

In working with the ASAP schools in Utah, we had several demonstrations that tested this formula. During the first two years of the project, these schools had great concern over the math placement of fifth- and sixth-grade students. Very few sixth graders placed in the sixth level or even the fifth level of *Connecting Math Concepts*. Some barely passed the placement test for the fourth level of the program—Level D. This level assumes that students have mastery of a wide range of math facts and operations. Therefore, we were reluctant to place new students in D unless they had a strong performance on the placement test. The schools, like the teacher in the example above, assumed that the fastest way to get sixth graders into sixth-grade material was to start them as close to that material as possible.

On three occasions, we had the opportunity to split groups that were fairly homogeneous in performance and to place half the group at the beginning of D and the other half at the beginning of C, where they would learn the facts and operations that are assumed by Level D. The strategy for these students was to make sure they performed according to the ideal percentages of first-time performance, and to move as quickly as possible. If students were clearly firm on something, we would either direct the teacher to skip it in half the lessons or present the problems as independent work. As soon as the percentages started to drop, we would return to presenting full lessons and continue at that pace until it was clear that the students could be safely accelerated. (Note: We tend not to skip material when we accelerate students. We simply go through the material faster. We've discovered that when teachers start skipping material, they often skip too much or skip material that should not be skipped even if students perform at acceptable percentages.)

In all cases, groups that started in C performed much better and actually passed up groups that started in D. In two cases, this occurred before the end of the first year. For the last case, it occurred in the middle of the second year. The students who started in D tended not to perform near the ideal first-time percentages. They often failed the 10-lesson tests, and teachers had to spend a great deal of time reviewing and reteaching things the students were expected to have learned. In contrast, the students who had been placed in C were able to do more than one lesson a day (until they reached about lesson 30 in D) and had a very high rate of passing the 10-lesson tests. For these students, the sequence of the program was congruous with their skill level, and the steps in the program were small; for the students who started in D, the program steps were too large and the climb too steep. The overall effect was that the D-starting students didn't like math as much as the other students did and had far less confidence about their ability to learn math. We later adopted the practice of starting all students with marginal understanding in Level C, not D.

Rule 4: Move students as quickly and as reinforcingly as their performance permits—This rule opposes the notion that teaching to mastery is somehow synonymous with having picky or punishing standards. For instance, I recently observed a teacher who seemed to confuse teaching to mastery with being a "taskmaster." She was teaching reading to a group of 10 first graders. Students were attempting to read a sentence in unison. After the second word, the teacher stopped the group because one of the students did not have both feet on the floor. On the second trial, one of the students did not point to a word on time. The third time, one of the students did not clearly respond to the last word in the sentence. On the fourth trial, three students did not read the second word, etc.

This teacher, and many others who attempt to teach to mastery, confuse form with function. The goal is to give the children the information and practice they need as quickly and efficiently as possible, secure evidence that they have mastered the material, and move on. While military precision may indicate mastery for some things, effective tests should be used to determine mastery. After observing the teaching of the reading lesson for a while, I pointed to a student who had unwittingly been responsible for the group going back to the beginning of the sentence at least twice and asked the teacher, "Does he know all the words in this sentence?"

She said, "I don't know."

I asked, "If you presented an individual turn to him, would he know all the words?"

She said, "I'm not sure."

Her responses indicated that she had been largely looking at the wrong things. The student was at mastery, but his performance was being judged according to standards that were simply barriers—not indicators of mastery. The teacher was trying to teach to mastery without actually evaluating what was happening. She was being a taskmaster, not an evaluator. The teacher's behavior showed the students that they were failing, even though they were actually quite firm on the material. And it wasn't apparent to them what they should do to please her. It seemed inevitable that they would have to read each sentence many times, regardless of what they did.

Although these students were placed properly in the instructional sequence, the teacher's method of firming preempted her from being able to meet the criterion of getting through the lesson in a reasonable amount of time. That fact should have been a signal that something was wrong.

I told her to use a different format for presenting to this group. She would tell students that they would read the sentence only one time. If they made a mistake, the teacher would tell them the correct word and then they would move on. After the group read the sentence one time, the teacher would call on two or possibly three students to read the sentence individually. If they all read it correctly, everybody in the group would receive a point for the sentence. (Also, when students read the sentence, they were permitted one, but only one, re-read or self-correct of a word.)

Although this format is not appropriate in all situations, it was good for this teacher because it helped her separate the mechanical details from the substance of what is being learned and helped her present in a way that gave students a chance both to achieve mastery and to feel good about their success. When she was able to observe the performance of individual students, she was able to see more clearly whether they were at mastery. She also was able to increase the pace of the lesson so that it was far more enjoyable for her.

BENEFITS OF IMMERSING STUDENTS IN MASTERY

Teaching to mastery has benefits for students, teachers, and the school system. Students benefit by becoming much more competent and by gaining options for their futures they otherwise would not have. Teachers benefit because students who are taught to mastery tend to succeed; therefore, teaching becomes easier. Schools benefit because students are much easier to teach in the upper grades if they have a solid mastery foundation starting in kindergarten. In the upper grades, students are able to learn new material at a good rate, and the bottom end of the student population performs more like traditionally taught students.

Two types of performance change occur in students. The most obvious is that students learn more material during a specified time period. The second change is in their ability to learn new material. There is a simple relationship between the amount of material they master and their overall facility to learn new material: The more success students have with a particular type of material, the better they become at it.

Teaching to mastery also instills self-confidence in students because they learn they are capable of learning whatever new skills or material the teacher presents. Their positive attitude is firmly grounded in experience. Because students have learned everything the teacher has taught, students understandably have confidence that it will happen the same way for future instruction.

What governs these changes in student performance and self-confidence? The degree to which students benefit from being taught to mastery depends on the extent of the mastery teaching and on the number of areas in which students experience mastery.

Early work in the Direct Instruction Preschool provided many examples of the acceleration achieved in specific areas of knowledge by teaching to mastery. One of the cleanest demonstrations came from the teaching of classification concepts—vehicles, clothing, food, animals, etc.—to 4-year-olds. For this demonstration, the order of introduction for the classes differed from one group of children to another. (One group started with food, another with clothing, etc., and learned the classes in different orders.)

Children learned one class to mastery, then learned the next in their sequence. Children were considered to be at mastery if they could name members of a class and correctly respond to inference games that asked about the larger class and the smaller class. For instance, after children had learned about clothing, the teacher would say, 'I'm thinking of something that is clothing. Is it a shoe?" The answer is, "Maybe," or, "We don't know."

The teacher also would present tasks that referred to things in the class of clothing. "I'm thinking of something that is a shirt. Is it clothing?" The answer is, "Yes." Also, "I'll name some things. Tell me if they are clothing or not clothing. Truck…glass…hat…etc."

The number of trials required for the children to learn different classes followed a predictable trend regardless of which class they learned first and which they learned fourth or fifth. The class that required the largest number of trials was the first class or second class in their sequence. The fourth or fifth class in the sequence required less than half the number of trials required for the children to learn the first class.

One of the reasons for this accelerated learning is that the children did not have to learn as much to master the fifth class as they had to learn to master the first. In learning the first class, they had to learn the names of higher-order class (vehicles, for instance) and some members of this class (boat, train, bus, etc.). Children also had to learn the relationship between the higher-order class and the members of the class. They had to learn basically that all trucks are vehicles, but that all vehicles are not necessarily trucks. This relationship is tricky and requires practice.

All the classes have this same structure. Children who learn the structure for the first class do not have to relearn it for each of the other classes. They still have to learn the name for the new higher-order class and the names for the various members. But the children do not have to relearn the structure or relationship of the higher-order class to members. Therefore, the children do not have to learn as much to master later examples. Consequently, children are able to master these classes faster, in fewer trials, and with less learning. Note, however, that these children could not benefit from the savings in how much learning is required unless the children thoroughly learned the structure of at least one class. If the children "sort of" learned the earlier classes, there would not be a dramatic change in the number of trials or amount of practice the children needed to "sort of" learn later classes. These children could not "transfer" the structure from one class to another because the children did not thoroughly understand the structure.

Because they had more experience learning to mastery, they developed more effective strategies for categorizing new information or operations in a way that permits them to recall and use this information. In other words, they are better at learning how to learn, simply because they have had more successful practice in thoroughly learning new information and skills. This practice permits them to learn new material faster than students who don't experience mastery.

The same benefits that occur in this example apply to all bodies of related knowledge. If students learn one particular subject, such as math, to mastery, but don't learn spelling, reading, handwriting, language, and other skills to mastery, the students gain an advantage in math. Students develop the facility needed to learn new math concepts and applications faster. However, the benefits of the mastery instruction would not be greatly evident in other content areas. Not a great deal of "transfer" would be expected to affect the students' reading performance or writing performance.

Students who are immersed in mastery, in all subjects for at least three years, will become much smarter than comparable students taught in a traditional manner. Mastery-taught students not only will know more—these students will be far more proficient and faster at learning new academic material of any kind. Because these students have been immersed in mastery, the students have thoroughly learned everything taught and have developed generalized mastery-learning skills that permit them to achieve mastery quickly with any academic content. In other words, if students experience mastery instruction in all subjects for a substantial period of time, they are changed. They become smarter. They learn faster. They retain new information better.

Students who are taught to mastery in all subjects for only a short period of time (a school year or less) will benefit, but not as much as those who receive mastery instruction for a much longer period. They tend to learn more skills during a given time period than students of the same initial performance level who are not taught to mastery. But these mastery-taught students will not receive the extent of learning to mastery needed to greatly change their rate of learning new material. If a student who starts at 7 years old has had no previous experience in being taught to mastery, the student's new learning performance probably will not be greatly different than it was before this instruction.

What this means is that mastery teaching provided for several years has the power to take students who enter school performing at a relatively low level and transform them into students who are much smarter, as measured by any method we might choose to assess intelligence and skill. Through mastery teaching for several years, the school has the power to change lower-performing students into higher-performing students. In many Title I, full-school DI implementations, the lowest-performing fourth graders complete Level 4 in reading, math, and language programs. Furthermore, the higher performers in fourth grade frequently complete Level 6 of these programs. Mastery learning is the only vehicle that is capable of achieving this transformation.

RESULTS OF NOT TEACHING TO MASTERY

Just as teaching to mastery has a positive effect on students' self-image because it provides students with evidence that they are learning, failing to teach to mastery promotes a negative self-image. The student who is consistently incapable of performing correctly on the material presented is quite aware of this failure rate. In time, the student comes to the unfortunate conclusion, "I am a failure."

This attitude is dangerous because students who know they fail are quick to give up after experiencing evidence of failure. Failure is punishing; they understandably do not want to engage in punishing activities. Therefore, they often avoid the kind of practice that would actually help them become successful.

Reteaching students who have learned inappropriate strategies and negative attitudes requires great amounts of time. When students are not taught to mastery, they often mislearn the skills and concepts the teacher attempts to teach. For instance, they may learn to guess at words in sentences. Reteaching them requires many more trials and much more work than that required to teach them to mastery initially. Initial teaching may require only 10 or fewer trials on some skills. Reteaching the same skill after students have mislearned it and have practiced inappropriate strategies for years may require several hundred trials. Even with careful remedial instruction, however, the student leaves the school with unnecessary scars of failure. The student has experienced unnecessary pain and has drawn unfortunate negative conclusions about self and school. These conclusions could have been avoided by teaching to mastery.

SUMMARY

Teaching to mastery represents the most effective use of available instructional time. It accelerates students' performance, provides students with demonstrations of success rather than failure, and reduces the total amount of work that must be done to transmit a given body of skill and knowledge to students. If students are immersed in mastery, they become smarter because they acquire information faster, and they develop efficient strategies for learning and retaining new material of any type.

For mastery to occur, the program design must be like a stairway, distributing new learning in small amounts and providing for mastery of each step before moving on to a new step. After being introduced, new learning is firmed for several days, then systematically reviewed across time. Students learn that once something is learned, it must be remembered and used again and again.

In addition, the teacher and the system must have provisions that permit continuity, appropriate placement of students according to their performance, close coordination of schedules within the school, ample models of what students are to do, and provisions for celebrating academic achievements of students. Teachers must be able to make predictions about student performance.

Teaching to mastery is difficult for schools to orchestrate because of the various details that must be coordinated, and difficult for teachers to learn because the implications of teaching to mastery often contradict conventional wisdom about how to teach, place, and challenge students.

Mastery is difficult for teachers for three reasons:

1. It is contrary to their practices and expectations about how students will perform.
2. It therefore forces the teacher to view students and instruction in a way that hinders success.
3. Schools do not have good models of doing it the right way.

At the core of teaching to mastery is information about student performance, which is expressed as the percentage of first-time-correct responses for material that is introduced the first time and for material that is assumed to be at mastery.

Students taught with a mastery approach will change in three ways:

1. They will be able to learn new material that has the same structure in fewer trials.
2. They will know more information and more operations.
3. They will have more skill in applying what they have learned.

Students taught to mastery have learned how to learn. They have developed generalized mastery-learning skills they can apply to all subjects. When done properly, mastery is able to change the lives of children and provide them with a far brighter future than they would have in the absence of mastery.

SECTION II

DEVELOPING EFFECTIVE CURRICULAR MATERIAL

Coinciding with the promotion and development of his philosophy of learning, Engelmann used the principles of his philosophy to design instructional programs that could be widely used. In the 1960s, Engelmann began reporting on the success of these programs and how they were related to his theories of learning and instruction. His publications not only promoted his programs, but also legitimized them by demonstrating their strong effectiveness in comparison to other curricula. Throughout his career, Engelmann has tried to explain the differences between his instructional programs and traditional programs. He has critiqued educational theories and programs that, in his judgment, are not able to serve as strong instructional tools. These critiques were written not to promote his work, but to elucidate what principles do and do not lead to effective instruction.

The publications in this section were selected to illustrate the development of Engelmann's instructional programs and how they were based on his philosophy of learning. They demonstrate the validity of his theories and how the Direct Instruction model is not only successful with at-risk students, but *all* students, even those thought to be unteachable before. The broad application of the Direct Instruction model has helped countless students achieve, and also given hope that all children can succeed at the highest levels.

Engelmann's early publications discussed the development of DISTAR reading, language, and math programs, and their implementation in the Bereiter-Engelmann preschool. These articles, one of which is reprinted as Chapter 6 in this section, detail how the programs were designed and implemented to maximize the effectiveness and efficiency of the lessons, while aiding an underserved population. The programs were structured to teach core content at an accelerated rate. This acceleration propelled students to levels where they could be competitive with their more affluent peers.

Engelmann's publications discussed the success and difficulties of implementing the programs as well as the need to take a scientific approach to instruction where all the variables affecting instruction are recognized and controlled. Thus, his earliest publications demonstrated the validity of his philosophy of learning while explaining why traditional programs were not as successful as Direct Instruction programs. He was able to identify the weaknesses of these programs and how the Direct Instruction model accounted for these factors. Engelmann's scientific approach to instruction created a blueprint for the development of future programs, which would cover more topics and grade levels.

In line with his belief in scientific reasoning, Engelmann has always incorporated the collection of data during instruction to make sure that students are learning the material. He has also been a strong proponent of the use of data to determine the effectiveness of an instructional program and whether it should be implemented. The creation of Project Follow Through in the late 1960s gave Engelmann the opportunity to develop a large data set to demonstrate the effectiveness of Direct Instruction.

Project Follow Through was the largest and most expensive experiment ever conducted in the field education. The experiment was funded by the U. S. federal government and designed to determine the most successful academic program for teaching at-risk children. The Direct Instruction model and over twenty other instructional models were systematically implemented in schools across the country in urban and rural settings. Thousands of students from very diverse backgrounds were administered the Direct Instruction programs. The results of Project Follow Through were clear-cut. Students taught with Direct Instruction had stronger academic growth and stronger self-concepts at the end of the intervention. No other curriculum produced these changes. Thus, the results demonstrated the success of the Direct Instruction model. They showed its success with at-risk students, as well as more affluent peers. Both groups experienced accelerated growth and success in comparison to students in other programs. The results also showed its success across all types of community settings. Engelmann has written extensively about the outcome of Project Follow Through and its demonstration that the Direct Instruction model was by far the most effective program overall. The expansive data set provided strong evidence of the effectiveness of the Direct Instruction model, but also extensive material to analyze and report on in the following decades. One of Engelmann's summaries of the Follow Through results is in Chapter 12.

Following the development of the original Direct Instruction programs, Engelmann applied the theoretical principles to instructional programs for various other topics such as algebra, writing, science, and social studies. He and his colleagues also began to test the effectiveness of the Direct Instruction model with a broader range of students, providing validation of his theories on learning. They applied Direct Instruction principles to teach students with autism, severe handicaps (Chapter 9), and those who were deaf or hard of hearing (Chapter 7). Through these experiments Engelmann demonstrated how the Direct Instruction model is not only successful with at-risk students, but with all students, including middle-class and high achieving students (Chapter 8).

The success of the model with all students is due in part to its focus on maximizing the effectiveness and efficiency of instruction. By providing clear, concise lessons, designed to teach to mastery, students require fewer repetitions and less practice to advance. Some of Engelmann's work incorporated these principles into new modes of instruction. For instance, in the mid-1980s he pioneered the use of video disk technology for instruction (Chapter 10). His work with students who were deaf or hard of hearing involved the development of tactual vocoders to help the students develop proper speech by allowing them to feel the different vibrations for each sound in a word (Chapter 7). These experiments also included students without hearing difficulties, which helped advance Engelmann's understanding of unfamiliar learning, a continued focus throughout his career and illustrated in this section by his use of Direct Instruction to teach absolute musical pitch (Chapter 11).

Through his research on unfamiliar learning Engelmann gained a better understanding of what it means if a child requires hundreds of repetitions to learn an unfamiliar task and thus, a greater understanding of the process of learning and the importance of learning to mastery. Furthermore by understanding how children learn unfamiliar tasks or problems it becomes easier to teach them difficult skills. As in other work, Engelmann applied his scientific approach to analyze the situation, identify the variables, and control them to create change.

CHAPTER 6

The Bereiter-Engelmann preschool provided an environment to test Engelmann's theories of instruction with at-risk children and an opportunity to teach students the academic skills needed to prepare them for elementary school. In this article, the authors discuss the process of creating an academically oriented preschool for culturally deprived children and their experiences in teaching at-risk children. They discuss their objectives for the preschool and how they were to be obtained, specifically the development of language skills. Key goals outlined for the preschool included analysis of the formal characteristics of language, reading, and arithmetic that were pertinent for their students. They created instructional goals based on these characteristics, determining feasible means of implementing Direct Instruction with the students, determining how much these particular students could learn, and assessing the rate of learning that could be achieved. Additionally, the article discusses the children's achievement in three individual instructional programs following a three month period. Examples of the lessons taught are included to provide greater clarity on the principles of Direct Instruction.

The authors demonstrate the effectiveness of the Direct Instruction model and the importance of creating an academically oriented preschool so all students are prepared to enter elementary school and succeed. This article represents one of many written to promote the effectiveness of the Direct Instruction model, argue for the need to restructure the organization of preschools, and demonstrate how a properly designed program could help struggling students succeed.

AN ACADEMICALLY ORIENTED PRE-SCHOOL FOR CULTURALLY DEPRIVED CHILDREN (1966)[*]

Carl Bereiter, Siegfried Engelmann, Jean Osborn & Philip A. Reidford[1]

The experimental pre-school represents radical departures both in methods and in goals from any existing pre-school programs for the culturally deprived of which we are aware. These departures are based on two premises which we can defend only very briefly here. One premise is that mere enrichment of experience is not sufficient to enable the culturally deprived child to overcome his backwardness in skills necessary for later academic success. Analysis of available data on the effects of enrichment, principally that of Lee on the effects of selective migration on Negro intelligence[2] and that of Kirk on the effects of early education of the mentally retarded,[3] indicates that the most that can be hoped for is an average gain of one year in mental age for each year of enriched educational experience. From this it is a matter of simple arithmetic to show that a four-year-old child who is already a year retarded in the development of verbal intellectual abilities cannot be expected to overcome his deficit through a year or two of enriched experience. Indeed, he should never entirely overcome his deficit, even with continuing enrichment.

---

[*] Bereiter, C., Engelmann, S., Osborn, J., & Reidford, P. A. (1966). An academically oriented pre-school for culturally deprived children. In F. M. Hechinger (Ed.), *Pre-school education today: New approaches to teaching three-, four-, and five-year-olds* (pp. 105–135). Garden City, NY: Doubleday & Co. Reprinted with permission of the publisher.

[1] The authors are members of the Institute for Research on Exceptional Children at the University of Illinois. The material in this article was originally presented as part of a symposium at the American Educational Research Association Convention in Chicago, February 12, 1965. The research reported herein was supported through the Cooperative Research Program of the Office of Education, United States Department of Health, Education, and Welfare.

[2] Lee, E. S., "Negro Intelligence and Selective Migration: A Philadelphia Test of the Klineberg Hypothesis," *American Sociological Review*, 16:227-233, 1951.

[3] Kirk, S. A., *Early Education of the Mentally Retarded.* Urbana: University of Illinois Press, 1958.

For this reason we were led to reject the approach of the typical nursery school, which appears to be based upon mimicry of those aspects of the culturally privileged home environment which are deemed significant for intellectual and personality growth. A more fruitful approach appeared to be that of selecting specific and significant educational objectives and teaching them in the most direct manner possible, as is done in the intermediate and secondary school grades.

The second premise has to do with the selection of those educational objectives. It is no news that the outstanding deficiencies of culturally deprived children are in the area of language. Language covers such an enormous territory, however, that setting up language development as an objective for pre-school education narrows the field hardly at all. The field can be narrowed considerably by separating out those aspects of language which mainly serve purposes of social communication from those aspects which are more directly involved in logical thinking. The former include lexical terms—nouns, verbs, and modifiers—and idiomatic expressions. The outstanding feature of the latter aspect of language is the manipulation of statement patterns according to grammatical and syntactical rules.

This is an artificial division, of course, but it has some value for curriculum planning. A great deal of effort can be and often is expended in building up the child's repertoire of idioms and concrete words and teaching him conventional usage patterns. All of this mainly serves to enable the child to get along better in the language environment. It is much like what a tourist gets out of studying a list of useful words and phrases in a foreign language. A child may be able to accumulate a great deal of learning of this kind and still be unable to reason verbally, to draw inferences from statements, and to generate the statements that are called for by questions. To do this requires a mastery of the formal aspects of language.

Our second premise was that training in the formal, structural aspects of language would have more value in the improvement of academic aptitude for culturally deprived children than would training directed toward "getting along" linguistically. From our earlier work in teaching concrete logical operations it became evident that culturally deprived children do not just think at an immature level: many of them do not think at all. That is, they do not show any of the mediating processes which we ordinarily identify with thinking. They cannot hold onto questions while searching for an answer. They cannot compare perceptions in any reliable fashion. They are oblivious of even the most extreme discrepancies between their actions and statements as they follow one another in a series. They do not just give bad explanations. They cannot give explanations at all, nor do they seem to have any idea of what it is to explain an event. The question and answer process which is the core of orderly thinking is completely foreign to most of them.

The curriculum that we worked out, starting from the two premises discussed above, is an academically oriented one, using direct instruction that focuses upon the basic information processes that are necessary for thinking. Three content areas were chosen. One is basic language training and the other two are reading and arithmetic. The same information processes are involved in all three areas, but their application is different. These three areas were seen therefore, not as different "subjects" in the traditional sense, but as different areas of application in which a child must be proficient in order to succeed in the elementary school.

At the present time our work is largely developmental. We have not yet run a controlled comparison of the effects of our program with the effects of other possible treatments. Rather, our present concerns include:

(1) analysis of the formal characteristics of language, reading, and arithmetic that are relevant to young culturally deprived children,

(2) translating these into instructional goals,

(3) discovering feasible means of carrying on direct instruction with young culturally deprived children,

(4) determining how much of what we would like to teach actually can be taught to children of this kind, and

Chapter 6: An Academically Oriented Pre-School for Culturally Deprived Children (1966)

(5) assessing the rate of learning which can be achieved.

Our subjects are fifteen children selected in the following manner. Public school teachers in a low income, almost totally Negro district made visits to the homes of children in their classes. They were asked to note families in which there was a four-year-old child, in which the older sibling whom they had in class showed educational problems, and where the home environment struck them as particularly deprived. Of the families approached, all but one agreed to send their child. We rejected two children—a pair of identical twins who were almost completely non-verbal, unmanageable, and showed indications of severe brain injury. Thus, the fifteen children represent a fairly unbiased selection from the lower stratum of a culturally deprived ghetto.

The school runs for two hours a day, five days a week. The typical school day consists of three twenty-minute sessions, one each devoted to language, arithmetic, and reading instruction. These periods are separated by one half-hour period for refreshments and singing and a shorter period of relatively unstructured play activity. For the instructional sessions the children work in groups of four or five. Each subject has its own teacher, who works with each of three groups of children in turns, as in a high school. Groups are constituted on the basis of over-all rate of progress, with children being frequently shifted from one group to another as their relative achievement level shifts. Two children whose learning rate is far below that of the others compose a fourth group which receives training in all three subjects from a single teacher. This arrangement is required by scheduling problems, however, and is not a matter of preference. In a larger school with more teachers it would be possible to accommodate even such retarded children in the regular program.

The school as a whole is run in a highly task-oriented, no-nonsense manner. Full participation of all children in the learning tasks is treated as a requirement to which the children must conform (much like the hand-washing requirement in a conventional nursery school) rather than as a developmental goal toward which the children are allowed to progress at their own rate. Emphasis is placed upon effort, attention, and mastery, but not upon competition, as is so damagingly done in many of our more achievement-orientated elementary schools. It may be mentioned in passing that the morale and self-confidence of the children appears to be very high and that there are relatively few signs of psychological stress.

We will discuss in detail the three separate instructional programs and the achievements of the children in them after three months of work. Here, by way of a more general indication of effectiveness of the program, we may consider changes in scores on three subtests of the Illinois Test of Psycholinguistic Abilities (ITPA). The auditory-vocal automatic and the auditory-vocal association subtests were administered to the children several days before the school began. The auditory-vocal automatic is essentially a test of ability to use grammatical inflections for the formation of plurals, comparatives, and tenses. It is a test on which culturally deprived children have been found to be especially subnormal. The auditory-vocal association subtest consists of simple verbal analogies and has been found to be highly correlated with Stanford-Binet scores. At the time of first testing the children had a median chronological age of 4-3. They were as a whole over a year retarded on both subtests. Not one child, in fact, was performing up to his age level on either subtest.

Approximately three weeks after the beginning of the school the full ITPA was administered. On the two subtests that had been given previously, median scores went up nine and ten months. (Medians are used throughout, because the existence of some scores that were below norms for the subtests made calculation of means impossible.)

Three months after the beginning of school selected subtests of the ITPA were again administered. Gains of thirteen months over pretest scores were obtained on both subtests, with gains of four and three months respectively over those obtained on the first retest. Retesting was also done at this time on another subtest: vocal encoding. This is a relatively unstructured test. Subjects are presented various objects and told to "tell me all about it." Scores are based on the number of different appropriate things that the subject says. This subtest was of interest as a check on the possibility that direct training in language patterns might have little or no transfer value to language usage in unstructured situations. The results showed, however, that performance of this freer, more "creative" type improved more markedly than any other—a median gain of fifteen months, bringing the group as a whole up to near normal on this scale. Since this test gets fairly directly at the social uses of language, it would appear, paradoxically enough, that the best way to teach young culturally deprived children to verbalize more freely and expressively (which is the major concern of many pre-school programs for the culturally deprived) is to ignore the matter and concentrate on more fundamental language processes.

In terms of the traditional achievement quotients, these children gained approximately 20 points in three months in three highly significant language areas. On two of them they are now close to normal. We do not, however, regard these results as the most important indications of the effectiveness of the program. The more specific achievements in language, reading, and arithmetic, to be reported in the following sections, indicate more directly what it is that these children have been able to accomplish. Judged by absolute standards, it will be found that most of these children are still a long way from mastery of language, reading, and arithmetic. On the other hand, their progress in three months' time seems to compare rather favorably with that of culturally deprived children in the first grade, and these children are two years younger. In this sense the children are academically precocious, and in their general attitude and approach to learning this is how they act. There is every indication that the children will be able to maintain their present rate of academic progress. How much of this will be reflected in more global measure of intellectual ability remains to be seen, but it is more or less beside the point. Our strategy, as indicated earlier, is not to try to do everything in an attempt to increase intellectual abilities across the board, but to concentrate our efforts on what seems most significant for academic success.

STRUCTURAL LANGUAGE TRAINING

Almost every experimental pre-school program for culturally deprived children that we know of makes some serious effort, however informal, to improve children's language abilities. Though methods vary from program to program, there is an order of emphasis on different aspects of language behavior which appears to be almost universally accepted. Primary emphasis is given to encouraging the children to make fuller use of whatever language skills they possess—to merely getting the children to talk, in some fashion or other. Then, in descending order of emphasis, attention is given to vocabulary building, improving pronunciation, and finally to improving grammatical structure. The last two are often given no methodical attention at all, but are expected to emerge as natural consequences of progress in the first two.

We establish a program which essentially reverses the usual order of emphasis. The program's major concern is the acquisition of grammatical statement patterns and a grasp of the logical organization of these patterns. Precise pronunciation is seen as a critical requirement for mastery of grammatical structure, for even in our relatively uninflected language a good deal of grammatical structure is mediated by little affixes, variations, and particles which cannot be differentiated by the blurred pronunciation typical of culturally deprived children. The child who says "Ih bwah" for "This is a block" is in a poor position to understand, much less communicate, such contrasting statements as "This is not a block," "These are blocks," and "These are not blocks." For this reason, and not because we were interested in niceties of diction, we have given a great deal of emphasis to perfecting pronunciation.

As for vocabulary development, we have allowed much of it to occur as an incidental outcome of work on grammatical structure. Where direct teaching of concepts has been done, it has been concerned with concepts chosen because of their value in organizing experience and in making logical distinctions—for instance, inclusive class concepts such as *people, food,* and *vehicles.*

Perhaps our most radical departure from tradition has been our treatment of the child's already established language patterns. It seems to have been taken for granted by other educators that one must begin by encouraging the child to make the fullest possible use of the language he already possesses before one may set about improving it. Our estimation of the language of culturally deprived children agrees, however, with that of Bernstein, who maintains that this language is not merely an underdeveloped version of standard English, but is a basically non-logical mode of expressive behavior which lacks the formal properties necessary for the organization of thought.[4] From this point of view, the goal of language training for the culturally deprived could be seen as not that of improving the child's language but rather that of teaching him a different language which would hopefully replace the first one, at least in school settings. The two languages share lexical elements and these we made use of, but apart from this we proceeded much as if the children had no language at all. This led us naturally to adopt many of the techniques of modern oral methods of foreign language teaching, which, as Ausubel has pointed out, proceed upon the same assumption.[5] While we have not actively suppressed children's use of their "native" language in ordinary social intercourse, neither have we gone out of our way to encourage it. Rather, we have strived to get the children to extend the language patterns they were being deliberately taught into less structured social situations.

INITIAL LANGUAGE ABILITY

The success of the language training program, at this early date, at least, must be judged against the language abilities which the children brought with them. These children exhibited the severe and general language impoverishment which has been described by Deutsch and others.[6] This is borne out by the pretest data, which showed them to be on the average a year to a year-and-a-half retarded in language development.

---

4 Bernstein, Basil, "Language and Social Class," *British Journal of Sociology,* 11:271-276, 1960.

5 Ausubel, D.P., "Adults versus Children in Second-Language Learning: Psychological Considerations," University of Illinois, Bureau of Educational Research, n.d. (Mimeograph.) Ausubel criticizes audiolingual methods for this fact, but it should be recognized that this criticism applies to their use with older students who have already mastered a first language which has considerable transfer value to the second.

6 Deutsch, M., "The Role of Social Class in Language Development and Cognition," *American Journal of Orthopsychiatry.*

When the children first arrived, they had, as expected, a minute repertoire of labels to attach to the objects they used or saw every day. All buildings were called "houses," most people were called "you." Although Urbana is in the midst of a rural area, not one child could identify any farm animals. As obvious as their lack of vocabulary was their primitive notion of the structure of language. Their communications were by gesture (we later discovered that one boy could answer some questions by shaking his head, but that he did not realize that a positive shake of the head meant yes), by single words (Teacher: "What do you want?" Child: "Doll"), or a series of badly connected words or phrases. ("They mine." "Me got juice.")

The pronunciation of several of the children was so sub-standard that, when they did talk, the teachers had no notion of what they were saying. One of the brighter girls would ramble on and on, using a lot of poorly enunciated words and loosely connected phrases, but in an order that made little or no sense to any of the teachers or (as we learned later) to her mother.

Typical of their social non-use of language was the time it took to teach the children each others' names, and for them to learn to use these names in playing with each other.

Dramatic as these deficiencies are, they impressed us as much less significant than other, more subtle differences that appeared as we began trying to teach them. Although most of the children could follow simple directions like, "Give me the book," they could not give such directions themselves, not even repeat them. Without exaggerating, we may say that these four-year-olds could make no statements of any kind. They could not ask questions. Their ability to answer questions was hampered by the lack of such fundamental requirements as knowing enough to look at the book in order to answer the question, "Is the book on the table?"

TEACHING PROCEDURES

How can a four-year-old child be taught the logical structure of our language? The basic technique we have used is similar to what foreign language teachers call "pattern drill." The children learn basic statement patterns and how to answer the fundamental questions about those patterns.

For example, in the teaching of "*big*" and "*little*," the following standard procedure was observed.

REPETITION OF THE VERBAL STATEMENT CONTAINING THE CONCEPT
Teacher: "This block is big."
Child: "This block is big."

LOCATION OF CONCEPT
Teacher: "Show me the block that is big."
The child touches the big block.

VERBAL STATEMENT
Teacher: "Tell me about the block."
Child: "The block is big."

Rhetorical questions are used at every stage, "Is this the big block?" These questions demonstrate the questions inferred in every statement. Since the children did not have a storehouse of statement and question patterns, in which, by varying the subject and predicate to match the topic at hand, they could communicate an observation or ask a question, much time was spent learning such patterns.

After learning big, and in the same fashion, little, they learned that these antonyms were comparatives, that if a big block and a little block were drawn on the chalkboard, the big block could become the little block if the little one was erased and an even bigger block drawn next to the remaining block.

Antonyms were also used to teach positive and negative statements and the deductions inherent in them. After each child learned the positive statement pattern, "This block is big," the question was asked, "Can you show me the block that is not big?" Not one of the children could make the deduction that something that is not big was little. So, again, the patterns were repeated: "This is the one that is not big." "Show me the one that is not big." "Tell me about this block." "This block is not big; it is little." This pattern was soon condensed to, "Show me the one that is not little."

Positive and negative statements had immediate application to the school discipline—Teacher: "Do we run down the hall?" Child: "No, we do not run down the hall. We walk down the hall." By substituting various subjects (balls, people, sticks, blocks, voices, dolls) and predicate pairs (fat-skinny, tall-short, long-short, loud-soft, fast-slow, heavy-light, soft-hard), the children were able, by varying the vocabulary, to apply these statement patterns to many situations.

In all of the work with statement patterns, special emphasis is given to achieving clear pronunciation of the particles which distinguish one statement from others that may involve the same lexical elements. If the child cannot clearly pronounce the words "is" and "in" in repeating, "The crayon is *in* the box," he will have difficulty grasping the difference between this statement and "The crayon is *on* the box" or "The crayon is not *in* the box." Many of the important logical distinctions in our language are conveyed by small words or particles which are easily slurred over: *and* versus or, *than* versus and, *big* versus bigger, *is* versus isn't.

The children were not able to pronounce, use, or understand the functions of prepositions and conjunctions in a sentence. Prepositions selected to be learned were *in, on, above, under, beside, between, in front of, in back of.* A child was instructed to sit on a table; if he didn't do this correctly, the teacher helped him and said, "You are sitting on the table." The child and teacher repeated the statement. The teacher repeated the statement. The teacher asked the child "Where are you sitting?" The child would say, "On the table." Teacher: "Now say the whole thing." Child: "I am sitting on the table." Eventually, one child was able to give another child the orders to sit under the table, stand beside the table, hold a hand above the table, etc. In translating words into actions the underlying logic of grammatical forms becomes apparent to the child so long as the specified or implied operation is physically possible. In correctly following an instruction to sit under the table, the child demonstrates to himself the connection between word and action. The next and more difficult step is to have the child describe the relationship between action and word. The teacher puts a pencil between a red block and a green block; the child must describe the action.

Tasks of this type give children practice in manipulating the verbal machinery necessary to transfer words into action, action into words.

In teaching the conjunctions *and* and *or*, we placed objects such as toy furniture on the table. The child was requested to pick up a chair and a stove. He was asked to tell in sentence form what he had: "I have a chair and a stove." The process was repeated with *or*. Soon the students were giving each other the orders, with the teacher requesting one child to give another an *and* order, than an *or* order. Children who had difficulty differentiating between the two words were given the instruction, "When you hear *and* it means you take two things; when you hear *or* you must decide on one." (One boy, when given an *and* instruction paused with his hand above the objects and said aloud, "*And* means two, I got to pick up two things," and proceeded to pick up two objects.)

The lessons on *and* and *or* extended to using sentences in which the instruction was "Pick up a table and a chair and a refrigerator," thus extending the number of things that could be obtained by using more *ands*. Next, requests were given to pick up all the white blocks and all the yellow blocks, introducing the notion of groups connected by *and*. All the above lessons were repeated with *or*. Then, *and* was taught as a conjunction connecting words that describe one object: "She has a red and white dress." "This cookie is big and round." Now the children are learning about the reversibility of the subjects around *and*. The teacher says, "I have a green block and a red block. Can you tell me another way I can say it? I have a red block and a green block. Is this saying the same thing?" This is a good example of a word pattern which has direct transfer to and from a mathematical concept that was being taught in the arithmetic class: $3 + 1 = 4; 1 + 3 = 4$.

This kind of practice does relatively little in expanding concept formation when compared to enriched play situations, field trips, and extensive story-reading. What it does do is teach the children directly those elements of vocabulary which they would have difficulty learning from casual experience.

As we have said, straight vocabulary teaching is not a major goal in this program; when we do teach vocabulary, the words are not chosen so much for their social usefulness as for their value in making logical distinctions and in organizing experience. On this basis we decided to devote a good deal of attention to the teaching of colors and the more inclusive class names. In teaching color the classification rule, "If it looks the same, it is the same; if it's not the same, it's different," became most useful. We started with blocks and pieces of colored paper. If two red blocks were placed side by side they belonged to the same classification, red, and therefore had the same name. If two blocks, one red, and one green, were placed side by side, the statement, "If this one is red, this one is not red," could be made even if the child did not know the second color. This rule gave the children a means of discriminating and matching the properties of color in objects. Blocks, picture books, the children's own clothing, their toys, the juice they drank, the cars they rode to school in, were all used to teach color names.

In teaching categories of objects we used pictures in books, toys and furniture in the room, drawings on the chalkboard, and the children themselves. They learned a system for classifying objects, while simultaneously expanding their repertoire of concepts and vocabulary. When the children learned cow, horse, pig, sheep, rooster, and duck, they also learned that these were all farm animals, and that they were called farm animals because they lived on a farm. They learned that apples, bread, potatoes, and butter were food, and that what they ate was defined as food. Similarly they learned about the categories of people, furniture, clothes, toys, wild animals, birds, buildings, letters, and numbers, and the names of many members of these groups.

The gains in scores on ITPA subtests, reported in the introduction, provide one form of evidence of the effectiveness of the program. Of the three subtests cited, only the auditory-vocal automatic subtest can be construed as showing direct teaching effects, however. It tests mastery of grammatical inflections which, in English, are so few in number that it would be impossible to teach grammatical usage without "teaching for the test." The other two subtests may be taken to indicate generalization of language learning. The analogy form employed in the auditory-vocal association subtest was never employed in teaching, and the unstructured describing behavior called for in the vocal encoding subtest was quite foreign to our instructional procedures.

In the Color Test the children were required to name the colors of squares on the color chart. The teacher pointed to the squares in random order and the child was required to name the color. A plus indicates success on the first trial. Although none of the children knew even the basic colors when they started school, all but one showed fairly complete mastery of colors at the end of three months.

Items on the *Prepositions Test* required the child to accomplish two things in order to earn a plus–follow an instruction, and give a correct verbal description. Example: Teacher: "Put the scissors in front of the box." The child had to put the scissors in front of the box and then, in response to the question, "Tell me, where are the scissors?" the child had to make a complete statement equivalent to "The scissors are in front of the box." This kind of statement-making, which was beyond all the children at the outset, may be seen to have been quite thoroughly mastered.

The *Categories Test* required the child to give the proper category word when shown pictures of various objects within a given category. For example, in the category, furniture, the child was shown pictures of a table, a chair, a lamp, a bed, and a chest of drawers, and asked, "What is the word that we can use that means all of these things?" He was then asked, "What do we do with furniture?" To be given credit for a correct answer he had to know the category word and to be able to make a general statement about the category on the first trial.

The *Identity Statement* is a test of a child's ability to understand the structure as apart from the content of a sentence. The teacher drew identical figures, pointed to the first and then to the second as she said, "If this ⌒ is a blurp, is this ⌒ a blurp?" If the child said, "Yes," it is assumed he understood the principle of labeling: if two things look the same, they have the same name. The next task involves two different figures, the question is the same, "If this ⌒ is a blurp, is this ⌒ a blurp?" Passing criterion: correct response on first trial.

For the *And Test*, the child was asked to pick up a green block and a red block, then asked, "What's another way of saying it?" If the child picked up both blocks and was able to restate the instruction to "pick up a red block and a green block" he passed both sections of the *And Test*.

For the *Or Test*, the child has to pick up one object when told to "Pick up a red block or a green block." If he could do this and restate the instruction to "pick up a red block or a green block" he passed the *Or Test*.

All children could handle the meanings of *and* and *or* adequately, though none of them could respond appropriately to *or* previous to instruction. Reversal or commutation of elements about *and* and *or* was not yet fully mastered, but work on it had only begun at the time of testing.

For the *Size Test* the child was shown two books and asked which one was bigger. To pass he had to point to the bigger one and say, "This is bigger than that one." The other two parts of the test were similar in form.

In the *Statements Test* the child was shown a picture with two squirrels, one in a tree and one on the ground. The teacher, pointing to the squirrel in the tree, asked "Where is this squirrel?" The correct response was, "The squirrel is in the tree." Next, the teacher pointed to the squirrel on the ground. "Is this squirrel in the tree?" The correct answer was "No, this squirrel is not in the tree." If the child said, "This squirrel is on the ground," he was asked to give the "not" answer. To pass, the child had to make two complete statements, but was allowed to rephrase incomplete statements into complete sentences.

What these results indicate is that all the children have begun to operate at the statement level, which is to say that they have begun to master those formal grammatical patterns which are lacking even in the speech of their parents. Although this kind of linguistic achievement is commonplace among culturally privileged four-year-olds, and therefore tends to be taken for granted when it is observed, we have found that this is the single most impressive achievement of these children in the eyes of experienced teachers of culturally deprived children—the fact that they speak in sentences. From our point of view, however, it is not the speaking in sentences itself which is important, but what speaking in sentences enables the children to do. It enables the children to "unpack" meaning from statements, to convey meanings which they otherwise could not, and to draw inferences which carry them beyond the immediately given facts.

TEACHING ARITHMETIC THROUGH LANGUAGE OPERATIONS

The new mathematics treats arithmetic as a system of statements and statement forms. In the present project, we have carried the "new math" orientation even further; we have endeavored to teach arithmetic as a language. This is not a completely arbitrary position. Mathematics is a system of language, and it shares four fundamental assumptions with statements in everyday language.

(1) The first is the assumption of classification and transition. If you can make identical statements about two things they are the same; they can be classified together. Also, if two things are the same as a third, they are the same as each other.

(2) The second major assumption is what might be called the reality assumption. The statement, "The coins are in the box," implies an operation. It implies that if, for instance, you assemble more than one coin and a box, you can create a model of the statement, "The coins are in the box." So it is with statements in arithmetic such as $3 + 2 = 5$. The statement implies that if you begin with three anythings and acquire two more anythings, you will have a sum of five anythings. The reality assumption is quite the same for both the statement that is capable of being true or false and the statement in arithmetic. *Neither specify a physical operation; both, however, imply one.*

(3) The third common assumption is that both arithmetic statements and everyday language statements imply questions and answers. "The coins are in the box," implies such questions as "Where are the coins?" ... "Are the coins in the box?" ... "Are the

coins under the box?" ... and so forth. The arithmetic statement, 3 + 2 = 5, implies analogous questions. "Three plus two equals how many?" ... "Does three plus two equal five?" ...and so forth. Note that these questions and answers derive from the statement and not from the individual components of the statement. A set of questions and answers derives even when the statement is reduced to a propositional function, such as "A + B = C" or "The glack is in the gleep." The statement has a meaning which *cannot* be reduced to the meaning of the constituent elements. The statement, therefore, is in this respect the basic unit of the language.

(4) The final shared assumption is that parts which compose a statement have a meaning. *Three* has a meaning in terms of counting. *In* has a meaning in terms of the position of objects.

What does all this mean? Simply that the extent to which arithmetic and everyday language share assumptions is the extent to which arithmetic is nothing more than a foreign language. *To this extent it can be taught as a foreign language.* However, the analogy between the two types of statements is not precise. Although arithmetic statements share every assumption that characterizes everyday language, they possess an additional assumption which is not shared by statements in everyday language. *Arithmetic statements such as 3 + 2 = f provide for their own completion.* If one understands how the system works, he can complete a statement without knowing the completed statement in advance. The statement implies that one can translate the statement into an operation and then *count* to discover the completed statement. Furthermore, any of the five elements in the statement can be eliminated and the completed statement can be discovered.

Because arithmetic statements provide for their own completion, arithmetic cannot be treated precisely as a foreign language. The extent to which the presentation should be different is the extent to which the content is different. In other words, arithmetic is primarily a language; however, many arithmetic statements possess a peculiar property.

Our presentation began with the individual concepts that make up a statement. The individual members were defined in terms of counting. The signs were defined in terms of the operations they imply. Thus, the symbol + is read as "plus" but is translated as the operation, "Get more." Similarly, the = sign tells you to *end up*. Next, after concepts we presented the fundamental statement forms of the arithmetic language. We began with the identity statement. The parallel in everyday language would be such a statement as "This is a stove." In a sense, it says no more than the word *stove*, and yet it is capable of generating a series of questions and answers that cannot derive from the word alone. So it is with arithmetic. After the dust has settled, the statement "$A + 0 = A$" says no more than "A," and yet it is capable of generating a series of questions and answers.

The identity statements were taught as a rote pattern. "One plus zero equals one, two plus zero equals two," and so forth. The purpose of presenting statements in the counting order was to establish the parallel between the identity statement and the familiar counting elements. We wanted the child to understand that since the identity statement held for every number in the familiar counting series, it should hold for any new numbers that are introduced.

After the identity relationship came the basic non-identity conclusion. These parallel the pattern in everyday language, "If it's not hot it must be ____." If it's not the same it must be ____." The basic non-identity conclusion in arithmetic holds that a non-identity statement is not an identity statement. Or, stated operationally, "If 1 + 0 = 1, 1 + 1 can't equal 1. It equals 1 more than 1–2." The non-identity conclusion was again presented as a pattern, in an attempt to demonstrate that if the +1 conclusion holds for every number in the familiar series, it should hold for any new number introduced into the series.

In connection with these tasks, the basic substitution assumption of arithmetic was introduced as an operation. "If $A = 2$ it means that you can put a 2 wherever you have an A." The final language-type parallel that was taught was the reversible-element notion. Some elements in a compound statement can be reversed without affecting either the questions the statement generates or the answers to these questions. In arithmetic, this is the so-called commutative law: $a + B = B + a$. We presented the law as a language task. "What's another way of saying 2 + 0? 0 + 2."

All arithmetic problems were presented as "questions." An algebraic type symbol was introduced as the question asker: $3 + 2 = a$. The children were taught to read the problem first, then translate it into a question, then answer the question. If the children did not know the answer to the question, they were taught how to "figure it out." This involves first understanding what question the problem is asking, then somehow translating the problem into a counting operation. We noted earlier that the open statement in arithmetic implies a physical operation but does not specify one. For several reasons, we chose a finger-counting operation as the "reality parallel" of the statement. "Start with 3" means to hold up three fingers on the left hand. "Get 2 more," meaning to hold up two fingers on the right hand. By counting the extended fingers, the child arrives at the answer, which hopefully is five. Since the total number of fingers is five, he can, according to the substitution assumption, put a five in place of the a. Thus, $3 + 2 = 5$.

A number of minor conventions had to be introduced to make the system operational—for instance, the idea that the answers to the question, "How many?" is always the name of a single number, not a series of numbers. Also, since the basic questions were sometimes presented visually, the children had to know how to "read" the statement. Therefore, the symbols 0, 1, 2, 3, 4, 5, 6, 10, +, and = were introduced, together with several symbols for "how many."

The extent to which the language of arithmetic parallels the language of everyday usage is the extent to which the culturally deprived child should have difficulty with the type of arithmetic presentation we used. Obviously, a child who does not understand the statement, "It's not in the box if it's on top of the box," is going to be at a disadvantage when he tries to understand the statement, "1 + 1 can't equal 1, if $1 + 0 = 1$." Similarly, he's going to have trouble understanding the relationship between questions and answers in everyday language.

Our children had a very slow start. Only two of them came to the school with any knowledge of counting. None could repeat a simple arithmetic statement, such as $2 + 3 = 5$. None could read symbols. Only two or three knew that the answer to the question "How many?" is a single number. Only about a third of them knew the concepts *same* and *different*. None could reverse elements in a statement, 2 + 0 (which, by the way, is probably the most difficult task they have encountered in arithmetic).

Despite the initial deficit of our children, they are presently showing good progress.

The children were tested on three major areas of achievement—verbal tasks, visual tasks, and more difficult tasks—the solution of which involves the interplay of visual, motor, and vocal elements. Tasks were presented in roughly the order of difficulty.

Task 1: Children were asked to count as far as they could, and they were encouraged to keep going if they stopped. All but one child counted to 10 without a mistake.

Task 2: Children were asked, "What comes after one?" … "What comes after two?" … etc. Each incorrect response was corrected before the next question was presented. The slowest group did not perform as well as the other two, but the poorest performer missed only three, and nine children did perfectly.

Task 3: Children were presented with a mathematical statement, such as 2 + 2 = 4. They were then asked "Two plus how many equals four?" The children in the top two groups had no trouble with this task.

Task 4: The identity series was presented in the counting order, "One plus zero equals ____, two plus zero equals ____." All but one child went through the entire 1–10 series without a mistake.

Task 5: Identity statements were presented out of context. "Tell me, what would four plus zero equal? …" The children in the slowest group had more trouble with this item. This suggests that though they can produce the identity pattern, as in *Task 4*, the slowest children have not yet grasped it as a rule.

Task 6: Plus-one problems were presented in the counting order. "One plus one equals ____, two plus one equals ____" and so on through "nine plus one equals ____." Highly variable success is shown on this task.

Task 7: Plus-one statements were presented out of the context of the counting order. A child in both of the top two groups, as well as two children in the slowest group, had trouble with the task.

Task 8: Children were presented with a statement such as "Eight plus two," then asked, "What's another way of saying, 'eight plus two?'" This is probably the most difficult verbal task. The members of the top group have worked on it considerably longer than those in either of the other groups. The slowest group had had only slight exposure to the operation (although in their language studies they have worked on the reversibility idea using the word *and* and two subjects).

Task 9: Children were asked to identify the thirteen symbols that have been presented. Eight of the children show complete mastery, and only one could be considered seriously backward in learning symbol identification. Again, the faster groups have been exposed to the full set of symbols for a longer time.

Task 10: Children were asked to read a relatively simple problem. All children passed on this item.

Task 11: In this, the easiest of the interpretation tasks, children were asked to solve a problem never presented before: $3 + 5 = a$. To arrive at the solution the child was required to read the problem; then interpret into an operation (a counting operation using fingers); and finally indicate how to change the problem (through substitution) so that it became a true statement. All but one child was able to solve at least one unfamiliar problem.

Task 12: Children were presented with a standard, simple algebra problem, which they were asked to solve. This is the most advanced level of problem which the children have been presented, and only the top group had worked with it for an appreciable length of time. Four of the five children in this group were able to solve such a problem, and in addition one child in the intermediate group was able to do so.

These results indicate that culturally deprived pre-school children are able to learn formal arithmetic operations when these are presented primarily as part of a language. They are able to read the statements of the language, phrase the open statements (those involving an unknown) as questions, answer the questions, and substitute the answers for the question-asking elements. In short, they are able to learn arithmetic operations from a procedure that places emphasis on the formal meaning, not on the concrete things that are normally treated as primary elements in arithmetic education. Since this procedure enables a more direct, articulate presentation and also ties in with other language skills being mastered by the child, it has great potential application in educating the culturally deprived pre-schooler.

TEACHING READING AS A LOGICAL PROCESS

Among some primary school educators there seems to be a long-standing belief that arithmetic is something intrinsically meaningless to young children whereas reading, if it is taught through suitably lively and realistic materials, is a highly meaningful learning experience. If meaningfulness is defined in any non-trivial sense, however, the exact opposite appears to be true. Arithmetic statements always have counterparts in concrete operations. Arithmetic rules permit abundant testing in the real world. Moreover, they are marvelously consistent, and a rule that works for some numbers will usually be found to work for all other numbers that the child encounters. Reading, on the other hand, is based on a completely arbitrary and closed set of rules relating printed letters to speech sounds. The rules for decoding print have no applicability to anything outside of reading, and they even run contrary on certain points to cognizing rules that are valid in the outer world (for instance, the rule that a letter may change its identity when it is turned upside-down is directly contrary to the rule governing object identification in the physical world). Moreover, the rules are numerous, unrelated, inconsistent, and incomplete, so that an enormous amount of rote learning is required. There is nothing at all to commend reading instruction except that it is necessary. In teaching arithmetic one can at least take pride in introducing children to one of the more elegant creations of the human intellect; in teaching reading all one can hope for is to make the best of a bad thing.

This pessimistic view could lead one to postpone reading instruction until the child had become sufficiently accomplished in prerequisite skills to learn it in the least possible time and with the least possible effort. Unfortunately, the realities of educational life do not make such postponement practical. In order to progress far in other areas of learning the child must learn to read, and academic progress as a whole is pretty much held down to the rate at which children learn to read. Because culturally deprived children typically have more than their share of difficulty in learning to read, it seems that one should try to give them as rapid a start in it as possible. To delay reading instruction, it seemed, would be merely to dodge one of the major problems in the education of the culturally deprived.

We decided, therefore, to attack the problem of reading head-on, but to try to teach it in such a way as to gain from it whatever secondary educational benefits it might be able to provide. Even though the rules for decoding print are arbitrary and have virtually no transfer value to other problems, they are rules nevertheless, which involve the same logical and language operations as other rules. It therefore seemed that the preferred approach to reading instruction would be one in which children gained a maximum amount of experience in the explicit handling of rules and statements.

Most popular approaches to reading instruction, whether of the whole-word or the phonic type, try to keep rules behind the scenes. In extreme versions of the whole-word approach, reading is taught as if it followed no rules at all. But even in phonic methods, which are worked out on the basis of rules connecting graphemes with phonemes, the rules are not taught explicitly. The child is expected to absorb them unconsciously in the course of practice. These covert approaches to reading may be effective in accomplishing their major objective of enabling children to read, but in keeping the rules hidden they of necessity exaggerate the meaninglessness of the reading process, and deny the child whatever secondary benefits he might draw from working with an at least partially logical system.

By introducing certain artificial restrictions, we were able to reduce the inconsistency and complexity of English orthography and highlight its logical aspects. We restricted the initial vocabulary to three-letter, consonant-vowel-consonant patterns, and avoided use of some of the more troublesome consonants. For further simplification we used only lower case letters. Within this restricted set of words, the following six sets of rules hold:

(1) A word has a beginning and an end. (The beginning is the initial consonant; the end consists of the vowel and the final consonant.) If it has a beginning and an end, it is a word. The beginning always comes before the end.

(2) If the beginnings are the same and the ends are the same, the words are the same and they look the same.

(3) If the words are the same, they sound the same. If the words sound the same, they are the same.

(4) If the words look the same and sound the same, they are the same.

(5) If the endings of the words are the same, the words rhyme. If the words rhyme, the endings are the same.

(6) If the beginnings of the words are the same, the words alliterate. If the words alliterate, the beginnings of the words are the same.

Parts of words were presented to the children on cards, the initial consonant (the beginning) on a white card and the last two letters (the ending) on a yellow card. All letters were printed in black, and the cards contained a black border which served as a cue for orienting and sequencing the cards. Three pieces of three-by-one board were affixed horizontally at different intervals on the back of a standard sized portable chalkboard. The boards were grooved so that the cards could be slid along. The only other addition to this apparatus was an arrow drawn on the middle board which indicated left-right direction.

Rules were taught in the order given above. The following is a sketch of the procedures employed:

Rule 1—a word has a beginning and an end—demanded that we present the words in two parts. This was facilitated by having the beginning and end cards of different colors and lengths. This first rule was a difficult one to teach. To begin with, it was the children's first learning experience in a formal situation. Next we were dealing with culturally deprived children most of whom did not know what beginning or end meant, none of whom had more than about a two-second attention span, and many of whom had difficulty articulating simple words and phrases. We demanded the children's attention by continual questioning; we demanded that they look and respond, with or without understanding. We spent a lot of time trying to improve each child's pronunciation by continual correcting and encouragement. Finally, we got across the idea of beginning and end by always making up each word by a left to right action, taking the white beginning and exaggerating its primacy and directionality and moving it to the center of the display rack and then bringing the end in place with a final motion. Through this latter action we de-emphasized directionality. The second part of this rule—if it has a beginning and an end, it is a word—is a logical extension of the first part. And the third part—the beginning always comes before the end—is a clarification of the first and second parts.

Rule 2—if the beginnings are the same and the ends are the same, the words are the same and they look the same—was important for it taught the children to look for the distinctive characteristics in the elements of each word and to relate the parts as well as the whole to other words. Many of the children had very poor visual discrimination and this rule and the teaching that was necessary to make the rule functional to the children has increased their visual discrimination abilities. This rule has also helped to teach the children the important concept of same and different.

Rule 3—if the words are the same, they sound the same—is an extension of rule 2, and has served to teach the children auditory discrimination as well as more correct pronunciation of the words.

It should be interjected here that in conjunction with the teaching of these rules, we were teaching the phonetic values of consonants which we used with three endings; the total product of which was about fifty words.

Rule 4—if the words look the same and sound the same, they are the same—pulled together everything which we had previously taught them.

Rule 5—if the endings of the words are the same, the words rhyme—was designed to exploit their previous knowledge. The children could now hear different parts of words and to some extent distinguish sounds. By establishing the rhyming rule in their minds, we were setting up the framework for pattern similarities among words. Cat, sat, bat, mat, hat patterning was now not a series of unfamiliar disparate words, but a family of words—all closely related and almost known. After this rule was well learned, we set up endings and began to flip through the initial consonants they knew. With many of the children rhyming is now a simple process; as the test results show, many of them can use the rhyming principle to figure out the unfamiliar words. The children initially showed no ability to recognize rhymes when they heard them. After making little progress in getting them to hear the rhymes in the one-syllable words we were using, we were able to achieve a breakthrough by using a three-syllable rhyming pattern—by using what might be called "over-rhyming." A picture of Superman was drawn on the chalkboard and the children were shown how by placing different consonants on his chest one could change his name from *Superman* to *duperman, buperman, guperman, muperman, huperman,* etc. The children quickly learned how to determine the name from the letter and to choose the right letter to go with a name. It was then possible for them to transfer this to series like *get, net, met, set.*

Rule 6—if the beginnings of the words are the same, the words alliterate—identified a point of similarity that one finds over and over again in language. Although teaching the word "alliterate" to four- and five-year-olds might seem affected, it really was not, for it identifies for all times a pattern that is often not really recognized until high school poetry classes. Many of the children benefited right away by being able to carry on a list of alliterative words to words especially familiar to them. For example, in one class that has a

Tina, a Tony, and a Steven, Steven finished off this list with a smug look at his two classmates: truck, tire, tree, timid, terrible, trouble, time, table, Tina, Tony.

After three months of instruction the children have covered all six rules. How stably they have learned them and how well they can apply them differs a good deal between children in the slowest and in the fastest group; however, we have passed beyond the point where major attention is given to work with the rules. Compared, for instance, to the number of rules involved in arithmetic, this is a huge number of rules to master for children who are so deficient in language structure. We feel they served the purpose of developing a basic awareness of what printed words amount to and how they are constructed, while at the same time giving them valuable experience in the use of statements; but to hold up progress in reading until the rules were thoroughly mastered would be unreasonable. They are not, in the end, that essential for learning to read.

Recent work, therefore, has dealt with phonic blending, figuring out what words are when the ending remains the same and the beginning changes and vice-versa. Most work has been concerned with the changing of beginnings—what is popularly called "first-letter phonics."

The over-all progress of the children in reading is quite favorable compared to what we observed previously with culturally privileged children who were younger in chronological age but comparable in mental age but who were taught by a less structured method. The progress is, of course, inferior to what one would expect with children of similar chronological age but with better developed language abilities.

Over and above the children's progress toward learning to read, we are encouraged by the development in the children of a conviction, coupled with some competence, that printed words are things that can be figured out. Had we used one of the more covert approaches to teaching reading, the children might have progressed as far in reading ability, but considering how slow the rate of progress is, it is likely that many of them would have become discouraged and bewildered. As it is, the children have a clear awareness of what they are able to do and why it works. They are solving very difficult problems, problems which might have been avoided by more rote procedures; but by approaching reading as a logical problem they may well be developing abilities and the confidence necessary to deal with logical problems of all sorts. This should in the end pay dividend not only in reading but in all kinds of academic pursuits.

CHAPTER 7

Working to apply the principles behind Direct Instruction to a larger population of students, Engelmann conducted research on the development and application of tactual vocoders to assist students who are deaf or hard of hearing to develop oral communication skills. In the experiment described in this article, Engelmann and Robert Rosov used tactual vocoders with four hearing and four deaf students to determine if they could recognize words transmitted through the device. The experiment was designed to find an alternative form of instruction for deaf children, and results indicated deaf students could be taught to hear fine speech discriminations. Similar results occurred with the hearing students. Engelmann's research on tactual vocoders assisted his understanding of unfamiliar learning, demonstrated the effectiveness and applicability of the principles of Direct Instruction, and helped another underserved population succeed.

TACTUAL HEARING EXPERIMENT WITH DEAF AND HEARING SUBJECTS (1975)[*]

Siegfried Engelmann & Robert Rosov

For over four decades investigators concerned with the problems of the deaf child have tried to develop a device that would function as an external ear. Such a device would provide information about pitch, loudness, and the characteristics of each phoneme. The deaf child would then receive the feedback information needed to begin matching his own utterances against those of an outside model.

Investigators have taken two different approaches: the visual approach and the tactual approach. The visual approach is characterized by the use of an oscilloscope. The child looks at the patterns that appear on the oscilloscope and matches them by saying something to produce a picture like the model picture. The problem with this approach is that the analogy between the oscilloscope and the ear is poor from a psychological standpoint. While it may be possible for an oscilloscopic presentation to provide information about phoneme structure, loudness, and pitch, the device involves volition. The subject chooses certain features to attend to, possibly irrelevant details.

For a device to be more analogous to an ear it would have to ensure that:

1. The subject receives the sound information whether or not he chooses to receive it.

2. All relevant aspects of each sound are presented as discriminable details that are felt by the subject. For example, something loud would *feel* different from something not loud.

---

[*] Engelmann, S., & Rosov, R. (1975). Tactual hearing experiment with deaf and hearing subjects. *Exceptional Children*, *41*(4), 243–253. This research was supported by Siegfried and Therese Engelmann, Linda Youngmayr, Laurie Skillman, Carol Witcher, Milly Schrader, The Collins Foundation, The Oregon Research Institute (Paul J. Hoffman, Director), and in part by National Institute of Health General Research Support Grant No. MH-05612. Reprinted with permission of the publisher.

3. The subject would be able to receive sound information in the range of situations that a hearing subject receives the information. The information would not be restricted to situations in which the subject looked at another person or looked at a device.

The tactual-vibration approach would allow for construction of an external mechanical ear that is consistent with the psychological characteristics of hearing. The device would convert words or sounds into vibration, which would be delivered to the subject. Ideally, it would contain information needed for the subject to identify what is said, how it is inflected, how loud it is, and so forth. Hopefully, the nervous system would be adequate to handle this information and allow for accurate perception of what is presented in the form of vibration.

TACTUAL DISPLAYS

The first tactual device was reported by Gault and Crane in 1928. This device amplified sound from a speaker and presented it to a subject as vibration. The device was crude and investigators did not find the results encouraging. During 1949 and 1950, Wiener, Wiesner, David, and Levine briefly experimented with a tactual glove, Felix, that was connected to a vocoder. Vocoders were first developed to transmit speech over long distance telephone cables. Vocoders divide the speech spectrum into frequency bands or channels. For example, one channel might cover the frequency range of 200 to 240 Hz. Every time energy is present in this range, the channel is activated. The more energy present in the channel the stronger the signal becomes. At the other end of the long distance line, the signals from all of the channels are reconstructed as speech.

Felix was designed so that different parts of the speech spectrum were displayed on different parts of the hand. The energy from the one part of the spectrum activated vibrators on one finger, while energy from other parts of the spectrum activated specific vibrators on other fingers. Apparently Felix was used only a few times before the investigators abandoned it. Later attempts to construct a vibratory prosthesis also ended in discouragement (Guelke & Huyssen, 1959; Kringlebotn 1968; Pickett & Pickett, 1963).

The present experiment was based on the idea that the vocoding devices used in the past were adequate to provide a suitable display of speech. However, adequate training was lacking. Analysis of the training provided with previous vocoder devices disclosed that the investigators seemed to assume that if the display provided the information needed for adequate speech perception, the subject would learn quickly, if not instantly. The assumption underlying the present study was that a great deal of practice would be needed (probably at least 1,200 corrected trials) before a healthy subject could be expected to perform consistently on each of the early words to be discriminated.

CONSTRUCTION OF A TACTUAL VOCODER

The tactual vocoder constructed at Oregon Research Institute (the site of the training experiments) incorporated several new features but was not radically different from previous tactual vocoders. The final version used with hearing and deaf subjects employed a 23 channel vocoder. The frequency ranged from 200 Hz through 4,000 Hz, was divided into equal logarithmic intervals and transmitted through 15 channels. Four low frequency channels extended the lower range to 85 Hz, and four high frequency channels extended the upper range to 10,000 Hz. The purpose of the low frequency channels was to provide information about fundamental pitch of speech (Flanagan, 1972). The high frequency extension allowed for discrimination of fricatives (sh, ch, s, f), which are not adequately discriminated at the 4,000 Hz level for some speakers (Hughes & Halle, 1956; Heinz & Stevens, 1961).

To receive tactual information through the system, a subject attached five metal boxes (each about 3 inches long) to the surface of his skin (using elastic bandages to hold the boxes in place and upright). The boxes contained 23 vibrators, 1 for each channel. Three boxes held 5 vibrators each; two held 4 vibrators each. The vibrators consisted of miniature solenoids which drove 1mm diameter metal plungers. The plungers were spaced at half inch intervals and protruded slightly through the base plate of the boxes. When speech energized a vocoder channel, that channel's solenoid was activated at 60 Hz and its plunger vibrated against the skin. Two microphones were attached to the system, so that a trainer could talk into one and the subject could respond into the other (see Figure 1).

Figure 1. Tactual Vocoder

TRAINING HEARING SUBJECTS

The hearing subjects were four female instructors employed by the Engelmann-Becker Follow-Through Program at the University of Oregon. All were in their 20's. Training began in September

1972 and terminated in August 1973. Subject 1 received 80 hours of training, subject 2 received 70 hours, subject 3 received 50 hours, and subject 4 received 20 hours.

The basic procedure used in all training sessions was for the trainer to sit next to the subject. The trainer spoke words into a microphone, and the subject responded by identifying the word. The subject did not look at the trainer during the word or sentence drill. Furthermore, the subject wore headphones that transmitted about 85 dB of white noise, rendering the subject artificially deaf. Since the subject neither looked at the trainer nor was able to hear the trainer, the only source of information about the words presented came through tactual vibration.

Training sessions lasted 20 to 60 minutes (usually 30 minutes). Although there was an attempt to schedule daily sessions, the subjects' university training activities took them out of town regularly, often resulting in absences of 1 or 2 weeks at a time in the training. The training time was divided roughly in the following ways:

1. Isolated words presented randomly (70% of available training time).

2. Vocabulary words presented in connected sentences (15%).

3. Inflection copying (5%).

4. Rhyming (2%).

5. Face to face work (3%).

The Word List

The isolated words presented to the hearing subjects and those used to compose the sentences they identified were taken from a list of 60 words. The word list contained samples of the following word types:

1. Words that are minimally different, that is, different in only one phoneme.

2. Single syllable words beginning with either consonant sound or vowel sound.

3. Two, three, or four syllable words.

4. Words occurring frequently in statement tasks and instructions used with deaf children (words such as *what, is, that, not, touch, why*).

Performance Tests

The subjects were regularly tested on the words in isolation. Words were presented in random order. If the subject correctly identified a word on the first run through of the list, that word was dropped and the subject received a score of "1" (first trial). If the subject misidentified a word, she was told the word; the word was set aside until the end of the first run through. All words not correctly identified on the first trial were then presented in random order in a second run through. If the subject then correctly identified a word, a "2" was entered on the score sheet for that word and the word was dropped. The procedure was repeated until all words had been correctly identified or until the subject had received three trials.

RESULTS WITH HEARING SUBJECTS

Isolated Words

Although the subjects often received no training for periods of 2 or more weeks at a time, the number of words they identified on first trial generally increased with additional time. Subjects 1 and 2 (who received training for the longest period of time) frequently achieved above 90% correct on the first trial when working with the complete list of 60 words. The relative degree of difficulty of different words diminished with training. During the first month of training, 18% of the words were not identified after the second trial. After the first 2 months, however, only 1% of the words were not correctly identified on either the first or second trial. Also, the more quickly a subject mastered a new word, the better she remembered that word.

The rate of acquisition seemed to be associated with the criterion used for introducing new words. The lower the criterion, the faster the subject mastered new words. Subject 4 was on a 60% new word criterion. After 2 months, she outperformed the other subjects. Subjects 1 and 2, who progressed fairly rapidly, were on a new word criterion of 70%. Subject 3, who progressed the slowest, was on an 80% new word criterion.

Words in Sentences

Over half of the arbitrarily constructed sentences presented to the subjects were correctly identified on the first trial, even when these sentences were quite elaborate. The most frequently missed word in the sentence was the first word. In longer sentences, the subjects would sometimes fail to identify the last words; however, actual misidentifications did not frequently occur near the end of the sentence. A possible explanation is that the first word of the sentence is presented against a baseline of silence. The word appears suddenly. The remaining words in the sentence, on the other hand, are presented against the characteristics of the preceding words. The performance of the subjects on sentences and the relatively small amount of time devoted to the sentence identification implies that the perception of connected speech is easier than the perception of individual words.

Voice Pitch Patterns

With a minimum of training, subjects 1 and 2 could not only copy the relative pitch of a complex pitch pattern but could also imitate the pattern precisely, varying no more than a quarter tone from each pitch produced by the trainer. This performance was achieved on over 90% of the trials in which the subject responded to a female speaker whose voice fell in the same register as the subject's voice. When a male speaker presented pitch samples, the subjects copied the relative pitch but with diminished accuracy.

A minimum degree of facility with the vocoder seemed to be required before subjects could perform on pitch discrimination exercises. Attempts to train subjects 3 and 4 on pitch discriminations after they had received between 12 and 20 hours of instruction produced only modest results. Subjects 1 and 2, however, spontaneously began to match inflections of the trainer after they had received around 60 hours of instruction. Possibly attention to pitch assumes a familiarity with the other speech variables which are transmitted through the vocoder. This familiarity may be attainable only after so many words or types of words have become familiar.

Placement of Vibrators

Subject 2 worked with vibrators attached to her fingers. The other subjects had vibrators attached to their forearms. No difference in performance seems attributable to the placement of the vibrators since subject 1 performed at least as well as subject 2. Subjects 1 and 4 performed as well when the vibrators were transferred to their legs. The same relative position of the vibrators was maintained, and the transfer was instant, which would indicate that performance observed was a function of mastery of the patterns, not of any neurological adaptation or increased sensitivity of particular body parts.

TRAINING DEAF SUBJECTS

In August 1973, training of the hearing subjects was terminated and work with three deaf subjects began. A fourth subject was added in November 1973. Subjects were young males, each with a bilateral hearing loss exceeding 85 dB in the range of 250 to 8,000 Hz.

Subject 1, an 8-year old boy, was alert but at the beginning of training lacked all except the most rudimentary speech behaviors. He was substantially behind in academic skills and tended to "act out" in school.

Subject 2, a 14-year old boy, was verbal and articulate on phrases used in everyday exchanges. At the beginning of training his verbal performance when reading a third grade book, however, was largely incomprehensible. With his hearing aid, he was able to hear voices and identify some words when he was not facing the speaker.

Subject 3 was a 13-year old boy who had a history of behavior problems. He seemed eager and cooperative, although his speech behavior (as well as written communication skills) were grossly deficient.

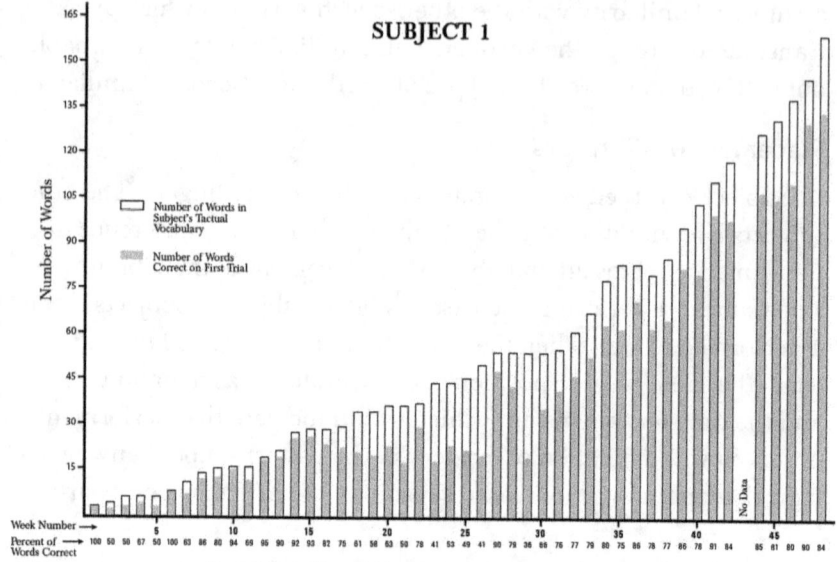

Figure 2. First trial word indentification performance for deaf subject #1

Subject 4 was an 8-year old boy who lacked all but the most elementary speech behaviors.

Subjects 1, 3, and 4 were prohibited from using hearing aids during training sessions with the tactual vocoder. During most of the experiment subject 2 was allowed to use the combination of tactual information and what information he could secure through his hearing aid.

Although the procedures used in the training session were similar to those used with hearing subjects, there were differences.

Specifically:

1. Vibrators were placed on the subjects' thighs (three boxes on one thigh, two on the other) so that the subjects' hands would be free to touch objects or pictures.

2. Particularly during the first 2 weeks of training the subjects responded by touching rather than by producing verbal responses.

3. Some time was spent during each period to work on articulation (both to prepare the children for verbal responses and to break up the period).

4. Because of the need to teach basic speech skills in connection with the perception of speech patterns, longer periods were introduced (initially 1 hour a day for 6 days a week and later 1 hour a day for 5 days a week).

5. A reinforcement system was introduced to "turn on" the subjects and keep them on task. Children worked for pennies or nickels. The rules for earning these rewards varied with each child's proficiency.

6. The emphasis of the training sessions was on the identification of words contained in sentences. The goal was to provide the deaf subjects with as much "imprinting" of syntax as possible. To achieve this goal, the various tasks were designed so that all work, including word identification tasks were presented in a syntactical context, for example, "Get ready…touch the glass." "Get ready…say the word (pause) *glass*. Glass."

7. A variety of "phrases" was introduced so that work on word identification could be conducted in different syntactical contexts. Each subject was taught five or more phrases, such as "pick up…," "touch…," "hand me the…," "this is a(n)…," "I am a…," "this is not a(n)…," "I am not a(n)…"

The Training Sessions

Our rationale for each activity presented during the training sessions follows.

Face to face work on articulation (15% of available training time). We were faced with a difficult trade-off in terms of showing results with the vocoder. Perhaps the greatest potential of the system lies in the area of helping a deaf child speak in a conventionally acceptable manner. Since the perception of speech is a prerequisite to sophisticated articulation training, the investigators established *speech perception* as the highest priority.

The context of the face-to-face articulation work varied with each child. The rule followed by the trainers was this: If the child is to give a verbal response to any of the tasks presented, work on the articulation of those responses. Make sure that the subject can produce an acceptable, if not perfect, response. Limit the amount of time spent on face-to-face work to no more than 8 minutes a session.

The initial face-to-face work concentrated on the production of basic sounds. For example, subject 1 initially could not say words beginning with an "m" sound. He stopped the "m," saying "mmbe" instead of "me." Subject 2 had a similar problem with "s" saying "s(t) itting" instead of "sitting." Later face-to-face work focused on more advanced skills, such as saying a sentence without stopping between each word, for example, saying, "Iamuman" rather than "Iyn amm oay monn."

Words and sentences (65% of available time). – As noted above, the goal was to introduce words in a syntactical context as early as possible. Because of the management and articulation problems of the first days of training, however, the trainers had to present a series of "touching tasks." A display of three or more objects was placed in front of the child. The trainer sat slightly behind the child so that he could not see her face. The trainer would say, for example, "Get ready ... touch the (pause) monkey ... Monkey." The child was not required to produce a verbal response. He was required simply to touch the appropriate object. After perhaps 6 hours of training a format requiring a verbal response from the child was introduced, for example, "Get ready ... touch the (pause) monkey ... Monkey." The child is now required to touch the appropriate object and say the appropriate name, "Monkey."

As part of the work on words and sentences the children were tested at least twice a week. A test consisted of the presentation of all the words in the child's vocabulary. Words were presented only one time, in random order. Trainers recorded the first trial performance for each word. During the tests, the words were presented in sentence contexts, using a format familiar to the child ("say the word..."). The convention of using the same phrase for all words was introduced to simplify the recording of data.

Isolated sounds and rhyming (10% of available time). – During the early training sessions, work with letter identification was implemented with subjects 1, 3, and 4. The children identified letters by their sound (the letter s being identified as "ssss," for example).

Deaf subjects who received training for at least 20 weeks were introduced to rhyming tasks. For example, the trainer says, "rhymes with at ... mmm." The child responds, "mat". The rationale for work with rhyming was that it could be a useful source of information about the individual sounds within words (and that the words are composed of individual and different sounds). The rhyming tasks rarely exceeded 4 minutes during a session and usually involved the presentation of these sounds: "rrr," "mmm," "sss," "shhh," "c," and sometimes "lll."

Language action tasks (10% of available time). – The work with language action tasks involved a less structured format. The trainer would present tasks from a book. The subject was not prohibited from looking at the trainer; however, the trainer pointed to illustrated matter on the page and often presented tasks while the child was looking at the page. The trainer would typically present tasks such as: "What is this?...Is this a man?...Say the whole thing...What is the girl doing?...Say the whole thing...Is the girl sleeping?...Is the girl riding a horse?...Is the girl sitting?...Is she climbing a tree?"

The child was not required to repeat the questions presented by the trainer; however, from time to time the trainer would follow a question by saying, "What did I say?" The child received points for correct responses.

Language action tasks comprised as much as 20% of the early training periods. They were used as a change of pace to reduce the high degree of concentration required by the word identification tasks. After the children had been in the training program for 15 weeks the language action tasks assumed a position of less prominence. On many days, they were not presented at all (particularly on test days, when the list of words became quite long); however, these tasks were often used as reward for a good performance.

The Word Lists

Each child worked from a slightly different word list, and none of the lists was identical to that used by the hearing subjects. The lists were constructed primarily according to the individual child's ability to articulate different sounds. Also, difficult words were introduced from time to time in an attempt to see how long it would take the subject to master these, whether they had a deteriorating effect on the other words the child had mastered, whether their introduction facilitated the child's ability to generalize to new words, and whether more practice was required for these words or for words presented at the beginning of the program.

During most of the training, the trainers followed a performance formula for introducing new words. The formula was based on a 70% to 80% first trial performance. If a child's performance level fell below 70%, the trainer dropped words in the vocabulary and firmed the remaining words. When the first trial performance exceeded 80%, the trainer introduced new words and integrated these with the others in the child's vocabulary.

Reinforcers

Positive reinforcers were used with all subjects on sentence identification tasks. The reinforcement schedule varied according to the task presented and to an individual child's behavior. Initially, each child received 1 point for every correct response. After earning 10 points, he received a penny or a nickel. If a child developed a pattern of guessing, the schedule was changed so that the child had to make a set number of consecutive correct responses before earning a nickel or a penny. At the end of each training period, the child was given an opportunity to purchase items that had been placed in the "store," or he was allowed to keep the money.

Initially, no points or money were awarded for face-to-face work. Later, contingencies were introduced so that the child was reinforced for performing acceptably on words or phrases that had been practiced in face-to-face work. For example:

Trainer: Get ready. (pause) Touch the glass.

Subject: Touch…the…glass.

Trainer: Good.

The trainer then awarded 2 points to the child and said face-to-face, "Two points. You said *glass*. So I gave you a point for good talking."

Results with Deaf Subjects and Discussion

Subjects were tested weekly on words in isolation that were presented in random order: The performance of the deaf subjects was similar to that of the hearing subjects, although perhaps slightly slower during the early stages of training.

Subject 1. Subject 1 was the most experienced deaf subject, with 48 weeks of practice. His performance is summarized in Figure 2. The top of each bar indicates the number of words in his vocabulary. The shaded part of each bar indicates the number of words correctly responded to on the first trial of each week's test.

As the figure indicates, the rate of subject 1's mastery accelerated as a function of continued practice. By the 36th week he had mastered only 1.94 words per week on the average. From the 36th week through the 48th week, however, he averaged 4.75 new words mastered a week. The rate of vocabulary growth paralleled identification performance. At the end of the 36th week, the subject had a tactual vocabulary of 81 words, which was larger than the hearing subjects' vocabularies. By the 48th week, however, subject 1's tactual vocabulary had nearly doubled, to 152 words. In 12 weeks, 71 words were added to his vocabulary. During these 12 weeks his new word mastery rose from 70 to 127, an increase of 57 words. (Subject 1 had required about 33 weeks to master his first 57 words.)

Subject 1's performance is even more impressive when the number of trials involved in the word mastery is considered. He required 14 weeks of practice to master the first 27 words that were introduced. These were the only words in his tactual vocabulary; therefore, the practice time was devoted exclusively to these words. He required approximately 14,000 trials to master these words. From week 31 through 36 (a 5-week period) 27 words were introduced. Subject 1 required approximately 1,400 exposures to master these words. Another 27 words were introduced between the 45th and 48th week. These words required less than 300 exposures. The rate at which subject 1 was able to identify new words increased about 46 times during the period reported.

The following is a sample of subject 1's performance on mastering 5 new words presented during the 34th week of instruction. The words were *eat, go, jump, give,* and *put.* The 5 words were presented in random order until the child achieved two consecutive perfect runs. Then the words were randomly integrated with 16 familiar words and again presented until the child achieved two perfect runs on the 5 new words. Four trials were needed on both occasions to achieve the two consecutive perfect runs.

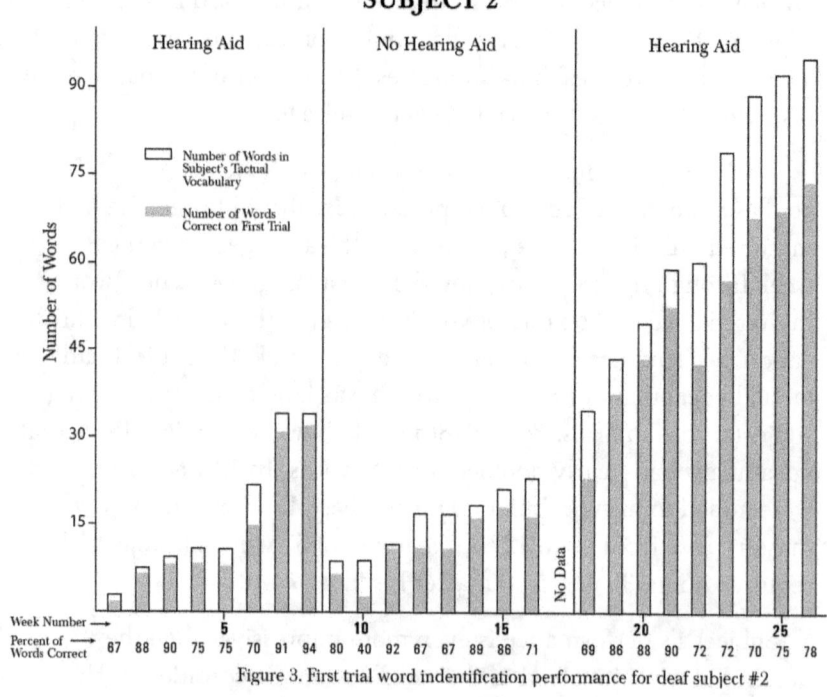

Figure 3. First trial word indentification performance for deaf subject #2

Subject 2. Figure 3 summarizes the performance of subject 2 on first trial correct identification for his 26 weeks of participation in the experiment. The heavy vertical lines on the figure mark the period during which the subject did not wear his hearing aid (weeks 9 through 17). During the remaining weeks (1 through 8 and 18 through 26) subject 2 used both his hearing aid and the vocoder during the training sessions.

Subject 2 progressed quite rapidly during the first 8 weeks of training. When he was prohibited from using his aid, he virtually had to start over. His rate of progress without the aid, however, seemed reasonable. By the end of the 16th week, his vocabulary consisted of 24 words, only 4 less than subject 1's vocabulary at this time.

With the reintroduction of his hearing aid, subject 2 again progressed rapidly, particularly during weeks 23 and 24. Twenty-nine words were added to his vocabulary during these weeks, while his performance consistently remained at or above 70%.

The extent to which the subject relied on information received through his hearing aid is not easy to determine. What seems to have happened during the training was that the subject became more proficient at "hearing" the training words through his aid. When tested during the 8th week he performed at about 65% accuracy in response to training words when he used *only* his hearing aid (not using the vocoder and not looking at the trainer). His performance with only the vocoder was about 40% accuracy on the same words. His performance when both the vocoder and aid were used was about 94%. We were quite surprised, however, to find that the subject's performance on common words not in the vocabulary was only about 20% accurate when the subject used the hearing aid only. The conditions were the same as those used to test the training words. Apparently, the subject learned to use his hearing aid with far more precision than he had in the past. Perhaps the repetition and focus of the training taught the child to attend to information to which he had not previously attended.

Subject 2 was dropped from the experiment after the 26th week, at which time he was able to perform acceptably with a vocabulary of 95 words. The primary reason for dropping him was that the training sessions were conflicting with other activities in which the subject wanted to participate.

Subject 3. Figure 4 shows the performance of subject 3 on first trial accuracy. At the end of the 12th week his word list consisted of *elephant, cow, monkey, glass, chair, shoe, book, table, tape, recorder, Rodney, paper, light, sister, M & M,* and *ashtray*. The performance of this subject was slower than that of the others. During a 2 week period, he was not available for training and during most of the experimental period (12 weeks) he was experiencing a number of personal problems. We make no assumptions about the extent to which these affected his performance, except that they resulted in frequent absences.

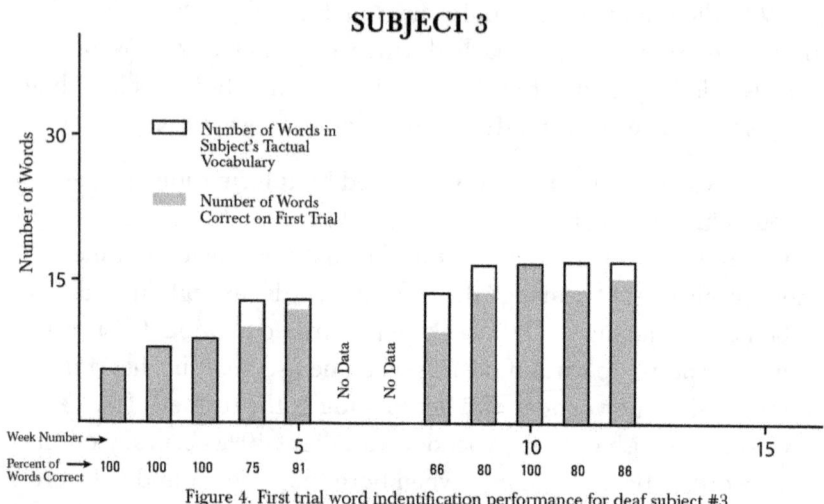

Figure 4. First trial word indentification performance for deaf subject #3

Subject 3's rate of progress during the first 4 weeks was as rapid as that of subject 2 and surpassed that of subject 1. Subject 3's performance deteriorated somewhat following a 2 week absence from the training; however, his performance was not substantially behind that of subject 1 at the end of the 12th week (at which time subject 3 withdrew from the experiment).

Subject 4. As Figure 5 indicates, subject 4 progressed less rapidly than the other deaf subjects. During the 16th week of training subject 4 had trouble adjusting to new firming procedures. At that time, the number of words in his vocabulary was reduced from 29 to 22. Eight weeks passed before the number of words in his tactual vocabulary exceeded 30. What seemed to be lacking from his performance was the acceleration apparent with subjects 1 and 2, particularly after the 30th week of instruction.

Subject 4 averaged only 1.25 words mastered per week through the 37th week (compared to nearly 2 words per week for subject 1).

There was some increase in subject 4's mastery rate near the end of the reported period. From the 27th week through the 37th week, subject 4 averaged 1.7 new words mastered per week. This figure is substantially behind that of subject 1.

Possibly, subject 4 required more practice before his rate of mastery would begin to accelerate. Possibly, his absences accounted for his poor performance. (He averaged slightly more than one absence a week from the 30th through the 37th week.) According to his trainers, he learned quickly but had trouble remembering the words. In the 29th week, he required six run throughs or 30 trials to master five new words.

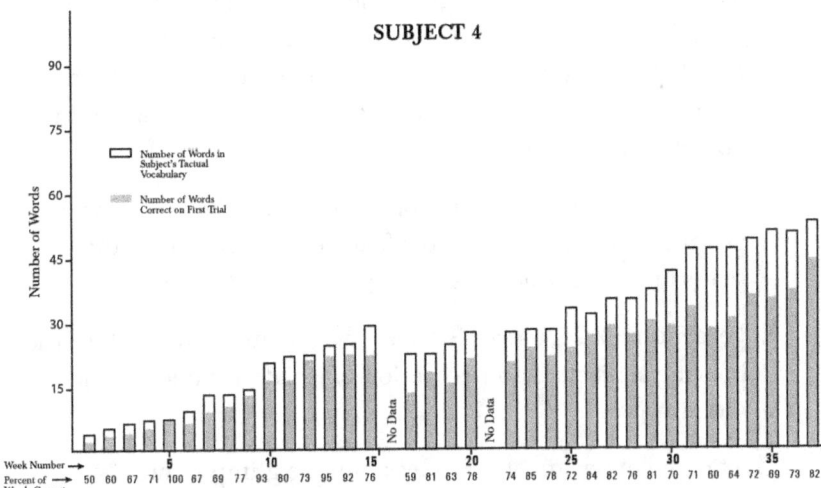

Figure 5. First trial identification performance for deaf subject #4

CONCLUSIONS

The following observations have been made in our experiment with the vocoder:

1. Deaf subjects can be taught to hear fine speech discriminations through the tactual mode, even discrimination as fine as those involved in "fly...sly" or "teef...teeth."

2. The performance of subjects is positively correlated with practice and seems to be clearly a function of training.

3. The quest for the appropriate tactual display of speech, therefore, must be conducted *within the training context*. The adequacy of a display is evident only after sufficient training has been provided.

4. Hundreds of corrected repetitions are required for either a deaf or hearing subject to learn simple tactual discriminations.

5. Initially deaf subjects learn more slowly than hearing subjects; however, their rate seems to match that of hearing subjects once an initial set of perhaps 30 to 40 words is reliably mastered.

6. The rate at which a subject is able to learn new words increases with the number of words the subject has mastered (a relationship that cannot be maintained indefinitely but which is apparent during perhaps the first year of instruction and probably will hold for a longer period).

7. It was observed that deaf subjects as well as hearing subjects are able to attend to prosodic features of speech including stress and pitch when speech is presented tactually.

8. Perception of sentences is apparently no more difficult for the hearing subjects than perception of isolated sounds or individual words.

The tactual experiment provides a unique glimpse into the amount and type of practice needed for a person to learn to use a new sensory modality. The performance of these deaf children is encouraging. With more sophisticated and portable hardware, we believe that a deaf infant could learn to "hear" using tactual input in exactly the same way a hearing child learns to hear.

REFERENCES

Flanagan, J. L. *Speech analysis, synthesis and perception.* New York: Academic Press, 1965.

Gault, R. H., & Crane, G. W., Tactual patterns from certain vowel qualities instrumentally communicated from a speaker to a subject's finger. *Journal of General Psychology*, 1928, *1*, 353-359.

Guelke, R. W., & Huyssen, R. M. J., Development of apparatus for the analysis of sound by the sense of touch. *Journal of the Acoustical Society of America*, 1959, *31*, 799-809.

Heinz, J. M., & Stevens, K. N. On the properties of voiceless fricative consonants. *Journal of the Acoustical Society of America,* 1961, *33,* 589-596.

Hughes, G. W., & Halle, M. Spectral properties of fricative consonants, *Journal of the Acoustical Society of America,* 1956, *28,* 303-310.

Kringlebotn, M. Experiments with some visual and vibrotactile aids for the deaf. *American Annals of the Deaf,* 1968, *113,* 311-317.

Pickett, J. M., & Pickett, B. H., Communication of speech sounds by tactual vocoder. *Journal of Speech and Hearing Research,* 1963, *6,* 207-222.

Wiener, N., Wiesner, David, E. E., Jr., & Levine, L. Operation "Felix." *Quarterly Progress Reports,* Research Laboratory of Electronics, Massachusetts Institute of Technology, Cambridge, 1949-1951.

CHAPTER 8

Responding to the critique that the Direct Instruction model would only be effective with at-risk children, Engelmann conducted research to examine its effects with more affluent children. This article analyzes a study of the effectiveness of the DISTAR instructional program on 30 middle-class second grade students. The students were tested on their academic achievement and attitude towards the Direct Instruction program. Results replicated those found with at-risk populations, with the middle-class students having higher levels of achievement and more positive attitudes toward learning. The authors suggest this study provides good support for the implementation of Direct Instruction programs with all students, not just children who are difficult to teach. The Direct Instruction model can maximize the effectiveness of teaching all types of students, not just those who are at-risk.

DIRECT INSTRUCTION OUTCOMES WITH MIDDLE-CLASS SECOND GRADERS (1982)[*]

Siegfried Engelmann & Doug Carnine

Because the Distar programs are used extensively with lower performing children, many educators have assumed that the programs are designed only for low performers and that they are either not appropriate or are even stultifying for "average" children. The Distar authors, on the other hand, maintain that the programs are designed for any child who has not mastered the skills necessary to read, to solve arithmetic problems, or to handle basic language operations.

Data on the Engelmann-Becker Follow Through Model (Becker & Engelmann, 1978) tend to substantiate the authors' contention that Distar does not inhibit middle-class children's achievement. Within Follow-Through classrooms are some 20 percent middle-class children. At the end of second grade the average performance in reading decoding for 3,363 poor children who started in first grade was level 3.7 (based on the Wide Range Achievement Test norms); for 898 middle-class children, the average reading performance was grade 4.5.

To further document the effects of Direct Instruction on the attitudes and achievement of "average" children, data were collected on a classroom of 30 middle-class second graders in Springfield, Oregon. The top half of the total second-grade enrollment–as determined by teacher assessment–was placed in the experimental classroom (28 children). These children had been in Distar as first graders also. Two low-performing children were added to the experimental classroom. One was a repeater (the only student who had been retained). The other was placed in the classroom on the recommendation of the reading specialist.

During both the first-grade year and the second-grade year, the children were taught primarily by trainees (students at the

---

[*] Engelmann, S., & Carnine, D. (1982). Direct Instruction outcomes with middle-class second graders. *ADI News*, *1*(2), 4–5. Reprinted with permission from Siegfried Engelmann.

University of Oregon enrolled in a practicum on Direct Instruction techniques). Two academic skills – reading and arithmetic – were taught by trainees each morning during a two-hour period. For reading the second-grade year, each child received one-half hour of small-group instruction in level III Distar (which focuses heavily on science content), one-half hour of independent reading seatwork, and one-quarter hour of entire class instruction. The daily arithmetic instruction involved one-half hour of entire class presentation and one-quarter hour of independent seatwork.

The second-grade classroom teacher was rated as a superior teacher; however, the trainees were responsible for the bulk of the academic instruction in reading and arithmetic.

A supervisor was responsible for training the trainees and for monitoring their performance. A total of six trainees taught the children over the two-year period. The trainees usually switched subject areas or small groups at the beginning of each new quarter, which meant that the children were frequently taught by three different "teachers" during the year, some of whom initially had never taught children before. Based on training data and children's performance in Follow Through, one would expect that the inexperienced trainees would not be able to achieve performance gains as great as those of experienced teachers.

These tests were given from late April to early June of the second-grade year:

Stanford Achievement Test (Primary Battery 2) for Reading, Arithmetic, and Science. Wide-Range Achievement test for oral reading.

The ten children who performed best in reading achievement also received the Gates-MacGinitie test of *Speed and Accuracy* (for fourth through sixth graders).

An attitude questionnaire (developed by the investigators) was designed to tap the children's feelings about their reading program, their teacher, and themselves. (See Table 1.) The attitude questionnaire was presented to the entire class. The tester told the students that he was going to ask questions about their reading program and that the children were not to write their names on the test form. The tester then read each item aloud and the children circled the words that indicated how they felt. (The questions did not appear on the children's answer sheets.)

TABLE 1
Distar Reading Attitude Questionnaire and Children's Responses

	1	2	3	Mean
A. Enjoyment				
1. How much did you enjoy the stories?	a little (4)*	some (6)	a lot (20)	2.5
2. How much did you enjoy the workbook?	a little (6)	some (11)	a lot (13)	2.2
3. Were the materials:	too easy (5)	just right (22)	too hard (3)	1.9
4. Which part of the program did you enjoy the most?	beginning (4)	middle (15)	end (12)	2.3
5. Which part of the program did you enjoy the least?	beginning (16)	middle (7)	end (7)	1.7
B. Interest and Curiosity				
6. How much did you talk about what you've learned with other people?	a little (8)	some (10)	a lot (12)	2.1
7. Have you read other books to find out more about something you read in a story?	Yes (20)	No (10)		1.3
C. Self-Image				
8. How smart are you compared to other kids you know?	smarter (9)	just as smart (16)	not as smart (5)	1.9
9. How well are you going to do next year in school?	very well (19)	O.K. (10)	not too good (1)	1.4
10. How smart are you going to be when you grow up?	very smart (24)	average (6)	below average (0)	1.2
11. How much did the teacher expect you to work?	a little (1)	some (2)	a lot (27)	2.9

*Numbers in parentheses indicate the number of children who circled that response

RESULTS

Figure 1 presents bar graphs of the reading test scores. The first bar shows the mean reading (comprehension) score for all 30 children on the Stanford Achievement Test and the publishers norm (dark). The mean performance for the 30 subjects was at the 4.6 grade level. The only two children who scored below grade level (below 2.7) were the two low performers added to the classroom. Both scored 2.6.

FIGURE 1

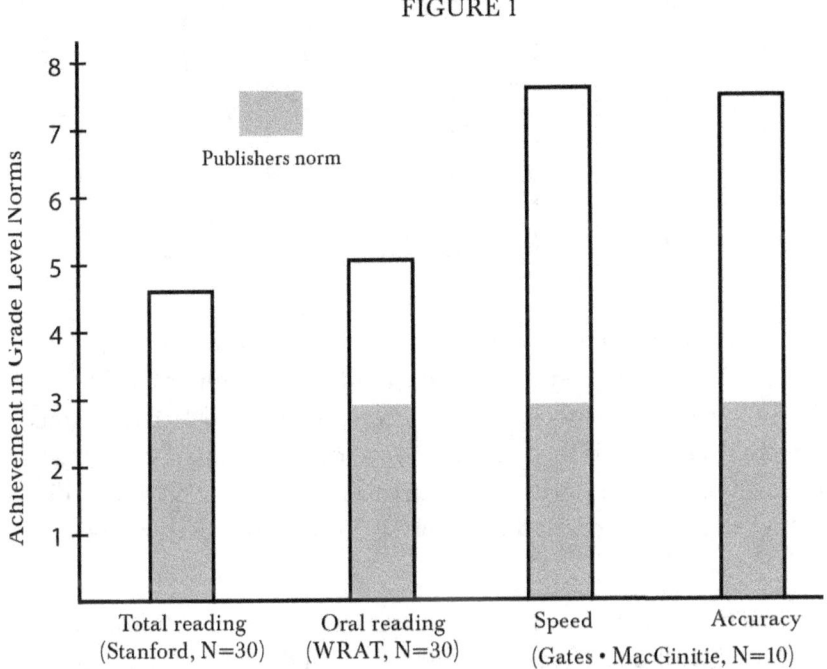

The second bar shows the mean performance for all children on the WRAT Reading (oral decoding). No child scored below grade norm.

Results of the Gates-MacGinite tests of *Reading Speed and Accuracy* appear on the third and fourth bars. Only the top ten children received this test. Although the children were in the second grade, they received the fourth through sixth grade battery because that is where they were performing. The ten children's mean performance was grade level 7.6 for speed and 7.5 for accuracy. The lowest score for speed was 4.6 (both scores achieved by the same child.)

Figure 2 shows the performance of all 30 children in Science and Arithmetic as measured by the Stanford second-grade battery.

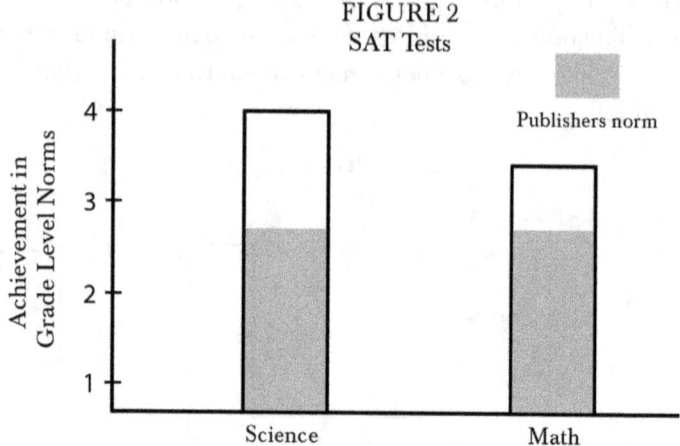

FIGURE 2
SAT Tests

The children were not taught science as a subject. What they had learned about science derived from Distar Reading III. The 15-minute daily entire class activity could be labeled "science" since the children learned the various science rules presented in Distar III during the time. In science performance, the mean of 4.0 is significantly above the expected norm of 2.7. Only four children scored below grade level.

The mean Arithmetic performance (grade level 3.4) is not as high as that of reading and science. The standard deviation for arithmetic performance was only .83, indicating a narrow score distribution. Five children were below grade level.

The results of the attitude questionnaire are summarized in Table 1.

Items 1 through 5 deal with the student's enjoyment of the level III material. In response to item 1, 67 percent of the children indicated that they enjoyed the text material (the stories) a lot. The group enjoyed the workbook less, however, the highest category (a lot) was marked by 43 percent of the children. Most children

(73 percent) indicated that the material was "just right" in terms of difficulty (item 3). In items 4 and 5, the students indicated that they enjoyed either the middle (47 percent) or the end of the program (40 percent) far more than the beginning.

Items 6 and 7 may be considered as a crude indicator of the extent to which the children's interest was either stimulated or stifled by Distar Reading III. The summary of item 6 indicates that almost three-fourths of the students (73 percent) talked about the content some or a lot with other people. Also, 67 percent of the children read other books to find out more about specific content presented in the reading program (Item 7).

Items 8 through 10 deal with "self image" as it relates to being smart and performing well academically. Responses to item 8 indicate that the children do not consider themselves smarter than other kids they know; however, according to item 9, 80 percent of the students believe they will be very smart when they grow up. Almost two-thirds of the children (63 percent) indicate that they will do very well in school during the following year (item 10).

While there is no comparison group reported in the study, the performance of the children seems to be far above what would be expected in middle-class second-grade classrooms. There were no non-readers at the end of the second-grade year. In fact, the two lowest performers on the Stanford were only one-tenth grade level below norm. Both of these students scored above grade level on the WRAT. If we consider the publisher's norms as a basis for comparison, the children reported in the study were significantly accelerated, although the children had received no kindergarten instruction and although the classroom situation was less than optimal for achieving maximal performance or attitude gains. The constant switching of trainees meant temporary breaks in continuity. The inexperience of the trainees frequently meant that the children did not progress as rapidly as a more experienced Distar teacher would have moved them.

SOME CONCLUSIONS

This study is not presented as a definitive statement about the effectiveness of highly structured, direct-instruction techniques with average and above-average performers; however, the data suggest that many statements like the following are false.

1. Highly structured programs either retard or hold back average or above average performers. The teaching procedure is basically the same for both above- and below-average children; however, where they start and where they end is different. As soon as the children show that they can perform on a particular skill, the teacher moves to the next skill. The children in the study completed an average of 460 lessons during the two-year period (an average of 2.6 lessons per school day, based on 180 days per year).

2. While highly structured programs may be successful in teaching very basic skills, such as decoding, they are not well designed to teach comprehension and reasoning skills. The comprehension mastery as measured by the Stanford (4.4) was 1.7 years above grade level.

3. Children who learn from highly structured programs find the instruction boring. Neither the behavior of the children in this study, nor their responses to the questionnaire provide any evidence that they found the highly structured presentations boring. While recognizing that their teacher required them to work hard, the children generally enjoyed what they did. An interesting point is that they enjoyed the program more as they progressed through it.

4. Structured programs stifle curiosity and instill passive, stimulus-response behavior. The children reported that they discussed the content of the program outside of class and two-thirds of them read books about specific concepts taught in the program. Discussions and independent projects are generally taken as signs of both independence and curiosity.

5. Structured programs do not promote positive self-images. Self-image is difficult to measure because there are many facets to a positive self-image. (Confidence on the basketball court does not imply a positive self-image in a reading group.) Although the measures used to judge "self-image" in the present study are, at best, crude, the children seem to be saying that they feel confident about themselves, that they are smart, that they will do well in school next year, and that they will be smart when they grow up. The only item that provides an apparent inconsistency with this interpretation is 8, to which the children responded that they generally consider themselves as smart as other children. A possible interpretation is that the children are using their classmates as a basis for this evaluation. The fact that they feel they will do very well next year and will be very smart when they grow up implies that they currently consider themselves quite smart. If these statements actually reflect their feelings, the children exhibit a quite positive self-image with reference to academic performance.

In summary, this study provides good support for the use of Direct Instruction programs with all children, not just the difficult-to-teach children.

REFERENCE

Becker, W. C. & Engelmann, S. *Analysis of achievement data on six cohorts of low-income children from 20 school districts in the University of Oregon Direct Instruction Follow-Through Model.* Technical Report 78-1: Eugene, Oregon. University of Oregon Follow Through Projects, 1978.

CHAPTER 9

The struggle to help all children succeed academically has been a recurring theme in Engelmann's publications. Beginning with his research on at-risk students, Engelmann identified the need to design instruction based on the students' skills. He continued his research to demonstrate how his theories of instructional design could be successful with students of varying backgrounds and abilities. This article discusses the difficulties of teaching students with severe handicaps and how the authors used aspects of the Direct Instruction model to more effectively teach these students new skills and prevent social failure. Multiple examples of applying Direct Instruction principles to teaching severely handicapped learners with various conditions are provided, and statistical results regarding behavioral change are included. By demonstrating how the principles of Direct Instruction could be utilized to teach new skills and alter behaviors in severely handicapped learners, the authors provide additional evidence of how these principles can accelerate the learning process of all students.

DI FOR SEVERELY HANDICAPPED LEARNERS (1983)[*]

George Singer, Dan Close, Geoff Colvin, & Siegfried Engelmann

If you teach students with severely handicapping conditions, you probably have taught individuals who were either recently released from an institution or who were in danger of being sent to an institution. You probably wondered what to do with these problematic students. They often exhibit severe behavior problems and limited skill repertoires. They are also likely to have a variety of handicaps. For example, Ron, a ten-year-old, was admitted to a large state hospital in California. Along with a very limited skill repertoire, Ron exhibited severe behavior problems including regurgitating food, smearing feces, and placing dangerous sharp objects in his eyes, ears, and nose. Another student, Jess, not only exhibited severe behavior problems, but also had multiple handicapping conditions including partial vision, cerebral palsy, and a seizure disorder. Estelle, an eleven-year-old girl, required a wheelchair to move around because of her cerebral palsy. She had a very limited range of skills and several maladaptive behaviors, including biting and scratching her mother and teachers, and refusing to eat any solid foods. Also, she rarely initiated any activity. Teaching children with such limited skills presents many instructional and programmatic problems.

While there has been great progress in the behavioral treatment of the severely handicapped in the past 15 years, there is still a need for new technology to reach those who do not respond to current approaches. Because of our failures, extremely low performing students are still placed in large state hospitals where they are subjected to neglect, isolation, and impersonal custodial care.

---

[*] Singer, G., Close, D., Colvin, G., & Engelmann, S. (1983). DI for Severely Handicapped Learners. *ADI News*, 2(4), 3–4. This research was funded by contract #300-80-0743 between the U.S. Department of Education and the Oregon Research Institute. The views expressed herein are those of the authors and do not necessarily reflect the opinions of the U.S. Department of Education. Reprinted with permission of Siegfried Engelmann.

The principles of direct instruction offer an innovative approach for teaching extremely low performing students that promises to add to behavioral technology. Direct instruction is based upon a logical analysis of learning (Engelmann & Carnine, 1982). While it was initially developed for mildly delayed learners, we believe that by applying the component principles and procedures of direct instruction to severely handicapped students, we can help teach new skills to these students and prevent their social failure.

The purpose of this paper is to describe some of the problems we have encountered in teaching extremely low performing students and to relate how we have used the principles of direct instruction to solve them.

PROJECT S.A.I.L. NORMALIZATION THROUGH DIRECT INSTRUCTION

For the past two years we have been working with children and young people similar to the three students described below. They are residents of a demonstration group in Mount Shasta, California. The home is the main product of Project S.A.I.L. (Systems Adaptation for Integrated Living), a federally funded demonstration project conducted by the Oregon Research Institute. The project serves young people, ages 8 to 21, who were residents of a California State Hospital or who were awaiting admission to a state hospital. All of the clients have severely handicapping conditions, including mental retardation.

Take Henry as an example. He was born with Downs Syndrome. Henry lived in northern California, until he was six years old. No school services were available for him in his hometown. When he contracted juvenile arthritis, there was no community service to help with his many needs. His mother placed him in a state hospital where he was the only verbal and ambulatory person on a large ward. He soon lost his speech and become socially withdrawn. Thirteen years later, when Henry moved to Mount Shasta to live in the S.A.I.L. training home, he exhibited few adaptive behaviors. He simply sat all day in a chair. He occasionally moaned. He had few self-care skills. When faced with this young man's needs, the question arises, "Where do we begin?" At Project S.A.I.L. the beginning is a statement of human values (Singer, in preparation).

The ideas of normalization and personalization suggest the ultimate goals of instruction. They focus the direction of our instruction on the demands of a normal household and community. They provide a set of values. We must keep these values constantly in mind when deciding what and how to teach our students. They tell us if our vehicle (instruction) is on course, but they do not tell us how to design and construct the vehicle. They do not tell us where to begin to teach. We must examine what a person must know in order to enter a simple human community. What are the basic elements of human communication and interaction? What must a person know to benefit from instruction? We have identified the following concepts as essential to the learning process.

The first principle that must be demonstrated to these young people is the contingent relationships inherent in social communities. The students we work with often do not conform to basic standards of human interaction. Their behavior appears random and unpredictable. Tantrums seem to develop without external provocation. These inappropriate behaviors imply a failure to comprehend the relationship between their action and social or environmental consequences. These students need an understanding of the rules and standards for acceptable and unacceptable behaviors. They must learn that acceptable behavior leads to reward and unacceptable behavior leads to punishment.

Another major principle is the meaningful nature of language. Many of our students possess little receptive or expressive language. They do not know the rudiments of communication. A basic concept which must be taught is that people can direct each other's attention in a civilized and purposive manner. If we point to a bar of soap, we are attempting to direct the student to use the soap. When we give an instruction, we are indicating to the learner what is expected.

These two principles, that the social community is orderly and that language is meaningful, directly relate to the issue of compliance. Compliance with instructional requests is a requisite of any instruction. We must carefully and deliberately teach our students to comply with instructions if they are to benefit from training. The following section will present examples of instructional procedures we have utilized to teach our students new skills, thus increasing their participation in society.

COMPLIANCE TRAINING

Simple contingency management procedures are a powerful tool in changing behavior. However, these procedures are often not effective with persons who have firmly established inappropriate behavior of a serious nature (self-abuse, aggression, tantrumming, etc.).

When contingency management procedures did not produce adequate behavioral changes at Project S.A.I.L., a second procedure, generalized compliance training (Engelmann & Colvin in press) was implemented. This program attempts to teach compliance behaviors that generalize to a variety of settings while developing new skills. In addition, it attempts to eliminate noncompliance and other undesirable behaviors. The following example is for purposes of description. It does not provide a set of guidelines or a prescription for programming. The reader is referred to the book *Generalized Compliance Training* for a detailed description of these procedures.

One of the first skills taught in compliance training is to follow simple instructions reliably. Once students learn to follow instructions, it is possible to teach longer, more complex tasks. During later sessions, instructions incompatible with inappropriate behavior are also practiced. If inappropriate behaviors appear during the compliance training session, the student is corrected with a loud command, e.g. "No tantrumming!" and required to follow a simple instruction, e.g. (stand up and sit down). If the inappropriate behavior persists, the student is required to perform the simple instruction until the behavior stops. Social reinforcement is provided only after correct performance of simple instruction. Furthermore, the procedures are carefully programmed to achieve generalized compliance across all relevant people, materials, and settings. An important lesson learned in compliance training is that appropriate behavior or following directions leads to reward. Inappropriate behavior, disobeying directions, leads to simple repetitive tasks without reinforcement.

GENERALIZED SKILL TRAINING

Generalized skill training refers to a method of teaching that incorporates many direct instruction principles (Engelmann, Colvin, & Singer, in preparation). Of interest in the present paper are the notions of *teaching core skills* that generalize to a variety of functional tasks, and *removed-component instruction* to focus training on essential features of tasks. These innovations have been used to teach self-care and domestic-living skills to students in Project S.A.I.L.

Core skills. A detailed analysis of the skills required to perform self-care and domestic-living tasks indicates that 10 basic core skills account for over 99% of all the motor movements (Close, Halpern, Slentz, and Taylor, 1982). Of these motor movements, the vast majority are variations of a simple manual grasp. Other core skills include push, pull, turn, insert, place, lift, stand, set, and rub. At Project S.A.I.L. we teach these basic core skills within the context of functional self-care and domestic skills. For example, teaching handwashing allows us to present the core skills of grasp and turn the faucet, grasp and rub the soap, rub hands and soap together, place hands under the faucet, etc. These core skills appear in a variety of hygiene tasks such as showering, bathing, and shampooing. Once the core skills are mastered, they are easily applied to other tasks. Tasks are selected for instruction because they include core skills common to other functional skills, not because they are easy to learn.

Removed-Component Training. Several students at Project S.A.I.L. could not perform basic core skills. Other students could perform the component response or core skill but not when it was needed. Both of these groups of students could benefit from removed-component training. The essential part of the task is practiced in isolation and then reintegrated into the task. Several rules guide this technique: (1) select skills or components that can be performed in less than 10 seconds; (2) present the massed trials instruction rapidly using functional reinforcement; (3) once the learner reaches criterion on the removed component, present it in a sequence juxtaposed to a variety of other skills; (4) finally, reintegrate the component back into the task and teach the task as an entire sequence. For example, one of our students was having difficulty washing his hands with soap. We removed the core skill of rub. He practiced several forms of rub (e.g. rub his arm, rub his hands together, rub his face, rub the table with a cloth, etc.). He then was required to perform different tasks requiring rub with the simple cue of, "Jack rub," paired with a gesture of where to rub. Finally, instruction of the entire hand and facewashing task was resumed.

RESULTS

On a norm referenced measure of adaptive and maladaptive behavior, the clients of the training home have made statistically significant gains in adaptive behavior (domestic, leisure, self-help, and community skills) and shown significant reductions in maladaptive behaviors (tantrums, running away, public masturbation, destruction of property, aggression, and self-abuse). To date, three of our students have been able to return to their natural homes or to foster homes in the vicinity of their home communities. Three other clients are scheduled to leave for foster homes as this article is in press. The home has a waiting list of referrals for other children with severely handicapping conditions and a replication home will be opened soon in Chico, California. Global data for the efficacy of our demonstration model is described in detail elsewhere (Singer & Close, in preparation).

The following descriptions are presented to provide a better understanding of the young people we are teaching and the techniques being used in the home.

Freddie. Freddie is now 17 years old. He is a tall, thin, and handsome young man. However, when he entered the program he possessed very little language, constantly engaged in some form of self-stimulatory behavior, and tantrummed violently an average of five times a day. He lived most of his life in institutions because of his frequent tantrums.

For several months his tantrums were treated with a contingency management system. He was rewarded with praise and activities when he behaved appropriately. He was placed in a time-out corner when he tantrummed. The number of tantrums decreased, but their intensity worsened, and he began to smash windows. A staff member's wrist was broken during a tantrum. The generalized compliance training procedure was implemented at this point.

The procedure dramatically reduced the frequency and intensity of Freddie's tantrums. This decrease has maintained for eight months. When tantrums did occur, they appeared to be triggered by an unplanned and improper change in instructions or in general group home management procedures. In other words, the causes of the tantrums were clearly identifiable and easily remediated. The graph in Figure 1 illustrates the change in Freddie's behavior.

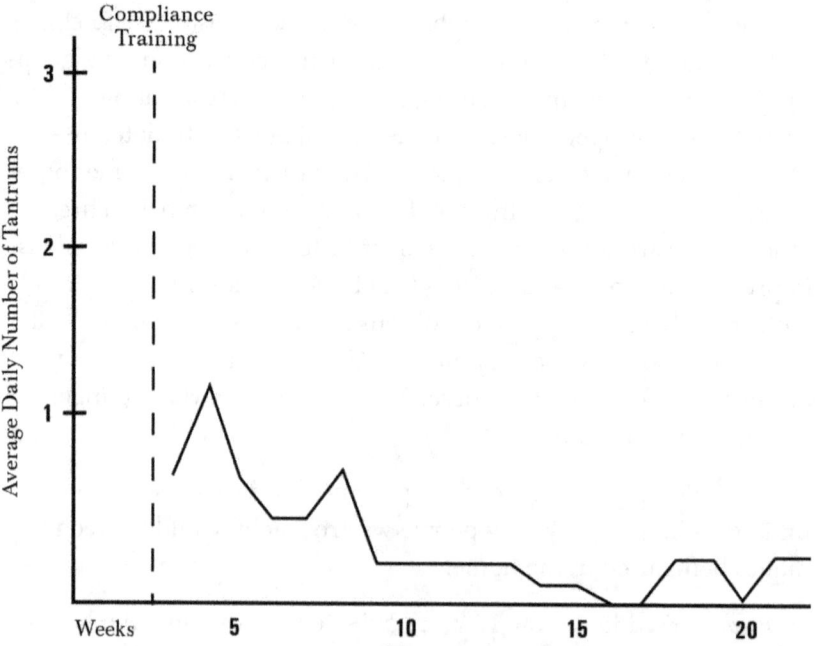

Figure 1. Average daily number of tantrums per week before and after generalized compliance training.

Jack. Jack is 16 years old. He was born with only one eye, has cerebral palsy in half of his body and is physiologically incapable of speech because of distortion of his face. He has been in and out of

Chapter 9: DI for Severely Handicapped Learners (1983)

the state hospital system since birth. Each foster placement has failed because of Jack's inappropriate behaviors that include loud sustained yelling, self-biting, throwing objects, spitting food, and falling on the floor to resist manual guidance.

Jack's skill training was a problem. He often performed most of the steps of a chain, but then showed decreases in correct responding before reaching criteria. Changes in reinforcers and changes in instructional content did not remediate this problem. The strategy that has proved to be promising with Jack and with other clients involves teaching a removed component of the task.

Figure 2 represents the steps completed with the assistance of a verbal prompt on the task of facewashing. The erratic character of the line is typical of Jack's performance during skill training. The dashed line represents the point at which skill training was suspended and the component response of rub was practiced. Jack reached criterion on the second training session and maintained it for three consecutive sessions. The task was reintroduced with the rub integrated and Jack was quickly able to perform the whole task.

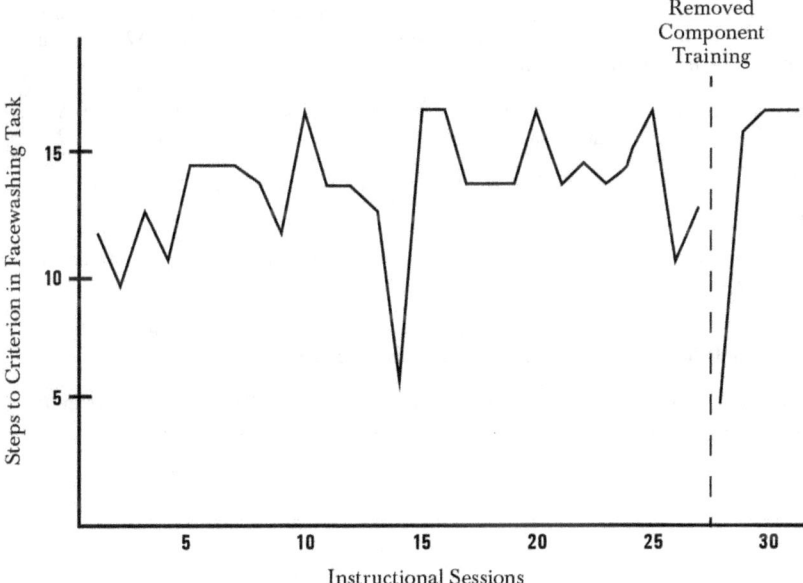

Figure 2. Number of steps performed on a 17-step task before and after removed component training.

SUMMARY

Severely handicapped students with behavior problems are frequently in danger of being removed from society. They are placed in large congregate care institutions or nursing homes where they are treated as indigent medical patients. They are not exposed to the normal challenges and rewards of community living and are treated as a deviant population rather than as fellow citizens. New techniques and service delivery systems are needed to allow institutionalized students to reenter society or to prevent placement of those who are at risk for institutionalization. Project S.A.I.L. developed a service delivery model that has made use of compliance training and generalized skill training to allow young people to participate in a normalized home setting. All of this has taken place in a remote rural area. We believe that this model and the emerging technology offers hope for the 130,000 citizens with severely handicapping conditions who remain in large hospitals or institutions.

REFERENCES

Close, D., Halpern. A., Slentz, K., & Taylor. Evaluation and Training of Severely and Profoundly Retarded Persons for Community Adjustment, Final Report. Washington, DC: Office of Special Education, 1982.

Engelmann, S. & Carnine, D. *Theory of Instruction: Principles and Applications.* New York: Irvington Publishers, Inc., 1982.

Engelmann, S. & Colvin, G. *Generalized Compliance Training.* Dallas, TX: Pro-Ed, Inc., In press.

Engelmann, S. & Colvin, G., & Singer, G. *Direct Instruction for very low performers.* Book in preparation.

Singer, G. & Close, D. Deinstitutionalization of school-aged persons with severely and profoundly handicapping conditions: demonstration. Paper in preparation.

Singer, G. An overview of Project S.A.I.L. In G. Singer (Ed.) *Project S.A.I.L. Replication Guide.* Eugene, Oregon: Oregon Research Institute. Book in preparation.

CHAPTER 10

Utilizing advancements in technology, Engelmann and his colleagues conducted research on the use of video disk instructional programs as teaching aids. They examined the capabilities of this new technology and how they could incorporate the Direct Instruction model to create an aid for teachers and instructional programs for home schooled students. This article describes the effectiveness of video disk instruction and the issues associated with its implementation in schools. The authors describe the video disk as "one of the most potent technologies available to educators," because of its ability to store and present tens of thousands of images as well as offer easy navigation. Video disks are able to provide tutorials, as well as simulations and drill and practice sessions, while still allowing the teacher to maintain a central role in the instruction process by determining areas of focus and review. The use of video disks has been shown to simplify the instruction of scientific concepts because of the ability to utilize slow motion and freeze frames. A video disk program titled Core Concepts is discussed in terms of effectiveness, specifically its focus on teaching to mastery and teacher feedback. This article documents the broader application of the Direct Instruction model through advancements in technology and the ability to enhance instruction in the study of science.

VIDEO DISK INSTRUCTION (1984-1985)[*]

Douglas Carnine, Siegfried Engelmann, & Alan Hofmeister

One of the most potent technologies available to educators is the video disk. One side of a laser disk can project 64,000 different still frame screens, making it the world's most efficient slide projector. If the frames are presented quickly, motion sequences are produced. The teacher can play the disk forward and backward at different speeds, freeze the action for a moment while making a comment, or leave the image on the screen for the entire period. If a different portion of the disk is needed for class discussion, the disk player can jump to another portion of the disk in a few seconds. The ability to quickly jump from place to place is called random access. Moving from place to place on video tape is much slower.

The potential of video disk instruction is limited only by the dynamics of the video sequences (Morris, 1984), the simplicity and power of the instructional content (O'Loughlin & White, 1982), and the presence of a mastery learning management plan (Block, 1971). A well conceived and executed video disk instructional system would both motivate students and increase their understanding and mastery of the subject area content (Bunderson, Baillio & Olsen, 1984). Video disk instruction can include drill and practice, tutorials, and simulations.

PREVALENCE OF VIDEO DISK TECHNOLOGY

For all the advantages of the video disk, the technology is only slowly beginning to appear in schools. Stereotypes about how the technology can be used may account for this slow emergence. Most educators hook a disk player to a computer and provide instruction for a single user. Limited user access makes video disk technology too expensive for widespread public school adoption. Most schools cannot afford the hardware and software for video disk if only a few students can use the system each day.

---

[*] Carnine, D., Engelmann, S., & Hofmeister, A. (1984–1985). Video disk instruction. *ADI News, 4*(2), 3, 5, 2. Reprinted with permission of Siegfried Engelmann.

However, breaking the stereotype that disk players must be hooked to a computer and used with one student at a time makes disk technology affordable. Presenting video disk instruction to an entire classroom, not to a single student, is cost efficient. Then 25 or more students at a time benefit from the disk technology. Moreover, the teacher maintains a central role in the instructional process, deciding when to review or to elaborate content presented on the disk. Entire class instruction, directed by a teacher, also makes it feasible for a teacher to use a video disk course as a primary means of presenting course content. An example of the potential of video disk technology is a system now under development called *Core Concepts*, a system which brings together video disk technology, instructional design, and mastery learning procedures to address a central challenge in American education—math and science instruction in high schools and colleges. Math and science teachers are too aware of the trade-offs between "finishing the book" and making sure the students come away with a basic understanding of the central concept of the course. The growth of textbooks over the last five years makes compromise all the more difficult. The appeal of video disk instruction in *Core Concepts* is that it can compellingly convey what's most important to learn.

DYNAMIC VIDEO

The advantage of dynamic video sequences are apparent. A textbook diagram of RNA's role in assembling proteins does not as clearly convey the process as would a video sequence of the process in operation. Video can also highlight crucial events, like inclusion of the wrong amino acid in an RNA chain. The integration of video and audio, to give explanations while phenomena are being shown, or to ask questions, makes possible realistic instruction through the disk medium.

INSTRUCTIONAL DESIGN

The dynamics of video ("a motion sequence is worth ten textbook pictures") allows concepts to be conveyed in a relatively simple fashion. The notion of economy (and power) in instructional design came from Bruner's *Toward a Theory of Instruction* (1966). Economy comes in the simplicity of an analysis for portraying knowledge. Power refers to the generalizability of an analysis, the degree to which the analysis applies to many different examples. Economy and power are important because they provide a lens for transforming the growing information in science into more manageable chunks that are relatively easy to understand and that have great explanatory power. An example from the *Core Concepts* physical science program is harmonic motion. Students are first taught about generating and restoring forces in a pendulum.

A generating force (a push) sets the pendulum in motion (from position B in Figure 1). As the pendulum rises, a restoring force (gravity) slows the pendulum and momentarily stops it (position A in Figure 1). The pendulum then falls back, overshooting its starting point (position B) and rises on the other side, stopping at position C. The cycle then repeats itself–the pendulum falls back, overshoots, rises, stops, falls back, overshoots, etc. In short, the pendulum forms a system to which energy is added (a generating force) and that energy is then transformed by a restoring force.

Figure 1. An Example of Economy of Explanation (simplicity in representation of knowledge): Harmonic Motion

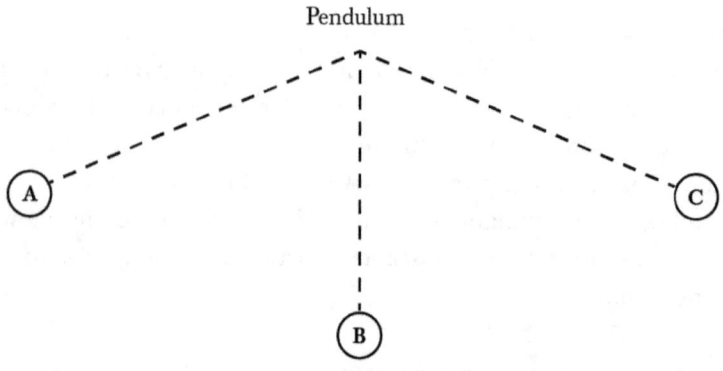

Conservation of Energy: Potential Energy + Kinetic Energy = a Constant

When the potential energy is maximum (position A), the kinetic energy is zero.

When kinetic energy is maximum (position B), the potential energy is zero.

Figure 2. An Example of Power in an Explanation (it applies to many examples).
Conservation of Energy: Potential Energy + Kinetic Energy = a Constant
When the potential energy is maximum (position A), the kinetic energy is zero.
When kinetic energy is maximum (position B), the potential energy is zero.

Gravity Waves in Fluids

Generating Force: wind
Restoring Force: buoyancy

Wind moving across the water causes waves beginning at position B and the water moves to position A. The water at position A becomes less buoyant and drops back, overshooting B to C.

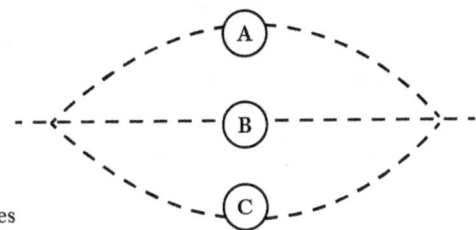

Electricity

Generating Force: particle collision
Restoring Force: electric field

Particles collide at position B and a particle moves to position A. The force of the electrical field pulls it back overshooting B to C.

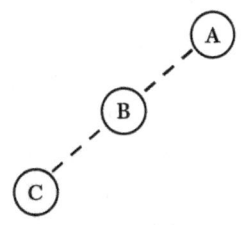

Cloud Movement

Generating Force: wind, heat
Restoring Force: angular momentum

Wind and heat push the clouds from B toward A. Angular momentum (circular motion) pulls the clouds back overshooting B to C.

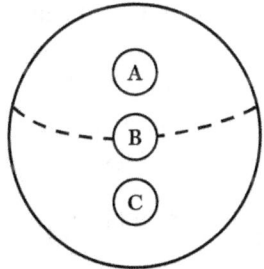

The economy of this explanation of the operation of a pendulum can be compellingly conveyed with a video disk, particularly with freeze frames and slow motion. The economy also sets the stage for the power of the instructional design. Harmonic motion, with a generating force and a restoring force, is then used to explain water waves, electricity and cloud movement. (See Figure 2.) By using a single relatively simple model for harmonic motion, students can fairly readily come to understand one of the core concepts that underlies the seemingly unrelated phenomena of water waves, electricity, and cloud movement.

Power in instructional design not only shows relationships among seemingly different topics, but also reviews core concepts. Each time important concepts, like generating and restoring forces, are applied to a new example, these concepts are also reviewed. Thus, power contributes to both generalization and retention.

MASTERY LEARNING PROCEDURES

Dynamic video and well-designed instructional sequences will not ensure adequate learning by the full range of students found in secondary and post-secondary classrooms. The *Core Concepts* course has numerous check points for evaluating how well students are learning. At each check point, the teacher decides whether enough of the students are performing acceptably on test items. If class performance is deemed satisfactory, the teacher presents the next new segment on the disk. If performance is unsatisfactory, the teacher replays an instructional segment from an earlier disk lesson and then presents practice problems. These problems are presented as still frames (like slides) on the screen. After students work a problem, the next screen, which shows the steps for working the problem, is presented. The teacher presents problems one at a time until reaching the next check point. Depending on how students perform, the teacher either goes on in the lesson or replays an appropriate instructional segment from the disk.

The check points occur at these stages:

1. After each new instructional segment from a lesson. These practice problems serve as an immediate check.

2. Before the beginning of the next lesson. This brief quiz is a one-day delay check.

3. After every fourth lesson. This mastery test is a one-week delay check.

4. At the end of each grading period. This exam is a multi-week delay check.

Immediate checks reveal how well initial learning is progressing. Teachers can quickly review troublesome material, before initial confusions grow unwieldy. Delayed checks measure retention. Having checkpoints at various intervals allows teachers to quickly review skills before serious misconceptions develop. In classes with a wide ability range, the mastery learning system gives a teacher feedback needed to decide how much additional explaining and practice are needed by the students. This feedback does not eliminate the problems caused by students with heterogeneous skills, but it does allow teachers to react efficiently and effectively to students' errors.

BENEFITS TO ADMINISTRATORS

The primary benefits of a video disk instructional system like *Core Concepts* have already been discussed:

1. The clarity and motivating capacity of dynamic video.

2. The simplicity and power of the instructional design.

3. The mastery learning procedures.

Some of the capabilities of *Core Concepts* are particularly relevant to a major administrator concern—staff development. In school districts where, for one reason or another, finding qualified math and science teachers is particularly difficult, the *Core Concepts* system offers the opportunity to ensure that students receive high quality instruction. In classrooms with qualified instructors, the *Core Concepts* system can provide vivid, compelling visuals. Experienced teachers build on the video presentation.

In all situations, the full course video disk system could provide a model of important aspects of instructional design and of mastery learning that would be informative for most teachers.

Finally, the frequent check points in the mastery learning procedure also make it relatively easy for administrators to gauge the progress of students in classes taught by reassigned teachers, or by any group of teachers for that matter.

REFERENCES

Block, J. H. (Ed.), (1971) *Mastery Learning: Theory and Practice.* New York: Holt, Rinehart, & Winston.

Bunderson, C. V., Baillio, B., & Olsen, J. B., (1984) Instructional effectiveness of an intelligent videodisc in biology. *Machine-Mediated Learning* 1(2), 175-215.

Morris, J. D. (1984) The Florida study: Improving achievement through the use of more dynamics in TV production. *The Journal*, October, 104-107.

CHAPTER 11

This study addresses issues in teaching highly unfamiliar skills and its relation to understanding human growth and development. Paul Williams and Engelmann studied the use of Direct Instruction strategies to teach a group of first graders to develop absolute pitch. The majority of the students could not sing on pitch prior to the study, but at the end of the intervention they had significantly greater skill in discriminating and producing musical notes. The authors concluded that the process of learning absolute pitch follows the same pattern of learning other highly unfamiliar content. Furthermore, the use of reinforcement, models, and basic instructional techniques that are integral to all Direct Instruction programs were effective in teaching new skills. Apart from showing the successful application of Direct Instruction strategies to teach unfamiliar skills, this article demonstrates how Engelmann further developed his understanding of how children learn and the importance of teaching to mastery.

TEACHING ABSOLUTE PITCH (1989)[*]
Paul Williams & Siegfried Engelmann

Learning highly unfamiliar skills is a topic that is important to understanding human growth and development, but something that has not been studied extensively. Unlike the learning of familiar skills, learning unfamiliar skills requires much, much practice. This study was done as part of a series of investigations involving highly unfamiliar skills. The objective was to teach first graders, most of whom could not sing on pitch, to develop "absolute" pitch–the ability to identify notes played on a piano or sung.

The incidence of absolute pitch is not precisely estimated and apparently has not been studied to a great extent. Wynn (1971) has noted the relationship between absolute pitch (AP) and other "rhythmic bodily functions" such as menstrual cycles and androgen cycles.

Brady (1970) and Wynn (1971) suggest (and other investigators aver) that AP is probably instilled very early in life. At least one investigator (Brady, 1970) tried to train himself in absolute pitch at the age of 32. He improved considerably over the estimated eight months of training and testing. Wynn (1971) reports that Brady was the only known adult to achieve substantial gains in AP.

The question of what constitutes AP is not answered precisely by the literature. Perhaps the most detailed classification is offered by Bachem (1937), who identifies three main levels, each with subcategories. The highest level is called Genuine AP and is characterized by, at most, an occasional half-tone or octave error. Another characteristic of Genuine AP is short latency (one or two seconds). The middle level, quasi AP is characterized by the subject's apparent use of an internal standard, typically, humming a note of known pitch and then "figuring out" the note that had been presented for identification. Bachem's third level, pseudo AP, is characterized by very long latency ("tens of seconds") and by relatively poor accuracy

---

[*] Williams, P., & Engelmann, S. (1989). Teaching absolute pitch. *ADI News, 9*(1), 23–26. Reprinted with permission of Siegfried Engelmann.

(judgments that may be inaccurate by as much as four and one-half notes).

Brady (1970) and Cuddy (1968) state that positive effects in AP training are dependent upon the subject's relative-pitch performance. The literature is quite vague on the incidence of genuine AP, although all investigators apparently agree that it is quite rare.

The present study was designed to teach absolute pitch of the genuine AP type using effective DI strategies. The experiment involved subjects who: (a) had very little previous experience, (b) had poor relative pitch, and (c) were past the age of infancy, but not yet to the age when estrogen and androgen cycles would potentially interfere with their performance in pitch discrimination (if such really happens).

The investigators' interest was not in AP *per se,* but in AP as an example of highly unfamiliar learning. The investigators had done studies to show that hearing subjects could learn to identify tactually presented words and sentences (Williams, Granzin, Engelmann, and Becker, 1979). The learning was characterized by no initial acuity by the subjects, hundreds of trials to achieve apparently simple discriminations, and an acceleration of learning that is at least partially controlled by the sequence of examples presented to the learner and the practice provided. In brief, the investigators assumed that the learning of AP should follow the same general pattern as learning tactually presented words. The initial performance should be characterized by many mistakes, however, over time, there should be a definite growth pattern toward the AP type of performance.

METHOD

Subjects

Subjects for the experiments were first-grade students in a semi-rural, near-average performing, elementary school. Initially, investigators asked for the higher-performing students in the school's only first grade classroom; however, all 18 students were initially placed in the program. Students dropped from participation if they seemed to have trouble attending to the presentation or had extreme difficulty responding. By the 6th week of instruction, 12 students remained in the program. All but one of these students remained until the end of the program.

Control subjects were high-school-age volunteers from a music theory class being conducted during the summer session at the Music Department of the University of Oregon for high school music students. Subjects reported that they had studied music, voice and/or a specific instrument for from 4 to 11 years.

Procedure

The same investigator taught the experimental students on a nearly daily basis. The students who were tested received a total of 152 teaching sessions from October 23 through May 15. Each session lasted for about 20 minutes and consisted of activities involving perception of tones and production of tones. During the first few months, over 70 percent of the periods was devoted to relative-pitch production—e.g., singing simple phrases and songs.

Notes were introduced so that the children discriminated each note from other notes and sang each note—in isolation as part of "songs." The order and date of each noted introduction is indicated in Table 1.

Table 1
Dates of Note Introduction

Date	Note
October 23	C
October 25	F
November 1	A
November 20	D
November 24	Octave Discrimination
February 14	B
March 5	G
April 2	E

During each lesson, each student responded an average of 15 times to pitch-production and pitch-discrimination tasks. Approximately 33% of the responses were production tasks (requiring the students to sing notes that are identified by letter name) and the remaining 67% of the responses required the students to discriminate between notes.

The production tasks required students to:

a. Sing isolated notes.

b. Sing songs composed of familiar notes.

c. Sing the scale, starting with middle C.

The following is one of the songs that was introduced after the notes C, A, F, and D had been introduced: CEE, DEE, EFF, AAE, CEE, DEE, EFF, AAE; CEE, DEE, EFF, AAE; CEE, CEE, EFF. The investigator would sing the song with students, direct the students as they sang it by themselves, call on individual children to sing the song, and call on subgroups to sing it (all the boys, all the girls, all children in front rows, etc.). For most discrimination exercises, the investigator played the note on the piano or played a group of notes on the piano (out of student view). The students identified what the investigators had played.

The rate of introduction for the notes was determined partly by the performance of target students in the group and partly by the need to reduce the possibility of students getting the right answers by guessing. When only three notes had been introduced, the strategy of guessing about the name of a single note that had been played led to correct responses one third of the time. A fourth note was introduced quickly (before students had reached a very high criterion of discrimination performance with C, A, and F) to reduce the students' odds. Also, at this time, the single-note identification tasks were replaced by three notes identifications. The investigators played three notes on the piano (which was still shielded from the students' view), repeated the three notes, then called on an individual or on the group to identify the notes. After January 15, virtually all perception or discrimination tasks involved three-note identifications.

To make the identifications relatively easier for the students, three-note phrases were taken from songs. The phrasing used in the songs was not used in the three-note sequences, which were played about 47% of each session. For instance, the notes CCF appear in the song "CDFA" above. Typically, after students sang two or three songs, they would do discrimination exercises. One group of notes selected from "CDFA" was "CFF" (i.e., CEE, CEE, EFF). This group was presented during discrimination exercises approximately 19%.

The following is a list of the three-note sequences taken from the various songs that were introduced. Each three-note sequence was presented at least 200 times.

AFA CCF CFA AFC FAC CAA CDC CDF

AFC CCF CDA CFA ADD DFA FCC DCD

For the reinforcers, the investigators used praise, stickers, and during one period of training, old buffalo-head nickels. The investigator had never taught early elementary children, had never taught in the public schools, and had taught academic-type skills for only one quarter in a practicum prior to the experiment. The investigator taped some sessions, which were critiqued. Judgment of the investigator's presentation skills was that they were quite good, perfectly capable of inducing the desired learning.

Student Assessment

At the end of the training period, students were assessed on: (a) discriminating notes and (b) producing notes. These tests were not administered at the same time and were administered at least 5 days after the last instructional session had been completed. Each student was presented with fifteen, three-note sequences. Each sequence was played twice in succession on the piano. The student was then asked to identify three notes. No feedback was given about the correctness of the identifications. All fifteen sequences were composed of notes the students had been taught; C D E F G A B. Seven three-note sequences were sequences from songs that had been sung and practiced as discrimination sequences. Eight three-note sequences were generated from a table of random numbers by assigning a number value to each note and then generating the random numbers.

The following is a list of discrimination test items:

1. CFA	5. CCF	9. EGB	13. ABD
2. FAF	6. FAD	10. CCA	14. CBF
3. CDC	7. FGA	11. CEB	15. FAB
4. DFA	8. DED	12. BAG	

Production Assessment

The production test was administered at least 48 hours from the time the discrimination test had been given.

The production test consisted of three tasks:

1. "Sing the note C."

2. "Sing the note A."

3. "Sing the note F."

To score each subject's response, productions were recorded and then played by judges who demonstrated virtual absolute pitch. Each subject's production was judged on three occasions. If a judge was in doubt about the note produced by the subject, the judge could compare the recorded production with the output of a Wavetek Signal Generator. The judge's reliability was 87.2%. If judgments varied across three separate occasions that the tones were evaluated, the modal judgment was taken as the scorable response.

Students in the comparison group were tested about a week after the experimental students had been tested. The procedure for testing the comparison subjects was basically the same as the procedure for the experimental subjects; however, comparison subjects were practicing musical skills at the time testing occurred.

RESULTS

The discrimination of the two groups was assessed by adding the number of notes identified correctly plus one-half the number of notes missed by only one full note. This scoring procedure allowed each subject to have a familiar-sequence score and unfamiliar sequence score that included weighted correct responses ($X=1.0$) and near-misses ($X=.50$). Table 2 summarizes the discrimination performance by subject. Maximum mean score for the three-member sets was, of course, three.

Table 2

Discrimination Performance by Subject

	Experimental Subjects		
Subject Number	Means of Familiar (Sets 1-7)	Means of Unfamiliar (Sets 8-15)	Combined Means (Sets 1-15)
1	2.78	2.06	2.40
2	1.14	1.25	1.20
3	1.00	1.38	1.20
4	0.93	0.87	0.90
5	2.50	1.94	2.20
6	2.50	1.56	2.00
7	2.07	1.81	1.93
8	3.00	2.44	2.70
9	2.64	1.81	2.20
10	2.93	2.99	2.80
11	2.64	1.88	2.23
Mean	2.19	1.70	1.98 (SD =.63)

(continued)

Table 2 *continued*

	Control Subjects		
Subject Number	Means of Familiar (Sets 1-7)	Means of Unfamiliar (Sets 8-15)	Combined Means (Sets 1-15)
1	1.50	1.19	1.33
2	1.50	1.25	1.37
3	0.71	2.13	1.47
4	3.00	3.00	3.00
5	3.00	3.00	3.00
6	0.07	0.97	0.97
7	0.93	1.50	1.50
8	1.14	1.53	1.53
9	2.43	2.37	2.37
10	3.00	2.97	2.97
11	0.71	0.97	0.97
12	0.14	0.70	0.70
13	1.50	1.07	1.07
14	0.50	1.03	1.03
15	0.57	0.43	0.43
Mean	1.38	1.76	1.58 (SD =.85)

Production comparisons of the two groups take into account each subject's ability to approximate the correct response. For each note judged to be "right on," the subjects received one point. For each production that was not exact, but that was no more than one note above or one note below the appropriate note, subjects received one-half point. Production performance of experimental and comparison groups is summarized in Table 3.

Table 3

Production Performance by Subject

Experimental Subjects		Control Subjects	
Subject Number	Production Means	Subject Number	Production Means
1	0.167	1	0.000
2	0.833	2	0.500
3	0.333	3	0.167
4	0.167	4	1.000
5	0.500	5	1.000
6	0.333	6	0.833
7	0.500	7	1.000
8	0.167	8	1.000
9	0.500	9	1.000
10	0.500	10	1.000
11	0.667	11	0.000
		12	1.000
		13	0.000
		14	0.167
		15	0.000
Mean	0.424	Mean	0.578
SD	0.22	SD	0.460

Discussion

Typically, tone acuity is assessed by such instruments as the Seashore Measures of Musical Talents (1939). Test items require the student to either distinguish the higher of two notes or to name the ordinal position of a note that is changed from one passage to another. The first subtest assesses the students' ability to make relative, not absolute pitch judgment and the second subtest is seriously confounded by student memory and ability to accurately count notes. The results of this test imply that very, very few subjects in an opera company had absolute pitch, only 0.8% of conservatory students had absolute pitch and only 2% of the performers in a philharmonic orchestra had absolute pitch.

In the present study, 2 of 15 *comparison students* had perfect scores on unfamiliar sets, which is 13%. Another subject had a nearly perfect score, (missing only 1 of 45 notes). Possibly, the three-note sequences provide a more valid test of production skill. Probably the incidence of the skill is far, far more prevalent than one would gather from the scant literature on the subject.

Amenability of Absolute Pitch Instruction

Although no experimental subject performed perfectly on either the discrimination or production exercises, it was apparent that their performance had been affected by training. The seven-year old experimental subjects had better overall ability to "approximate" the notes than the comparison subjects and even though the comparison group contained three subjects with virtually perfect scores, the experimental group out-performed them.

The ultimate conclusion is that the learning of absolute pitch follows the same pattern of learning observed with other highly unfamiliar content. The initial slow learning is expected, but this does not imply that the learning is impossible. Once the students learn the "game," their performance improves. They learn "benchmarks" or reference points for new learning. The performance of the students in this study would have been more impressive if they had reliable relative pitch at the beginning (the ability to carry a tune). The results, however, demonstrate that even though initial learning is very slow, the use of reinforcement, models, and basic instructional techniques are effective in teaching the skill. The study has implications for slow learners in academic skills and for remedial learners, whose performance is much like that of the subject learning something that is highly unfamiliar. The message is that the slow initial learning is not an indication of either what the student is capable of learning or of the learning rate that will occur after the initial learning has occurred.

REFERENCES

Bachem, A. (1937). Various types of absolute pitch. *Journal of the Acoustical Society of America, Vol. 9*, 146-151.

Brady, P. T. (1970). Fixed-scale mechanism of absolute pitch. *Journal of the Acoustical Society of America, 48*, 883-887.

Cuddy, L. L. (1968). Practice effects in the absolute judgment of pitch. *Journal of Acoustical Society of America. XLIII/5*, 69-76.

Williams, P., Granzin, A., Engelmann, S., & Becker, W. (1979). Teaching language to the truly naïve learner–An analog study using a tactual vocoder. *Journal of Special Education Technology, 2*, 5-15.

Wynn, 1971. (Complete reference not available at press time.)

CHAPTER 12

The wealth of data accumulated in Project Follow Thtrough provided strong evidence of the effectiveness of the Direct Instruction model. After more than two decades following the beginning of Project Follow Through, Engelmann and Wesley Becker continued to examine the data by comparing the outcomes of the Direct Instruction model with its competitors. In this article, they report findings from the results of the National Evaluation of Project Follow Through. They describe the structure of Project Follow Through, the groups included in the study, the tests used to determine success, the final report's findings, teacher opinions, and implications of the findings on Direct Instruction.

Results indicate the Direct Instruction model was by far the most effective of all the programs tested. Additionally, results showed the Direct Instruction model was almost as effective with low-IQ students as with high-IQ students. Follow up studies showed Direct Instruction students continued to outperform the comparison students in high school. The Department of Education's Joint Dissemination Review Panel reviewed the Direct Instruction Follow Through projects and certified all of them as exemplary in reading and mathematics for the primary grades. This publication reveals years of research and evaluation of the Direct Instruction model and how its design was demonstrated to be effective with large and highly diverse populations.

SPONSOR FINDINGS FROM PROJECT FOLLOW THROUGH (1996)*

Wesley C. Becker & Siegfried Engelmann

The final report of the National Evaluation of Project Follow Through, a comparative study of different approaches to teaching economically disadvantage children in the primary grades, shows that the Direct Instruction Model (University of Oregon) was largely successful in assisting disadvantaged children in catching up with their middle-class peers in academic skills. This demonstration is the first to show that compensatory education can work.

The Direct Instruction Model emphasizes small-group face-to-face instruction by teachers and aides using carefully sequenced lessons in reading, arithmetic, and language. These programs were designed by Siegfried Engelmann using modern behavioral principles and advanced programming strategies (Becker, Engelmann, & Thomas, 1975), and are published by Science Research Associates under the trade name DISTAR. The program directors, Professor Wesley C. Becker and Siegfried Engelmann, attribute its success to the technological details, the highly specific teacher training, and careful monitoring of student progress. The closest rival to the Direct Instruction Model in overall effects was another behaviorally-based program, the University of Kansas Behavior Analysis Model. Child-centered, cognitively focused, and open classroom approaches tended to perform poorly on all measures of academic progress.

DESIGN

The National Evaluation of Follow Through used a planned variation design to provide a broad-range comparison of educational alternatives for teaching the disadvantaged and find out "what works." Different models of instruction were tested in 139

---

* Becker, W. C., & Engelmann, S. (1996). Sponsor findings from Project Follow Through. *Effective School Practices*, 15(1), 33–42. Reprinted with permission of Siegfried Engelmann.

communities and evaluated for stability of results over successive program years. Model programs were implemented in kindergarten through third grade. The descriptions of the nine major models in the National Evaluation are taken from the Abt Associates descriptions of the report.

The Open Classroom Model (Education Development Center, EDC) which is based on the British Infant School model;

Cognitively-Oriented Curriculum Model (High/Scope Educational Research Foundation) which is based on Piaget's theories;

The Responsive Education Model (Far West Laboratory for Educational Research) which is based on Glen Nimnict's work in structuring a teaching environment and uses a variety of techniques;

Bank Street Early Childhood Education Model (Bank Street College of Education) which is concerned with the development of the whole child;

Tucson Early Education Model (TEEM, University of Arizona) which is based on the language-experience approach of Marie Hughes that initially focused on teaching bilingual children;

Language Development (Bilingual) Model (Southwest Educational Development Laboratory-SEDL) which utilizes programmed curricula for bilingual children (and others) focusing on language development;

Behavior Analysis Model (University of Kansas) which used modern principles of reinforcement and systematic classroom management procedures; and

Direct Instruction Model (University of Oregon).

For each sponsor, children were followed from entry to third grade in 4 to 8 kindergarten-entering sites, and some first-entering sites. Comparison groups were also tested. The evaluation, referred to as "the largest controlled education experiment ever," included measures of Basic Skills, Cognitive Skills, and Affect.

Basic Skills were based on four subtests of the Metropolitan Achievement Test (MAT)-Word Knowledge, Spelling, Language, and Math Computation.

The Cognitive Skills included MAT Reading, MAT Math Concepts, MAT Math Problem Solving, and the Raven's Coloured Progressive Matrices.

The Affective Measures consisted of the Coopersmith Self-Esteem Inventory and the Intellectual Achievement Responsibility Scale (IARS). The Coopersmith measures children's feelings about themselves and school; the IARS measures the degree to which children take responsibility for their successes and failures.

RESULTS

Adjusted Outcomes

Abt Associates used covariance analysis to adjust third-grade scores according to entry differences between experimental and comparison groups. An adjusted difference was defined as educationally significant if the difference between experimental and comparison group was at least one-fourth standard deviation unit in magnitude. This convention was adopted because when dealing with large groups, statistical significance can be very misleading.

Figures 1 to 3 show the performance of the various sponsors on the adjusted outcomes in comparison to control groups. An Index of Significant outcomes (ISO's) is used to show relative effects across models. ISO's are derived by taking the number of educationally significant minus outcomes for a sponsor and subtracting this from the number of significant plus outcomes.[1] This number (which may be negative) is divided by the total number of comparisons for a model and multiplied by 1000 to get rid of decimal points. The result is a number either positive or negative, that shows both the plus-minus direction and the consistency of each model's effects. If the

---

[1] The Abt analysis provides the two comparisons for each measure. One with a local control group and the other with a pooled national control group. A comparison was counted plus if either comparison was plus, and minus if either was minus. Use of alternative decisions rules would not change the relative rankings of models.

direction is positive, it means that the model outperforms the controls. The larger the number, the more consistently the model performs. If the number is negative, the control groups outperform the model.

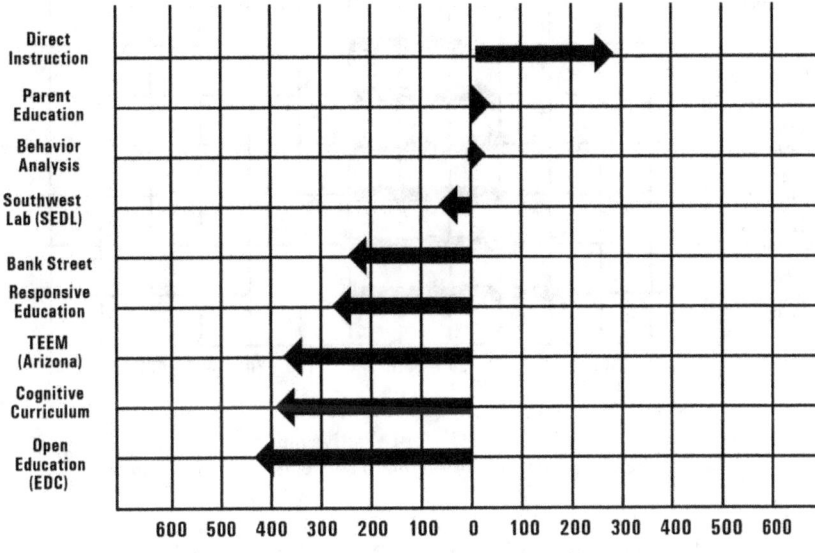

Figure 1
ISO's for basics measures
(word knowledge, spelling, language, math computation)

Figure 1 compares the performance of different models on Basic Skills. Only three models achieve positive ISO's. The Direct Instruction Model is more than 270 ISO points above the nearest comparison (Florida). The Direct Instruction Model is about 700 points above the lowest program, EDC's Open Education Model.

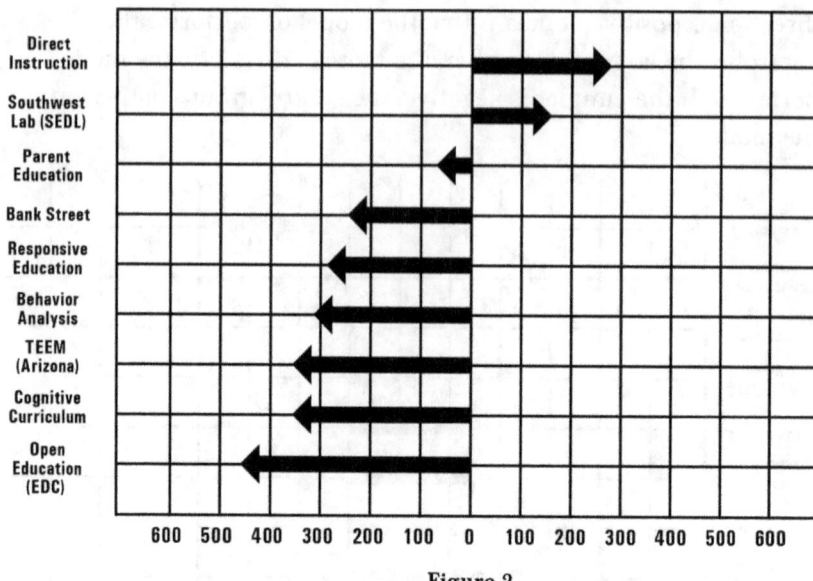

Figure 2
ISO's for cognitive measures
(reading comprehension, math concepts, math problem solving)

Figure 2 compares models on academic Cognitive-Conceptual Skills. Only two models have positive outcomes, and again the Direct Instruction Model is in first place (this time by over 225 ISO points above the second-place finisher and by over 800 ISO points above the lowest program [EDC]). The performance on Cognitive-Conceptual Skills demonstrates that those programs based on cognitive "theories" do not have the technological know-how to achieve positive results with poverty children, and that the behaviorally-based Behavior Analysis Model also lacks the technology to teach Cognitive-Conceptual Skills.[2]

---

[2] The Raven's Coloured Progressive Matricies result is not included with the data graphed because it is not an academic skill. Only 3 of 27 comparisons for all nine sponsors showed a positive outcome on the Raven's suggesting that this test does not reflect what was being taught by sponsors. Direct Instruction shows a negative ISO on this measure, but would still rank 1 if it were included.

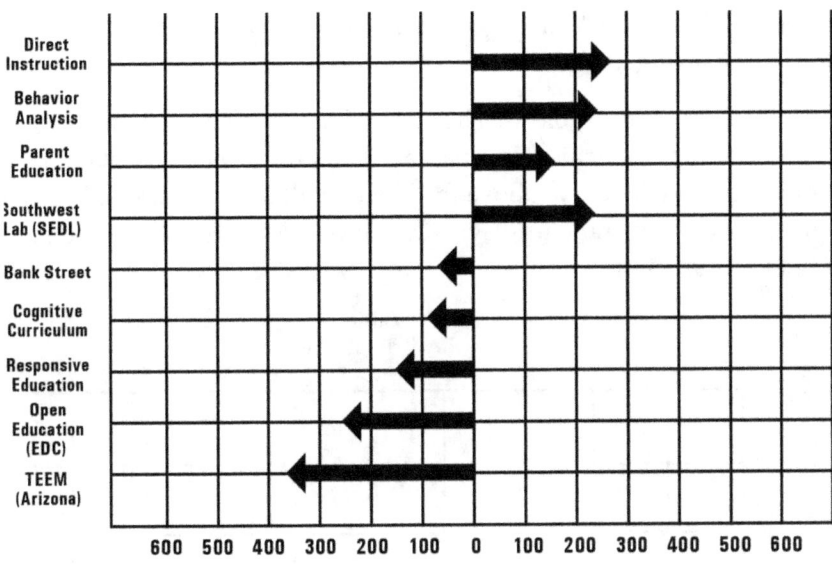

Figure 3
ISO's for affective measures
(cooperation, self-esteem, intellectual achievement, responsibility scale)

Figure 3 compares models on Affective Measures. The Direct Instruction Model achieves the highest positive effect. Behavioral Analysis, Parent Education, and SEDL also have positive ISO's. Note that only those models that achieved positive effects on Basic Skills or Cognitive-Conceptual skills produce positive outcomes on Affective Measures. Note also that the cognitively-oriented programs (with the exception of Parent Education) perform as poorly on Affective Measures as they do on Academic Achievement. The high correlation between academic and affective outcomes suggest a need to re-evaluate some interpretations of what turns kids on and how they learn to feel good about themselves in school.

Grade-Equivalent and Percentile Performance

The Abt IV Report provides performance level data for four MAT measures: Total Reading, Total Math, Spelling, and Language. Tables 1 to 4 display percentiles on a one-fourth standard deviation scale. With this display, differences between sponsors of a quarter-standard deviation (e.g., an educationally significant difference) are easily detected, while the percentiles provide the "norm reference."

The baseline at the 20th percentile represents average expectation for disadvantaged children.

Total Reading (Table 1). The Direct Instruction Model, the only one to show achievement above 3.0 grade level, is about one-half standard deviation above the mean of all other sponsors. It is nearly a quarter-standard deviation above the second-place model, Behavior Analysis.

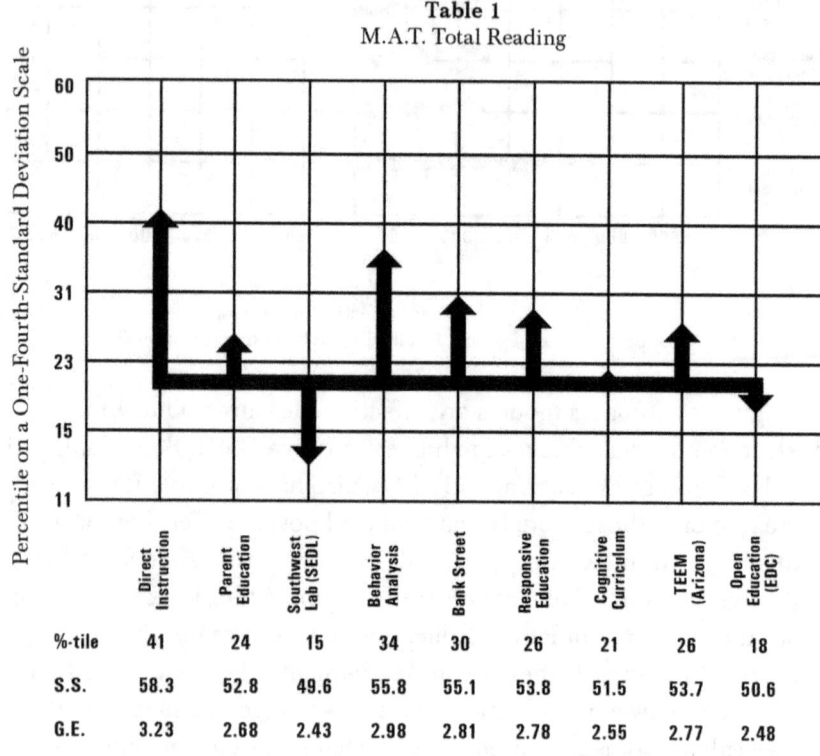

Table 1
M.A.T. Total Reading

	Direct Instruction	Parent Education	Southwest Lab (SEDL)	Behavior Analysis	Bank Street	Responsive Education	Cognitive Curriculum	TEEM (Arizona)	Open Education (EDC)
%-tile	41	24	15	34	30	26	21	26	18
S.S.	58.3	52.8	49.6	55.8	55.1	53.8	51.5	53.7	50.6
G.E.	3.23	2.68	2.43	2.98	2.81	2.78	2.55	2.77	2.48

Grade equivalent for 50th percentile is 3.5

Total Math (Table 2). The mean grade-equivalent scores for the Direct Instruction Model is 3.71, which is at the 48th percentile, and one full standard deviation about the average of all other sponsors. The Model is one-half standard deviation above the second-place model, again, Behavior Analysis.

Table 2
M.A.T. Total Math

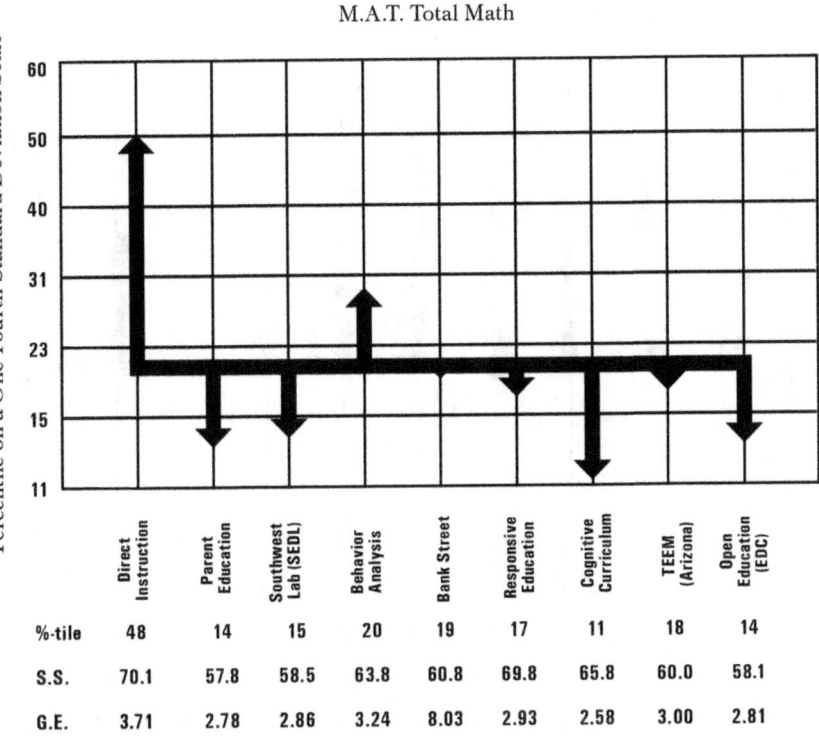

Grade equivalent for 50th percentile is 3.75

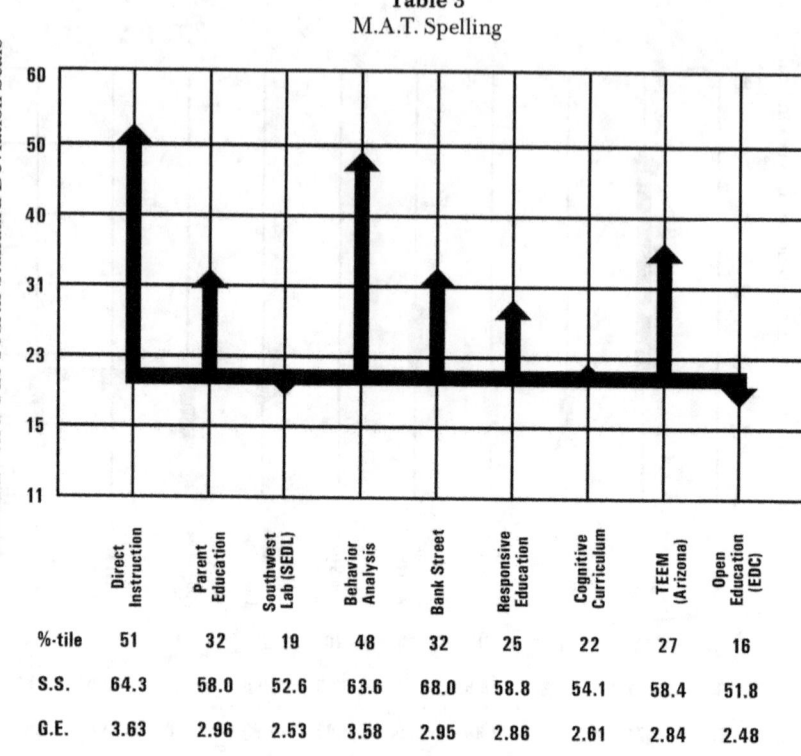

Table 3
M.A.T. Spelling

Grade equivalent for 50th percentile is 3.6

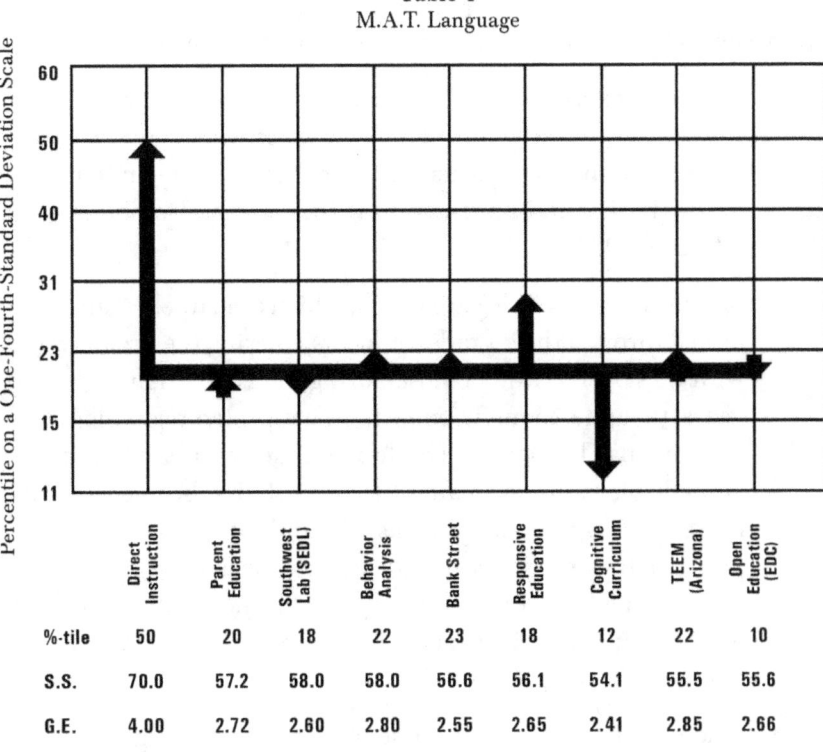

Table 4
M.A.T. Language

Grade equivalent for 50th percentile is 4.0

Spelling (Table 3). The Direct Instruction Model achieves the 51 percentile and again leads all sponsors. The Behavior Analysis model, however, is a close second (49th percentile).

Language (Table 4). The Direct Instruction Model performs at the 4.0 grade level, or 50th percentile. It is three-fourths of a standard deviation above all other models. (No other model scores were within one year of the Direct Instruction Model on grade-equivalent score.)

Sponsor Findings

Sponsor-collected data further support the above conclusions:

- A greater measurable and educationally significant benefit is present at the end of third grade for those who begin Direct Instruction in kindergarten than for those who begin in first grade (Becker and Engelmann, 1978; Gersten, Darch & Gleason, 1988).

- Significant gains in IQ are found, which are largely maintained through third grade. Students entering the program with IQ's over 111 do not lose during the Follow Through years, though one might expect some repeated regression phenomena. The low-IQ children, on the other hand, display appreciable gains, even after the entry IQ has been corrected for regression artifact. Students with IQ's below 71 gain 17 points in the entering kindergarten sample and 9.4 points in the entering first-grade sample; gains for the children entering with IQ's in the 71-90 range are 15.6 and 9.2, respectively (Gersten, Becker, Heiry & White, 1984).

- Studies of low-IQ students (under 80) show the program is clearly effective with students who have a higher probability of failure. As indicated in Figures 3 and 4, these students gain nearly as much each year in reading (decoding) and math, as the rest of our students with higher IQ's; more than a year-per-year on the WRAT (Wide Range Achievement Test) Reading and a year-per-year on MAT (Metropolitan Achievement Test) Total Math (Gersten et al., 1984).

- High school follow-up studies of Direct Instruction and comparison students were carried out in five districts. All the significant differences favored Direct Instruction students: five on academic measures, three on attendance, two on college acceptance and three on reduced retention rates (Gersten and Keating, 1987).

- The model generalizes across both time and across populations. The Department of Education has a Joint Dissemination Review Panel that validates educational programs as exemplary and qualifies them for national dissemination. During the 1980-81 school year, the last of the 12 Direct Instruction Follow Through projects were submitted for validation. Of the 12 districts, 11 had 8 to 10 years of data on successive groups of children. The schools sampled a full range of students: large cities (New York; San Diego; Washington, D.C.); middle-sized cities (Flint, MI; Dayton, OH; E. St. Louis, IL); rural white communities (Flippin, AR; Smithville, TN); a rural Black community (Williamsburg, SC); Mexican American communities (Uvalde, TX; E. Las Vegas, NM); and an American Indian community (Cherokee, NC). One hundred percent of the projects were certified as exemplary in reading and mathematics for the primary grades, thus providing replication over 8 to 10 years and in a dozen quite diverse communities.

- Research on implementation found consistent high-to-moderate relationships between observed level of model implementation and classroom achievement gains in reading. At least for highly structured models of instruction, degree of implementation can be measured in a reliable and valid fashion (Gersten, Carnine, Zoref, Cronin, 1986).

Two conclusions seem of special interest, especially in view of the wave of programs recently initiated in major urban areas to improve the teaching of basic skills. The first is that teachers at first may react negatively to or be confused by intensive, structured, in-class training (or technical assistance). Yet, ultimately at least half of the teachers found this to be one of the most positive features of the intervention.

The other key finding is that many teachers altered their reactions to structured educational models after they saw the effects of this program with their students on a day-to-day basis. Often this transformation took many months. At the beginning teachers were far from enthusiastic about the program and tended to feel that too much time was devoted to academics. Not enough was set aside for "fun" or creative activities. Yet their strong support by the end of the second year was unequivocal. From teacher interview data collected over two years, there can only be one main explanation for this, namely, the effect of the Direct Instruction Model on student performance. Time and again the teachers marveled at the new academic skills their pupils demonstrated. Teachers reported anecdotal evidence of growth well before the standardized achievement tests were administered (Cronin, 1980).

IMPLICATIONS OF THE DIRECT INSTRUCTION FINDINGS

The Follow Through data and our extensive experience in the field attempting to generate changes in school systems permit tentative answers to a number of major issues in the field today.

Will Money and Comprehensive Services Do the Job?

Each of the sponsors in Follow Through had about the same amount of money to provide comprehensive services and an educational program. Most sponsors had two aides in most classrooms, and spent about $350 per child above basic school support on the educational component. The Abt data provide a convincing demonstration that money, good will, people, material, Hawthorne effect, health programs, dental programs, and hot lunches do not cause gains in achievement. All Follow Through sponsors had these things, and most failed to do the job in basic instruction.

Does Individualization Require Many Approaches?

The programs that failed the most in terms of educational achievements were those oriented to individual needs in instruction. The popular belief that it is necessary to teach different students in different ways is, for the most part, a fiction. The requirements for sequencing an instructional program are determined by what is to be taught, not who. In the DISTAR programs used by the Direct Instruction Model, each child faces the same sequence of tasks and the same teaching strategies. What is individualized is entry level, when corrections are used, reinforcement procedures, and number of practice trials to mastery.

Is Self-Directed Learning Best?

A common assumption arising from dominant subjective education philosophies is that self-directed learning is the only meaningful learning. Direct Instruction is said to produce isolated rote learning, not "meaningful" learning. The Follow Through results obviously demonstrate such an assumption to be false. The students performing best on all measures of higher cognitive processes were from the Direct Instruction Model. The assumption about the value of self-directed learning probably arises from observing young children (as Piaget did) interacting with the physical environment. The physical environment directly reinforces and punishes different responses. However, there is no way a child can learn the arbitrary conventions of a language system without someone who knows that system providing systematic teaching (including modeling of appropriate language usage). In addition, there can be no question that smart adults can organize and sequence experiences that will teach concepts and problem-solving skills better than children.

Why is Improvement in Reading Comprehension Hard to Achieve?

The Abt IV Report notes that successful outcomes were harder to come by in reading comprehension than in other skill areas. Only the Direct Instruction program made significant and sustained gains in this area. Even then, we only reached the 40th percentile on MAT Reading. Becker (1977) analyzed the Follow Through data and other data on reading, and concluded that schools are not designed to teach the English language to "poor kids" (e.g., to children whose parents, on the average, are less well-versed in knowledge of standard English). Schools are basically designed for white, middle-class children, and leave largely to parents the teaching of a most basic building block for intelligent behavior, namely, words and their referents.

Why Do Economically Disadvantaged Students Continue to Do Poorly in School?

In general, economically disadvantaged students come to school with less knowledge relevant to succeeding in school. Thus, teaching these students requires teachers with different attitudes and skills, and more patience than is typically required. Colleges of education and schools are not organized or administered to develop and support teachers with these attributes. To coin a malapropism, "there is a way, but no will." Students from low-income families do not need to fail in schools. They can be taught.

In summary, through the careful design of curricula, classroom procedures, and training procedures, the DI Follow Through Model was able to achieve a major goal of compensatory education; improving the academic performance of economically disadvantaged children to (or near) median national levels. Only one other major model in the Follow Through experiment (the University of Kansas Behavior Analysis Model) came close to matching this achievement. The DI Model also performed best on measures of affective outcomes, such as self-esteem. Follow-up studies, through primary and secondary levels, show strong continuing effects in terms of academic performance at the primary level, and better attendance, fewer grade retentions, and increased college acceptance at the high school level.

THE COMMUNITIES

The communities which have used the Direct Instruction Model are Providence, RI, Brooklyn, NY (P.S. 137), Washington D.C., Cherokee, NC, Williamsburg County, SC, Dayton, OH, E. St. Louis, IL, Flint, MI, Grand Rapids*, MI, West Iron County*, MI, Smithville, TN, Tupelo, MS, Racine*, WI, Todd County, SD, Rosebud Tribe, SD, Flippin, AR, Uvalde, TX, Dimmitt*, TX, E. Las Vegas, NM.

*No longer in Follow Through.

REFERENCES

Abt Associates. (1977). Education as experimentation: A planned variation model (Vol. IV). Cambridge, MA: Author.

Becker, W.C., Engelmann, S., & Thomas, D.R. (1975). Teaching 2: Cognitive Learning and Instruction. Chicago: Science Research Associates.

Becker, W.C., & Engelmann, S. (1976). Analysis of achievement data on six cohorts of low income children from 20 school districts in the University of Oregon Direct

Instruction Follow Through Model (Technical Report #76-1). Eugene, OR: University of Oregon, Office of Education, Follow Through Project.

Becker, W., & Engelmann, S. (1978). Analysis of achievement data on six cohorts of low income children from 20 school districts in the University of Oregon Direct Instruction Follow Through Model (Technical Report #78-1). Eugene, OR: University of Oregon, Office of Education, Follow Through Project.

Bereiter, C. (1967). Acceleration of intellectual development in early childhood. Final Report Project No. 2129, Contract No. OE 4-10-008. Urbana, IL: University of Illinois, College of Education.

Cronin, D. P. (1980). Implementation study, year 2, Instructional staff interviews. Los Altos, CA: Emrick.

Engelmann, S. (1967). Teaching formal operations to preschool children. Ontario Journal of Educational Research, 9(3), 193-207.

Engelmann, S. (1968). The effectiveness of direct verbal instruction on IQ performance and achievement in reading and arithmetic. In J. Hellmuth (Ed.), Disadvantaged Child, Vol. 3. New York: Bruner Mazel.

Gersten, R., Becker, W., Heiry, T., & White. W. A. T. (1984). Entry IQ and yearly academic growth in children in Direct Instruction programs: A longitudinal study of low SES children. Educational Evaluation and Policy Analysis, 6(2), 109-121.

Gersten, R. M., Darch, C., & Gleason, M. (1988). Effectiveness of a Direct Instruction academic kindergarten for low-income students. *The Elementary School Journal, 89*(2), 227-240.

Gersten, R., & Keating, T. (1987). Improving high school performance of "at risk" students: A study of long-term benefits of direct instruction. Educational Leadership, 44(6), 28--31.

Nero and Associates, Inc.. (1975). Follow Through. A description of Follow Through sponsor implementation processes. Portland, OR: Author.

McLaughlin, M. W. (1975). Evaluation and reform. Cambridge, MA: Ballinger Publishing Co.

Weisberg, H. I. Short-term cognitive effects of Head Start programs: A report of the third year of planned variation-1971p; 72. Cambridge, MA: Huron Institute.

SECTION III

PROMOTING REFORM AND CHANGE IN EDUCATION

Engelmann has written extensively about the need to restructure the world of education. He has identified a number of the key components: school districts, teachers, teacher colleges, administrators, instructional programs, publishers, the creators of assessments, and education researchers. Engelmann's first publications in this area discussed the need to restructure preschools to become academically oriented so that children entering elementary school would be better prepared to succeed. He later moved to examining the education system as a whole, writing about the lack of advocacy for students, how the actions of school systems often harmed vulnerable children, and how these actions could be viewed as "academic child abuse." Engelmann has observed the failure of students across the country and determined the root of failure to be the school system as a whole. He has argued that teachers are not always trained in the most efficient and effective practices, administrators don't always have firsthand experience working with students and do not always choose programs based on data of proven success, and researchers and publishers often promote inferior programs.

Beginning with the creation of the Bereiter-Engelmann preschool, Engelmann recognized the lack of advocacy for at-risk children. He determined schools were failing these students because the instruction was not adequately designed and executed for them, but rather it was more appropriate and effective with their more affluent peers. Engelmann's work at the Bereiter-Engelmann preschool strengthened his understanding of the most effective ways to organize and orient preschools to heighten children's skills and prepare them for their future education. His observations and analysis led to the conclusion that the present organization of preschool education was problematic for all children and that a restructuring could lead to the greater success of all children.

To determine why students struggled to learn, Engelmann examined various traditional instructional programs to determine how they were designed and executed, and whether it was possible for these programs to succeed if they were followed exactly as designed. By thoroughly analyzing these other programs, Engelmann demonstrated how they failed to serve a large percentage of students. He also compared these traditional programs, with Direct Instruction programs, showing how the careful design of DI countered the weaknesses in the traditional programs. These direct comparisons provided data on the greater effectiveness of Direct Instruction, as well as explanations for why they worked when other programs failed. Chapters 13 and 14 in this section provide examples of these writings.

As important as the selection of an appropriate program is for the success of students, proper implementation is essential. In order to help ensure that teachers implement the carefully designed curricula, Direct Instruction programs use scripted lessons and instructions for presenting information and determining students' acquisition of that information. But just providing the teacher with the content does not ensure the successful transmission of information. The teacher's skills are an essential element in the process of learning. Recognizing the importance of both adequate programs and teaching, Engelmann analyzed the role of the teacher, how teachers are the vehicle by which children are educated. Engelmann argued that the teacher's role is much greater than just presenting information. The teacher must be able to observe problems, identify them before they become chronic, provide appropriate feedback, be able to understand the design of the program being taught, recognize any inadequacies in the instruction and correct for them when needed. Furthermore, teachers need the support of supervisors to ensure the proper implementation of these programs; they need to be properly trained to administer the necessary assessments to ensure all students are mastering the content. Chapter 15 in this section discusses the importance of supervision in helping teachers promote their students' success.

After striving for decades to implement solutions for failing students, Engelmann determined the current education system could not evolve enough to create significant change. Thus, a true revolution would be needed. He argued the current procedures and principles for instruction and education were so ingrained in the current system that change could not come easily. Every aspect of the system would need to be reevaluated from the ground up, with focus directly placed on the success of all students. Utilizing his scientific approach, Engelmann examined every variable of the education system and determined there was a need for a philosophy of education that would clarify the role of the schools, teachers, administrators, programs, and tests. Each element needed to abide by this philosophy in order for all children to succeed. Just as in the proper implementation of Direct Instruction, all variables needed to be controlled to ensure success. To revolutionize the world of education, adequate programs would need to be selected. Teachers would need to be properly trained in these programs and receive adequate supervision from administrators who had in-class experience and an understanding of what it means to teach. Decision makers would need to make decisions based on data. Education researchers would need to support the most effective programs. Success would depend on the cooperation and coordinated execution of each entity. Chapter 16 in this section, titled "Change Schools Through Revolution, Not Evolution," summarizes this argument.

Engelmann's analysis of problems in education being the result of multiple interconnected factors was the basis for numerous articles, using various different approaches to provide greater clarity and new perspectives on the issues he discussed. Later in his career, as the problems he identified remained ingrained in the world of education, he used his website zigsite.com to address them. Beginning in 2008, Engelmann began publishing fictional dialogues between the philosopher Socrates and participants in the world of education. Following the work of Plato, Engelmann constructed these dialogues in a question-answer format to analyze important issues such as teacher training, program selection, and "gold standards" in education. The dialogues are designed to decipher a problem by ruling out competing possibilities until the truth becomes evident. These articles address serious problems in education that Engelmann had addressed previously but were still present and devastating to the success of children. Furthermore, these writings provide insight into the logical thought process of his mind as well as his notable wit and style of writing.

Engelmann has viewed his philosophy of learning as essential to the success of all students. Not only is it critical for this philosophy to be applied to those working directly with school systems, but it should also permeate the work of everyone in the world of education, including researchers, publishers, and policymakers. Everyone must have the same goal and follow the same principles and guidelines to ensure the success of children. Through the fictional dialogues with Socrates, Engelmann delineates the importance of sound teacher training and effective schools of education (Chapter 17). He describes the moral responsibilities of publishers for both educational successes and failures (Chapter 18). He stresses the importance of education researchers using logical and scientifically sound policies and procedures (Chapter 19).

Throughout his career, Engelmann has documented how there was–and still is–a lack of advocacy for students, the education system is harmful, and its treatment of children should be viewed as a form of academic child abuse. In his publications, Engelmann has stressed that students should not be held accountable for their failure to learn; instead, administrators and teachers must be viewed as the cause of their failure. If a student fails to learn, it is the result of faulty instruction, not the student. Engelmann's progressive and thorough analysis of the world of education has successfully identified the problems within it, but, equally importantly, he has provided solutions to the problems described. The guidelines and philosophy of education Engelmann has written about so extensively provide real answers and steps for creating educational equality among all students.

Each of the publications in this section was selected to represent Engelmann's dedication to the education of all children. Beginning with his philosophy of learning – that all children can learn when properly taught – Engelmann sought to understand all of the factors that affect the learning process and how to produce the ideal environment for learning. His relentless approach to helping children succeed inside and outside the classroom can be seen in his dedication to the issue over the decades, the different approaches he has taken to understanding the issue, and his attempts to create viable solutions.

CHAPTER 13

Engelmann's theories of learning guided his design of instructional programs that maximize effectiveness and efficiency. In his Direct Instruction programs, all of the details in presentation, word choice, and review of material are carefully controlled to avoid miscommunication and unnecessary review. This article examines curricula that do not embody these elements. It reports on a study that analyzed major basal reading programs used in grades 4, 5, and 6 and the behaviors of teachers using those programs. The analysis focused on the clarity of communication, the adequacy of the practice, and other aspects that would be controlled by an effective program.

Results indicated that if a teacher followed the average program precisely, students would be exposed to many spurious prompts, could be confused by distractors and variation in teacher wording, would be misled by the set of examples, would receive poorly designed practice, and would experience ambiguous and confusing instructions. Interviews with the teachers revealed that they would deviate from the programs about twenty percent of the time. Engelmann concludes that teachers were aware of students' problems learning with the curricula, but were not trained to effectively fix them. This article demonstrates the importance of instructional design in the success of students and how traditional programs can hinder teachers' ability to teach and students' ability to learn.

A STUDY OF 4TH-6TH GRADE BASAL READING SERIES: HOW MUCH DO THEY TEACH? (1982)[1]*

Ziggy Engelmann

As part of the development of the Direct Instruction reading programs for grades 4, 5, and 6, we did a rather elaborate study to gain more precise information about teacher behavior and how teacher behavior relates to "the ideal." The design of the experiment was basically simple. We first analyzed the major basal reading programs that are used in grades 4 through 6 – Ginn, Scott Foresman, Houghton Mifflin, and Holt. We analyzed the programs, we considered the clarity of the communication that was provided, the adequacy of the practice, and other aspects that should be controlled by an effective program. Next, we interviewed the 17 teachers who participated in the study. We provided them with no information about the nature of the study. (They knew only that they would receive some free materials for participating.) Their participation involved answering questions during two taped interviews and video taping two lessons in their reading program. They were told that they would be taped teaching a main idea lesson and another lesson (whatever lesson came up during the time scheduled for the testing). The teachers were selected from various regions of the United States, from Bridgeport, Connecticut, to Eugene, Oregon.

After the students received a lesson, they received a simple test of the material that the teacher had just covered. There were no trick items, no extensions of concepts, and basically nothing more than what the teacher had taught. The test was sufficiently long to provide a reasonable sample of each student's understanding.

With the information from the analysis of the program, the teacher interview, the record of the teacher's teaching, and the

---

[1] This project was conducted by Engelmann-Becker Corporation and coordinated by Don Steely.

*Engelmann, Z. (1982). A study of 4th–6th grade basal reading series: How much do they teach? *ADI News*, *1*(3), 1, 4–5, 19. Reprinted with permission of Siegfried Engelmann.

student outcomes, we had the information needed to perform a rather thorough analysis that we felt would answer the following questions:

1. Based strictly on an analysis of the program material, how well would the program be predicted to teach the average student?

2. How much do teachers actually deviate from the specifications of the basal programs, and if they do deviate, to what extent do these deviations facilitate communication? (In other words, how much better do the teachers teach than they would if they followed the program to the last detail?)

3. How well do students perform in response to the instruction that the teachers actually provide.

4. How do the facts about the teacher's instructional program, the teacher's actual teaching behavior, and the actual student outcomes relate to the teacher's verbal descriptions of these areas? (Are teachers accurate and knowledgeable about the details of their programs? Do they know specifically the types of problems their children have? Do they accurately evaluate their own teaching?)

Figure 1. Four Areas of Investation

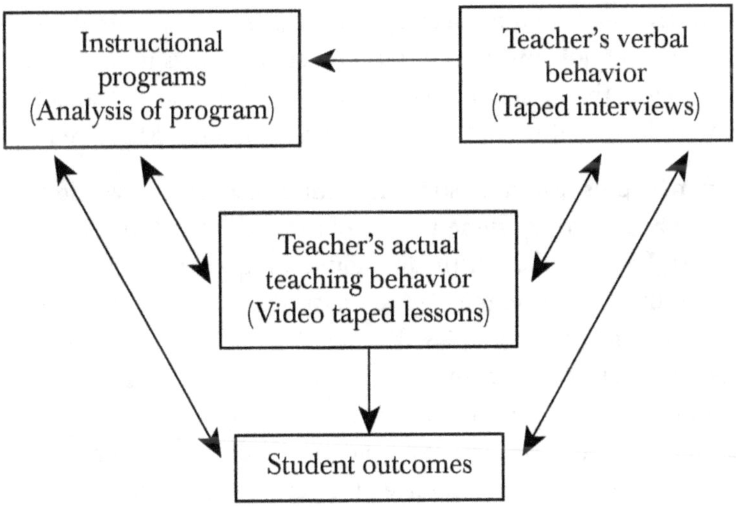

```
┌─────────────────────┐         ┌─────────────────────┐
│   Instructional     │ ◄────── │  Teacher's verbal   │
│     programs        │         │      behavior       │
│(Analysis of program)│         │  (Taped interviews) │
└─────────────────────┘         └─────────────────────┘
          ▲  ▲                           ▲   ▲
           \  \                         /   /
            \  \    ┌─────────────────┐/   /
             \  \   │ Teacher's actual│   /
              \  \  │ teaching behavior│  /
               \  \ │(Video taped lessons)/
                \  \└─────────────────┘ /
                 \  \        │        / /
                  \  \       ▼       / /
                   ┌─────────────────┐
                   │ Student outcomes│
                   └─────────────────┘
```

Figure 1 shows the four areas that were investigated. The arrows indicate the various comparisons that were possible from one area to another area.

PROGRAM ANALYSIS

Perhaps the greatest new contribution the study provided was a basis for analyzing instructional programs. The analysis was based on fairly reliable information that we had received when developing Direct Instruction programs. Tryouts consistently disclosed that skills must be taught for a minimum amount of time, that the wording should be simple and consistent, that the skill must be reviewed on a regular basis, that distractions result in mislearning, and that the set of examples and rules that are presented must be unambiguous (so that the learner will not learn a misinterpretation). The misinterpretation is perhaps the most important single consideration, because there is a very reliable rule that if the presentation is ambiguous, some students will learn an unintended interpretation. A simple example would be a presentation that showed all examples of the concept "red" as being round balls and all examples of "not-red" as squares. Clearly, this demonstration cannot teach the naïve learner what red really means because the learner has the option of concluding that the word "red" refers to the color or that "red" refers to the circular shape (or that something is called "red" only if it is both circular and red in color). The problem with presentations that present possible misinterpretations is that while students may perform perfectly on the initial examples (red balls, for instance), it is not until later that we discover that they don't understand red.

A more sophisticated illustration of misinterpretation would be provided by a poorly designed series of examples used to teach main idea. Let's say that for the first four examples, the main idea is expressed by the first sentence in the passage. The students perform marvelously on these examples. The next example, however, may be one that contains no sentence that expresses the main idea. The prediction, based on this poor set of examples, is that when some of the students reach this last example, they will identify the first sentence as the main idea sentence and that it will require great effort to teach them the real concept of main idea. The point is that these students are not behaving in an unreasonable way. The series of examples the teacher presented strongly prompted them to attend to the "first sentence," just as certainly as the red balls would teach some children that red means round.

The results of the program analysis were, at best, frightening. Table 1 summarizes the averages of the five basal programs for the teaching of main idea in grades 4, 5, and 6. Note that the number of lessons and examples refers to a three-year period.

The asterisked items provide some indication of the lack of precision exercised by these programs. Item 1 indicates that only 14% of the examples are taught. An example is considered "not taught" if the question of the type asked about the example had not been presented in the last 50 teaching days. (These basal programs, as you know, are not divided into daily lessons. To compute the lessons, we counted the total number of pages presented over the 3-year period, divided the total by 480 [160 lessons a year times 3 years].) The resulting number provided an arbitrary, average number of pages that should be covered during a "daily" lesson.

Table 1

Program Analysis Results Across Programs

	Means Across Programs	Ideal
*1. Percentage of examples taught	14	100
2. Percentage of questions ambiguous and not taught	88	0
3. Percentage of answers to questions that were misleading and wrong	12	0
4. Percentage of minimum discriminations not taught	5	0
5. Percentage of variation in teacher presentation wording	14	0-15
6. Percentage of variation in student workbook wording	44	0-15
7. Percentage of variation in items, teacher presentation	10	0-50
8. Percentage of variation in items, student workbook	18	0-50

(continued)

Table 1 *continued*

9. Percentage of questions relevant to concept, teacher presentation	62	100
10. Percentage of questions relevant to concept, student workbook	75	100
*11. Percentage of probability of correct interpretation	27	100
12. Percentage of response variation	13	0-50
13. Percentage of visual distraction, student workbook	25	0
14. Percentage of academic distraction, teacher presentation, student workbook	31	0
15. Percentage of strength of teacher presentation responses	89	100
16. Percentage of strength of student workbook responses	72	100
17. Percentage of prompted, teacher presentation	24	0
*18. Percentage of prompted, student workbook	49	0
*19. Days since two examples were presented	62	?
20. Total number of examples in program	66	?
*21. Number of student examples on same day as teacher material	9	?
22. Percentage of student examples on same day as teacher material	14	?
*23. Total number of lessons	22	50-80
*24. Percentage of examples for which correction is specified	0	100

*Large discrepancy between program and ideal.

Item 11 shows that the probability of a correct interpretation (based on the set of examples presented by the program) is only 27%. In other words, there are approximately 4 possible interpretations that are perfectly consistent with the set of examples presented by the program. Item 18 shows the percentage of prompted examples (49 percent). These are items that give the student the answer. Item 19 indicates that a period of 62 days elapses before two or more examples of main idea are presented in the program. Over the three-year period, only 66 examples of main idea are presented, only nine of these appear on the same day in the teacher and student material, and only 22 lessons deal with main idea at all. No specific correction procedures were specified in any of the five programs (item 24).

This analysis of main idea suggests that if the teacher follows the average program and teaches precisely according to the program specifications, the programs are incapable of teaching the average student. The student will be bombarded by spurious prompts, will possibly be confused by distractors and variation in teacher wording, will be misled by the set of examples the teacher presents, will receive practice that is sparse and poorly designed, and will receive ambiguous and confusing instructions from the teacher.

The analysis of other skills paralleled that of main idea. Fact-versus-opinion, for example is frequently taught so that it is perfectly misleading. Fact and opinion are taught as exclusive categories, which means that a person could not have an opinion that was a fact. (John said, "It's Friday today." It's a fact that John said that it's Friday today. If it is Friday, it's a fact that it is Friday. It is further a fact that in John's opinion, it is Friday. The material provided by these basals does not typically make these distinctions. Instead, it suggests that if something is an opinion, it is not a fact.)

HOW THE TEACHERS TEACH

The programs are basically incapable of teaching the average student, but possibly the teachers embellish these programs with good teaching that makes them work for the students. Certainly, we've all heard talk from teachers about how they don't follow the program and how they improved on it. (We received the same kind of information from the teacher interviews, where the teachers indicated that they deviated from the program specifications about 20% of the time.)

Probably the most interesting fact about the performance of the teachers in the study was that not one teacher deviated in any way from the specifications for the primary part of the lesson. Teachers sometimes didn't do the enrichment or additional activities provided by the teacher's guide, but followed the lessons precisely. Note that they were given no instructions about how to present other than, "Just present the lesson the way you normally would."

The tapes of the teaching were analyzed two ways—they were first analyzed without referring to the instructional program; next they were compared with the specifications provided by the program.

The teaching provided by the teachers (regardless of the program used) was not sound from a technical standpoint. The following is a brief profile of how the average teacher in the study taught:

1. The maximum rate of the teachers' presentation produced an average of 4.2 responses per minute. On student-reading tasks, the maximum rate was slightly higher—4.6 responses per minute.

2. The teacher presented 84% of the tasks to individuals and 16% to the group.

3. The teachers gave the answer to 34% of the tasks, either by responding with the students or by modeling the answer.

4. The teachers praised nearly half of the correct student responses (46%). Most praise was directed to individual students (95%). Only 2% was behavior-specific praise, rather than general praise.

5. The teaching presentations produced a student error rate of 27%. Only 37% of these errors were corrected. Of those mistakes for which a correction was provided, only on 10% was the student retested to determine whether the information provided by the correction was actually communicated to the student.

Table 2 compares the average teaching behaviors with ideal teaching.

Table 2

Teacher Behavior Data Across Programs

	Grand Mean	Ideal
Total percent questions with errors	27	10-12
Total percent questions that were group tests	16	25-60
Total percent questions that were individual	84	40-75
Total percent errors that were corrected	37	100
Total percent errors that were corrected & retested	10	100
Total percent of tasks that were models	20	0-20
Total percent of tasks that were leads	14	0
Total percent of tasks that were models or leads	34	0-20
Total percent of responses that were given general praise	44	0-10
Total percent of responses that were given specific praise	2	15-30
Total percent of responses that were praised	46	15-25
Total percent of responses that were given negative feedback	1	0-2
Rate per minute	4.4	9-15

As mentioned earlier, all teachers followed the specifications that were provided by the programs they used. If we compare their teaching with the teaching that would have resulted if the program were presented by some kind of recording device, we do notice some differences, however. These differences are caused by one problem—student mistakes. The teachers responded to these mistakes, and when they did, it typically increased the number of questions that were judged irrelevant or ambiguous. For example, students read a main idea passage that does not contain a topic sentence that expresses the main idea. The students had just finished reading three passages in which the main idea was expressed as the first sentence in the passage. The passage they read now indicates a host of problems that the railroads encountered after they crossed the Mississippi River-railroad wars, disease, Indian raids, etc. When asked, "What's the main idea of this passage?" a student raises her hand and when called on, reads the first sentence in the passage. The teacher nods and adds a question that does not appear in the teacher material. "Yes," she says, "that was one thing that happened. But what is the whole main idea of this passage?" The students frown knowingly, return to the passage, and raise their hands. The next child called on (of course) reads the last sentence. Again, the teacher repeats, "Yes, that also happened. But what is the whole main idea?" The question the teacher asked was judged irrelevant because the students had never been presented with this kind of task and the only way they could know what the whole main idea is would be to receive direct information about how the main idea is formulated when no topic sentence expresses it. So the teacher typically asks more questions than the program specifies. These questions are presented in response to mistakes. And questions added by the teacher are either irrelevant, ambiguous, or misleading.

Table 3 shows a comparison of the average teacher behavior with the average program specifications. Note the teachers asked 151% more questions than the program specifies.

The comparison of the program specifications with the teacher's presentation disclosed one important fact: Not one teacher (on either taping) taught as well as or better than the program specifications. In other words, the instructional program tends to function as a limiter of what the teacher does. The teachers follow the program, are aware of the problems that the students experience, but are quite incapable of responding to the problem with effective remedies.

Table 3
Average Teacher Behavior and Average Program Specifications

Total number of questions asked in the program lesson.	8
Total number of questions asked by the teacher.	20
Percent more teacher questions over program questions.	251%
Percent of program questions that were ambiguous or misleading.	42%
Percent of teacher question that were ambiguous or misleading.	48%
Percent of program questions that were relevant to the topic.	69%
Percent of teacher questions that were relevant to the topic.	24%
Student correct interpretation probability from the program.	22%
Student correct interpretation probability from the teacher.	27%

(continued)

Table 3 continued

Strength of student responses from program questions.	78%
Strength of student responses from teacher questions.	77%
Percent of prompted responses in the program.	12%
Percent of prompted responses from the teacher.	22%

Table 4
Mean Percent At or Above Different Criterion Percent

	Criterion Percent Correct		
Topic	90%	75%	50%
Main Idea	10%	33%	58%
Key Words	8%	32%	65%
Map Skills	30%	33%	56%
Inferences	15%	30%	62%
Context Clues	0%	0%	15%
Relevant Details	24%	82%	99%
Cause Effect	10%	30%	60%
Fact/Opinion	0%	25%	70%
Means Across All Topics	12%	30%	55%

STUDENT OUTCOMES

After the taping, students were presented with test worksheets that tested the material that had been presented during the taped lesson. Table 4 summarizes the student performance on 8 topics. These outcomes dramatically confirm that the programs are incapable of teaching if presented as taught, and that the teacher's presentation was technically poor and presented a sequence of tasks that was actually inferior to that presented by the printed program. Although there was some variability from topic to topic, the tests disclosed that the students did not generally understand the concepts and information the teacher had just presented. The three topics that are of most interest to traditional educators are main idea, context clues, and inferences. No more than one-third of the students taught these topics scored more than 75% correct on what the teachers had just finished teaching. When we consider all the topics that were tested, we see a very frightening trend. Only about one-half of the students scored 50% correct on the material just presented.

The first response to these results is perhaps shock. Imagine only about 30% of the students understand even 75% of what the teacher is trying to convey. When we look at the results in a broader context, however, we may draw the conclusion that the results are the inevitable outcome of traditional education. Consider achievement tests. Items for these tests are designed so they will maximize individual differences and "spread the distribution." The test designers achieve this spread by designing items that are passed by about half the children (so the average child will correctly answer about half the items). The same pattern of correct responses appears in the results of the tests for the various topics. The average student correctly responds to about half the items. The basal programs, therefore, seem to be quite consistent with the achievement tests that are used to evaluate programs; however, neither the programs nor the traditional evaluations are appropriate for good instruction.

Table 5

Teacher Reports on Main Idea and Student Performance

T:	What percent of the students should master any skill?	86%
S:	Percent of students at 90% criterion on all topics	12%
	Percent of students at 75% criterion on all topics	30%
T:	What percent of the students could do the workbook exercises after the lesson was taped?	72%
S:	Percent of students at 90% criterion on all topics	12%
T:	What percent of the students need more practice on the topic taught?	58%
S:	Percent of students below 75% criterion level on all topics	70%

(continued)

Table 5 continued

S:	Percent of students below 50% criterion level on all topics	55%
T:	What percent of the students master main idea?	56%
S:	Percent of students at 90% criterion on main idea	10%
	Percent of students at 75% criterion on main idea	33%
T:	What percent of students remain unchanged?	40%
S:	Percent of students below 75% criterion on main idea	67%
T:	How deficient is the program for teaching students main idea?	16%
S:	Percent of students below 75% criterion on main idea	67%

TEACHER VERBAL RESPONSES

The reports by teachers generally showed that the teachers were not familiar with the details of the program they used, were not greatly aware of their teaching behavior, and greatly overestimated their students' understanding of the material presented. Table 5 gives a summary that compares their verbal responses to seven questions on student mastery on the topic main idea.

The final step that we took in this study was to determine the extent to which the teachers we sampled were typical of a broader population of teachers. To make this comparison, we designed a questionnaire that was sent to 3,000 teachers in grades 4, 5, and 6. The same questionnaire had been presented to the experimental teachers as a part of their first interview.

Sixteen percent of those receiving the questionnaire responded (493 responses). The responses provided by the experimental teachers showed that the teachers gave atypical responses on 12 of the 94 scoreable items on the questionnaire. The experimental teachers, in other words, seemed to be a representative sample of teachers who were interested enough in instruction to return the questionnaire. Table 6 gives part of the questionnaire, with the means for each item marked with a dot, and the range of responses indicated with a bar. If you want to compare yourself to the average traditional teacher in grades 4 through 6, answer the questions and compare your responses with the dots.[†]

A FINAL WORD

This study made me feel very sad, not so much because the results surprised me, but because the tapes of the teachers revealed both concern and a lot of raw talent. Most of the teachers who volunteered for this study were clearly intelligent people who were trying very hard to do an important job. Their verbal responses and the questionnaire responses suggest that these teachers are quite aware of the more obvious learning problems that their students experience. They know, for example, that students tend to confuse the title or the first sentence with the main idea. They simply don't know how to avoid this problem, how to teach in a way that will help solve it; and how to provide explanations and examples that correct the problem. As it is, their talent, their potential to be super-teachers, is unfulfilled, in the same way that the potential of their students is.

[†] Editor's Note: To enhance readability, the data in Table 6 are presented, in this version, with the range and mean given in numerical form.

Table 6

Section 1

1. What reading program do you use? (If you use more than one, list the one you use most and answer the questions based on that program.)
2. What grade do you teach?
   Range: 4 to 6, Average: 5
3. How many students do you have for reading?
   Range: 21 to 33; Average: 27
4. How many years teaching experience do you have?
   Range: 4 to 7; Average: 5.7
5. How would you describe your reading class?
   Range: Mid-Low to Mid-High; Average: Mid-Range
6. How would you describe the teaching instruction in your class?
   Range: Small group to Whole Group; Average: More whole group
7. How many hours per week do the students spend in reading instruction?
   Range: 3.9 to 7.5; Average: 5.9
8. How many hours per week do you spend actually teaching reading?
   Range: 3.5 to 8.2; Average: 5.8

Section 2

1. In oral teacher directed activities, how closely do you follow the procedures that are specified in the teacher's guide?
   Range: 52% to 98%; Average: 76%
2. If a good student makes a mistake on an orally-presented reading activity, what percentage of the time will at least one other student repeat the same mistake?
   Range: 9% to 36%; Average: 22%
3. If a low student makes a mistake, what percentage of the time will at least one other student repeat the same mistake?
   Range: 4% to 31%; Average: 18%
4. During an average lesson, what percentage of the student responses will be incorrect?
   Range: 8% to 30%; Average: 18%
5. As a generally acceptable guide, what percentage of the students *should* be able to master any particular skill in this reading program?
   Range: 71% to 91%; Average: 81%

(continued)

Table 6 *continued*

6. What percentage of the mistakes made during oral presentations do you correct?

    Range: 40% to 95%; Average: 68%

7. Indicate the percentage of time you use each of these corrections:
    - Call on another student
      Range: 20% to 95%; Average: 50%
    - Tell the student the answer is wrong and repeat the question
      Range 20% to 65%; Average: 40%
    - Tell the answer and then repeat the question
      Range 20% to 41%: Average: 21%
    - Tell the answer, repeat the question, then repeat the question to the whole group
      Range: 20% to 36%; Average: 22%
    - Ignore the mistake and permit the students to discover a natural consequence of their error
      Range: 20% to 48%; Average: 23%

8. Most reading programs make general comments about praising and reinforcing students for correct responses. What percentage of the student responses do you reinforce in some way?

    Range: 55 to 90%; Average 72%

9. What percentage of the time do you call on individual students to answer questions (rather than the whole group or class)?

    Range: 50% to 90%; Average: 70%

10. In what percentage of the lessons do worksheet exercises for a topic appear the same day as teacher activities for that topic?

    Range: 24% to 86%; Average: 56%

11. There are places in the program where it says to help or guide the students. In what situations is this appropriate? (Check all that apply.)
    - Students have just learned the skill: Checked by 79%
    - Students rarely use the skill and tend to forget it: Checked by 55%
    - Students need the help or they will never master the skill: Checked by 59%
    - Students have never really been taught the skill: Checked by 54%
    - Students must answer an open-ended question: Checked by 35%

12. How would you describe the teacher directions of your program?
    - General statements of what to do: Checked by 19%
    - Specific steps you are to follow: Checked by 19%
    - Specific steps you are to follow and some direction on what to say: Checked by 47%
    - Detailed scripts of exactly what to say and do: checked by 15%

13. What kind of mastery testing is specified in the program?
    - Repeated items from student workbook: Checked by 5%
    - Items similar to those in student workbook: Checked by 58%
    - Items not similar to those in student workbook: Checked by 5%
    - Standardized tests specified: Checked by 16%
    - No mastery testing specified: Checked by 9%

(continued)

Table 6 *continued*

14. What kind of follow-up activities are specified for students who do poorly on the mastery tests?

    - No follow-up exercises specified: Checked by 23%
    - Lessons to be repeated: Checked by 13%
    - Supplemental exercises, the same for any student below mastery level: Checked by 34%
    - Supplemental exercises, different for different mastery test results: Checked by 21%
    - Lessons to be repeated with specified criterion for those lessons: Checked by 4%

Section 3

1. About how many lessons in the level you teach focus on this skill?

    Range: 3 to 33; Average: 19

2. About how many minutes long are lessons or parts of lessons that focus on the main idea?

    Range: 12 to 22: Average: 18

3. What percentage of the students knew main idea before the lessons?

    Range: 30% to 70%: Average: 52%

4. What percentage of the students master main idea?

    Range: 40% to 80%; Average: 60%

5. Here are some typical types of main idea exercises. Put a P by those that are in the program you use. Put a U by those that you think are particularly useful in teaching main idea. You may mark both P and U for any items.

    - Students underline main idea sentence when it is topic sentence:
      Majority marked U and P
    - Students decide if first or last sentence tells the main idea:
      Majority marked U
    - Students indicate which of three sentences tell the main idea:
      Majority marked U and P
    - Students decide if paragraph contains a main idea sentence and, if so, they underline it:
      Majority marked U
    - Students write their own main idea sentence:
      Majority marked U
    - Teacher goes through paragraph one sentence at a time and asks if that sentence tells the main idea:
      Majority marked P
    - Teacher asks students to tell the main idea and then has students try to find a main idea sentence in the paragraph.
      Majority marked U

(continued)

Table 6 *continued*

6. Indicate the percent of students that have these problems:

    - Confuse main idea with title: Checked by 30%
    - Think that main idea is first sentence: Checked by 42%
    - Think that main idea must be a sentence that comes from the text: Checked by 46%
    - Cannot pick out the correct main idea sentence if it does not contain any phrase from the passage: Checked by 42%
    - Cannot generate main idea sentence: Checked by 36%
    - Other: Checked by 24%

7. How closely do you follow the specified directions in your program for teaching main idea?
   Range 57% to 95%; Average: 76%

8. Indicate how you generally change your program's specific activities for teaching main idea. (Check all that apply.)

    - I skip the following percentage of specified activities
      Range: 20% to 35%; Average: 21%
    - I add the following percentage of activities
      Range: 20% to 56%; Average: 38%
    - I change the following percentage of specified activities
      Range: 20% to 44%; Average: 25%

9. If you change specified activities, how do you change them? (Check all that apply.)

    - Provide more directed teaching: Checked by 71%
    - Provide more review: Checked by 55%
    - Do more testing: Checked by 7%
    - Give more examples: Checked by 79%
    - Give harder examples: Checked by 25%
    - Give easier examples: Checked by 32%
    - Spend more time on teaching the main idea: Checked by 59%

CHAPTER 14

To evaluate the effectiveness of an instructional program and determine why it may succeed or fail, Engelmann has promoted analyzing every detail of the program's design. By examining the design of a program, it is possible to determine its weaknesses and how it can be improved. In this article, Engelmann compares the Direct Instruction program Reading Mastery with traditional basal programs. He explains how Reading Mastery was designed to solve the typical problems students encounter in traditional basal reading programs, including poor instruction for developing decoding and comprehension skills, the lack of integration of skills, and the use of less effective literature. He then explains how these problems are accounted for within the Reading Mastery program. The article provides examples of literature used by Reading Mastery and basal programs, highlighting how the Reading Mastery literature is more effective. Engelmann describes how appropriate literature selection aids the development of vocabulary, comprehension, inductions, and perspectives. This article explores the importance of instructional design and how, even though programs may appear to be similar, the outcomes that they produce can be significantly different.

ENGELMANN COMPARES TRADITIONAL BASALS WITH SRA'S NEW *READING MASTERY 3 & 4* (1983)*

Siegfried Engelmann

Reading Mastery 3 and *4* are designed to solve the typical problems students experience when they go through traditional basal programs. The basic goal of a reading program is to teach students how to become more proficient at decoding different types of material and how to understand this material. The approach taken by the basal programs is to identify a list of skills, such as main idea, context clues, fact versus opinion, relevant detail, etc. The basals then provide passages or intermittent exercises designed to teach these skills. The programs, however, have serious problems. (See Reading 4, 5, 6 study, DI News, Spring 1982. Also reprinted as Chapter 13 in this book.)

THE PROBLEMS

1. Basals typically do not have adequate provisions for teaching decoding, for testing students on their ability to decode, or for guaranteeing that students receive regular practice in applying decoding skills to a variety of materials (Beck & McCaslin, 1978, Chall, 1967). Typically, students read silently. Whether they read accurately is not determined, either by their silent reading performance or by their responses to written comprehension questions.

2. Basals do not provide adequate teaching for comprehension skills. Part of the problem relates to the categories that have been created to "measure" comprehension skills. There are hundreds of important comprehension skills in addition to those listed in the traditional-basal format. These skills are not taught, except incidentally. Also, the targeted comprehension skills are taught in a very poor manner. Typically, the teaching for a particular skill is

---

* Engelmann, S. (1983). Engelmann compares traditional basals with SRA's new *Reading Mastery 3* & *4*. *ADI News, 2*(3), 28–31. Reprinted with permission of Siegfried Engelmann.

not coordinated, which means that once a skill is taught, students do not continually use the skill. Also, the introduction is typically ambiguous (with the presentation being consistent with more than one possible interpretation). For instance, in most programs, *fact* and *opinions* are treated as opposites, which they are not. The teaching does not typically suggest that somebody could have an opinion that was a fact, or that it is fact that the person had a particular opinion. Finally, the programs are built around a "spiral curriculum" format, in which different lessons deal with different topics. Typically, however, about 60 school days elapse between the presentation of two or more examples on a particular topic (such as *fact* versus *opinion*).

3. The skills are not integrated. The lack of integration occurs on the level of daily lessons and is observed in the frequent discrepancies between the workbook items for the lesson and what the students are "taught." As a rule, students are not tested on what they are taught during a particular lesson. On the level of lesson-to-lesson integration, the programs seem to operate from the assumption that continuity is not necessary. Typically, the student readers are anthologies, with relatively uncontrolled vocabulary, uncontrolled sentence forms, and no careful gradation from one author or selection to the next. (Vocabulary and sentence forms are not systematically introduced, practiced, and then integrated.) The programs have no review tracks or activities that systematically review things that had been taught (word meanings, information, decoding words, skills—such as drawing inferences or using "context clues"). And the programs have no performance criteria or solid expectations for either the students or the teacher. (Lessons or expected units of progress are not specified.)

4. Perhaps the most distressing aspect of these programs is that most stories—the heart of the program—are not very interesting or highly motivating. (Generally, the good basal stories introduce far more vocabulary and are therefore much more difficult to decode than the poor stories, which often require many inferences, because important information is missing and must therefore be supplied by the reader.)

Students would generally be much better off reading good novels than they would engaging in traditional basals. If they read a single author, they would receive enough repetition of particular sentence forms and particular vocabulary to learn something. They would also read interesting stories. Students are deprived of these opportunities by the basals because of their author's lack of concern with details. Another problem is that there are almost no good novels available for students performing on the third-grade level and very few for students on the fourth-grade level. (Most of the novels judged appropriate for fourth graders by Scholastic Book Club and other book clubs are not actually appropriate for fourth graders. They are possibly suited for the average mid-fifth grader. We determined this fact by comparing performance on achievement test items with the novels.)

Because the basal stories are not greatly interesting and because there is no continuous new content control from story to story, the basals tend to reinforce terrible strategies for all but the highest performers. The learner is taught to approach reading material with the attitude, "I probably won't understand much of this stuff, but it doesn't matter, so I'll just skip over the parts that don't make much sense."

THE SOLUTIONS

The problems imply the solutions. If the program is to overcome the problem of inadequate decoding, it should provide adequate decoding practice. The program should also provide adequate teaching for comprehension skills, should teach all new words, syntactical constructions, and facts that are needed if students are to understand the stories. The program should provide for the systematic integration of skill into the stories. Finally, the program should revolve around stories that are interesting. The stories, obviously, should not be part of an anthology, because too many details must be controlled—the types of inferences or comprehension questions supported by the text, the specific vocabulary words, the syntax, the integration of facts and information, and interest level of the stories.

From a mechanical standpoint, the objectives of *Reading Mastery 3* and *4* are obvious from the major activities in the daily lessons. Students begin by orally reading isolated words. These words are pretaught before they are presented in stories. (Vocabulary words appear on 1-4 lessons before being introduced into stories.) For some words, the teacher provides information about word meaning and tests students on word meaning. These words are those that may be unfamiliar to the students (and also words that will appear in stories that follow the preteaching.)

Next, the students read selections. On all regular lessons, students read a main selection, which is usually a chapter of a longer serial. The chapters are designed to end on a cliff-hanging note (to promote interest). Students read part or all of the selection orally. They have an "error limit" for the oral story reading. If they read within the error limit, all students receive points. Also, during the reading of the selection, the teacher asks specified comprehension questions. These questions are keyed by circled letters in the student reader. When a student reads to the end of the sentence that is followed by a circled letter, the teacher asks the question for that letter. During the oral reading of the main selection, the teacher asks between 15 and 30 questions.

On some lessons, students read information passages before reading the main story. These passages present facts and rules that relate to stories they will read. For instance, if students are going to read a selection about a flea circus, the information passage presents information about the fleas and how they are trained.

Following the structured work, students do their independent work. They are presented with around 40 items each day. The items deal with the information that had been taught—vocabulary words, facts and rules from the information passage, and questions that relate to the main story. The students' independent work also includes a review section that tests important information skills (such as map skills) taught earlier in the program.

Although an examination of the daily lessons discloses the major objectives, it does not suggest the degree of control and integration that occurs within the program. Because such control is not exercised in other reading programs, I would like to illustrate some of the things that may escape the casual observer.

Easy Reading Material

As I indicated above, our greatest concern is setting up the main reading selections of the program so they teach new things, (new perspectives and new information) and so they are interesting. I mentioned that traditional stories of high interest usually have elaborate vocabularies (because the author is explaining things that are happening in a way that permits the student to identify with the events), while the stories with simple prose usually require incredible inferences on the part of the reader. The reason is that the author has left out important details in an attempt to make the prose "simple." Below is a passage from a biography of Jane Addams written by Hellen Peterson. It illustrates the amount of inference that is implied if the text appears to be "simple."

> One day in Spain, Jane knew what she would do. She told Ellen. "I will rent a house in the poorest part of Chicago. I will live with the poor people and be their neighbor."
>
> "But what will you do there?" Ellen asked.
>
> "Whatever I can to help them. Oh Ellen, let's do this together. Will you?"
>
> "I – I..." Ellen stammered. Then suddenly she was smiling. "Yes! I believe all men are brothers. I'd like to live those words."
>
> Jane was overjoyed. A short time later she was back in London. Some college men were living together in the East End now and helping the poor people. The name of their home was Toynbee Hall. She saw classes where college men taught working men and women. She heard a young man from Oxford University tell stories to a roomful of eager children.
>
> Jane had an idea. "Young women can come to work with us!" she thought. "College women like myself who haven't known what to do will be happy to help."

She hurried home to start her settlement house.

That prose is not the type that grabs kids (or many other people). It is unintentionally very difficult for a number of reasons. It introduces names that should be explained, such as Oxford University, but mentions them only once, (which means they are irrelevant). The strategy that some students will develop is to simply read over any strange names with the understanding that they are probably incidental and probably play no real role in the story. The problem with this strategy is that it will not work on some occasions. The "strange name" that is introduced may both recur and may have an important bearing on the story. So the students are punished either way—punished if they are forced to read incidental words and references, or punished if they do not and later fail to comprehend what is happening in the story.

But the Jane Addams excerpt has many other problems. It flits from setting to setting with nothing to hold the settings together. Although the sentences and the declarations about the different events are not generally hard to read, they create bizarre characters who have apparently random and unmotivated thoughts. Can we really picture a person who had the thought about college women helping in this home and then who hurries across the ocean on her way home so she can start a settlement house? This distillation of events is very artificial and hard to identify with. (She would probably do what everybody, including fourth graders, would do, which is to chew on the plan, develop it, anticipate the problems, talk, rehearse, plan, plan, plan.) Very sophisticated readers may be able to interpolate the necessary information between the lines of the truncated account above. But the formula for making descriptions easier is to provide more details about the significance of events. The more thorough the information, the less likely it is that students will fail to extract the meaning and emotions the character experiences.

Below is an excerpt from one of the early *Reading 4* stories. The characters are Oomoo and Oolak, Eskimo siblings, and a full grown polar bear named Usk, which the children had raised from a cub and which they were no longer supposed to play with. Despite their father's other warning about not playing on the ice floes, the youngsters went on the ice floe and began to play on an ice chunk, which drifted north, toward the open water, where a band of killer whales waited for any unhappy prey that tried to venture toward the open sea. The excerpt starts as the youngsters are drifting toward the killer whales.

> Oolak looked very frightened and cold. His eyes were wide. Oomoo tried to hold on to him and keep him from slipping off. "Are we going to die?" he asked.
>
> "No, we're okay," Oomoo said. She was lying. She didn't see any way that she and Oolak could survive.
>
> Then suddenly the wind died. The waves still rolled and continued to push the ice chunk beyond the ice floe. But the big wind had stopped. Rain and hail started to fall. The rain and hail made more noise than the wind had made. "Help!" Oomoo shouted. But she was starting to lose her voice. "Let's shout together," she said to Oolak. "One, two, three: help!" They repeated the shout again and again, until they could not yell anymore. Still the rain and the hail pounded down. Even though the rain was cold, it was much warmer than the ocean water.
>
> After half an hour, the rain began to die down. When the rain had been coming down very hard, Oomoo had not been able to see more than a few meters. Now she could see where they were. The ice chunk was near the top of the C-shaped ice floe and it was still moving north. Oomoo looked to the ocean, past the ice floe, and she could see them—five or six of them. Sometimes they would roll out of the water so that she could see the black-and-white markings around their heads. Sometimes they would move along with only their fins above the water. Oomoo saw the killer whales, but she didn't say anything to Oolak. (*Reading Mastery IV*, page 67.)

This passage is less difficult for students than the Jane Addams excerpt because it gives information about why the characters do what they do, and how they feel. Fourth graders have no trouble identifying with characters if they have enough information about how the characters feel and why. Because the passage provides that information, it does not require incredible inferences to transform the characters into people they could identify with.

Controlled Vocabulary

A common feature of beginning reading series is a controlled vocabulary—an introduction of a limited set of words that are to be used in all stories. Typically, the controlled vocabulary applies only to the words to be decoded, not with word meaning (although the teacher may "discuss" the meaning of the words). The controlled vocabulary usually vanishes in the third and fourth levels of these programs because the reading material is an anthology.

Reading Mastery 3 and *4* have a very careful vocabulary control. All words that are new for decoding are pre-taught (during the first part of the lesson). A given decoding word appears in more than one lesson. In addition, specified vocabulary exercises are presented for all words whose meanings may not be understood by the students. Word-meaning exercises are presented on more than one lesson, and these meanings are reviewed throughout the program. With minor exceptions, if a word is introduced, it will appear at least 15 times in the reading material presented to the students. The cumulative review and application of new words guarantees that students learn these words and become facile in using them.

Oral Reading

A good program should provide students with models of good oral reading and lots of practice in oral reading. The oral reading is functional when reading to a group, when reading poetry, when reading plays or other speeches. Oral reading is also important because it is closely related to comprehension. Comprehension assumes that the reader first reads the words that the author presents, then understands them. If the reader does not accurately read the author's message, the reader is preempted from understanding, in many situations.

Reading Mastery 3 and *4* meet the oral reading objectives. The program contains daily provisions for the teacher to re-read the first part of the daily reading selection, providing students with a good model of oral reading (with inflection and appropriate feeling). Also, as noted earlier, the students read either all or most of the selection aloud (all of the selection in *Reading 3* and most of it in *Reading 4*).

The program also promotes accuracy through daily points that are awarded to all members of the group if the group reads the selection within a specified error limit. The limit is set in a way that permits some mistakes (about 2 per hundred words) but that encourages accuracy.

Comprehension

Oral items. The main reading selections are the focus of the program, the integration of all skills into an interesting context. Therefore, for the program to be highly successful, there should be provisions to assure that students understand—in detail—what they read. To achieve this objective, the program presents oral-comprehension questions and written comprehension questions. The oral tasks are specified in the teacher's script and are keyed to the student text. The place at which each comprehension item will be presented is prompted by a circled letter in the student text. During the oral reading, the teacher will ask 20-30 oral questions that sample the full range of item types—from viewpoint to literal information. The circled letters in the student text serve as a prompt to the students as well as to the teacher. Students quickly learn that the teacher will ask a question at the end of a sentence that is followed by a circled letter. They therefore attend carefully to the text and learn the important strategy of anticipating the question that will be asked.

Written comprehension items. Developing student skill in writing answers to comprehension items is an important objective for any reading program. For this objective to be met, the program should be designed so that students retain important information and demonstrate their retention through written items. The written items should make sure that students understand everything that has been taught, and the items should be designed so that students receive continual review and application of important facts, relationships, and rules.

In *Reading Mastery 3* and *4*, many oral questions also appear as worksheet items, and the more important questions become part of a cumulative review that continues throughout the program. The recurrence of these questions helps shape student strategies for retaining information. Basically, the rules for designing written comprehension questions are:

1. Items sample the important information presented in the stories.

2. They test facts that were provided in structured teaching demonstrations, such as the information passages (which present the facts in a way that permits them to be firmed by the teacher).

3. They require students to apply rules, strategies, and skills that had been taught (such as map skills or rules about ocean currents).

The questions are not "picky," which means that they usually do not require students to go back to the story and find specific words that answer questions. The main goal is to teach students to retain the information. ("Study skill" items are different, however, because they require students to find specific information. The program presents study skill exercises that require students to refer to story information that students probably would not remember.)

Controlled Syntax

Students often do not know what different types of sentences are attempting to say. The students' problems are reasonable, because many sentence forms that appear in stories are not widely used in conversations. The use of qualifiers (such as generally), appositions, passive voice, gerunds, and other forms that are infrequent in conversations should be taught in the same way that any skill is taught. All examples of a particular sentence form are the same with respect to how they are interpreted. So the strategy for introducing each form should be to give students repeated practice in "translating" sentences of that form. The process should be cumulative, so that once a form is introduced, it continues to appear in the material the students read.

Basals, and other texts, do not generally follow this procedure. Instead, relatively short passages may contain a variety of sentence forms that may be ambiguous to students simply because the students have not had much experience with them. The sample below comes from a fourth-grade science text. The problem parts are italicized.

> ...Listening and watching in the stern as the clanking, churning paddle wheel sprays you with water can be exciting, too.
>
> The early river boats depended upon steam for power. Wood or coal *was* burned to heat water in the boilers. The water changed to steam. Steam, *under pressure*, caused parts within the steam engine to move. The *movement of these parts, in turn,* caused other parts to move. One very big part *which* moved was the large paddle wheel...

The syntactical problems interact with the vocabulary problems and render the passage very difficult for the average or below-average student. (Questionable words include *stern, depend upon, coal, boilers, in turn,* and *caused.*) Aside from the vocabulary problems, the passage introduces gerunds (listening and watching–without an actor to perform these actions), passive voice, and/or construction, needless qualifiers, and questionable use of *which.*

To solve the syntax problem, *Reading Mastery 3* and *4* present a controlled syntax (to go along with the controlled vocabulary and controlled information). At the beginning of level 3, sentences are designed so that the first part designates something that is happening and each subsequent part unambiguously adds more information. No "loops" or ambiguity are possible with these sentences, which means that the sentences do not become barriers for student understanding. Sentences like these would never appear early in the program because they break the rules:

> "When he went home, Jokey ate four cans of dog food."
>
> "Jokey, when he finally got home, ate a huge meal."

The first sentence is a "no-no" because it does not name the actor in the first part of the sentence. (It should say: "When Jokey got home, he..." because this order presents the information unambiguously.) The second sentence contains a kind of apposition and creates an unusual word order, which makes the sentence potentially difficult.

The only violation to the progressive-meaning structure of sentences occurs with speeches that characters make. In these sentences, the name of the speaker comes after the quote. However, these are set up so that: (a) the sentence preceding the quote makes it clear who is talking; or (b) the content of what is said makes it apparent who is talking. Below is an excerpt from a series about Jokey, a beagle who is very fat because he eats everything.

> There was a cat peeking through the fence on the other side of the yard. "That's right," the cat yelled. "Everybody thinks I'm so ugly, but I'm beautiful next to you."
>
> Jokey tried to pull in his big belly so that he wouldn't look so fat. It didn't work. His belly was still touching the ground. "I can't help if I'm fat," Jokey said. "It's not my fault."
>
> "Wrong," the cat said. "It is your fault. Don't you know the rule: The more you eat, the fatter you get. If you don't eat as much, you won't be so fat."

It is possible to identify who is talking by referring to content of what the character says or by clues that are provided through the preceding paragraph.

As students progress through the program, new syntactical forms are systematically introduced. For instance, passive voice constructions are introduced in level 3. The introduction involves the easiest type of passive-voice construction, which is a verb at the end of the sentence. This form is easiest because the verb functions in the same way an adjective functions.

"She was finished" is structurally and semantically similar to "She was carried."

When each type of syntactical form is introduced, students receive "massed practice" in dealing with the new form. Below is an excerpt from a story about the word bank, an imaginary place in the land of Hohobo in which words are seated according to the frequency that the people in Hohobo use the words. The most frequently said words are in the front row and the least frequently said are in the last row. When the people in Hohobo started to do things (which was new behavior for these people), great turmoil occurred in the word bank. The excerpt below takes place on the day that new seats are announced for the words.

> At 9:00 announcements began and they were not finished until late at night. Nearly every word in the word bank was moved. Sometimes whole rows of words were moved. And some words moved more than 100 rows. The most amazing announcement of the day came about 10:30 in the morning, after two or three hundred words had been moved. Here was that announcement: "The words run and walk will move from row 110 to row 1." (*Reading Mastery* IIIA, page 280.)

Note that the passage provides repeated practice with the new form. The sentences tell about *was moved, were moved,* and *had been moved.* The passage begins with a sentence that uses *were not finished,* which is a particularly easy transition sentence. Note that the introduction of the passage firms some earlier-taught vocabulary words (such as *announcement*). The passage deals with time notations. The passage supports inferential comprehension questions based on the word-frequency rules that govern the seating in the word bank. And the passage presents a sentence that describes what *had happened,* a sentence form that had been introduced earlier. Although the intertwined objectives may be perfectly invisible to the casual observer, they are disclosed by careful analysis of the text. Everything that had been taught is reinforced in the text material, and the text material provides sufficient practice with the various teaching objectives to assure that students become firm in applying all the targeted skills.

COMPREHENSION SKILLS REVISITED

When we look at the problem of comprehension as it relates to the word-by-word, sentence-by-sentence progression through a passage, we realize how fragile the traditional comprehension-skill categories are and even worse, how inadequate they are.

There are only three major "categories" of comprehension skills: (1) the structural details that are unique to the written page (and that have no counterpart in spoken language), (2) information that is treated literally, and (3) information that promotes some sort of inference.

Structural Details

Included in this category are: dots or spaces between paragraphs that indicate some "time lapse" or lack of transition, italicized or bold-faced words that are to be stressed or said loudly, ellipses following partial utterances (…) to indicate that the person stopped talking or was interrupted.

Each of these details is taught in *Reading Mastery 3* and *4*. For instance, students learn the rule that dots at the end of a paragraph indicate that part of the story is missing. Students then read to the dots, interpret them, read the following part of the story and then draw a conclusion about which part of the story was missing. If one scene is in a school, and the next is in the character's home, students conclude that the missing part would tell about the character going home.

Similarly, students learn to interpret bold-faced words by stressing them. If a character says, "I don't want to do **that**," students say the speech the way the character said it, stressing the word *that*. Again, students receive repeated practice in "interpreting" bold-faced words.

Literal Comprehension and Inferential Comprehension

The test for literal comprehension is simply: Do words in the story answer the question that is asked? If so, the item tests literal comprehension. Literal comprehension practice is important because it tests the stated aspects of the passage. Students therefore receive repeated practice in literal comprehension.

In levels 3 and 4, however, students also learn and apply various inferential comprehension skills. There are two basic types of inference—those that are based on a deduction and those that are based on induction. For deduction, the rule is specified and is then applied to instances. (The cat who talked to Jokey presented such a rule: The more you eat, the fatter you get. This rule supports the rest of the deduction: You ate more, so you got fat.) Inductive inference does not present a rule. It simply presents examples that permit future predictions. For instance, let's say that a character in a story lies again and again. These instances suggest the rule: He is a liar. When a new situation occurs, we can predict how the character will behave. He will probably lie.

Figure 1

---

6. The people who owned Jokey got madder and madder as Jokey got fatter and fatter. Circle the Jokey that made the owners the maddest.

| A | B | C | D | E |

7. What do you do when you go on a diet? _____

The traditional comprehension categories of cause and effect, relevant detail, context clues, etc., make very little sense within this framework. In the example about the liar, for instance, how could we draw a conclusion about future behavior without attending to context clues? How could we attend to context clues without perceiving relevant details? When the character appears in a new situation, how can we predict the behavior unless we know what causes it? Furthermore, how could we even follow the story unless we attended to literal information presented in the story? Certainly, *Reading*

Mastery 3 and *4* teach cause and effect, relevant detail, context clues, and all the other traditional skills, but they teach these skills within a more comprehensive framework that treats various inferences as either deductions or inductions (not always by labeling them, but by referring to the information presented in the story). At the beginning of level 3, students receive repeated practice in performing deductions. Figure 1 shows an example from worksheet 13.

Deductions are applied to a variety of content, throughout levels 3 and 4, including content in which the "rule" that determines the conclusion of a deduction is embedded in a story. For instance, the passage below is the opening paragraph from a level 4 serial.

> Going places with Grandmother Esther was fun, but it was also embarrassing. It was embarrassing because Grandmother Esther had a lot to say, and she talked in a very loud voice. She talked the loudest and the longest about inventing. So when Leonard went to the museum with Grandmother Esther, Leonard was ready to hear a lot of talk about inventing. (*Reading Mastery IV,* page 121.)

Questions such as "How loudly will she talk at the museum?" and "Why?" are derived through a deduction (and are asked by the teacher).

The deductions sometimes apply to a variety of complex behavior. In the serial about Leonard, for instance, Leonard invents an electric-eye device that automatically turns off lights in a room that is empty and turns on the lights when somebody enters the room. During the first afternoon of the invention fair, Leonard is disappointed by the lack of response to his invention.

> Grandmother Esther explained:

> "Things aren't always what they seem to be. Smart manufacturers will never let you know that they're interested in your invention. They're smart. They know that you'll want more money for your invention if they're very interested. So they'll act as if they're not interested. Don't let them fool you. The ones that seem the most interested are the ones who will never want to buy your invention." (*Reading Mastery IV,* page 158.)

The next chapter of the serial tells about the last day of the fair. The excerpt below presents one of the many complex interactions that are based on the "rule" Grandmother Esther had presented. The excerpt begins when manufacturers' representatives casually approach Leonard's booth.

> Grandmother Esther whispered, "Leonard, they're going to try to make a deal with us. Let me do all the talking."
>
> The man and woman approached Leonard's display. They stopped. They didn't smile. They just stood there.
>
> "Hello," Leonard said at last.
>
> The woman said, "Do you have a patent on this device?"
>
> "Yes," Leonard replied.
>
> The woman said nothing for a few moments. Then she said, "I'm with ABC Home products." The woman continued, "I don't think many people would be interested in an invention like yours. But I may be able to talk my boss into working out a deal. But that deal must not involve a lot of money."
>
> Grandmother Esther pointed to the large clock in the center of the hall. "It's already after eleven o'clock," she announced loudly. "This afternoon we're going to be very busy. This evening we're going to win first prize and there will be many manufacturers who are interested in this invention. If you want to make a deal, you'd better start talking about a lot of money, and you'd better start right now." (*Reading Mastery IV*, page 159.)

The discrepancy between the woman's speech and her motives are explicable in terms of the rule that Grandmother Esther had presented earlier. Although "inferences" of this type are common and important, how do we categorize them in terms of traditional basal classifications? I don't know of any category that deals with overt behavior versus real motives.

Inductions

Just as there are thousands of possible deductions that deal with anything that can be expressed as a "rule" (from the rule about how words are seated in the word bank to rules about the discrepancy between what manufacturers say to inventors and what they really think), there are thousands of possible inductions. Various types are presented in level 3 and 4. They range from simple examples to those that are very complex. One of the more complex inductions occurs in the Leonard stories. After the students read about how Leonard solves different problems in designing a workable electric-eye device, the serial ends with Leonard being a successful inventor (after winning second prize and making a deal with ABC Home products). In the last chapter of the serial, Leonard and his mother go to the store. As they approach the car, carrying bags of groceries, his mother complains because she must put down the bags and search for her key to the trunk. Leonard examines the car. The trunk of the car is dusty.

> He drew two little circles in the dust. One circle was on each side. Then he looked at his mother, smiled, and said, "I have figured out an invention that will solve your problem."
>
> Now it is your turn to think like an inventor. See if you can figure out the device that Leonard was thinking about when he told his mother that he could solve her problem with an invention. The end. (*Reading Mastery IV*, page 167.)

To solve the problem, the students must apply what they have learned about the electric-eye devices and figure out how to make the trunk open in a way that would occur only when somebody was standing very close to the trunk. This task is inductive. (By the way, during field tryouts of the program, most students came up with very clever inventions.)

Perspectives

Cutting across both inductions and deductions are perspectives. There are perspectives based on importance (with a person responding one way to things that are important to the person and another way to things that are not important), perspectives of size or distance (with some things looking big when viewed from one perspective and small when viewed from another), perspectives of time (with a given time period apparently short to one person and long to another), and perspective of viewpoint (with the reader receiving information about what one character is thinking, but not what others are thinking). Each perspective is taught in levels 3 and 4. In level 3, students learn about size and distance perspectives through a serial about Nancy, a spoiled little girl who shrinks to the size of a drop of water. She learns many things about being small, such as the rule that very small animals are not hurt if they fall from high places, and that their voices become higher as they become smaller. She has adventures trying to drink from a drop of water (which has a skin around it that presents problems when she tries to penetrate the drop). The students practice switching viewpoints by indicating how large things look to us and how large they look to Nancy. (For instance, students indicate how small a crumb of toast looks to us and how large it would be for Nancy if she held it.)

Other viewpoints are presented in the level 3 serial of Herman the Fly. Herman wanders into a jet plane that travels all around the world, stopping at different places. Herman has different adventures. Things that are seen through his viewpoint are juxtaposed with the same events seen through the eyes of the passengers on the plane. The excerpt below illustrates one of the many perspective switches. Herman is caught in a spider web as the plane approaches Japan.

> Herman gave a great buzz with his wings. He gave the hardest buzz he could make. Suddenly, he was in the air, with some sticky stuff still on his legs.
>
> Get out of the dark, Herman thought. He flew from the closet to the bright parts of the jet. A moment later, Herman landed on a warm red[1] and rubbed his front legs together. As Herman sat on the seat back, he did not remember what had just happened. For Herman, things were warm and red. And he was tired. Time to nap.

---

1 Editor's note: In this reading passage Herman does not know the name of the object he lands on because he is a fly. Thus, the name is not included in the text.

Chapter 14: Engelmann Compares Traditional Basals with Reading Mastery 3 & 4 (1983)

> For the passengers it was a time for excitement. Look off in the distance. The green strips of land and a great mountain. "Look," they said as they crowded near the windows. "Japan." (End of chapter, *Reading Mastery III*, page 243.)

The culmination of all the perspectives and all the information presented in levels 3 and 4 is the last serial in level 4, a 38-chapter story about Al, who was a very poor student, and his sister Angela. They encounter a strange old man who operates a shop on a strange street in the city. The old man has magical powers and takes the youngsters on trips to exotic places, but the trips are contingent upon Al and Angela being able to pass a test on the information learned from each trip. Through different adventures, all perspectives are reviewed and integrated into the new story context. On Al's first adventure, he finds himself in a racing car, zooming along at a speed of more than 180 miles an hour with the engine screaming and wind roaring. Suddenly a jet speeds past the racing car.

> The old man said, "This car is really very slow. Let's get into something that has some more speed."
>
> "I think I better go home," Al yelled. "It's getting late and..."
>
> Suddenly, Al was no longer in the racing car. He was in the front seat of a jet plane. Everything was quiet inside the plane. Al looked out the window. He could see the racing car below.
>
> When Al looked at the speedometer, he couldn't believe it. One thousand kilometers per hour. (*Reading Mastery IV*, page 321.)

At the end of the chapter, Al and the old man were hurtling through space at the speed of light. The old man pointed to a far off galaxy and said that at the speed they were traveling, it would take 200 million years to reach that galaxy. The test that Al received following this trip consisted of one question. What does it mean to go fast? Al explained that in the racing car, he felt that he was moving at a frightening speed, but the speed of light is actually very slow when you consider how long it would take to get to places that are far off in the universe.

In later adventures, Al becomes so small that he can observe molecules; he goes to Neptune and Saturn (where air is solid); he and Angela go to the bottom of the ocean where they observe how pressure affects a small balloon as it ascends, and observe the strange creatures that are adapted to the ocean floor; they go to the Sun, and the Milky Way, where they see our sun from a new perspective—as a medium-sized star near the edge of the disk. They go inside the human body and observe the workings of bones, muscles, the brain, the eye, the ear; they go to the poles of the earth. After Al and Angela pass the test on this trip, the old man explains why there will be only one more trip.

> "You don't need the trips anymore. When you first came to me, you needed to see things. You needed to learn about the world. And you needed to learn that it is fun to learn. Now you have learned these things, so you no longer need the trips." The old man selected the last trip, the library. After reading parts of books about modern animals and dinosaurs, the old man asked, "Did you like this trip as much as the trip to the poles or the human body?"
>
> "No, I didn't," Angela said.
>
> The old man smiled. Then he said, "Taking a trip from a book is not as easy as taking a real trip. You have to use your imagination to take a trip from a book. The old man then reminded the youngsters that they could no longer go on real trips. "But you can still go back to the bottom of the sea with a book. And if you want to visit other planets, take a trip from a book."
>
> The old man stopped talking. The library was quiet. Al was thinking, "Maybe the trip from a book would not be as good as a real trip, but it would still be a good trip. It would be fun to take a trip to Africa to learn about the baboons. It would be fun to go back to the Mesozoic and read about Plateosaurus." (*Reading Mastery IV*, page 430.)

As Al learned, books represent the ultimate culmination of different perspectives. *Reading Mastery 3* and *4* are designed to present this ultimate perspective to students in a way that is both plausible and emotionally compelling. By the time students complete *Reading Mastery 4*, they, like Al and Angela, will have experienced many things through books—vivid experiences that make them laugh (such as the foibles of Jokey), and make them cry (such as the death of Herman), that transform ordinary things into centers of excitement (such as a drop of water), and that transform vocabulary and information into tools that permit the student to gain a great sense of achievement and to open new doors to exciting places and events.

The programs have the potential to achieve these goals—which should be the goals of all reading programs. The intertwined objectives assure that students will not become overwhelmed or bored, if the program is presented properly, and the format guarantees that students use the information and vocabulary they learn and that they use it in a broad range of contexts so there is an ongoing payoff to the students for learning the words, inferences, and knowledge of structure that serve as the basis for not merely "learning to read," but "reading to learn."

REFERENCES

Beck, I. L. & McCaslin, E.S. *An analysis of dimensions that affect the development of code-breaking ability in eight beginning reading programs.* Learning Research and Development Center, University of Pittsburg, 1978.

Chall, J. *Learning to read: The great debate.* New York: McGraw-Hill, 1967.

Engelmann, S. and Hanner, S. *Reading Mastery III.* Chicago: Science Research Associates, 1982.

Engelmann, S. and Hanner, S. *Reading Mastery IV.* Chicago: Science Research Associates, 1983.

CHAPTER 15

Continuing his pursuit of understanding how children learn and how to maximize the success of all students, Engelmann has examined characteristics of teacher supervision. In this article, he describes six key components of effective supervision and solving problems in the classroom: direct observation of teachers' behaviors, timely identification of problems before they become chronic, careful analysis and correction of program design and inadequacies when required, provision of extensive teacher practice in structured settings and additional supervised practice in the classroom, and recognition that the supervisor must be well trained in the specific skills needed to be effective. Engelmann also provides a series of facts about teaching and supervision, and a conclusion about each problem or assessment presented. He argues that controlling teacher behavior in the classroom is essential for managing what students learn, how they learn, and how their attitudes change.

THE LOGIC AND FACTS OF EFFECTIVE SUPERVISION (1988)*

By Siegfried Engelmann

The behaviors teachers exhibit in the classroom when working with students are the principal determinant of what students learn, how well they learn, and how their "attitudes" are shaped about the content and about being taught. According to the rhetoric of educators, the objective is to arrange instruction so that it is very close to being optimal for each student being taught. If this objective is for real, supervision of teachers is implied at this point. The argument can be presented as follows:

- Either we assume that things are perfect in the classroom or we don't.

- If we don't make the assumption that things are perfect, we must rely on data of some sort to determine what is not perfect.

- Either we respond to data that suggest problems or we don't. If we do respond, we are involved in supervision.

The details of effective supervision derive from facts about teachers, students, and learning. Many of these facts are supported by the research literature; however, all of the facts can be ascertained simply by working closely with large groups of teachers.

Fact 1: Teachers' verbal reports are unreliable.

a. Teacher reports are often interpretations and do not suggest the actual problems (which have to do with the antecedent events and the consequent events surrounding the problem behavior). Teachers are often unable to provide an articulate statement of what happened before the student made a mistake or misbehaved, or to describe the behavior in a way that would clearly imply a remedy. Interpretations often focus attention on details that are far removed from possible instructional remedies, such as "Oh, he just has an indifferent attitude."

---

* Engelmann, S. (1988). The logic and facts of effective supervision. *Education and Treatment of Children, 11*(4), 328–340. Reprinted with permission of the publisher.

b. Teachers also omit details. For instance, teachers who do not recognize that pacing is an important instructional variable and that poor pacing may cause lack of attention, off-task behavior, etc. will not refer to pacing in their verbal reports of the problem.

c. Teacher reports may be "politically" motivated. A teacher may want a particular student removed from the classroom, or may want to keep the supervisor from observing in the classroom. For instance, the teacher might meet the supervisor in the corridor and say, "Things are just going wonderfully. Thank you so much for the help you gave me earlier." (Things are actually very dismal in the classroom.) Another ploy is for teachers to request the supervisors to "demonstrate." "I'm having a real problem teaching _____. Please show me how you do that the right way." While this request may be based on legitimate concerns, it is an effective way of disarming the supervisor and keeping the supervisor from observing the teacher.

d. The information presented in reports may be misleading. As an informal study, we responded to teachers' requests to help by requiring the teacher to explain the specific problem the targeted learner was experiencing, without identifying the learner by name or by sex. We then went into the classroom and tried to identify the targeted learner, based on the description of the problem (such as "unable to read multisyllabic words," or "takes too long to finish written assignments"). We could not identify the targeted learners because (in a class of 28) there were at least four others in the classroom who had the same problem.

Conclusion 1: Effective supervision does not rely on teacher verbal reports.

This conclusion is not intended to deny that some teachers may provide very reliable reports. However, a supervisor cannot tell who is reliable without careful observation (Adler, 1982, 1983-4; Carnine, 1981; Zoref, 1981).

Fact 2: Effective remedies for specific problems, both behavioral and academic, must be more extensive if the problem is "habitual."

Much data support this fact for behavioral problems. Academic problems follow the same pattern. To teach the average six-year-old to reliably decode the word *the* requires possibly 30 trials (distributed appropriately over time). At the end of this training, the child will reliably discriminate between *a* and *the* when they occur in sentences. For the typical corrective reader in grade 6 to achieve the same criterion of accuracy may require as many as 600 trials. On a less dramatic scale, the effects of timely intervention – correcting student problems before they become habitual mistakes – can be demonstrated to increase the rate of student mastery.

Conclusion 2: Effective supervision must involve an observational scheme that permits timely identification of problems.

Fact 3: The solutions to problems are a function of both the stimulus prompts (sequences of tasks) presented to the learner and the structure of the reinforcement.

Even if a supervisor observes a problem in a timely fashion, this does not imply that an effective solution will be forthcoming. Let's say that the student is not firm on a series of elementary arithmetic facts, and let's say that the problem the teacher is using tests the facts in this order:

$$0 + 1 = \square, 1 + 1 = \square, 2 + 1 = \square, 3 + 1 = \square, 4 + 1 = \square$$

(which is done in quite a few level-1 arithmetic programs.)

If the supervisor simply introduces a good "reinforcement" program, and demonstrates that after practice the child performs perfectly on the series ten consecutive times, the problem is apparently solved. But the solution probably creates new problems because the learner could achieve a perfect performance by simply "reciting" the number that are said when you count "1, 2, 3, 4, 5". The learner could be reinforced for an inappropriate "private" solution for the task.

A knowledgeable supervisor would obviously recognize the potential problem and would specify changes in the "test sequence" so that the items were randomized. However, this problem is only one of many. Analysis of traditionally basal programs discloses that many would have to be completely scrapped if the criterion was to fix them up so that the program was not a possible cause of serious learning (or mislearning) problems. When we were engaged in Project Follow Through, we recommended a particular social studies text to be used in participating sites. The text was probably better than others; however, it needed a lot of "fixing up" before it would be capable of communicating clearly. So we began fixing it up. When the number of pages of fix-ups exceeded the number of pages in the text by a factor of two, we stopped trying to fix it up. It was hopeless.

The implication for supervision is that if instructional sequences are poorly designed, a supervisor (or somebody) would be required to redesign them before an effective remedy would be possible. A supervisor typically would not have time for this undertaking with more than one or two teachers. If programs are well designed, the supervisor can work on supervising teaching in the delivery of tasks and reinforcement for appropriate responding. The supervisor can therefore work with a larger number of teachers (a dozen or more). If programs are poorly designed, the supervisor must first redesign the sequences, then work on delivery (Becker, Engelmann, Carnine and Maggs, 1982; Brophy & Good, 1986; Engelmann & Carnine 1982; Englert, 1984; Fabre, 1983; Gersten, 1985; Reith, Polsgrove, & Semmel, 1982).

Conclusion 3: Programs should be carefully selected for their technical fidelity in presenting the stimuli for teaching various skills and concepts.

Fact 4: For teachers to master basic presentation techniques in the simplest situation, they must practice the techniques a great deal.

The simplest situation would be in a structured practice session. The supervisor would first demonstrate (model) the format or exercise that is to be presented; the teachers would then present it (in unison) as the supervisor gave the appropriate student responses (lead). Next, the teachers would pair up – one playing teacher, the other playing student – and would practice the same exercise. After working on other selected exercises the same way, the supervisor would return to the earlier exercise and *test* the teachers on it by having them again present it to their partners.

The average teacher would have to practice an average exercise in a subject like beginning reading about 12 times before becoming adequately proficient at presenting. An adequate presentation would be one that was rapidly paced with the appropriate words stressed. It would be delivered as something important followed by functional reinforcement. Functional does not mean elaborate. For component tasks *within* an exercise, reinforcement should be behavior specific, but quite quick. If it is elaborate, the students may go off task. At the *end* of an exercise, more elaborate reinforcement is appropriate.

An appropriate presentation requires orchestrating many details, each of which has been shown to affect student mastery – teacher wording, pacing, pointing to a word in an unambiguous way, reinforcement, etc. Most teachers haven't been taught such skills.

Conclusion 4: Provisions must be made for structured practice of selected activities in a "simple" setting where prompts and feedback are provided by the supervisor.

Teachers who cannot orchestrate the various details in this setting will certainly never be able to do it in the more complicated setting that involves students.

Fact 5: Transfer of skills from the practice setting to the classroom is variable among teachers. In our experience less than 30 percent of what is practiced will transfer to "live teaching" settings.

Transfer is based on one consideration: The perceived "sameness" shared by two situations. As a rule, teachers who have taught for more than two years before receiving DI training will have the greatest problems in transferring. They are like the "corrective reader," who must practice extensively to override old habits. The presence of students is a very strong discriminative stimulus (S^d) for these teachers to revert to old behaviors, regardless of what they had been taught or how many times they had been told that they will use these procedures in working with students. New teachers who have never taught will tend to "transfer" about twice as fast as experienced teachers. Some, however, have notions of "teaching" that inappropriately dominate their behavior when they are faced with students. For example, they may do things like reinforce children for inappropriate responses to make these students "feel good," etc.

Conclusion 5: Additional practice, prompting, and training must be provided after teachers have matriculated from the training sessions into the classroom.

Without this practice, the performance of many teachers will be disappointing and will be reflected in the relatively poor performance of their students.

Fact 6: About six months of periodic observations, prompting, practice sessions, and assignments are required for the average teacher to become proficient in the classroom.

One might ask, "Well, if it takes that long, why don't' we just eliminate the initial practice sessions and start right in the classroom?" There are two reasons. The first is that the mock-training provides teachers with skills. These skills can be "prompted" in the transfer setting (the classroom). Often a gesture or few words from the supervisor as the teacher is teaching is sufficient to remind the teacher of appropriate behavior. Second, the types of details teachers have trouble with in the classroom are typically those associated with "interactions" with students. Some teachers "learn their lines" and initially present as if they are a "solo" act. Students fail to respond appropriately, but teachers do not correct them. Some have trouble "getting their group under control" or start presenting when the children are not attending. Some have troubles with the mechanics of presenting group tasks; for instance, some display words to be sounded out in a way that half the kids in the group can't see them. Some may be punishing when correcting, suggesting that they are disappointed with students (or that the students are trying to spite them). Some exhibit poor timing with corrections (e.g., waiting much too long). Some have trouble correcting the children, and so on.

Conclusion 6: Supervision schedules should parallel teachers' needs, with very frequent observations when teachers first move into the classroom (daily), and less frequent observations later.

Again, there will be great variability among teachers. Some will be quite proficient after two months; other will still require a relatively heavy observation schedule after four months (Glang & Gersten, 1987; Joyce & Showers, 1980, 1982; Showers, 1984).

Fact 7: The specific behaviors of the supervisor are strongly correlated with teachers' rate of learning and performance.

The frequency of "supervision" does not insure that it is effective. What occurs during the interactions between supervisor and teacher determines both the immediate changes in the teacher's behavior and the teacher's generalizations to the situations that had not been responded to by the supervisor. The list of details that make a difference in teacher performance is very long. Some of the more critical details are these:

a. If the supervisor overloads the teacher (as she teaches), the teacher will learn more slowly. For instance, the supervisor may call attention to a student who should be reinforced, then remind the teacher about how to hold the presentation book, then remind about signaling clearly so that the students are able to respond together, and so forth.

b. On the other hand, if the supervisor does not provide the teacher with some demonstrations, of "doing it the right way," the teacher will learn more slowly. If the supervisor demonstrates, shows the appropriate teaching behaviors, and secures the appropriate student behaviors, the teacher has a model that correlates how the activity is supposed to look with the appropriate student behavior.

c. If the supervisor does not require the teacher to *verbally* reconstruct what happened when a problem occurred, the teacher will learn more slowly. The S^ds provided by accurately reciting what happened immediately before a problem occurred, what the teacher did in response to the problem, and what the kids did, provide a basis for self-management of improved teaching in the future. Specifically, the teacher should describe what happened before the "problem" occurred and what behaviors occurred during the problem. This description suggests the *cause* of the problem. The cause is always assumed to be something the teacher did. Once the cause of the problem is clearly identified, the solution is implied. The basic assumption is that the performance of students is a function of what the teacher does.

One of the most easily misinterpreted things a supervisor can do is demonstrate the right way to teach a task and assume that the teacher understands exactly what happened. I recall a teacher who insisted that the kids in a group could not perform on a spelling activity. "They can't do it." I tried to point out that they could do it if the teaching behaviors were different. The teacher disagreed. So I demonstrated with the group. The kids performed perfectly. I said, "There you are. They can do it." Her response, "For YOU they can do it."

Variations of this problem are pandemic. The supervisor supposes that the demonstration is perfectly clear, the teacher, however, is not making the appropriate connections or is interpreting the outcome according to criteria that have little to do with the controlling stimulus events. To pre-connect this type of potential misinterpretation, the supervisor should take the teacher through the following argument step-by-step:

- "The kids had a problem. What was that problem? Describe exactly what happened."

- "They had a problem because of something you did. Can you identify what that was?" (If not, the supervisor will provide the answer.)

- "So how could you change their behavior by doing something different?" (Again, the details of the solution would be provided by the supervisor. The purpose of the prompt is to demonstrate the kind of "thinking" that should be going on.)

- "I'll change that part of the presentation. When I present, I want you to observe both what I do differently and what the kids do."

- After the demonstration, "What did I do that was different?" How did the kids respond?" "Why did they respond differently when I did it?"

Now the knot is tied. Teachers learn what to do far more quickly when they are helped to verbalize the nature of the problem and its solution.

d. If the teacher does not receive an "assignment" that is expressed in specific behavioral terms, the teacher will learn more slowly. After discussing the problem and solution with the teacher, the supervisor can provide either a "general" assignment ("Remember how to respond to that kind of problem.") or one that contains very precise expectations that are referenced to specific activities. The second alternative speeds learning and avoids many types of possible "ambiguous" communications between supervisor and teacher. "Tomorrow, when you present the second spelling activity, I want you to pause before… etc." This kind of assignment (which should be supported with a written one) makes the expectations very clear.

e. If the teacher receives the assignment *only* as a verbal description, learning is frequently retarded. If an assignment is presented verbally, the teacher may provide every "behavioral" indication that he understands. He'll nod, ask intelligent questions, and say the right things. When observed on the following day, he may do a terrible job. The supervisor can circumvent these possible miscommunications by requiring teachers to "demonstrate" the right way as part of the assignment. These practice sessions are important in another way: they demonstrate to the teacher just how much "rehearsal" is necessary to get the mind in "sync" with the body. This information is useful when the teacher is preparing to teach activities not taught before.

f. If teachers know the supervisor's schedule, learning is retarded. The reason is that the teacher's behavior may become "scalloped" – high performance when the supervisor is about to show up, relatively low at other times. For some situations – especially serious problems – the teacher should know that the supervisor will be in the classroom at a particular time. "I'll be here tomorrow, and I'll bet that if you do it the way we practiced, you'll see a big difference in the kids' performance." For less serious problems, the supervisor's schedule should be unpredictable.

g. If the teacher is given an assignment that involves more than three details, learning is slowed. If the teacher is required to attend to only a few things at a time, and if the teacher is prepared by the supervisor so that the probability of success with the students is quite high, the teacher will respond in a far more positive (and less anxious) way to the supervisor. If the teacher is doing eight things wrong and these things are handled in three sequentially-presented assignments – not one – the teacher will be more likely to master the eight points more quickly then she would if they were presented in a single assignment.

Conclusion 7: The supervisor must have a great deal of skill to provide well designed "shaping" programs for teachers being supervised (Gersten, Davis, Miller, & Green, 1986; Markel, 1982.)

Fact 8: Supervisors can be trained in the needed supervision skills in about two years, given that they have strong teaching skills when they enter the program.

Perhaps the greatest misconception in teaching is that if teachers are good, they will be good supervisors. The chances are good that they will be a very ineffective supervisor without a great deal of training. Consider the novice supervisor:

a. The supervisor may unintentionally model inappropriate behavior. How many times have we seen the "clinical" supervisor standing there, clipboard in hand, writing down numbers, taking notes, being "unobtrusive." All these behaviors are inappropriate. A supervisor must model the behaviors that we expect from the teacher. The teacher should be interested in kids. (That's where everything starts and ends.) So the supervisor should be very human – talking to kids, reinforcing them, and basically responding to them as if they were the supervisor's kids. (This doesn't simply imply that the supervisor should have a high profile in the classroom – no higher than that of a teacher, aide, or anybody else who is interested in kids.) Sometimes teachers – even good ones – who are elevated to the status of supervisor assume "aloof" behavior. This behavior doesn't demonstrate that the supervisor is working *with the teacher*. It shows clearly that the supervisor is an authority figure of the ancient floorwalker variety.

We want the teacher to be active and positive. We should model being active and positive. We want the teacher to be alert and relatively fast paced. The supervisor should behave in this manner. We want the teacher to understand that what she does is important. The comportment of the supervisor should reflect this attitude. The supervisor should always be busy – but approachable. The supervisor should not be late, should not socialize while supervising, but should convey, both through words and deeds, that she is there to work with the teacher at becoming better at teaching and helping kids.

b. The supervisor must prioritize the skills to work on with the teacher. If the teacher is making many different types of mistakes, the supervisor must make a judgment about what would be manageable for the teacher and which of the various problems are the "highest priorities." Intelligent selection of high-priority details often solves some of the other problems. For instance, the teacher has very slow pacing. He also has problems keeping the students on-task. He is reinforcing students for wrong responses. Students are not responding to his instruction, and so forth. If the supervisor works on pacing and reinforcing correct responses (not responses that are "sort of" correct) a lot of the problems will probably either disappear or become less prominent.

c. At the same time, the supervisor must follow the fundamental moral principle that CHILDREN OF TEACHERS BEING SUPERVISED MUST NEVER BE SUBJECTED TO POOR INSTRUCTION. Therefore, the supervisor's responses must be timely and must buttress against a situation in which the kids are not being taught well. The supervisor may have to change the structure of the classroom. "For a few days, I'll teach the kids and you keep data; after class you and I will practice." A variety of structural changes are possible, but one of them must be identified and implemented.

d. The supervisor must be able to use the least obtrusive means of intervening when there is a problem. If the teacher's problem can be corrected by prompting the teacher to do something she knows how to do, a prompt–a couple of words or a visual signal–is all the supervisor should present. If the least obtrusive intervention for a problem would be for the teacher to present the tasks to the students, that intervention would be the preferred one. If the teacher is floundering, the kids are having problems, and the teacher does not have behaviors that the supervisor can "prompt," the supervisor takes over the group and demonstrates, or (if this demonstration would be inappropriate for some reason) tells the teacher, "Skip that part and go on to..." (another part of the program that the teacher is able to handle).

Even the details of the demonstration are important. The supervisor is to follow the rule, "Don't demonstrate anything that you can't teach the teacher to do exactly the way you did it." The supervisor may know many tricks and techniques, but most of these may be perfectly inappropriate for demonstrating to the novice unless the supervisor wants to leave the teacher with the impression "I could never learn to do that." If the demonstration is to be functional, it must be teachable–now. If the supervisor is unable to demonstrate in that fashion, he must correct the problem in some other way. Also, the supervisor must succeed when demonstrating. There is nothing worse than a demonstration that does not show what it is supposed to show. Therefore, the supervisor must be a very proficient teacher–much better than what we consider to be a "good teacher."

e. The supervisor must be able to make intelligent judgments about what to assign the teacher, how to go through it verbally so that the teacher gets the message (or how to judge that the teacher already knows these relationships and it is not important to go through the verbal routes), how to specify the expectations for the teacher, how to reinforce the teacher for working hard, and how to make it clear that the supervisor is available (by phone) if the teacher has problems.

f. The supervisor must be able to schedule time so that each teacher receives relatively frequent (if sometimes short) visits. A classic mistake that novice supervisors make is to concentrate exclusively on those teachers who are having the most serious problems. Sometimes, they won't even schedule visits for the highest performers. When the supervisor finally gets around to a classroom of one of the "good" teachers, the supervisor may come close to fainting when she observes what's happening in the classroom. The supervisor will make the greatest gains for the group of teachers being supervised if all are visited relatively frequently, with obvious provisions for "brush fires" and work with the lower performers.

g. Above all, the supervisor must interpret the teachers' behavior conservatively; that is, in a manner that does not preempt the supervisor from finding out more about the teachers' problems. Sometimes, novice supervisors will misinterpret teachers' behavior, particularly those who are "smart." If the teacher is having problems, the supervisor may conclude, "She's not trying; she doesn't have a good attitude." This interpretation is not conservative. A conservative one would be, "She's doing the best she can." This interpretation suggests that the supervisor should help her, with additional practice.

Conclusion 8: The training of supervisors must provide for much hands-on practice and supervision by knowledgeable trainers of supervisors.

Just as the classroom teacher needs models, feedback, a step-by-step sequence that doesn't overwhelm them at first, and one that lets them spread their wings later, supervisors can master supervisory skills from a program that satisfies these needs. But obviously the trainers of supervisors must be one rung up on the ladder, which means that they have supervised successfully and have also mastered those skills that are unique to training supervisors in these behaviors. (Again, that a person is an excellent supervisor doesn't imply that she is an excellent *trainer* of supervisors. She may be a very good model of polished supervisory behaviors, but to efficiently train supervisors she must also know how to provide a step-by-step program that teaches these skills.)

Fact 9: A supervisory training program that incorporates the various details and commitments outlined in this paper exists at the University of Oregon.

Three staff-supervisors direct the training for practicum undergraduate students, graduate students working on the Handicapped Learner to Endorsement (HLE), and doctoral students electing the "supervision" alternative. Doctoral students for this option are screened on the basis of their teaching ability. If they are weak, they may provisionally enter the program; however, they must spend time working with kids and being supervised in basic teaching skills. After participating in the mock-training sessions (9 days, all day), each doctoral student is assigned to a super-supervisor who tutors the student supervisor. The first objective is "reliability" of observations. The supervisor and trainee observe teachers. The supervisor asks, "What are the big problems you see?" Once reliability in observations is established, the supervisor works on prioritizing targets for training. As the trainee masters this objective, others are presented in sequence – specifying the type of intervention called for, taking the teacher through the verbal recitation of a problem with kids she just had, identifying a possible problem with teaching behavior, generating a possible solution. Trainees are not permitted to intervene or to give teachers assignments until their second term or third term (depending on their progress). During their second year, supervisors in training are at least partly responsible for the training of an incoming supervisor. (However, this process is monitored very carefully by a super-supervisor.)

The program is very successful. The school districts that participate, by providing a setting for practica and supervision in training, recognize that the University is providing a real service. In fact, with as many as 30 practicum students in different classrooms and resource rooms during a year, the rate of complaints or reports of "problems" from the participating school districts has averaged less than one a year for the last four years.

The Handicapped Leaner Endorsement (HLE) graduates are quite skilled and are in great demand. Over the last five years, requests from the state of Washington alone for graduates has been about six times as great as the number of available graduates.

The demand for HLE graduates, however, is starkly contrasted with demand for trained *supervisors*, who are proficient in all criteria outlined in this paper. There is no waiting line for the doctoral students in the program, and not many candidates enroll in the program. The reasons for this lack of interest in supervisors seems to be a function of tradition more than anything else. To introduce expert teachers is to change many organizational details in school districts and in preparation of teachers. Although school districts have slots for supervisors, the supervisors are not trained, are very naïve about what is required to change teachers' behaviors, and spend most of their time in relatively pointless meetings.

The realities remain, however. The product of a typical supervision program is a naïve teacher who probably will never approach the level of expertise particularly needed to make a difference in the performance of lower performing students. And the system, perforce, will continue to flounder (and flounder it does) because the administration doesn't understand how to train or maintain high levels of teacher performance. The poor performance of teachers and school districts will continue as long as the current patterns of teacher-training and supervision continue.

Many of the component facts needed to make decisions about training and supervision are available from the literature. For example, Gersten, Zoref, and Carnine (1981) summarize the findings by an independent evaluator (Coresin, 1980) on the implementation of Direct Instruction in the San Diego Follow Through Project with the following: "Most teachers and aides found both the consultants from the University of Oregon and the local supervisors…extremely helpful…Most teachers liked the concrete, specific, 'hands on' type of supervisors and feedback offered." This finding strongly supports my conclusions 2 and 3.

Gersten et al. (1981) also report on a classroom observation study (Zoref, 1981) showing that teachers and aides continued to improve throughout the year in pacing, appropriate corrections, use of signals, and student accuracy of responding (the bottom line). Format accuracy was quite good after preservice training sessions. My conclusions 4, 5, and 6 are supported by these behavioral assessments of teaching process over a year-long period.

Recent research in a major California school district (Gersten, Davis, Miller, & Green, 1986; Gersten, Green, & Davis, 1986; Darch, Gersten, & Davis, 1987) found that instructional supervisors, though well-intentioned, were neither knowledgeable nor skilled enough to provide systematic teacher feedback that would result in improved instruction for difficult-to-teach students. Special education personnel were unable to offer sufficiently detailed recommendations that would lead to better teaching. The growing literature on effective educational leadership (Clark, Lotto, & McCarthy, 1980; Edmonds, 1979) is showing that effective instructional leaders—including special education administrators, supervisors, or professors at teacher training institutions—must be knowledgeable in the precise day-to-day details of education. This includes a thorough understanding of reading, language, and mathematics curricular programs; the ability to observe and analyze teacher performance; the use of student performance on academic tasks as criteria for placement and grouping of students; and procedures for consistent criterion-referenced monitoring of student progress.

When one analyzes successful adoptions of innovative educational programs (Berman & McLaughlin, 1978; Huberman & Miles, 1984; Loucks, 1983), two elements are consistently related to success: (1) the programs will work with hard-to-teach students if implemented appropriately, and (2) when teachers present classroom problems to consultants or supervisors, the consultants offer specific, concrete solutions that will work.

Even if these facts weren't available, someone could try working with teachers and would ultimately discover them, if the investigator were not satisfied with less than the best. (After all, the way we discovered many facts about training was through mistakes we made in our attempts to design an efficient system.)†

REFERENCES

Adler, E. (1982). *The effect of public posting of comparative classroom performance data on staff instruction related time.* Unpublished doctoral dissertation, College of Education, University of Oregon, Eugene.

Adler, E. (1983-4). An observational system to improve teacher performance. *Association for Direct Instruction News, 9*(2), pp. 4-5.

Becker, W. C., Engelmann. S., Carnine, D. W., & Maggs, A. (1982). Direct Instruction technology: Making Learning Happen. In P. Karoly & J. J. Steffen (Eds.), *Improving children's competence: Advances in child behavioral analysis and therapy* (Vol. 1). Lexington, MA: D.C. Health.

Berman, P., & McLaughlin, M. W. (1978). *Federal programs supporting education change. Vol. VIII: Implementing and sustaining innovations.* Santa Monica, CA: Rand Corporation.

Brophy, J. E., & Good, T. (1986). Teacher behavior and student achievement. In M. C. Wittrock (Ed.), *Handbook of research on teaching.* New York: Macmillan.

Carnine, D. W. (1981). High and low implementation of direct instruction teaching techniques. *Education and Treatment of Children, 4,* 42-51.

Clark, D. L., Lotto, L. S., & McCarthy, M. M. (1980). Factors associated with success in urban elementary schools. *Phi Delta Kappan, 61,* 467-470

Cronin, D. P. (1980). *San Diego Implementation Study, Year 2: Instructional staff interviews.* Los Altos, CA: John A. Emmrick & Associates.

Darch, C., Gersten, R., & Davis, G. (1987). Two consulting models – Their impact on teachers. *Association of Direct Instruction News, 6*(4), pp 10-12.

Edmonds, R. (1979). Effective schools for the urban poor. *Educational leadership, 37,* 15-24.

Engelmann, S., & Carnine, D. (1982). *Theory of Instruction.* New York: Irvington.

Englert, C. S. (1984). Effective direct instruction practices in special education settings, *RASE, 5*(2), 38-47.

Fabre, T. (1983). *An annotated bibliography of direct instruction research.* Unpublished manuscript, University of Oregon, Eugene.

Gersten, R., Davis, G., Miller, B, & Green, W. (1986). *The fragile role of the instructional supervisor in school improvement.* Paper presented at the annual conference of the American Educational Research Association, San Francisco, CA.

---

† I would love to demonstrate to any interested university what could be done in four years. Starting with practica for freshman and taking them through four years of practica with a *minimum* of class work to support the practica. I firmly believe that the average product would perform in the upper one percent of all teachers.

Gersten, R., Green, W., & Davis, G. (1986). The realities of instructional leadership: An intensive study of four inner city schools. *Association for Direct Instruction News, 5*(3), pp. 1, 11-14.

Gersten, R., Zoref, L., & Carnine, D. (1981). Large city implementation study. *Association for Direct Instruction News, 1*(1), pp. 8-9.

Glang, A., & Gersten, R. (1987). Coaching teachers. *Association for Direct Instruction News, 6*(2), pp. 1, 4-5, 7.

Huberman, A. M., & Miles, M. B. (1984). *Innovation up close: How school improvement works.* New York: Plenum Press.

Joyce, B., & Showers, B. (1980). Improving inservice training: The messages of research. *Education Leadership, 37,* 379-385.

Joyce, B., & Showers, B. (1982). The coaching of teaching. *Educational Leadership, 40,* 4-10.

Loucks, S. (1983). At last some good news from a study of school improvement. *Educational Leadership, 41*(3), 4-5.

Reith, H. L., Polsgrove, L., & Semmel, I. (1982). Instructional variables that make a difference: Attention to task and beyond. *Exceptional Education Quarterly, 2,* 61-71.

Showers, B. (1984). *Peer coaching and its effects on transfer of training.* Paper presented at the annual meeting of the American Educational Research Association, New Orleans.

Zoref, L. S. (1981). *A prototype for how to evaluate implementation of a structured educational program.* Unpublished doctoral dissertation, College of Education, University of Oregon, Eugene.

CHAPTER 16

In this article, Engelmann aggressively advocates for comprehensive school reform in response to the continued failure of public schools to ensure all students succeed academically. He argues that an extreme approach is needed to overcome the embedded practices currently present in school systems and promote the success of all students. Engelmann asserts school systems reject practices that are not in line with their guidelines and objectives, even if these guidelines and objectives have led to very poor implementation and underwhelming results. He provides examples of this level of failure in school systems and gives solutions that will promote the success of all students. In order to achieve success, the organization and priorities of these schools must be changed. They must become data-oriented, focused on what has been proven to be successful in the past. Additionally, administrators must have technical understanding, and both administrators and teachers must be viewed as causes of failure for students.

Engelmann provides guidelines to establish change in school systems. A key concept of his guidelines is accountability – firing administrators who fail to meet attainable student achievement goals and providing positive reinforcement to administrators when students achieve. Holding administrators accountable for student success would help ensure teachers are properly instructing students with the best methods and that students are in the best environment to succeed. This article marks the start of a trend in Engelmann's publications of advocating for a re-evaluation of the world of education and the need to rebuild to avoid the problems that have become too ingrained in its design.

CHANGE SCHOOLS THROUGH REVOLUTION, NOT EVOLUTION (1991)*

Siegfried Engelmann

The facts of failure within the school are pandemic. The rhetoric of the schools suggests great concern with improving instruction, creating equity for all children, maximizing potential, and reforming the system. Given this extensive rhetoric and the fact that the schools are engaged in what amounts to a continual reform or reorganization for reform, a rational person would assume that the schools would respond to data on what works and to suggestions about how to train teachers and students better, how to manage more effectively, and how to change behaviors faster and more systematically. The rational person would assume that if a successful demonstration were provided, the school decision-makers would quickly recognize its superiority to what is occurring now, would adapt the superior practices, and would nurture it, expand it, and even possibly improve on it.

The rational person who pursues these assumptions, however, quickly discovers the universal truths of the system. These truths are very sobering.

The system will reject practices that are not consonant with the system's guidelines and objectives. The system's guidelines and objectives have led to very poor implementations with very poor results. The obvious contradiction is that the district would hold to its guidelines even when the results clearly indicate that the guidelines and related practices are failures.

New guidelines are based largely on opinions that eschew data or that run counter to data. Although the decision-makers give the impression of addressing important social and educational issues, their posture is dramatically contradicted by fact. An example is the NCTM (National Council of Teachers of Mathematics) 1989 *Standards*. The *Standards* are outspoken in calling for

---

* Engelmann, S. (1991). Change schools through revolution, not evolution. *Journal of Behavioral Education*, *1*(3), 295–304. Reprinted with permission of the publisher.

"manipulatives," immersion in "problem solving," and scheduling practices that place very vague demands on the teacher and involve very tenuous methods of assessing what had been taught. The standards proclaim that one reason for publishing standards is to "... ensure that the public is protected from shoddy products" (p. 2). The *Standards* go so far as to assert, "It seems reasonable that anyone developing products for use in mathematics classrooms should document how the materials are related to current conceptions of what content is important to teach and should present evidence about their effectiveness" (p. 2). This statement suggests that the organization is not the mindless entity portrayed in points 1 and 2 above.

Furthermore, the NCTM's Research Advisory Committee (1988) pointed out problems with the draft version of the *Standards*. The Committee indicated that "...the draft version did not distinguish those recommendations that were well-grounded empirically or theoretically from those that were based more on the informed judgment of personal opinions of the authors... (p. 339). The final version of the standards was characterized by Bishop (1990) as containing recommendations and exhortations "...supported only by opinion—authoritative opinion, it is granted—but opinion nonetheless" (p. 366). Possibly, Bishop is being generous by suggesting that the opinions are authoritative. Since these opinions are easily contradicted by data, I'm of the opinion that the *Standards* are based on unenlightened—not authoritative—opinion.

In any case, the *Standards* represent a typical obstacle that is presented by educational decision-makers. Should math programs be designed so they are effective, they will run violently counter to the exhortations of the *Standards*. After all, the programs would have been shaped by facts and data.

By using the *Standards* as criteria for selecting programs, school districts will be assured of failure. At some future time, the failures will be recognized as failures. By then, however, the decision-makers will adopt new guidelines that are based on new opinions.

Although rational elements may exist in the decision-making chain or in the formulation of a "new approach," there is very little hope that the rational will dominate. Just as it was completely submerged by the NCTM 1989 standards, expert understanding of how to manage and train teachers to teach children effectively plays no role in the NCTE's (National Council of Teachers of English, 1987) recommendations for reading programs—in the "whole language" movement for teaching reading and related language arts. For reading and language arts, the rhetoric abounds—the call for reform, the need for equity, concern over the future of our children. At the same time, nobody within the adopting group is able to make the assertions:

"I have trained teachers so they uniformly do much better with whole language than they do with behaviorally based programs."

"I have taught children so they uniformly learn faster and better than they do with other programs."

No decision-maker is even able to say this:

"Although I haven't trained teachers or children myself, I have observed it and I know that it can be done."

If a person with this incredible knowledge deficiency adopts, recommends, or introduces the program on a large scale, the person has a problem of consistency and possibly morality. Theoretically, we do not experiment with children, particularly if instruction makes a difference in their performance and if there's a possibility that an experimental program will result in both emotional hardship and retardation of skills.

Historically and presently, the facts of educators' behaviors bear little relation to rhetoric. Nearly every aspect of school practices can be characterized as being consistent with "sorting-machine" logic. Sorting-machine logic, in its unadorned form, holds something like this: "We do what we feel like doing. If children do not learn, it's their fault." The position is roughly the opposite of a system of empathy, which would hold something like this: "If children fail, the teaching failed, and the teaching must be modified so that children succeed." The empathy position would dictate the following practices:

1. **Field testing and revisions of draft versions of instructional programs before they are published.** The system does not do this. As the NCTE (1987) *Report Card on Basal Readers* points out, "... books will almost always be in print before a child has an opportunity to respond to it, and it is only if teachers report these responses that they may have an impact on subsequent revisions." In the tradition of the sorting machine, however, the same report endorses whole language, which is an experiment of magnitude even greater than that of ineffective basals.

2. **Using information about child failure to modify teaching practices.** This step, although rational and reasonable within an empathic system, is never done traditionally. Alessi (1988) did a very nice informal study that illustrates this point. Through questions presented to school psychologists, he received information on approximately 5,000 children who were referred because they were failing. If the system entertained the possibility that it was less than infallible, a certain percentage of the children would have been diagnosed as having a problem that resulted from a poor instructional program, poor school practices, a poor teacher, or something along those lines. An arrogant system would conclude that all the problems were caused by defects in the children, none caused by defects in the system.

3. **Testing and evaluating performance so it can be referenced to the curriculum.** Among the more revealing practices in the school is "achievement testing," which is actually aptitude testing and which is designed to separate students on the basis of the "stuff" they bring with them rather than on what's taught in school. The achievement test doesn't test material that is taught on a particular grade level or in a particular program and therefore doesn't provide very clear implications about how the school failed or what to repair. The latest wave of "reforms" is critical of achievement testing but clearly for the wrong reasons. The current idiom is to replace "uniform" tests with teacher-constructed evaluations. This practice will

obviously serve the system in keeping the facts of failure from parents and possibly from those within the system.

Standardized, uniform tests should be provided. In an empathic scheme, however, they must be supplemented extensively with criterion-referenced measures to show where the current teaching is failing and to imply revisions that improve the system.

4. **Placing students at grade-appropriate levels.** This point relates to point 3. In an empathic system, students would not be thrown into deep water. They would not be placed in an instructional sequence that is far above their skill level and that will provide them with information that they are failures. Yet, we see, in virtually any school, students in the sixth grade who cannot perform on basic fraction problems of the type presented in the third grade. When we look at the students in the eighth grade, we see the same lack of understanding. The system has indeed been cruel to these students. It has confused them, convinced them that fractions (and math generally) are inexplicable, and provided them with compelling evidence that they are not "good" at learning math.

5. **Training and monitoring teacher performance.** The typical practices spring from sorting-machine philosophy. Teachers are not observed in the classroom, although data show that they perform better when they are observed. Teachers are not required to meet reasonable performance requirements before being permitted to teach in the classroom. Teachers are almost never removed from the classroom for not performing well with the children. (Removal might occur for some type of moral turpitude, child abuse, drunkenness, etc., but not for being a perfectly horrible teacher—as measured by child performance.

Training provided in most districts has not been shaped by data. Like other aspects of the system, training practices are the result of naïve opinion that becomes mandated practice.

IMPROVING EDUCATIONAL PRACTICES

The picture that I have painted of the schools is dismal, even hopeless. The picture, however, is accurate. There is little reason to assume that if we show schools what can be done, the schools will do it. It is even more dangerous to assume that the schools would know how to do it even if the steps were made very explicit. The schools have neither the structural nor the knowledge base to engage in successful implementations. After all, there are no experts in the district's administration; there are no precedents in place. And despite the rhetoric, there is no compelling evidence of a commitment from schools to serve as advocates for children. The system is currently built so that it can be run solely by people who have no technical knowledge of curriculum, effective training practices, or methods for teaching management skills.

These facts about the system come as very sad lessons to people who try to "shape" the system with the idea that if the system is provided with a demonstration of effective methods, the system will change, learn, and grow. Actually, a successful implementation will typically be removed by fiat at some later date—cancelled by the mandate of a new administrator or as part of a new plan. And it will die quite silently, with no great outcry from parents or teachers. Furthermore, six years later, there will be no official administrative memory of the project or its results.

I believe that anybody seriously interested in improving educational practices within the schools should start with the working premise that the foundations of the schools must be changed. The system must become data oriented. There must be administrators within the system who have technical understanding. Practices that are punishing to children or that result in serious retardation should be excised from the system. Possibly the most fundamental change that should occur involves putting administrators and teachers on the same side as the children. If teachers and administrators failed when children failed, it wouldn't be long before the system dropped its sorting-machine logic and the stance that failures are caused solely by child imperfections.

Here are some debatable guidelines:

1. *Don't try to work within the system to change it.* Work outside the system through those who have a stake in the product of the system—parents and possibly the business community.

2. *Focus the attack on the fundamental immorality and naiveté of the school's decisions.* The attack should be both concrete and should present a very concrete challenge. The attacks should point out that the people involved in the decisions have never demonstrated that they are expert teachers or trainers and that they have never been involved in a successful demonstration of their newly proposed plan. Therefore, why should anyone believe that they know what they are talking about? Why would parents sentence their children to their mindless experimentation? Why would a sensible board of education (which may exist) permit such abuse?

3. *Actively lobby for alternatives to current public schools.* Vouchers and the like have been proposed but at laughable funding levels, compared to the school's funding.

4. *Challenge the board's hands-off policy.* Board members are often oriented by a state agency in do's and don'ts. One of the don'ts is not to meddle in matters of instruction or technical aspects of what occurs within the school. This rule assumes that the board members are lay persons while the administration is composed of experts. Evidence, in the form of student performance, suggests that the administration is far from being expert. The board should, therefore, feel strongly obliged to monitor what goes on in the district, particularly with respect to instruction. (Tax dollars go to "orienting" board members in a way that prevents the board from being more than a rubber stamp for unenlightened practices.)

5. *Petition the board to involve parents in union negotiations.* These negotiations are a travesty because the children's interests

and those of the parents are almost never considered. The
negotiations center largely on the benefits and job security
teachers and aides have. The negotiations would assume a
completely different flavor if well-orchestrated parent groups
were involved to deal with such issues as: How many days per
year are the schools supposed to teach? What constitutes a
legitimate "contact day"? What are the bases for removing a
teacher or aide not on the ground of incompetence," but simply
of not performing? What are the plans for the second-graders
who cannot read? Why don't grade-level standards apply to
the school? How can a child be promoted to the fourth grade
when the child cannot read?

I am very sympathetic with teachers and aides. I feel that the
system does not recognize those who are real contributors and
doesn't help most of them learn very much about being expert
in their field. Much of what teachers are told is nothing less than
demeaning. However, the schools are not designed primarily for the
faculty and the staff. Schools are not merely sources of employment.
They are designed to instruct children. Anything that interferes with
this mission should be removed from the system.

6. *The board should be petitioned to get advice from expert teachers about pending decisions from the administration.* The board should be told how to go about finding expert teachers. (The outstanding performance of their students is the only indicator of their expertise.) These experts should report to the board on school proposals and point out aspects that seem "fishy" or inconsistent with the teachers' experiences.

7. *Irresponsible decisions by the board should be challenged.* The California 1988 reading adoptions were very discouraging, not so much because the state Department of Instruction and the board bought whole language and very soft-minded evaluation practices, but because nobody vigorously protested practices that will have an adverse effect on hundreds of thousands of children. Possibly the problem is that the public doesn't know how to challenge the board or the administration. The format of a very effective challenge involves concrete information:

a. Precisely where have you seen this practice installed so that it produces effective results?

b. Precisely where have you trained teachers so they can uniformly perform within the guidelines of this new system?

c. Where is the data that show you have achieved performance that is superior to that achieved by successful programs (not simply the administration's last unsuccessful attempt)?

d. Where are your endorsements from historically successful teachers (those whose students outperform demographic predictions)?

Typically, the administration will not be able to provide data or to answer any of the questions. That is what happened in California, for instance. On three occasions, I requested the data from the state. I received none, because the state had none, which sets the stage for the final concrete question: "By virtue of what magical formula do you expect your plan to work when you have precisely no information either that it will work or that you're able to train teachers in how to use it?"

When the concrete interrogation consistently comes to this bottom line (which it will), people will start to see that "the Emperor is as naked as a jaybird." The secret, however, is to be concrete. On levels of theory, traditionalists spin silken threads. On the level of the concrete, however, they are pathetically helpless because on that level they cannot conceal either their ignorance or their lack of concern for children.

8. *The central feature of "reform" should be performance standards for all administrators.* The standards for lower-performing schools should be expressed in terms of very detailed performance gains that the children must achieve. Unless the administrators associated with this school achieve the stated goals, they are fired.

A large number of details would have to be in place for this plan to be effective. The senior administrator would have to be provided with a sufficient amount of power to remove teachers or underling administrators who are not performing, and the terms of dismissal should be clearly specified, with the goals perfectly realizable by a person who knows how to achieve them.

If the superintendent in a district (along with all the underling administrators) accepted a contract under these conditions, there would most likely be a lot of firing within the district during the first year or two. The reason is that superintendents are incredibly naïve about what works. They don't know who to listen to or who to believe. When they try to find out, they'll probably make decisions that are very costly to their professional development.

But that's the whole idea. The single biggest problem with the current system is that the children fail, but the administrators who caused the failure by making irresponsible decisions are unaffected. They may even get a raise, while many children who failed to learn to read or who learned to hate math endure pain both now and later. The cornerstone philosophy of the schools survives only because administrators are able to "succeed" when children fail. If administrators failed when children failed (which is as it should be in any professional or quasi professional endeavor), the philosophy breaks down because the administrator is emphatically on the same side as the children. The administrator desperately wants them to succeed.

This administrator would have a very different set of priorities than the current ones in Ohio, New Jersey, or California. If a teacher was not performing, this administrator would not sit quietly by. Furthermore, this administrator would want advice from successful teachers, would be very interested in effective training, and would be generally receptive to sensible suggestions for reform.

9. *The final necessary ingredient needed to guarantee sensible reform is the establishment and strict enforcement of grade-level standards.* A large part of today's problem is that students in grades 6-12 cannot perform on the fourth-grade level in math. The writing of students in the eighth grade is largely horrible, characterized by a disregard for sentences, random punctuation and capitalization, and a low degree of continuity. If reasonable standards were established and honored for promotion, the

failures of the school would become more tightly focused. It wouldn't be possible for the fourth-grade teachers to blame the earlier teachers for not teaching children to read. Basic reading skills would be assessed at the end of the first grade with reasonable assessment devices (ones that actually showed whether the children could *read* and ones that would not permit teachers to "cheat" by "prepping" children for weeks on test items). Children who didn't pass would not go to the second grade in reading. The source of the problem would be quite evident.

Enforcement of grade-level standards would initially make most schools look pretty bad, but it would set the stage for sensible future reforms. So long as loose standards exist, sensible reform is impossible because there is no way in one year to make up for three years of poor teaching. The fourth-grade teacher who has students who perform on the first-and second-grade level cannot teach them so they will perform on the fifth-grade level at the end of the year.

If the administrators are held accountable and if grade-level standards are enforced, great reform would occur within three or four years. Children in reformed districts would make significant strides in catching up with their international peers, and the U.S. would start to accumulate a supply of brain power for the future.

For success in the 21st Century, the cornerstone philosophy and the practices that spring from the sorting-machine philosophy must be uprooted. Currently, there can be no significant reform in education because there is far less advocacy for children in school than there is for fur seals and spotted owls. There are no required "tests" for instructional programs before they are marketed, but there are for drugs and food. If administrators had a burning concern for child success, there would be uniform tests and commercial programs carrying warnings of the same order as those provided by the Surgeon General on cigarette packs. "This program may cause a high degree of failure among average and below average performers."

Although the first steps in establishing real reform may be painful, I believe that the only way to change school systems into responsible agencies is to reveal them for what they are and to help them only if they make strong, systemic commitments to serve as advocates for children.

REFERENCES

Alessi, G. (1988). Diagnosis diagnosed: A systemic reaction. *Professional School Psychology, 3,* 145-151.

Bishop, A. J. (1990). Mathematical power to the people. *Harvard Educational Review, 60,* 357-369.

Coles, G. (1978). The learning disabilities test battery: Empirical and social issues. *Harvard Educational Review, 48,* 313-40

National Council of Teachers of English, Commission on Reading (1987, November). *Report card on basal readers.* Paper presented at the NCTE Invitational Conference on the Basal Reader, Los Angeles.

National Council of Teachers of Mathematics (1989). *Curriculum and evaluation standards for school mathematics.* Reston, VA: Author.

Research Advisory Committee (1988). NCTM curriculum and evaluation standards for school mathematics: Responses from the research community. *Journal for Research in Mathematics Education, 19,* 338-344.

CHAPTER 17

Taking an alternative approach to his discussion of the importance of teacher training in the education of children, Engelmann wrote this fictional conversation as part of his Socrates series, in which Socrates engages in dialogues with educational "experts." Following the work of Plato, Engelmann deciphers problems by ruling out competing possibilities until the truth becomes evident. In this article, Engelmann presents a dialogue between Socrates and the fictional character Donald Dickerman, an executive of an organization that accredits teacher-training institutions.

Situated on the deck of a cruise ship heading to the Mediterranean, the two discuss teacher training programs, specifically examining their structure, goals, and accreditation. Dickerman explains how only five states require teacher-training institutions to be accredited by an agency recognized by the U.S. Department of Education and how there are over a hundred accreditation agencies that are not recognized. The two continue their discussion focusing on the goals and structure of an accreditation program and how to determine and teach the most necessary teaching skills. Socrates questions the validity of the accreditation agencies and the proof that they are indeed teaching the necessary skills, reinforcing Engelmann's view that the entire educational system is in need of dramatic change.

SOCRATES ON TEACHER TRAINING (2009)*
Siegfried Engelmann

Setting: Deck of cruise ship en route to the Mediterranean

Characters: Socrates and Donald Dickerman, Executive of an organization that accredits teacher-training institutions

Socrates: As I understand it, not all college teacher-training programs are accredited. How does that work?

Dickerman: It's complicated and sloppy at best. First of all, only five states require teacher-training institutions to be accredited by an agency recognized by the U.S. Department of Education. Some of the other universities choose to have their teacher-training programs accredited, but some choose not to. Until 2003 the National Council for Accreditation of Teacher Education was the only one recognized by the U.S. Department of Education. Now the feds recognize another agency, The Teacher Education Accreditation Council, which in my opinion is a sham.

Socrates: Why is that?

Dickerman: It permits colleges of education to set their own goals.

Socrates: And why do you see that provision as the problem?

Dickerman: Because most universities don't need to have accreditation for teacher training to make up their own goals. The university could simply drop the accreditation for the teacher-training program and run the program under the university's accreditation agency.

Socrates: As I understand it, not all accrediting agencies are recognized by the U.S. Department of Education.

---

* Engelmann, S. (2009). Socrates on Teacher Training. Available from http://zigsite.com/PDFs/SocratesTeacherTraining.pdf. Reprinted with permission of Siegfried Engelmann.

Dickerman: I'll say. There are over a hundred accreditation agencies that are not recognized. Some of them have impressive sounding names, like International Commission for Higher Education, World Association of Universities and Colleges, and Accrediting Council for Colleges and Schools.

Socrates: Is the main reason for being accredited that accredited programs are able to receive federal student loans and other financial assistance that are not available to non-accredited institutions?

Dickerman: Certainly that's a motivating factor, but most universities consider the main reason to be the assurance that the teacher-training program meets rigorous standards.

Socrates: And you believe that the programs you endorse deserve their accreditation and meet rigorous standards?

Dickerman: Yes, I do.

Socrates: Do people ask you why teachers are not better prepared by their college training?

Dickerman: Oh yes. We hear it and read about it all the time.

Socrates: How do you respond?

Dickerman: It depends on which aspects of training they are referring to. For instance, we work with a couple of institutions that complain about the lack of knowledge that high school math and physics teachers have. Their position is that the teachers should learn more math or physics before they enter the teacher-training program. Some other people we work with are complaining that our standards are too high and that much of the math and physics we require for high school teachers involves content that is not offered in many high schools. Also, most of them would never choose to teach mathematics.

Socrates: Let's focus only on the elementary schools. The central question I have for you is this: Why don't you limit your accreditation to institutions that use a scientific model for teaching teachers?

Dickerman: I don't know what model you're referring to.

Socrates: It's straight forward. You identify the skills that superior teachers have. You assess incoming students to determine the extent to which they have these skills. Then you set up the teacher-training program so it systematically teaches all the needed skills. Finally, you test graduating students to document that they have the various skills needed to be a superior teacher. Why don't you use that model for determining whether colleges of education are to be accredited?

Dickerman: I'm not sure I know where to begin to answer that question.

Socrates: Possibly the first step is to judge the soundness of the model. What do you think of the strategy of identifying what teachers need to be superior teachers, then systematically teaching those skills, then documenting that the skills have been mastered by the time they graduate?

Dickerman: We don't use those terms, but that's what the teacher-training program is designed to do.

Socrates: If that's the case, you should be able to give me at least a broad outline of the skills and knowledge that incoming students don't have but that superior teachers of at-risk children in elementary schools do have.

Dickerman: Indeed. The incoming students haven't learned how to meet the children's instructional needs, or how to achieve educational justice. They haven't learned about the importance of parental support, how school functions interact with the community, and the need for managing the children while meeting their emotional needs.

Socrates: Those are interesting words, but if graduates of institutions you have accredited are not proficient at teaching at-risk students effectively, there seems to be a serious contradiction somewhere. Specifically, the first-year teacher in an at-risk school typically lacks management skills, and management is one of the recurring in-service agenda items in school districts. How do you explain the fact that most graduates lack management skills?

Dickerman: Well, I'm not sure they do.

Socrates: But are you sure they don't lack these skills?

Dickerman: Personally, I think there's a range of individual differences, but on the whole, I believe that the average graduate does have a sufficient base in these skills?

Socrates: And what is your evidence base for drawing this conclusion?

Dickerman: Well, we're in touch with quite a few school districts, and they give us reports about the performance of our graduates.

Socrates: And what is your evidence that the reports correspond closely to the facts?

Dickerman: I don't have any reason not to believe the reports.

Socrates: Again, that's not relevant. What would be relevant is data that supports the accuracy of the report. Let's look at it a different way. Say you visited at-risk classrooms and observed the new teachers. How would those observations correlate with the reports you receive?

Dickerman: Well, I ... I don't know, but I think they would correspond to what the reports indicate.

Socrates: Have you ever done systematic classroom observations?

Dickerman: No, but I'm told ...

Socrates: Has your organization hired teachers whose students achieve superior performance to observe in classrooms and report specifically on the proficiency of new teachers' management skills?

Dickerman: Well, not really, but ...

Socrates: Which would give you better information, the reports of administrators you contact or those of a superior teacher who has firsthand knowledge of how to manage and who has performed systematic classroom observations?

Dickerman: I see your point, but I hesitate to conclude on the basis of a single person's observations.

Socrates: Good point. It suggests that you might need several superior teachers to observe independently and report their findings.

Dickerman: That sounds reasonable, but I think it may be beyond the scope of our role. We don't have money for such functions. Possibly the college should perform it.

Socrates: Would you say an organization that accredits institutions is like Consumer Reports, in that both organizations pass judgment on the effectiveness of something?

Dickerman: Yes, in that sense. But our goal is not to rank institutions, simply judge that their practices are sound.

Socrates: Could you imagine a consumer-reporting outfit that did not test products or services, but rather accepted anecdotal reports of unknown validity?

Dickerman: Not really.

Socrates: Well if you can appreciate what a sham such a consumer report could be, wouldn't it follow that your accrediting procedures could be as absurd?

Dickerman: I beg your pardon! We have been reviewed and recognized by the federal government as being worthy of providing valid evaluations of teacher training institutions!

Socrates: You make a good point, but it does not negate any of the problems we have discussed. Isn't it possible that the feds are unaware of the problems and have assumed that your practices are more appropriate than they really are?

Dickerman: Possibly, but you're impugning everybody's competence—recognized accrediting agencies, colleges of education, and the feds.

Socrates: If what I say is untrue, show where it is flawed.

Dickerman: You indicated that we don't concern ourselves with the skill level of the incoming student; however, we require high standards for students who are admitted to our institutions.

Socrates: By high standards do you mean that the students who are admitted have more of the skills that the successful teacher has or that they have more capacity to learn those skills?

Dickerman: More capacity. We require higher grade-point averages and we carefully review the records of all applicants. Some of our institutions select only one of three applicants.

Socrates: And am I correct in assuming that this is not simply a ritual but that you have strong correlational data to show that these students have a higher rate of being successful at teaching than the students you reject?

Dickerman: Well as I said earlier, we don't conduct such studies, but it makes common sense that students with higher overall ability to learn and who have a history of working hard in high school will do better than those who are rejected.

Socrates: Unfortunately, science is not in the business of common sense but of facts. Given that you don't even have an inventory of the skills that highly successful teachers have, and given that your curricular sequences are not specifically designed to teach these skills, how could you possibly know that you are not rejecting many students who are as likely or more likely to become highly successful than many of the ones you admit?

Dickerman: For one thing, if they don't have a strong academic background, they won't be able to pass the more-demanding courses.

Socrates: But do the students who pass these courses emerge with more of the skills an exceptional teacher has?

Dickerman: I already indicated that I don't know. But you're overlooking the fact that we have made the course of study more rigorous. Many of the institutions we accredit now require five years of study to complete the program, which includes a full year of supervised teaching. Certainly, these provisions should guarantee well-prepared teachers.

Socrates: Possibly, but the defining characteristic of an excellent teacher remains specific skills, and unless you assure that your graduates have these skills, your added rigor is simply a wish. Let me state it differently: Some who have successfully trained excellent teachers of at-risk elementary children declare that teachers can acquire all these skills in two or three years of training if the program focuses on these skills, not questionable peripheral content.

Dickerman: I totally disagree. The institution must instill a conception of teaching that frames the classroom in a broader context, one that is sensitive to students' realities and needs. Without it, we are left with a narrow recipe book and canned formulas for teaching.

Socrates: Your choice of words indeed suggests an emotional justification for your position, but Occam's razor addresses only those constructs that are logically unnecessary, regardless of emotional attachment to them. If something has no relevant function, it should be excised or at least not included until the central skills the students need have been addressed.

Dickerman: I think that kind of reasoning deprives students of important perspectives that go beyond the nuts and bolts of instruction.

Socrates: Consider a parallel situation. In the 13th century universities across Europe installed courses of study for doctors of medicine. This degree required *ten years* of rigorous, challenging work. Why didn't this extended program assure that the graduates were highly proficient practitioners?

Dickerman: I presume the answer you want is it failed because the content was flawed and didn't teach them what they needed to know. But I don't think that example is fair. Our content is not flawed.

Socrates: Did those who installed this rigorous content of the medical schools know it was flawed?

Dickerman: Of course not.

Socrates: Isn't the only basis you have for judging that its content was flawed the facts that reveal the flaws?

Dickerman: Yes.

Socrates: Is it possible that if you knew more about the skills a highly effective teacher has, you would be able to see how your conception of priorities about what should be taught is flawed?

Dickerman: Possibly, but I can't imagine an educated teacher who did not have a broad perspective of education and its role in society.

Socrates: Is teaching an art?

Dickerman: Yes, I would say definitely yes, and that's the point.

Socrates: Is medicine an art?

Dickerman: Well ...yes ... in the sense that the gifted doctor provides clever diagnoses and solutions.

Socrates: The course of study for doctors of medicine in the 13th century was also based on the belief that it was an art, which is why one of the required studies was original arts training.

Dickerman: You're kidding.

Socrates: No, and if you seriously viewed the priorities and content of your five- year program with the same skepticism that you show for original arts training, you would conclude "you're kidding" in response to many of your priorities.

Dickerman: Like what?

Socrates: Like the advertised criteria of leading colleges of education. Consider those espoused by a west-coast college of education that is consistently ranked in the top ten. Its descriptions for its unified teacher licensure program seem to be as unreasonable as original arts training. The first two standards are these:

- Prepares teachers to be aware of social and cultural influences in the classroom
- Focuses on educational justice

Dickerman: I fail to see anything unreasonable about these standards.

Socrates: Why are they so far removed from instruction?

Dickerman: I don't see that they are far removed.

Socrates: Why should teachers be aware of social and cultural influences in the classroom unless teachers are going to do something with the information?

Dickerman: I think it's assumed that the teacher is going to use them as guides for understanding how the structure of the children's families and patterns of social intercourse have shaped their attitudes. The teacher has to be sensitive to the powerful influence of their cultural and religious beliefs.

Socrates: And after the teacher has acquired this sensitivity, how is it to be used?

Dickerman: To do a better job of teaching.

Socrates: Then why doesn't the first item say, Prepares teachers to *manage* social and cultural influences in the classroom?

Dickerman: I think you're splitting hairs. Before the teacher can manage the influences, the teacher has to be aware of them.

Socrates: Indeed. But is it possible for one to be aware of these influences without having any understanding of how to manage them in the classroom?

Dickerman: Yes, that's possible, but I think it is reasonable to assume that if teachers know what the relationships are, they will know how to manage them.

Socrates: You are aware of these influences. So if I presented a specific example of cultural influences adversely affecting instruction, would you know how to solve the problem efficiently?

Dickerman: Not necessarily, but I'm not a teacher.

Socrates: Let's bestow a degree on you and declare that you are a teacher. Now do you know any more about how to do it than you did before?

Dickerman: No, but …

Socrates: Then you prove that mere awareness is not sufficient for one to manage these influences.

Dickerman: Mmmm.

Socrates: Furthermore and more relevant, wouldn't the teacher observe any specific examples of these influences in that classroom?

Dickerman: Yes, but then the teacher would have to have knowledge about how to provide solutions to these problems.

Socrates: That's the point I was trying to make. The training must provide instructional remedies.

Dickerman: Mmmm.

Socrates: The second priority the college advertises indicates that the program focuses on educational justice. How is this focus any more relevant to the teacher's skills as a teacher than original arts is to medical doctor's skills?

Dickerman: Teachers are agents of change. If they understand educational justice, they'll be able to communicate the need for it, and they'll be able to affect changes in how their students and others view educational injustice.

Socrates: Exactly what is educational justice?

Dickerman: It's a theory of justice that derives from economics. It assumes that a person's knowledge and skill level constitute an asset, that they influence the person's future earnings, lifestyle, and so forth. To be just, the educational system should be designed to distribute this asset fairly to the full range of students, not just to the advantaged students. The theory assumes that students have a role in determining their asset, but not at the primary grade level. Here, students are assumed to lack knowledge needed to make thoughtful choices. As children grow older and more skilled, they become increasingly responsible for their educational decisions.

Socrates: So, educational justice is a kind of affirmative action that is designed to insure that at-risk children acquire as much skill and knowledge as more fortunate students.

Dickerman: Correct.

Socrates: Here's a situation: A teacher has a class of 24 first-grade, at-risk children. Six of them are learning well; the rest are seriously behind in reading, math, and language. The teacher has no aide. She follows the school-mandated rules about what to teach and when. There is no language period. There are no waivers for teachers to use reading programs other than the one installed by the district. This program has a poor performance record with at-risk children. Exactly, how does this teacher go about meting out educational justice in the classroom?

Dickerman: Well, that sounds like a challenging situation.

Socrates: Yes, but would you say it is atypical?

Dickerman: In one sense. Not all teachers face this kind of challenge.

Socrates: But nearly all who work with children who desperately need educational justice do.

Dickerman: There are some things the teacher might do. Involve the parents more. Get more people in the classroom. Contact volunteers and public-service organizations, arrange with older students to partner with the younger children who are struggling. Possibly set up an after-school program...

Socrates: Is the teacher hired to engineer the means for teaching children or hired to teach?

Dickerman: Hired to teach. But in this case...

Socrates: Name one of the possibilities you listed that is the responsibility of the teacher, not of the school or the district.

Dickerman: That's hard to answer.

Socrates: If teachers in every classroom that needed educational justice had to do things like contact volunteers do you really think there would be enough volunteers to go around?

Socrates: Probably not.

Socrates: More relevant, do you think that the things you listed would significantly change the performance of the children?

Dickerman: They would certainly help.

Socrates: Where's the data supporting that claim?

Dickerman: Offhand I can't reference it, but there are a number of studies that confirm that more time on-task leads to better performance.

Socrates: Before we discuss time on-task, let's look at the problem another way. Some community groups have campaigned for educational justice. Do their recommendations target individual teachers or districts?

Dickerman: I'm not sure.

Socrates: The Coalition for Educational Justice lists some remedies. Are you familiar with them?

Dickerman: I'm familiar with the coalition but I don't remember the specifics.

Socrates: Here is a list of things the coalition assumes should be done.

- Add More Time to the School Day and Year
- Provide a Well-Rounded, College-Preparatory Curriculum for all Students
- Attract, Train and Keep the Best Teachers and Principals
- Provide Strong, Comprehensive Support for Every Child
- Put the Parents Back in Public Education

How many of those changes are under the teacher's control?

Dickerman: Possibly providing comprehensive support.

Socrates: The teachers who provide children with the skills and knowledge they need satisfy their part of comprehensive support. But do you agree that beyond this, the teacher has very little control over educational justice in the classroom?

Dickerman: Not entirely. One recommendation refers to attracting training and keeping the best teachers.

Socrates: That's not a teacher function, unless the policy calls for teachers to rate themselves.

Dickerman: Mmmm.

Socrates: The recommendations are apparently designed for action on the level of school districts and policymakers, not teachers. Note also that the recommendation to attract and train teachers assumes that teachers who are attracted need further training.

Dickerman: Yes, but that doesn't mean they need to be trained from scratch.

Socrates: True, but either way, it appears that teachers have no significant role in providing educational justice except to do the best they can within the educational framework that exists. However, if teachers are not in control of educational justice beyond their individual efforts, why would a teacher-training institution assert that it has a *focus* on educational justice?

Dickerman: Because teachers need to know about it and its manifestations in the classroom.

Socrates: How long would it take to provide smart college students, like the ones that are recruited, with information on what educational justice is and what the various recommendations are?

Dickerman: I'm not sure.

Socrates: I cannot imagine devoting more than 3 hours of class time to pretty well exhaust the topic both in the broad sociological sense and in terms of more specific classroom implications.

Dickerman: Why so little time?

Socrates: Aside from the fact that teachers have very little control over educational justice, the recommendations provided by you and by the Coalition for Educational Justice don't address *instructional causes* of the problem or *instructional solutions*, so they serve as something of a wish list.

Dickerman: How do you arrive at that conclusion?

Socrates: The core of the problem is that the teaching these children receive is not adequate for them to keep pace with more-advantaged populations. Yet, not one of the recommendations for achieving educational justice refers to *instruction,* not even in the broadest sense of installing instructional programs that have strong data of effectiveness.

Dickerman: That conclusion doesn't seem to follow at all. How can you deny that increasing the length of the school day and the school year would influence student achievement? Certainly, if the total school time were increased by several months, there would be a significant rise in performance.

Socrates: On average there would be improvement, but the solution is circuitous because it does not imply changing the instruction, just delivering poor instruction over more time with the hope that something positive will result.

Dickerman: If more time on-task is not an instructional solution, what is?

Socrates: A solution that is based on the assumption that if the time currently available in the schools is used more effectively, the rate of learning will increase, thereby reducing the performance gap between advantaged and at-risk populations.

Dickerman: Do you honestly believe that if a school used what you consider the most effective programs, it would eliminate the gap between at-risk and advantaged students?

Socrates: No, but good teachers using good material and practices can narrow the gap a lot more than poor teachers using poor material and practices for a longer period of time. Furthermore, the solution of improving the instruction is more consistent with the notion of educational justice.

Dickerman: Why is that?

Socrates: Because the teacher is the keystone of such justice, not a remote participant. The district can attain considerable justice by simply changing the teacher education and the tools they use in the current framework. Also, if the longer school day is provided only for at-risk students, the practice is more discriminatory than the solution of making better use of the available time with better teaching. Students are not punished by being subjected to a longer work day.

Dickerman: Well, let me play devil's advocate. Where is your hard data that teachers trained with what you call a scientific method are superior?

Socrates: The Follow Through study provides considerable evidence. Follow Through classrooms had either one or two aides. The Direct Instruction model, which outperformed all other models on everything measured, used all classroom aides as teachers, solely responsible for the instruction children received. In the typical first-grade classroom, the teacher taught reading. A parent aide taught language, and another taught math. Not only was the average aide rated by trainers to be as effective as the average teacher, classroom data totally confirmed the trainer rating. In fact, by the end of third grade, math and language performance of students exceeded that of reading.

Dickerman: Are you saying the parent aides outperformed the certified teachers?

Socrates: No, but they certainly performed as well, on average, and far above the average of current teachers of at-risk students.

Dickerman: Well, your report sounds suspicious. In the first place teachers are responsible for delivering instruction. I can't imagine school districts signing off on deploying aides as teachers.

Socrates: They didn't sign off. The teacher was "technically" responsible for the instruction. In practice this meant that the teacher assigned the teaching responsibilities to the aides. In extreme cases, the teacher had to present the first part of the first exercise each day, then turn the group over to the aide who actually taught the lesson. In all classrooms, however, the aides taught subjects.

Dickerman: And what made these aides so good?

Socrates: Training--preservice and in-class coaching. But it didn't take four years for both the teachers and the aides to become highly proficient. By the end of their second year teaching DI, both aides and teachers were about 90% as good as they would become after four years. Note, however, that a very small percentage of the aides would meet the entrance requirements of an average accredited college of education.

Dickerman: I'm at a loss for words. You seem to have all these insights that nobody else seems to possess. Where can I get the data you refer to?

Socrates: The technical reports submitted by Becker to the Office of Education provide training details. The Abt Follow Through final report on the performance of the Follow Through models provides descriptive statistical data.

Dickerman: Well, quite frankly, I'm skeptical.

Socrates: Skepticism is productive, so long as it doesn't serve as a prejudicial barrier to investigation.

Dickerman: What are you trying to say?

Socrates: If you're skeptical, investigate in a way that would clearly determine whether your skepticism is well grounded.

Dickerman: And how would I do that?

Socrates: Run a simple study, possibly like the one that Becker engineered in a couple of schools. He selected 16-year old students who were doing reasonably well in at-risk high schools and who expressed an interest in becoming teachers. They received high-school credit for working possibly two hours a day in primary classrooms of a neighborhood Follow Through school. They received an abbreviated version of preservice training, and were monitored in the classroom by good teachers. By the end of their senior year in high school they were rated by trainers to teach and manage as well as the better teachers and aides.

Dickerman: So you're saying that in two years these students learned more than our teacher-training interns learn in five years! I'm sorry but that sounds like a real fish tale to me.

Socrates: But it also sounds like a very cheap study that would be easy to replicate.

Dickerman: Well, I think you should talk to somebody in the study-replication business. That's certainly not me.

Socrates: But if you have healthy skepticism wouldn't it be worth your organization's time to conduct such a study?

Dickerman: I wouldn't know. I only work there, and I don't unilaterally make these kinds of decisions.

Socrates: But wouldn't you consider discussing this possibility with other decision makers in your organization?

Dickerman: No, I wouldn't. [He stands up and looks at his watch.] Listen, I'm late for lunch. But thank you for sharing your insights with me. Have a good day.

–End–

CHAPTER 18

This article examines how program adoptions and the role of publishers relate to students' success. Engelmann presents a dialogue between Socrates and the fictional character Henry Baxter, a marketing director of a leading educational publishing company. As they fly from New York to Los Angeles, the two discuss the publisher's role in the adoption of educational programs. Socrates questions the motives and possible ethical dilemmas of publishers who sell multiple programs when some have been proven to be more effective than others. Baxter explains each step of the adoption process for the programs and the rationale behind it. Socrates and Baxter debate the role of programs and instruction in a child's learning process. Through this article, Engelmann examines another complex element of the world of education, highlighting the need for all entities involved in education to adopt a common goal and philosophy to maximize the chances of success for all children.

SOCRATES ON PROGRAM ADOPTIONS (2012)[*]

Siegfried Engelmann

Scene: Plane flying from New York to LA

Characters: Socrates and Henry Baxter, marketing director of a leading educational publishing company

Socrates: In a phrase or sentence how would you describe U.S. publishing?

Baxter: A tough business, particularly with the economy where it is.

Socrates: I notice that your company markets more than one reading program for the elementary grades. Why would you have more than one program?

Baxter: To stay alive. Different districts have different philosophies, particularly with niche populations, like at-risk kids and non-English speakers. Some districts want balanced literacy, some want programs like Reading Recovery. Some want highly structured programs. If you don't have competitive programs for the various potential customers, you don't make sales. If you don't make sales, you don't stay in business very long.

Socrates: But aren't some of the programs you publish better than others?

Baxter: Sure. Some sell well; others don't perform as well as we'd like.

Socrates: I didn't mean how well they sell. I meant are some more effective at teaching students?

Baxter: If we publish them, we consider them to be effective. We have a large development and editorial division that oversees

---

[*] Engelmann, S. (2012). Socrates on Program Adoptions. Available from http://zigsite.com/PDFs/SocratesOnProgramAdoption.pdf. Reprinted with permission of Siegfried Engelmann.

programs being developed and checks on all the quality issues. If they say a program is effective, they ought to know what they're talking about.

Socrates: Do they test core programs before they are published?

Baxter (chuckles): Duh. Yes, they test core programs.

Socrates: What do they do?

Baxter: I'm not familiar with everything they do, but I know that they spend a lot of time studying how teachers respond to the material. They note exactly what teachers do. What do they look at first? What kind of comments do they make as they thumb through the material? They also have heavy-duty "product discussion seminars" where a group of teachers brainstorm the material, pointing out what they like, what they don't like, how the design might be changed to create more visual appeal, and other issues.

Socrates: This is a marketing investigation. I'm interested in how the students respond to the material.

Baxter: So are they. They ask teachers a battery of questions about what the students will like, what they might not like, and how things could be changed to have more overall appeal to the students and improve motivation.

Socrates: But this is simply their opinion and it may not be valid, particularly if teachers have only a cursory examination of the material and never actually try it out.

Baxter: We believe that teachers can judge the material. After all, they work with students and they are familiar with how students respond to different kinds of activities. Also, if they like the material, the chances are better that they may positively influence purchasing decisions.

Socrates: But why don't you test the material and get direct information on how students perform so you can know precisely which details of the program are ineffective and should be changed or dropped before the program is published?

Baxter: That might be something that's possible in Utopia, but not in the real world.

Socrates: Why not?

Baxter: Time. I gather you're not familiar with the adoption process. A quick summary is that districts and states that adopt material on a statewide basis make up a list of "standards" or criteria the new programs must comply with. Like some locusts, this comes up every seven years. We have some hints about new trends that will be emphasized by the new standards, but we don't officially receive the actual standards until 18 months before the final material is to be submitted to the state or district. Do you have any idea of what kind of scrambling and frantic activities have to occur in those 18 months?

Socrates: Tell me.

Baxter: Let's say we have to submit new reading programs for grades K through 5 or 6. That's six or seven levels of material, and there may be 10 or more components on each level. Even if we only have to revise 30% of the material we already have, you're talking about a mountain of new material. But before work begins on it, we have to make up schedules about each step and what the drop-dead deadline is for it to happen. We have to complete business cases that show bottom-line costs for each step of the development operation. Upper management must approve the expenditures before we can start anything. It usually takes weeks to figure out approximate page counts and costs. We also have to figure out how the current program will have to change to make sure we meet every standard, because if we don't, we will spend a lot of time working for nothing. We have to contract with creative houses to help us clarify what the material is to cover and what particular slant we want. Then the creative house develops the materials. Contracting with solid creative houses is not easy because all the other publishers are swarming over them to get their material in the hopper. When batches of material come back from the creative house, they go through our editorial department who checks for grammar, style, and equal representation of different groups—male, female, physically handicapped, black, brown, white. They have to make sure that none of the content promotes the taboo topics of Christianity, Christmas or political beliefs. While this is going on, the design department develops and tests new packaging, new looks, new formats. Before submission, we have to present at least roughs of the material to our sales force so they'll be up to speed. And last, but not least, the material has to be printed, which is not easy because the least expensive and reliable facilities in China or wherever are swamped. We may have to wait 6 weeks to get some of the material scheduled. The bottom line is that pre-publication editions of the material must be in the warehouse at least 60 days before the submission to states and districts. In actual practice some material may hit the warehouse 2 days before we submit it. There is not time for any field testing.

Socrates: So you never do any field testing?

Baxter: We have done some in the past for material that doesn't have to be changed much. We ran a 3-month test and another 7-month test.

Socrates: And what did you do with the results of this testing?

Baxter: The obvious. We take the data, write it up, give copies to all our sales representatives and trainers, so they'll be able to show potential purchasers that our product outperforms the competition.

Socrates: But you don't use field testing information to identify weak details of the program and to make changes in the material.

Baxter: How could we possibly do that and meet our production deadlines? Besides, you may not know this, but we are legally prohibited from conducting field tests in some states. Florida is an example. It outlawed any field testing by publishers during the 18-month period before the submission date. That's the only time we would even have information about what to field test.

Socrates: So if I understand the process, the first time new material is actually tried out with teachers and students occurs after the program has been adopted and in classrooms.

Baxter: That's an unflattering way of putting it, but yes, that's the reality of the adoption process. If we had more time, we could do more testing. But if we're going to be competitive, the unflattering truth is that we have to do a better job than competitors who are handicapped by the same rules we have to follow.

Socrates: But isn't it possible that these rules will result in poor instruction?

Baxter: Poor instruction? No. The truth is that no program will mesh perfectly with different learning styles. The people who make up the standards provide us with the formula about reaching a broader range of learning styles. Our role is to do a respectable job of creating instruction that reaches the broad segment. The rest is up to the teachers and the students.

Socrates: So you don't believe that instructional sequences can be designed so they are capable of teaching all students who have the skills needed to enter the program?

Baxter: Hell no, I don't believe that. I've got evidence in the form of my own kids that there's an enormous difference in learning styles. I have two daughters and a son. He's the youngest. The girls were learning machines through prep school. They just devoured everything the school taught (except math). Their scores on the SAT were around 780 in both reading and writing. My son, who is struggling to go through the same sequence, is a study in frustration. It's not because he doesn't try. He just doesn't have the same kind of learning wheels the girls have.

Socrates: What kind of program did they go through?

Baxter: The best that money can buy.

Socrates: So I gather your children did not go through public school.

Baxter: I live in New York and I don't have great confidence in the local public schools.

Socrates: Were the content-area programs used with your children the ones that your company publishes?

Baxter: No, the girls went through a cultural literacy program, based on E.D. Hirsh's standards. It's tough and the girls had to work hard, but my boy is trying to get through it, and he's just ...lost.

Socrates: And you believe that no program would have been successful with your boy?

Baxter: Damn right I believe it, and I've got the bills to prove it. Right now, he has a tutor every evening for one hour. She is the best, and at $135 per hour she better be the best.

Socrates: So you believe that your boy's failure is a product of his learning style and is not influenced in any way by the instruction.

Baxter: Here look. He wet the bed until he was five. He's been diagnosed as having hyperactivity, ADD, poor visual acuity, poor visual memory, and low self esteem. He couldn't learn as much about reading in three years as his sisters learned in three months. He's had to have drugs like Ritalin to calm him down. He's just a different kind of animal than his sisters. There's no comparison. And anybody who couldn't see the differences in how these kids learn or try to learn is blind.

Socrates: We're all different, and some of us learn more slowly than others. But there is strong evidence that all children in the normal range learn reading, math and other skills if the instruction is carefully designed.

Baxter: What evidence is that?

Socrates: In neighborhoods with children who typically perform below the 20th percentile, children who go through Direct Instruction reading programs score around the 50th percentile with all the children reading by the end of kindergarten.

Baxter: In the first place, I don't believe it. In the second place, if the group scores at the 50th percentile, some of them are above the 50th percentile and some are below. How do you explain the low ones?

Socrates: Individual differences in learning rate. But all of them are reading.

Baxter: Well, you'll never convince me of that.

Socrates: I can show you the data; you're the one who must decide whether it is sound. The data also shows that if the same programs are used properly with classrooms that historically perform in the 50th percentile range, they perform in the 75th percentile range, with only occasional students below the 50th percentile. If your son had been in such a classroom, he almost certainly would have performed above the 50th percentile.

Baxter: I don't know where you're getting this data, but I'm not buying it. Our kids had the best, and if Robbie has problems it's not because he hasn't had quality programs and teachers. Robbie is just Robbie and he learns the way he learns. Period!

Socrates: I understand your position. Getting back to the adoption issues, you indicated that you have the material developed through a creative house. Why do you farm out the development instead of doing it in house?

Baxter: Because it's more cost efficient this way. We can't afford a staff of writers, designers, and artists large enough to keep them on the payroll if they're only going to be needed possibly 2 out of every 7 years. The creative houses are set up so they have or contract with the people they need.

Socrates: Are all of the writers of material experienced teachers?
Baxter: I don't think so, but they're good writers, and our people read and evaluate everything they write. So, if some of them are not up to snuff, our people will know about it very quickly and work with the creative house to solve the problem.

Socrates: Are all of your editors experienced teachers?

Baxter: No, but they know what good literature is and what motivates students so they're good judges of the quality of the material.

Socrates: How do they judge what motivates students?

Baxter: They compare the offering with what they know to be good literature, clear writing, and topics that students like to read about. If there's a close match, it's good literature. If not it needs to be changed.

Socrates: Wouldn't it be more reliable to present material to students and note how well it motivates them?

Baxter: That may be true, but like I said, they are on a tight schedule and there's no room in it to run to schools and test each piece. We simply have to rely on the editors' judgment. And we have data that their judgment can't be very far off.

Socrates: What is that data?

Baxter: Program sales. Our best reading program captures 11% of the market. Our second best has 6% of the market, and our main niche program has 4%. Those are pretty damn good numbers.

Socrates: I notice that some programs have authors of high-visibility, like Marylin Adams and Isabel Beck. Are these working authors or do they just lend their names to the programs?

Baxter: I can't speak for all publishers, but when we contract with high-visibility authors, their role is to provide general directions and emphasis. They also read it and give feedback, but they don't do any of the grunt work.

Socrates: But how could their feedback lead to a superior program if their only basis for expertise comes from reading about results of research, not from the grunt work of teaching successfully or creating successful programs?

Baxter: If the author is an expert in reading, a reasonable assumption is that the author has more technical understanding than an ordinary author.

Socrates: But is that actually the case?

Baxter: I don't know that it's relevant. The program is going to meet adoption standards one way or the other. With a high-profile author, the program provides stronger evidence that it meets the standards.

Socrates: In the past and the present, the adoption standards for states and districts have been unrealistic. I recall that several years ago, one standard called for teaching fractions to kindergarten children. Currently, children in K and 1 may be required to learn very difficult phonemic awareness skills, like adding and deleting consonants. They also have to learn estimation in math, which is difficult to teach without first teaching rounding. How does your company respond to ill conceived standards?

Baxter: In a straight-forward, non-judgmental way. We try to give districts what their criteria indicate they want. If they want instruction that may strike us as being less sensible than it might be, we don't have much of a choice about what to do other than to give to them what they want. This may not be the best solution from an ideological point of view, but what's the option, to stand in the street with a protest banner and shout about poor standards? That's not going to change anything, except to cost us adoptions we could have been awarded.

Socrates: But shouldn't the system be changed so that publishers are given valid standards?

Baxter: That's not my bailiwick. I don't know how the system should be configured, and I sure don't conceive of our job as changing it. We're a publisher. We follow the rules and try to do a good job.

Socrates: Richard Feynman wrote a chapter, "Judging Books by their Covers," in which he pointed out some of the attempts publishers made to influence how he voted on their products. He indicated that representatives of one publisher not only offered to take him out for an evening of entertainment, but suggested they could get him laid if he wanted. Does your company try to influence textbook adoptions with bribery?

Baxter: If you're asking whether our sales force is authorized to get people laid, the answer is an emphatic no. If you're asking whether we try to develop a good, long-term relationship with our customers, the answer is yes, but everything is above board, no hanky panky. Some publishers lobby and probably go across the line in trying to influence members of adoption committees. Our approach is simply to view every customer as a potential long-term investment. So we try very hard to treat them as worthy individuals; we listen to what they want—professionally—and we do our level best to see that they're satisfied.

Socrates: Isn't it true that nearly every winter, larger purchasers of your material spend 4 days in Hawaii, with everything paid, and during this time there are only four short sessions, which are accompanied by food, ample refreshments, and entertainment?

Baxter: In the first place, there is nothing illegal or suspicious about the perks we provide. This is a chance for administrators to interact with others from all across the country and not only learn about some of our products, but share problems and solutions with people who face the same reality they have. Also, the setting provides us with the opportunity to get together with them, one-on-one, and learn how we might better meet their individual needs.

Socrates: And you don't feel that this treatment would influence them to purchase your products, even though they may be inferior to others?

Baxter: That's a very crude way of viewing it. In the first place we don't have "inferior products." In the second place, it's not a sin to establish customer loyalty. We treat our customers as colleagues who we are committed to serve. Of course we want them to turn to us first to meet their instructional needs. That's just good business. But understand that we do it through respect and through solid products, not through bribery or deception.

Socrates: If it is good business, it must have influence on what they buy.

Baxter: Of course it influences them, but not because we take them to nice places, but because these nice places provide us with ample opportunities to learn more about them as individuals and inform them about products that may serve their needs. It's a lot easier to talk to somebody in a comfortable setting than it is in their office while the clock is ticking.

Socrates: Earlier, I referred to the data achieved by Direct Instruction programs like *Reading Mastery.* Are you familiar with these products?

Baxter: Probably as familiar as I want to be. I understand that most administrators wouldn't consider using them because they dehumanize the teachers by having them follow scripts that tell them verbatim what to say and what to do. These programs even tell teachers when to pause when they are giving kids directions. I find that beyond insulting to the intelligence of teachers. I also understand that children are viewed not as choice makers and comprehenders, but as passive robots, who learn only by rote and who are to respond in unison whenever the teacher snaps her fingers or waves her hand. I see George Orwell written all over this method. The techniques might be appropriate for sheep or even monkeys, but not children.

Socrates: And how would you respond to data that the programs not only out-teach other programs, but motivate children because they are successful, without creating any of the ill effects suggested by your portrayal?

Baxter: I would say two things. First, I don't believe the data. Second, even if I did, I would reject Direct Instruction because I don't believe it could teach anything other than blind compliance while it snuffs out the creativity of children and their teachers.

Socrates: So even if the data showed that DI promotes smarter teachers and smarter students...

Baxter: I would say I want nothing to do with it. And I would also say that I have to read a proposal before we reach LA, so you'll have to excuse me for not continuing this conversation. But thanks for sharing your ideas.

–End–

CHAPTER 19

Responding to researchers and organizations who attempt to create "gold standards" for reviewing research, Engelmann sought to portray the dangers in creating standards for research studies that are overly restrictive and unrealistic. In this article, Engelmann presents a dialogue between Socrates and the fictional character Dr. Eugene Emry, an expert on experimental design of studies, inside Dr. Emry's office. Socrates and Emry debate the effect of gold standards on experimentation and its subsequent effect on conducting research. They discuss the importance of randomization in experiments and the problems that can arise when attempting to develop valid randomized studies in real-life settings such as schools. They also discuss contemporary practices of ignoring studies produced in earlier decades. This article critiques recent developments in education research, contending that the focus has swayed from the examination of what helps students be successful to a focus on unrealistic and unattainable "perfection" in research design.

SOCRATES ON GOLD STANDARD EXPERIMENTS (2013)*

Siegfried Engelmann

Setting: Dr. Eugene Emry's office

Characters: Socrates and Dr. Emry, expert on experimental design of educational studies.

Socrates: What Works Clearing House and agencies like the American Institute for Research reject experimental research that is more than 15 or 20 years old. What is the rational justification for this practice?

Emry: Several reasons. One is that the studies probably do not fit the current more precise analyses. Therefore, there are issues about how to interpret them. The most efficient solution is to either replicate them with more precision or simply ignore them.

Socrates: But why wouldn't the studies be addressed on a case-by-case basis to determine whether they are actually flawed?

Emry: We could do that; however, unless they provided for random assignment of experimental subjects, they would probably be rejected.

Socrates: What evidence is there that random assignment results in more valid outcomes?

Emry: Random assignment is justified on the grounds that it reduces possible confounds that could result from uncontrolled bias. It is one of the steps needed to assure that the only difference between the comparison group and the experimental group is the experimental treatment. For example, if the investigator is unaware of which individuals are assigned to the experimental and control

---

*Engelmann, S. (2013). Socrates on Gold Standard Experiments. Available from http://zigsite.com/PDFs/SocratesOnGoldStandards.pdf. Reprinted with permission of Siegfried Engelmann.

group, a possible bias is eliminated because the assignments are not directly controlled by the investigator, simply by chance.

Socrates: But how would somebody go about testing the effects of random assignment versus other reasonable methods of matching the performance of subjects in the control and experimental groups?

Emry: Possibly the best one could do would be to construct parallel experimental groups. The only difference between the two groups would be whether random assignment or some other means of assignment was used; everything else would be the same for both treatments.

Socrates: Was this method ever used?

Emry: Certainly. It was done in both medicine and education.

Socrates: And what were the results of these parallel designs?

Emry: (Chuckles.) The outcomes were probably more unusual than we would have predicted.

Socrates: Indeed. It is my understanding that the results of 500 randomized and non-randomized parallel medical studies led to two conclusions. The first was that the random assignment treatment performed higher than the other treatment on some occasions and lower on others. The second conclusion was that the differences were not predictable.

Emry: That's true, but the outcome data doesn't suggest that other assignment practices are as valid as random assignment.

Socrates: But does that same unpredictable relationship show up with educational parallel studies?

Emry: You could say that, yes. For example, comparison of randomized and non-randomized groups of high-risk males in training programs showed that differences between the parallel groups were large at times, small at times, and as the authors concluded, "Generally unpredictable."

Socrates: But in every case, you assume that the results achieved by the random-assignment groups are more valid, even though the unpredictable nature of the studies implies that some had serious confounds that were not identified, but that affected the results.

Emry: Yes, all things being equal, the random assignment would provide higher internal validity.

Socrates: The point is that all things are apparently not equal, even in studies that use random assignment and are judged to be of "gold standard" quality.

Emry: That seems to be an extreme conclusion.

Socrates: Well, let's be specific. A few years back, California spent millions to create smaller classes in the primary grades. What motivated that change?

Emry: I suppose you're referring to the Tennessee STAR study that compared class size and student performance.

Socrates: Exactly, and that study had large numbers of classrooms and used random assignment of classes. As I recall, a publication issued by the Brookings Institute observed "The STAR experiment offered convincing evidence that smaller class size can produce statistically significant and consistent, though modest, gains in student achievement." Is that an accurate statement of how the project was generally appraised by the professional community?

Emry: Yes, the study seemed very promising.

Socrates: And when California revamped grades K through 3 so classes were smaller, did the change result in statistically significant, though modest, gains in student achievement?

Emry: No. There were no gains. But there are possible reasons for this disparity. The fact that some classrooms in a school had smaller classes while others didn't could have created jealousies and concern about why some classes had fewer students. Also...

Socrates: You are confirming the point I am trying to make. Now there are possible reasons, but before the fact there were no possible reasons. So in this case, which was the most accurate predictor of a valid outcome, randomized assignment or "other unidentified factors?"

Emry: That seems to be a redundant question. But you must keep in mind that there is more to internal validity than randomized trials.

Socrates: That's exactly my point, and if the authors of the study and professional evaluators cannot identify these problems before the fact, what possible difference does it make whether random assignment was used to control what seems to be a minor contribution to internal validity?

Emry: You're creating a false dilemma.

Socrates: Not really. There is clearly an uncertainty principle that characterizes the internal validity of educational studies. Given the evidence of uncontrolled variables that affect the outcomes, isn't it possible that in some of the cases, the more valid assessment of student performance was obtained by a study that did not use randomized assignment?

Emry: From an argumentative point of view, yes. But we will never really know because we obviously have no way to compare the performance of either group to the "theoretically true performance." Therefore, we have to base our judgment on careful scrutiny of the internal validity of each study.

Socrates: I completely agree. Our agreement, however, implies that older studies should not be categorically dismissed, but should be evaluated on a case-by-case basis, with a clear understanding of the possibility that some older studies may actually be closer to the "theoretically true performance" than some later studies that are unquestioned. This is particularly the case with older studies that involved very large numbers of students, because we presumably agree that larger numbers tend to equalize irregularities that occur in smaller populations.

Emry: Your conclusion about older studies is not in accord with current thinking in the field; you're overlooking important factors in how life experiences of students have changed over the last 20 to 40 years.

Socrates: Did schools use normed tests 40 years ago?

Emry: Yes.

Socrates: Wouldn't it therefore be possible to use norms as an indicator of how current children compare to those 40 years ago?

Emry: Yes but the achievement tests are renormed as populations change.

Socrates: Have the tests been renormed so that 50th percentile today is higher or lower than it was 40 years ago?

Emry: Overall, lower.

Socrates: It would seem to follow, therefore, that older experimental studies involving at-risk students would be particularly meaningful today because a larger proportion of today's students would be in that low range. The older studies from 40 years ago that would have far less potential application today would be those that evaluated gifted students, because there would be proportionally far fewer students in that range.

Emry: Well, that's an interesting interpretation, but it doesn't consider the issue of stimulation differences between now and then.

Socrates: But doesn't learning to read and learning elementary math today require the same skills they did back then?

Emry: Well, essentially yes.

Socrates: And don't some programs achieve large gains both now and then?

Emry: Even if that were true, I'm not sure I see your point.

Socrates: These studies serve as a credibility bridge. If something works then and works now, it confirms that the older studies are probably as valid as the current ones.

Emry: But if the later studies were flawed, that formula wouldn't work.

Socrates: Let's try a different angle. In medicine, psychology and other fields, older studies are recognized. For instance, the works on memory, like memorizing a list of nonsense words, are still recognized as being valid. The U shaped curve that represents the general order of which items in the list are learned earlier and later is still valid. And what about the studies that identified the causes of scurvy and yellow fever, or the results of doctors not washing their hands before delivering babies? By your standards, these studies would have long since been discarded and Madam Curie, Semmelweis, and Salk would have been written off as oddities of the past, while education would have been officially born as a legitimate scientific endeavor around 1980. Doesn't that strike you as very inconsistent and without apparent reason?

Emry: It seems we're covering the same ground.

Socrates: Did it occur to you that only one educational approach is seriously affected by removing earlier studies?

Emry: No, it hasn't.

Socrates: As I understand it, Direct Instruction was validated by more than 50 studies that occurred before the cut-off date. No other approach has more than one or two scientific studies. Direct Instruction is also supported by more recent studies that confirm that the approach is as effective now as it was then. Some critics of the ban on referring to older studies suggest that the cut-off date was specifically designed to divest Direct Instruction of its rich data base.

Emry: That's absurd. I know of no such machinations.

Socrates: Possibly not, but I presume you do know that What Works Clearinghouse indicates that DI has virtually no evidence of effectiveness in teaching beginning reading, when in fact there are more than 100 studies that attest to DI's effectiveness in teaching reading.

Emry: You'll have to excuse me if I don't agree with your conspiracy theory.

Socrates: You seem to be denying what appears to be a clear pattern. But let's move on and look at the problem of what works from the standpoint of external validity. As I understand it, external validity is really nothing more than a rational argument about the extent to which the results of an experiment could be generalized beyond the population used in the study.

Emry: Yes, I suppose you could call it an argument.

Socrates: So what are the threats to external validity?

Emry: Well, in your terms a threat would be established by any argument that identifies a confound in the experimental procedures that could limit the generalizability of the outcomes.

Socrates: What are the unique threats to external validity in the context of what works?

Emry: I don't understand what you mean by "unique threats." The threats to external validity are aptitude-treatment interactions, pre-test effects, post-test effects, the Hawthorne..."

Socrates: Those aren't unique. The unique threats are those that have to do with the relationship between the experimental conditions and the conditions of the person who is looking for a program that works.

Emry: I'm not sure I understand.

Socrates: Let's say we are a school district that uses reading program X. We use achievement test A. The test results over the past few years show that our at-risk first graders perform in the 18th percentile at the end of the year. We want to find a better reading program. We read about a study that involves a population something like ours but with a lower percentage of blacks. The study used random assignment and is listed as meeting the gold standard of experimental design. The first-graders in the experimental group entered higher than our children but they scored considerably higher than our children at the end of the first grade. Also, the results are based on achievement test B, not A. To what extent are those results valid for us?

Emry: Assuming there are no confounds, quite valid.

Socrates: Wouldn't anything that is different between our situation and those in the experiment present a possible confound?

Emry: Yes, there are situational-specific confounds, but I'm not sure how they would apply here.

Socrates: We use achievement test A. The study used achievement test B. Is that a situational confound?

Emry: I suppose it could be if the norms for the two tests aren't the same, but you're talking a small difference if both instruments are normed.

Socrates: So you don't seriously question whether the achievement tests are valid measures of achievement.

Emry: No. If they are properly constructed, with all items having construct validity and being correlated with the total score, there is no reason to question the tests.

Socrates: But would the study have more validity or less validity for us if the study used our achievement test?

Emry: Possibly more.

Socrates: And could this confound possibly counter whatever benefits in validity were created by random assignment?

Emry: I have trouble with that conclusion. We don't know the magnitude of either variable.

Socrates: Let's try another item. The description of our hypothetical study indicated that the population in the experiment was ethnically different from ours. Couldn't that create a confound for us using the program?

Emry: Yes, I suppose so.

Socrates: So now we have two possible variables that could counter the possible benefits of random assignment.

Emry: I don't like the idea of keeping score in this manner.

Socrates: Here's another difference. The pretest performance of the students in the experiment is higher than ours. Couldn't that create a very serious confound?

Emry: I suppose you could argue that it's a confound, but I don't know about it being very serious.

Socrates: As I understand the instructional law of populations, a program that works well with lower performers will always work well with higher-performers, but I know of no data that suggest that if programs work well with higher performers, they will consistently work with lower performers.

Emry: Since I'm not familiar with studies that address this issue, I'll concede that a confound is possible.

Socrates: So on the negative side we have at least three possible confounds that should make us cautious about adopting the program, and logically these situational differences could more than offset the fact that the study used random assignment. In other words, it is not a gold-standard study for us. It might not even be a brass standard.

Emry: Mmmm.

Socrates: Do you agree that these context differences imply how we could conduct an experiment that would have gold-standard validity for our context?

Emry: I'm not sure I follow you.

Socrates: We simply design a study that avoids all the problems of external validity the reported study had. We run a trial that uses a representative sample of our at-risk students; we measure the performance on achievement test A; and we compare the results of the study to the performance of our current population. For the study to be perfectly valid for us, we wouldn't even need a comparison group, only an experimental group that uses the program we're considering adopting.

Emry: Now I think you've gone too far. You must have a concurrent comparison group if you hope to conduct a proper experimental trial.

Socrates: In terms of what you have said the comparison group is unnecessary.

Emry: What did I say that could possibly lead you to that conclusion?

Socrates: You said that you had great faith that appropriately normed instruments are reliable and valid measures of achievement. You also said that data based on our achievement test would probably be more valid for us than data on another normed test.

Emry: That's true but I don't see how those facts support the conclusion that you wouldn't need a comparison group.

Socrates: Well, let's say we have a comparison group that is perfectly representative of our at-risk population. At the end of the first- grade year, what do we do to show how well this group performed?

Emry: This question seems very elementary. We test the students, record the scores, and then analyze them to determine the gain.

Socrates: So is it fair to say that the only way we use the comparison group at the end of the experiment is to reduce these children to scores and numbers that are then analyzed?

Emry: That's an argumentative way to state it.

Socrates: Possibly. But could you describe how the data for the comparison group and the experimental group would be used differently if we didn't have a comparison group but simply made up a series of scores that are representative for our at-risk students?

Emry: There would be no difference in the calculation, but the scores are not authentic, whereas they are authentic if data are based on *actual responses.*

Socrates: True, but they are representative of our current student population. Therefore, what difference would it make if we used scores, instead of reducing live bodies into scores that we use in exactly the same way?

Emry: The procedure that you describe is not consistent with the intent of experimental trials. A real comparison is necessary.

Socrates: Really? What would we say if a real experimental group had representative scores on the pretest, but the real comparison group did not have representative pretest scores?

Emry: That the groups are not sufficiently matched.

Socrates: And what would we say if the groups were matched at pretest but the comparison group had post-test scores that were much higher than the post-test scores of our at-risk population?

Emry: Probably that there was some kind of confound, assuming that the control subjects used the same material that the rest of the population used.

Socrates: So in both conditions, if you don't like the numbers, you reject them or effectively change them through some kind of statistical "adjustment." Obviously, you feel you have license to change scores you don't like and substitute "unauthentic scores" for them. Yet, you reject the notion of having unauthentic scores for a comparison group even though these scores require no further adjustment, and are perfectly representative of our population. So is it simply an arbitrary decision on your part about when made-up scores are permissible?

Emry: No. Our scores are not made up. They are adjusted in a manner that does not jeopardize the internal validity of the study.

Socrates: Neither do the made-up scores I propose. Consider the internal validity of the study if the experimental group was perfectly representative of our at-risk population with respect to demography and scores, and the only difference in reading instruction was that the experimental group used program Z, not X. The instructional time and time of day were the same, the number of periods was the same, the experimental teachers had taught program X and obtained typical scores. How could the outcome of using program Z be caused by anything other than the program itself?

Emry: Well, since you're describing a setting in which the internal validity would be high, it would be high. But that doesn't mean that there would not be problems of external validity. There could be a novelty effect, a teacher-motivation effect and other possible confounds.

Socrates: You make an excellent point, but it is unlikely that any novelty effects would involve the students. For them the program is new, whether it is the experimental program or program X. There could be a novelty effect for the teachers, which could be estimated by having some of the other classrooms do something different, such as having visitors observe the reading period every Thursday. If these classrooms have a 2- point higher score than they had traditionally, we deduct two points from whatever score the experimental group had. In fact, however, whatever novelty effect the teacher might experience by having a new program would be more than offset by unfamiliarity with the program. Studies involving Direct Instruction teachers show that their performance improves during the first three years they teach the program.

Emry: The major problem I see with your analysis is that it does not take into account the fact that what you are describing is a norm-referenced design, which simply compares experimental scores to the norms. This design had been used somewhat in the 1970s, but has later been rejected.

Socrates: Two points. We are limiting our discussion to what works for us. In this context, the norm-referenced experiment has high internal validity. The external validity is also high because we are the ones who will use the results. The second point is that G. Kasten Tallmadge did several analyses of studies that showed good correspondence between results of true experiments with the results that would be obtained if they had only an experimental group that was referenced to the test norms.

Emry: What disturbs me is your apparent rejection of the gold standard. The standard has been established by thoughtful analysts who consider both the philosophy of science and psychology to create standards for proper experiments.

Socrates: As you may have gathered, I believe that you are depriving school districts of simple formulas that they could apply to perform experiments that do not require doing things much differently than the way they do them now. Yet, these experiments would provide quite valid information about what works in specific districts. These districts do not need random assignment or even comparison groups to perform experiments that are tailored to each district, its history, its achievement tests, and the specific details of its demography. Districts are intimidated by the aura of gold-standard "experiments" when in fact the task of discovering gold-standard information about what works is less complicated than installing a new reading program. Norm-referenced studies let districts do something constructive with their achievement test data, rather than going through the ritual of administering the tests and then filing away the results, with the hope that everybody will forget about them.

Emry: Well, I would prefer to think that the field would be much farther ahead if it conducted studies that have a sound scientific base.

Socrates: It appears however, that you are extremely selective with what you choose to recognize as scientific. For example, why would one have faith in the norms of tests, and yet fail to recognize the most obvious implication of the norms—if you have data on your students, and if this data is expressed in terms of norms, there are some contexts in which you don't need comparison groups.

Emry: I certainly don't agree with that conclusion. Our requirement for the use of randomly assigned comparison subjects is consistent with the philosophy of scientific inquiry.

Socrates: With respect to the philosophy of scientific inquiry, are you familiar with the works of Abraham Kaplan?

Emry: No.

Socrates: In 1964, he wrote *The Conduct of Inquiry.* In it, he postulated the Law of the Instrument. Are you familiar with that law?

Emry: No.

Socrates: Here's the law: "Give a small boy a hammer and he will find that everything he encounters needs pounding." I think that law describes the field's preoccupation with variables like random assignment, which are often impractical and are trivial in the overall scheme of what works.

Emry: It appears that you and I see the issues from irreconcilably different perspectives.

Socrates: I agree.

–End–

SECTION IV
RESPONDING TO CRITICISMS AND ROADBLOCKS

Engelmann's long career in education was not achieved without its roadblocks as critics from various fields questioned his theories and practices. Despite the strong demonstrations of success with his curricular programs and the soundness of his theories on education, prominent leaders in the fields of education and psychology were not convinced. Engelmann and his colleagues had to overcome a widespread belief that rigorous and/or demanding programs would be harmful to children, causing extreme anxiety, fear of school, and robot-like conformity. Yet, even though criticisms and roadblocks have persisted throughout Engelmann's career, he has continued to relentlessly pursue his goals of creating educational equality and success for all students. Engelmann's reliance on the data that showed the effectiveness of his programs supported his unyielding efforts to help all children succeed. Knowing that Direct Instruction is the most successful instruction program, he has been driven to continue to develop, extend, promote, and defend it from unfounded criticisms.

Engelmann's early criticisms of Piaget's theories on child development and learning (Chapter 3) were the beginning of a long fight to draw attention to poor systems of instruction and ineffective teaching techniques. He believed it was necessary to analyze other instructional programs to defend his programs by demonstrating how these other programs were inadequate. In some instances, Engelmann's responses to criticisms were intended to provide new perspectives on the issues discussed in order to have a greater understanding of the roots of the problems and how they can be solved. In others, he felt it was necessary to respond to maintain the integrity of Direct Instruction and protect it from outlandish claims and misinterpretation of data, which could be popularized if not directly confronted.

Apart from addressing other instructional theories and practices, Engelmann has written about the roles of education policies, education standards, and researchers who do not always promote the most effective programs. All of these entities play critical roles in the success of students and, as a result, can also lead to their failure. Throughout his career, Engelmann has demonstrated the importance of administering appropriate instruction based on the students' skills and preparing teachers to adequately communicate the content by being able to recognize skill deficits in children and respond accordingly. As important as these elements are to the success of children, they are not the only factors. Education policies and standards, and the actions that result from them, shape the education of students. To maximize the chances for success of students, all of these elements must work together under the common goal of providing the most effective instruction.

Beginning in the early 2000s, Engelmann has had an increased focus on these issues. With the greater acceptance of Direct Instruction theories and practices as well as the development of zigsite.com, Engelmann has been able to more directly address these issues and publish them in an easily accessible format. Engelmann's articles in response to these various factors provide greater insights into the mechanisms of the world of education. He has shed light on the relationships between researchers, publishers, and policymakers – how education researchers effect the promotion of academic programs, how the reviews of programs relate to state and national policies and standards, how programs are selected for implementation, and how this relates to the potential success of students. Utilizing a scientific approach once again, Engelmann has analyzed the process of education and determined how the process of learning is not solely determined in the classroom, but can be affected by forces based thousands of miles away.

The work of researchers to determine the most effective programs is essential to the promotion of programs and is a key factor in the decision making processes of states when selecting which programs to implement. States use the recommendations of researchers when establishing policies on adoption criteria for programs. Engelmann has written about how poorly executed research results in states looking for particular features of a successful program rather than if the program has documented its success with students and has data to demonstrate that success. These poor research practices create a trickle-down effect where faulty research procedures result in flawed state policies, which, in turn, create greater problems for administrators, teachers, and students. The determination of what works is not an easy question and that task cannot be taken lightly. Engelmann argues researchers must provide a more stringent analysis of programs to determine their effectiveness because their recommendations are key to the adoption of these programs and, ultimately, the success of children.

Working to bring greater attention to the complexity and disarray of the world of education Engelmann has had to defend the Direct Instruction model and the principles behind it from unfounded criticisms. Engelmann's responses were necessary to prevent the spread of flawed findings and illogical conclusions on the effectiveness of DI. He has demonstrated the effectiveness of his philosophy of learning for decades, yet researchers continued to attack it by finding ways to discredit the data, by manipulating it to create an alternative conclusion, and by making illogical conclusions about the effect of Direct Instruction.

The following publications were selected to show how Engelmann has reacted to criticisms and roadblocks throughout his career, the variety of criticisms, and the different approaches he took to respond. They include a specific response to a highly flawed study (Chapter 20) and critiques of illogical practices of educational researchers (Chapter 21), policymakers (Chapters 22 and 24), and schools of education (Chapter 23).

CHAPTER 20

When faced with criticisms he believed to be unfounded, Engelmann has scrupulously analyzed the critiques to decipher their arguments and identify their flaws. In this article, Engelmann responds to a Schweinhart and Weikart study entitled "The High/Scope Preschool Curriculum Comparison Study Through Age 23," which asserted that attendance at a Direct Instruction preschool was directly related to increased rates of antisocial behavior in late teenage and early adulthood. Engelmann determined there were many areas of concern over the design of the study and the interpretation of the data. Engelmann shows numerous errors and discrepancies in the data analysis and interpretation, and concludes that Weikart and Schweinhart's conclusions are unscientific and illogical.

RESPONSE TO "THE HIGH/SCOPE PRESCHOOL CURRICULUM COMPARISON STUDY THROUGH AGE 23" (1999)*

Siegfried Engelmann

Based on the follow up on three groups of children who had different preschool experience (Direct Instruction, High/Scope and Nursery School), Schweinhart and Weikart[1] suggest that Direct Instruction causes antisocial behavior. The follow-up, which occurred 20 years after the preschool exposure, is presented as a monograph, *Lasting Differences* (1997), and as an article in *Early Childhood Research Quarterly*, "The High/Scope Preschool Curriculum Comparison Study Through Age 23" (1997).

Most of the data that Weikart and Schweinhart present may be rejected out of hand because it is non-significant, and the only major finding that has not been presented in earlier High/Scope reports is the arrest data, which the authors declare shows that DI children had a significantly greater number of felony arrests than children in the other curriculum groups. The authors clearly implicate the preschool instructional practices as the cause of this difference. In the monograph, they write, "The increase in felony arrests might well be considered a harmful effect of providing a Direct Instruction program for young children living in poverty" (p. 66).

The problems with this conclusion are revealed only through some detective work because of the awkward way the data are presented. There were originally 68 children in the entire study —23 in DI, 22 in High/Scope, and 23 in Nursery school. Instead

---

* Engelmann, S. (1999). Response to "The High/Scope preschool curriculum comparison study through age 23." *Effective School Practices*, *17*(3), 18–23. Reprinted with permission of Siegfried Engelmann.

1 Editor's note: Schweinhart and Weikart developed the Cognitively-Oriented Curriculum Model (High/Scope Educational Research Foundation), which was one of the unsuccessful models of Project Follow Through. See chapter 12 for further information on its effectiveness.

of presenting tables with actual numbers of children, Weikart and Schweinhart convert them to percent values, which they sometimes add. Neither practice is reasonable. Adding percents sometimes yields a value that is impossible because it is not the correct percent for the actual number of subjects involved in the computation. Also, because the data tables do not indicate the number of subjects in the three curriculum models (only the total number for all), the only way to determine the actual number in each group is through inferences based on the percent values presented. The apparent reason for the percents is to make the study seem large, involving many subjects, when in fact the High/Scope sample is smaller than that of the other models and frequently has 14 or fewer subjects.

The authors attempt to establish statistically significant differences between the preschool programs. The procedures the authors use are probably inappropriate because the groups are small, and they are not well matched in number of subjects, sex, mobility, and differences in home environments. However, the data presentation has problems far more basic than those of statistical methods. The most severe problems have to do with elementary issues, such as the number of subjects actually involved in the comparison.

For the felony-arrest data, the number of subjects becomes a central issue. Of the 68 original preschool participants, 52 were reported to have been interviewed at age 23. In the monograph version of the table that deals with arrest records (Table 12, p. 53) the reported N is 68, which means that the table ostensibly reports on every subject who went through the preschool. This number assumes that the authors have data on every subject—data on whether or not each subject is still alive, data on where each resides, and data on the subject's arrest record.

In the *Early Childhood Research Quarterly* article, the reported N for the arrest-data table is 62, not 68 (Table 6, p. 133). The revised N is an admission that there are at least 6 subjects for which there is no valid arrest data.

A problem with these two tables is that both of them present some of the same percentage values, which means that not all the values are possible. If done correctly, the percentages for the subgroups would change as the Ns change. However, the two arrest tables present the same per-capita felony-arrest numbers for all three curriculum groups, and the same percentages for 1-2 arrests and 3-4 arrests. The percentages for the DI group in both tables are 22% and 17%. Both these percentages are impossible for a group of 21 subjects, which would be the size of the DI group if the total N were 62. Likewise, the Nursery School group has 4% and 13%. Both these numbers are impossible with an N of 22, which would be the size of the group in the *Early Childhood Research Quarterly* report.

The total N for the study is further complicated by the authors' description of which subjects were interviewed at age 23. The monograph's Table 3 (p. 23), which presents demographic data on the subjects, indicates that 52 subjects were interviewed. It even indicates where they were interviewed, with 75 percent of them (39 subjects) interviewed at home and the remainder (13 subjects) accounted for in a footnote (b). One irregularity with this table, however, is that there is no information about the whereabouts of three of these interviewed subjects. For the heading in the table *Current Home,* the N is indicated as 49, which means that the location of three of the interviewed subjects was unknown, even though there was a record of where the interview took place.

How is that possible? If the subjects were interviewed, how could their "home" be unknown —particularly if the classification will either be Ypsilanti, the county, the state, or outside Michigan? It seems impossible. Even if, for some incredible reason, the data on where these three subjects resided were lost, but all the other data on them were retained, the N for *Current Home* would still be 52, and the three orphans would be listed under a heading, *address unknown*. They would have been "interviewed," and therefore counted as interviewed subjects, not discarded from the group of interviewed subjects. The background-information table in the *Early Childhood Research Quarterly,* (Table 2, p. 125) also indicates that 52 subjects were interviewed, but the "home" was identified for 50 subjects, not 49. So apparently one subject was found. (A note at the bottom of the table indicates that the N for the table is 68 unless otherwise indicated. Yet, the headings for which no deviation is indicated have an N of 52).

Another irregularity with the three interviewed subjects whose home is unknown is that all of them were members of the Nursery-School group. If, in fact, only 49 subjects were interviewed, the nursery school group would not have 19 interviewed subjects, as claimed, but 16. This reduction in number attenuates the apparent "statistical" effectiveness of this group.

Some of the assertions the authors make clearly suggest that the total number interviewed was 49 and not 50 or 52. For instance, in the *Early Childhood Research Quarterly* account, the authors state, "The 19 study participants who were not interviewed were retained in the arrest records sample" (p. 127). For now, we will not consider the soundness of this procedure, merely the number of subjects not interviewed −19. If there were 19 subjects who were not interviewed and 52 who were interviewed, the total N for the study would not be 68, but 71. This total is impossible because previous records indicate that the total N for the group was 68. The only other conclusion is that the reported number of subjects interviewed (52) is false. If 19 subjects were not interviewed, the correct N for interviewed subjects is 49.

As noted above, the reported N for felony-arrest data in the monograph is 68, although the *Early Childhood Research Quarterly* account indicates that the N is 62. The argument that the authors presented for determining both Ns for felonies is tenuous. In the Monograph, they argue, "Unlike missing school records, which simply count as missing data, missing arrest records signify the absence of arrests, giving a particular study participant a score of 0 for *number of arrests*" (p. 31). This conclusion follows only if the arrest records for all the subjects are thoroughly searched. In fact, Weikart and Schweinhart searched only the records for Michigan, not those for other states. Yet, they report that they did not interview 19 subjects and did not have the address for these 19. Therefore, it seems unlikely that they know whether these subjects live in Michigan or even whether all of them are still alive. The possibilities are that they lived at least some of their adult life in Michigan or none of it in Michigan. In the former case, they could have committed some adult crimes in Michigan. For the latter, they could have committed no adult crimes in Michigan. The authors' conclusion, however, is that if there is no knowledge of where they live, they are assigned to live in Michigan.

In the *Early Childhood Research Quarterly* article, the authors present a somewhat moderated argument for establishing the total N of 62. They dropped 6 subjects from the group *that had been interviewed* because these subjects did not live in Michigan. The authors observe that "...study participants who were interviewed at age 23 in a state other than Michigan had a reduced chance of being arrested in Michigan....So...6 cases...were dropped from the sample" (p. 127).

This correction is reasonable, but it deals only with subjects who had been interviewed and who lived out of state. What about the 19 subjects who had not been interviewed and whose location was unknown? The authors argue that these subjects should be retained. Their rationale is that a search of Michigan state records resulted in percentages that are similar to percentages for the subjects whose location is known. The authors state, "Of the study participants not interviewed, 49% (8 of 19) had adult arrest records, only slightly less than the 56% (24 of 43) of the interviewed Michigan residents who had adult arrest records" (p. 127).

The argument rephrased goes something like this. "We don't know where 19 subjects reside. We have information that 8 of them committed crimes in Michigan; therefore, all of them reside in Michigan and all of the crimes they ever committed occurred in Michigan." This argument is not logically sound or even reasonable. The idea that the percentages of arrests this group achieved in Michigan is evidence that all the subjects reside in Michigan is conjecture, not fact. (Note that the authors tacitly admit that the number of subjects interviewed was only 49, not 52. They observe that there were 43 interviewed Michigan residents who had adult arrest records. If we add in the six cases interviewed in a state other than Michigan, the total for those interviewed is 49.)

A more serious problem with the arrest records for the 19 subjects not interviewed is that again, the numbers are inconsistent. The authors state that 8 of the 19 subjects not interviewed had arrest records and that the resulting percentage was 49%. In the first place the percentage for 8/19 is not 49%, but 42%. So the percentage is not as close to 56% as the authors suggest. In the second place, both percentages are contradicted by the authors' description of the resulting Ns for the three groups. The authors indicate that "1 of 4 Direct Instruction group members, 3 of 8 High/Scope group members, and 1 of 7 Nursery School members had adult arrest records" (p. 127). The description accounts for all 19 members, but it indicates that only 5 of them had adult arrest records. The resulting percentage of the 19 subjects who had adult records in Michigan was therefore not 49% or 42%, but 26%, which means that the authors' argument that the percentage of arrests for the missing 19 was the same as that for the interviewed sample is spurious. The arrest percentage for the 19 is less than half of that for the interviewed subjects, which means that if percentages are used as a basis for determining the number of the subjects assigned to live in Michigan, less than half of the subjects not interviewed live in Michigan.

A different comparison between the Michigan subsample and the entire group appears in the monograph (p. 55). Here, the authors refer to felony arrests, not to adult arrests, and they present data that purportedly demonstrates that the rate of felony arrests is substantially the same for the Michigan subset as it is for the entire group. The data actually shows a much higher rate for Michigan residents than for the others, but the numbers presented for the Nursery School group are particularly revealing. The average felony arrests for the Michigan subsample of NS is reported at 0.5, and for the entire NS group it is 0.3, which is mathematically impossible. There were 15 subjects in the Michigan subsample and (according to the authors' reckoning) 23 in the entire sample. 0.5 of 15 is 8 subjects, but 0.3 of 23 is only 7. So the authors would have us believe that part of the group had 8 felony arrests, but the entire group had only 7. Even if we assume that this is simply a rounding error and that the Michigan group had only 7 arrests, we would be faced with the obvious contradiction that the Michigan sample had a much higher rate of arrests than the non-Michigan sample –7/15 versus 0/7. A skeptic might conclude that there has been manipulation of this data.

So what is the proper total N and the Ns for the three subgroups' arrest data? If we remove the 19 not interviewed subjects and remove the subjects who were interviewed in a state other than

Michigan, the total number is 43. If we add in those 5 subjects whose address is not known but who committed crimes in Michigan, the N increases to 48. This may be the most reasonable number. It represents the group for which there is information about crimes in Michigan.

With a total N of 48, the Ns for the various subgroups would be: 18 for DI, 14 for H/S and 16 for NS. When these numbers are used, the statistically significant difference for felony arrests disappears.

Even if we disregard all these manipulations, however, the case that Weikart and Schweinhart present does not show that there were any statistically significant differences on *convictions for felonies*. The "significant" data that the authors have advertised as showing that DI promotes crime is based on "arrest" data, not on data about whether the subjects were judged to be guilty. The data reported by the authors on convictions shows that whether the total N is 68 or 62, there is no statistically significant difference between the groups on convictions for felonies. So even if the authors had the benefit of great doubt about whether there were significant differences in arrests, the data would not support the authors' assertions that DI causes more crime, only that it results in more arrests. If the authors are to make assertions about the rate at which crimes are committed, (rather than the rate at which arrests are made) the authors would need to refer to conviction data, which is something they do not always do. For instance, in a letter to the editor of the *National Review*, Schweinhart wrote, "... those who received Direct Instruction ...committed three times as many felonies...." Schweinhart's numbers are wrong and his judgment of guilt is premature.

One factor that the authors gloss over in their analysis of data is the mobility of the subjects. The goal in conducting a comparison is to be able to make statements about what caused outcome differences. Therefore, the groups that are compared should have matched experiences —except for one. The extent to which there is more than one great difference in the composition or experiences of the group is the extent to which it is not possible for us to determine which of the differences or which combination of differences accounted for the differences in outcome.

The groups in the High/Scope comparison differed in preschool experience; however, they also differed in other ways. Their gender balance was greatly different, with the High/Scope group having nearly two thirds of its participants female. The high-school experiences were greatly different. The percentages that attended Ypsilanti High School were 83% for DI, 69% for High/Scope and 39% for NS. The percentages that lived in Ypsilanti at age 23 were significantly different: 84% for DI, 64% for H/S and 44% for NS. Finally, the number of confirmed subjects within each group at age 23 is different, with DI having 18, High/Scope having only 14, and NS having 16.

The authors have a curious way of dealing with the possibility that mobility could have any effect on the outcomes. They don't address it. Instead, they make the following observation about the significant differences in mobility. "It seems unlikely that differential geographic mobility before high school is directly attributable to preschool *curriculum model;* it is probably best to treat it as a chance occurrence."

It's hard to imagine how any thoughtful person would suggest this obtuse relationship. The issue is not whether the curriculum model causes mobility; the issue is whether the differences in mobility cause differences in later arrest data. Given that pre-high school children are not usually in a position to determine whether they will move out of the city, the county, or the state, the idea that the preschool model would be related to difference in mobility is not only absurd; it displaces attention to a straw-man issue and completely ignores the very reasonable possibility that moving to a different environment may cause a difference in arrest rate, rates which are highly correlated with particular environments. The difference in mobility may therefore result in children growing up in greatly different environments, and being subjected to different pressures that relate to criminal activities. The difference in environments is a more recent possible cause than the differences in preschool curricula; the difference in environments has a longer duration and provides a more pervasive effect on the behavior of the subjects. Stated differently, the differences in environment, mobility, and sex between the curriculum groups could be used to make a far stronger case for differences in arrest data than any arguments based on preschool curricula.

Another problem with the arrest data presented by Weikart and Schweinhart is that these authors have a larger sample of subjects that show how atypical the performance of the High/Scope group is. The Perry Preschool project had a much larger number of preschool students than those involved in the High/Scope comparison study. The curriculum for the Perry Preschoolers was the same as that of the High/Scope group in the curriculum-comparison study. The estimated arrest performance of Perry Preschool subjects was quite different from that of the High/Scope children in the comparison study. In the *Early Childhood Research Quarterly* article, the authors acknowledge this difference. They write, "In the High/Scope Perry Preschool study, the estimated average felony arrests by age 23 were 0.7 for the program group and 1.5 for the no-program group" (p. 134). The reported number for the High/Scope group in the High/Scope comparison was 0.2, and DI was 0.9. It seems quite obvious that 0.2 is farther from the Perry Preschool mean of 0.7 than the DI number of 0.9 is. The DI subjects are only .2 from this mean; the High/Scope subjects are 0.7 from this mean. Given the magnitude of this difference, the authors should have recognized that their best data (the data for a larger sample of subjects) would strongly imply that the arrest rate for the small sample in the comparison study is not typical for High/Scope (and most probably not typical for N/S) but that DI performed quite similarly to the Perry Preschool program group.

The authors present a curious interpretation of the relationship between the Perry Preschool data and the DI group. They assert that "...The Direct Instruction program did not lead to more felony arrests than no preschool program would have, but neither did it lead to fewer felony arrests than no preschool program, as the other preschool programs did" (p. 134).

The felony arrests for no-program subjects and High/Scope subjects in Perry Preschool are 1.5 and 0.7 respectively. The arrests for the no-program group and DI are 1.5 and 0.9. The numbers in these comparisons contradict the assertion that the DI program did not lead to fewer felony arrests than no preschool program. If the High/Scope subjects in the Perry Preschool showed an advantage over the no-program subjects, the DI subjects likewise showed an advantage over the no-program subjects.

Note also that when the authors argued for categorizing all subjects whose address is unknown as Michigan residents, they appealed to the percentages they ostensibly discovered when searching the Michigan arrest records. They argued that if the percentages are close to those obtained for another sample, the entire group must be a Michigan group. In the case of overall program effect, they could have used a variation of the same argument, to wit: If the programs are the same, the numbers for arrests should be the same. Given that the arrest numbers are not the same for the Perry preschool High/Scope subjects and for the High/Scope group in the comparison study, the High/Scope comparison group is probably an outlier.

A final fact attenuates possible conclusions about arrest data being caused by particular preschool curricula. Eight of the original DI group and 8 of the NS groups had only one year of preschool (as four year olds) but all the High/Scope participants had two years of preschool (as 3 year olds and 4 year olds). So the duration of preschool for the groups was not well matched. Sixteen students experienced half of the preschool exposure that the other 52 experienced. If the preschool experiences caused lasting differences that manifested themselves in such outcomes as arrest rates, it would seem that the effects of the two-year program would be more pronounced than those of a one-year exposure. If no differences are observed between one-year subjects and two year subjects, the difference in preschool duration is not a possible cause in arrest rates, which means that the second year of preschool is apparently inert. But if the second year has no influence on arrest outcomes, and if there are other possible causes for explaining felony differences between the groups, it's possible that first year had no influence either. Possibly, whatever differences are observed for arrest rates are caused by differences in gender balance and place of residence.

In fact, the authors confirm that there are no differences between the one-year and two-year preschool experience. They write, "To see if the shorter preschool program influenced the curriculum group difference in felony arrests, the analysis was conducted with the subsample who attended their preschool programs for two years. In the two year subsample, the mean number of felony arrests for each of the three curriculum groups was almost exactly the same as it was in the complete arrest sample" (p. 134). This procedure is circuitous. The most straightforward comparison would be between the one-year sample and the two-year sample. It may have been that this comparison revealed some uncomfortable differences, such as the one-year subjects tending to commit more felonies than the two-year subjects. In any case, the authors suggest that the lack of difference in felony rates between the subsamples supports their case that DI causes relatively higher arrest rates and that the NS model causes lower rates. The absurdity of this logic is evident by extending their argument. If it's true that there is no difference between one and two years —both for programming the "good" attributes that occurred with the NS subjects and the "bad" that occurred with DI —would the authors predict that a subject who received only 2 weeks of DI or NS would have the same arrest rate as a two-year subject? If not, what is the "exposure time" required to program DI students to engage in activities that lead to a higher arrest rate and for NS subjects to become squeaky clean? Clearly, if length of preschool exposure is not a variable in arrest performance, either the preschool is not a principal variable in accounting for the arrest performance or we should give a serious consideration to the one-week preschool experience that programs children for life.

In summary the case Weikart and Schweinhart present falls far short of the mark of being scientific or even orderly. The numbers don't add up; the arguments are illogical; the presentation is so laced with inconsistencies that it smacks of questionable "manipulations." The most serious problem, however, is that there is no data to suggest that preschool experiences had an appreciable influence on the rate of felonies. There are too many intervening influences, too many differences between the groups and their experiences to single out the preschool as the cause for differences in felonies.

Yet, the authors proceed with confidence in identifying the preschool experience as the single cause of differences in felony arrests, despite the fact that their data comes from three woefully small groups of subjects who had begun preschool with an average IQ of 78, groups not well matched in number, in duration of preschool, in gender balance, or in pre-high school mobility. The case that Weikart and Schweinhart present lacks the endorsement of statistical significance, even with the most liberal interpretations. And their denial that influences other than the preschool could affect adult performance sets a new standard for fatalism.

Weikart and Schweinhart would like people to believe that DI is harmful. In fact, DI has *lots* of data to show that it is greatly beneficial, that it promotes a positive self image, and that it is effective in teaching children skills that permit later academic success. (See Adams & Engelmann, 1996.)

REFERENCES

Adams, G. L., & Engelmann, S. (1996). *Research on direct instruction: 25 years beyond DISTAR*. Seattle, WA: Educational Achievement Systems.

Schweinhart, L. J., & Weikart, D. P. (1997). Lasting differences: The high/scope preschool curriculum comparison study through age 23. *High/Scope Educational Research Foundation, Monograph 12.*

Schweinhart, L. J., & Weikart, D. P. (1997). The high/scope preschool curriculum comparison study through age 23. *Early Childhood Research Quarterly, 12,* 117-143.

Schweinhart, L. J. (1998, June). [Letter to the editor in reference to:] Nadler, R. (1998, June). Feature article: Failing grade. *National Review,* pp. 1-5.

CHAPTER 21

As a response to illogical reasoning by educational researchers, Engelmann's article "The Dalmatian and its Spots" examines the current state of education research and persistence of illogical reasoning. A primary focus of his concern is the practice of identifying various features of a successful program and concluding that if any program contains these features, the program will be successful. This contorted reasoning has resulted in the promotion of numerous curricular programs that have not demonstrated their success empirically, but simply have similar design features.

Engelmann argues, in his usual witty style, that just like the presence of spots on an object does not make it a Dalmatian, inclusion of a few features of a successful curricular program does not ensure that it, too, will be successful. All curricular programs are uniquely designed in terms of the content, presentation, review, and testing procedures. The nature and success of the entire program must be examined if valid recommendations are to be made. Engelmann shows how education researchers frequently conclude that a causal relationship exists, when the relationship is actually only correlational. By making this erroneous conclusion, they are not providing a thorough analysis of the available curricular programs. Instead, they are supporting inferior programs and ultimately diminishing the chances of students' success.

THE DALMATIAN AND ITS SPOTS: WHY RESEARCH-BASED RECOMMENDATIONS FAIL LOGIC 101 (2004)[*]

Siegfried Engelmann

At least part of the problem educators have in establishing effective instruction has to do with the illogical recommendations that researchers make. This illogical reasoning occurs in just about all research-based recommendations since 1985, when "Becoming a Nation of Readers" was published.

This illogical practice is the confusion about what follows from a true statement. Here's a noneducational example:

If a dog is a Dalmatian, it has spots.

Therefore, if a dog has spots, it is a Dalmatian.

The first statement is true. The second statement doesn't follow from the first.

The probable response from most readers is that nobody could be naïve enough not to recognize this flaw. English setters, some terriers, sheepdogs, and many mutts have spots. Unfortunately, there are many educational parallels to the argument that all dogs with spots are Dalmatians. Here's one:

If a beginning-reading program is highly effective, it has various features: phonics, phonemic awareness, and so on. Therefore, if a program has these features, it will be highly effective.

Current reform practices revolve around this logic, but the logic is as flawed when it refers to effective programs as it is when it refers to Dalmatians.

---

[*] Engelmann, S. (2004). The dalmatian and its spots: Why research-based recommendations fail logic 101. *Education Week, 23*(20), 34-35, 48. (Reprint available at http://zigsite.com/Dalmatian.htm). Reprinted with permission of Siegfried Engelmann.

Here's how the flawed reasoning occurs. Investigations like that of the 2000 report of the National Reading Panel start by sorting through research studies to identify specific programs that work. Call this group of programs *Dalmatians.*

Next, the investigators analyze the group of Dalmatians to identify their common features. Call each feature a *spot.* They find that the more effective beginning-reading programs have common features (phonics, phonemic awareness, decodable text, oral practice formats, and others). So they have formulated the true statement parallel to: *If a program is a Dalmatian, it has spots.* (If it is an effective program, it has the common features A through N.)

Next, investigators formulate their flawed recommendations, which assert (or imply) that if a program has phonics, phonemic awareness, decodable text, oral practice formats, and so forth, it will be highly effective. In other words, the investigators' conclusion is parallel to the conclusion, *If a dog has spots, it is a Dalmatian.*

The conclusion has no logical basis. There is a lot more to a Dalmatian than having spots, and a lot more to programs that generate superior outcomes than having the features that are specified in recommendations. The additional features would include the amount of new material introduced on each lesson, the nature of the reviews that children receive, the ways in which the program tests mastery, the number of times something is presented in a structured context before it occurs in other contexts, and many more technical details about how the material is sequenced and field-tested.

But the investigators do not simply flunk Logic 101. They set the stage for a daisy chain of illogic. Because the analysis has removed spots from Dalmatians, they are no longer Dalmatian spots, just spots. So the analysis moves from a more careful articulation of each *Dalmatian* (effective program) to an elaboration of *spots*, now freed from the constraints of the effective program.

Phonemic awareness is a spot. The analysis of the spot goes something like this: "Let's see, there are different types of phonemic-awareness activities. There's oral blending, rhyming, alliteration, segmentation, phoneme insertion, and phoneme deletion. Therefore, any combination of these activity types would meet the requirement of phonemic awareness, and the best versions of phonemic awareness would have all types."

If researchers conduct experiments to validate their notion of phonemic awareness, they typically don't compare their results with those of a highly effective program in terms of total time required and the performance outcomes. They are satisfied if their intervention results in a gain in performance on some standardized measure.

Note that the illogical formula for the design of programs would create benefits for districts that were using programs that had no spots. A program constructed from spots would probably produce results better than those of the programs the districts are using. So if a little better is what districts want, that's what the "spots first" reasoning will probably deliver. Unfortunately, the criteria become a double-edged sword that may reject truly effective programs.

The full circle of the daisy chain occurs when a state takes these "research based" recommendations and uses them as adoption criteria for programs that are supposed to be effective, but rejects a true Dalmatian because it does not meet the "standards" the state has set. For instance, a "standard" might indicate that the program had to have the full range of phonemic-awareness exercises (including activities that are ill-suited for beginning at-risk students, like phoneme deletion). If effective program X does not have *all of them*, it fails to meet a "research based" standard, even though it is highly effective and there is no evidence that the adopted programs are effective.

Not only is this type of reasoning possible, it happens with frightening regularity. For instance, California's *Ventura County Star* carried an article on March 15, 2003, titled "Effective Reading Program Must Go." A school in the district, it said, "was the only school in Ventura County and one of 109 in the state to get the citation ... for showing exemplary progress." The district was replacing the program with one that has no strong data of effectiveness, but that had been adopted by California because it meets the state "standards."

The county superintendent justified the move this way: "We want to make sure all schools are using the same curriculum. Why not something based on the standards that are going to be taught?" So in the end, the state not only identifies mutts as Dalmatians, but rejects true Dalmatians because they don't meet the state-created definition of "Dalmatians."

The solution is to excise this medieval logic and to be more straightforward about identifying *specific programs that work*, without pretending that the analysts are able to identify the full set of variables that make the program effective. This is not to say that the criteria for effective instruction are unspecifiable, only that the current standards are far from specifying them, and the effort of trying may be misplaced. If the goal is to identify programs that are effective, why not take the most direct route and simply identify them without the questionable analyses?

Another problem with "research based" recommendations is that the investigators apparently do not research the skill and capacities of the consumer of instructional practices (aside from possible verbal reports). The result is that even if their analysis disclosed all the vital characteristics of effective programs, their recommendations for using the evidence on effective instruction would completely lack research support.

For example, the April 2000 "Report of the National Reading Panel: Teaching Children to Read" discusses phonemic awareness, and the panel makes this recommendation: "There are many ways to teach [phonemic awareness] effectively. In implementing [phonemic-awareness] instruction, teachers need to evaluate the methods they use against measured success in their own students."

The assumptions are that a mix-and-match creation by the typical teacher will be effective, and that the teacher knows how to evaluate the methods he or she uses against measured success. There is no data showing that typical teachers are able to successfully combine components to make superior instruction, and none to suggest that a significant number of them have the knowledge or the resources needed to operate on the implications of "measured success," particularly if they are unaware of what a truly effective program is able to achieve. Before issuing this recommendation, a research-based panel would first have gathered data to address some practical issues:

How many years would it take for an average teacher to "discover" or "create" an excellent combination (given that it would be hard to try out more than one or two combinations a year in a classroom)? What kinds of records would be needed to make this enterprise systematic? How does this pursuit fit in with the district-adopted program and practices? Where does the teacher get the funds and the time that may be necessary to evaluate the results?

Two issues are even more serious: What concern do we have for the children who are being subjected to the teachers' experimentations, particularly if it takes the assiduous teacher years to come up with a program that has sufficient "measured success"? What in the history and demography of teachers in failed schools suggests that more than a very small percentage of them would be able to develop highly effective packages without extensive training?

The ultimate products of the National Reading Panel's spots-first logic are implications that true Dalmatians are not really Dalmatians. "[I]t is more common for phonics programs to present a fixed sequence of lessons scheduled from the beginning to the end of the school year," its report says. "In light of this, teachers need to be flexible in their phonics instruction in order to adapt it to individual student needs."

The central problem with this appraisal is that to accept it, one would have to deny that Dalmatians are Dalmatians. Highly effective programs have a fixed sequence. When the panel calls for adapting instruction to individual student needs, it is implying that the successful sequences are not successful, and that the teacher will be able to improve on the program by deviating from the program's "fixed sequence."

In fact, the highly successful program has evidence of being successful with the full range of beginning readers. This range comprises great variation in "individual student needs." The panel doesn't have to know how the program does it, but the panel must accept the evidence that the program must have successful procedures for accommodating "the needs of individual students."

Certainly, teachers would have to be trained to use the effective program to achieve individualization, but training would present specific practices that have been demonstrated to be effective and efficient. Teachers would not be encouraged to make changes in the sequence before they were very familiar with the details of the program. The training would show how to group children homogeneously, how to place them appropriately in the sequence. Groups may be started in different parts of the sequence and may be moved through the sequence at different rates, with lower performers repeating some lessons, and higher performers skimming parts of the sequence.

If the program is a Dalmatian, however, it has provisions for placing children, teaching them to mastery, and accelerating their performance. Researchers would learn a great deal about both program design and training if they studied effective programs carefully before drawing conclusions about what it takes to be a Dalmatian.

CHAPTER 22

The role and application of data have been critical in Engelmann's promotion of Direct Instruction and criticisms of inferior programs. Just as he has used data to determine if children are learning, he has always turned to data to demonstrate the effectiveness of a program in comparison to others. In this article, Engelmann argues that policymakers too often base their decisions on personal beliefs and prejudices, rather than data. Furthermore, these decisions have led to the implementation of less effective educational programs and the failure of some students in school and, later, as adults. He discusses how this is not a recent development, but has plagued the school system for decades. To stop this illogical approach to policy-making, Engelmann argues it is necessary to take a scientific approach to establishing policy, and insert people into positions of power who respect and understand data.

CHAPTER ONE, *DATA BE DAMNED* (2004)*
Siegfried Engelmann

Beginning in the 1960s, policymakers identified the failure of schools to teach at-risk students and have introduced various reforms, each designed to solve the problem, but each a fairly thorough failure. The failure of the educational system was not that research did not identify what works in teaching at-risk students, but that the facts of what works were not disseminated because they were not compatible with the educational policymakers' beliefs and prejudices. Because of policymakers' refusal to face facts, but instead to use their power to distort the facts, millions of children who became school failures and failures as citizens could have succeeded in school. The tactics that policymakers used are illustrated most emphatically by the history of compensatory education for disadvantaged children.

THE PROBLEM

Before any problem can be solved, there must be a clear identification of the problem. The problem with at-risk African Americans was outlined in great detail by the Coleman Report of 1966. Based on achievement data on 600,000 students, the report concludes that a great performance disparity existed between the at-risk black students and whites.

Part of the report compared schools of equal physical characteristics serving only African Americans with those serving whites. *The finding was that money spent on smaller classes, laboratories, counseling, higher teacher salaries, and higher teacher qualifications had no effect on academic achievement.* The irony of the finding is that proposals for higher teacher salary, higher qualifications and the like persist today.

Also, if the physical characteristics of the schools and all the other factors made no difference in performance, only two possibilities

---

* Engelmann, S. (2004). Chapter one, *Data be damned*. Unpublished book. Available from http://www.zigsite.com/AtRisk.htm. Reprinted with permission of Siegfried Engelmann.

remain. One is that black students are natively inferior to whites. The other is that the instruction blacks received was completely inadequate. Because there is no evidence of native inferiority, the second possibility should stand as a clear indictment of the educational system and a clear premise for resolutions that instruction had to improve. The most obvious and direct course of action would therefore be to search for instructional approaches and teaching techniques that had substantial evidence of increasing the achievement of blacks. If none are identified, a secondary tactic would be to commission various instructional designers and exponents of different educational strategies to create approaches and document their effectiveness. The test of effectiveness would be straight forward, an increase in achievement rates of blacks. If there is a lack of agreement about which specific instructional approaches produce the best results, the most direct response would be to set up a controlled experiment that fairly compared the approaches. No circuitry is implied by this description of the problem.

The facts of school failure imply that if there were effective practices, those responsible for the design of the instructional practices, the training of the teachers, and the management of the school lacked knowledge of them. Furthermore, all instructional programs, teacher trainers, and school management practices used in failed schools would be suspect until being vindicated by actual data. The ultimate implication is that those responsible for the design or implementation of these unsuccessful practices would not be considered experts. The outcomes they achieved-the performance level of the students—were inferior and unacceptable.

DEVIOUS SOLUTIONS TO THE PROBLEM

Educational policymakers did not pursue the direct implications of the problem. Instead they searched for circuitous ways to solve the problem, approaches that would not address the technical details of instruction and management. Instead, they searched for what amounts to non-educational magical solutions to address their educational problems.

The trick that they used was to redefine the problem. Instead of facing it as an instructional problem, they framed it as a *social problem*, rooted in history and caused by discrimination against African Americans. This solution did not require technical knowledge about teaching students or managing schools, and it completely avoided the problem of designing instruction that would accelerate the rate at which students master academic content.

By posturing the students' performance as a social issue rooted in historical inequities and segregation, the solution would now involve some form of non-segregation. Actually it would involve changing history, which is impossible. The next best thing would be to make amends.

The problem with this logic is that the issues of history beg the question about what should be done now. At the time the redefinition of the problem occurred, there were millions of black children in kindergarten, first, and second grade. How could any social agency change them without addressing their deficit in skill and knowledge and accelerating their performance of learning academic content? Changing society would certainly be effective over a long period of time. Income patterns would change, followed by changes in child-rearing practices. Within a few generations, the effects of the inequities would be erased. However, a third-grade student who reads on the level of a beginning reader needs a remedy that recognizes his problem and addresses it systematically while he is still in the third grade, not years after he is a grandfather.

Once the problem of poor performance was categorized as a social inequity, policymakers faced the practical task of how to achieve "equity." The vehicle for reform came from Thomas Pettigrew, who re-analyzed the Coleman data and discovered that black students attending mostly white schools had achievement levels much higher than those in segregated schools. Also, in these schools, the white students' performance was no worse than that of whites in segregated schools.

Policymakers used these correlations to solve the problem of poor performance without ever facing it. They confused correlation with causation and reasoned that if the black children in integrated schools performed higher, putting black children into white schools would cause them to perform as well as the blacks in integrated schools. The romantic transformation would occur because black children would bond with their white classmates, which would result in a kind of cultural exchange.

DISCRIMINATION THROUGH BUSING

Ironically, the solution was based on blatant prejudice. Policymakers apparently thought all blacks were the same, those who lived in neighborhoods that were integrated and those from the inner city. The analysis did not take into account the difference in the homes, the language models, and the other differences in child-rearing practices between integrated blacks and urban blacks. The relevant difference was that when integrated blacks entered school they were far advanced over the inner-city black in skill, knowledge, and language proficiency.

To integrate blacks and whites, decision makers turned to a completely non-educational vehicle–the bus. Inner-city children would be bused to predominantly white schools. The plan was costly, both in dollars and time. Some students would spend more than two hours a day on a bus. Even if a possibility existed that the integrated school would cause higher performance in blacks, rational decision makers would have tested the school-integration formula before committing thousands of black children to what proved to be certain failure. After all, delaying wholesale Busing three years is less damaging than gambling everything on a plan that has never been demonstrated to work.

A small-scale experiment with careful observations of the students would have revealed the inhumanity of this plan. The greatest irony of Busing is that it was conducted in the name of "equal opportunity". The contorted logic used to arrive at the conclusion that opportunities for all students were equal, assumed that most of the grades–like second and third–were really not necessary and that white children who were beginning second grade could skip both second and third grade and function in a fourth grade classroom with no problem. It apparently didn't occur to the decision makers that many of the black fourth graders performed at the beginning-second-grade level in reading, math, and language. To place them in the fourth grade of a well-performing white school would be to assume that they were able to skip second and third grades, and that the power of the integrated school would somehow provide the skills these students missed.

The fact that the policymakers and bureaucrats recognize that these grades are necessary for white children shows just how unequal the learning opportunities were for black students. Children who are placed far beyond their skill level will fail because the work is too difficult for them. Furthermore, they will be turned-off to instruction. The placement based on age, not ability, was both thoughtless and highly discriminatory. The blacks did not receive instruction that was proven to work well with lower performers.

The most tragic aspect of the decision to bus was that it would have taken decision makers only a couple of hours to secure dramatic data on just how outrageous the plan was. All they had to do was to go into a classroom of an at-risk black school, hand some of the fourth-graders fourth-grade reading material and tell them, "Read this out loud." I've seen such demonstrations provided for community workers. And I've seen tough male adults get tears in their eyes after observing the painful performance of the students and repeat, "I had no idea, I had no idea."

In 1970, a principal of a white school to which blacks were bused succinctly told me the reason for "white flight" from integrated schools. "We're supposed to have standards here. We don't do social promotions. So if I place black kids where they belong, more than 75% of them would be in special ed. If I put them in special ed, I'm a racist. If I leave them in the regular classrooms and flunk them, I'm either a racist or an ogre who doesn't understand affirmative action. So what do I do, close my eyes, sell out our standards and socially promote them, or go to another school?"

DIRECT INSTRUCTION

The equal-opportunity plan had addressed instructional issues principally through Head Start. Title 1 provided additional funds for schools to accommodate failed students, but there was no systematic compensatory education. Head Start was violently opposed to systematic instruction. It was designed to provide nutrition, a happy atmosphere, and "stimulation" for low-income preschoolers. Head Start was modeled after the traditional nursery school. There was no hard data that this format resulted in gains for inner-city blacks or even of affluent whites. Again, the policymakers did not search for programs that had data of effectiveness and fashion Head Start after these. Instead the Office of Economic Opportunity installed a playschool, even though there were other programs that had data of effectiveness.

The most effective preschool was at the University of Illinois which taught children through a method called Direct Instruction. The approach had significantly raised the IQ of black preschoolers and showed that disadvantaged four- and five-year-olds could learn beginning reading, mathematics, and a host of language skills.

This approach was not welcomed by early childhood educators or sociolinguists, who labeled it everything from an inhumane pressure cooker to a thoughtless approach that did not recognize "Black English" and tried to change healthy language patterns. Years later, in Meaningful Differences in the Everyday Experience of Young American Children, Hart and Risley vindicated the Direct Instruction practice of teaching language concepts directly. The investigators documented the differences in the exposure to concepts and language between affluent homes and those of at-risk children. The differences are enormous, amounting to hundreds of thousands of exposures per year for various language concepts. Even in 1966, however, anybody who seriously worked with at-risk children knew that they had serious language concept deficits and that any instructional effort would have to start there. If the policymakers had done something as simple as present three tasks to inner-city preschoolers, they would have quickly discovered how far behind some four-year-olds were.

The three tasks:

"Take this ball and put in on that table."
"Now take this ball and put it under the table."
"Now take this ball and hold it over the table."

For a lot of lower performing children, the ball would end up in the same place-on the table. Investigations of other language concepts would have disclosed the same order of deficiency.

Investigations later confirmed that both Busing and Head Start were disasters. A 1972 study, "The Evidence on Busing," showed that black students in Boston who were bused to white schools did not improve in performance over black students who were not bused. Head Start earned the same score as Busing. In 1968, an extensive evaluation of Head Start, the Ohio-Westinghouse Study, concluded that children going to Head Start showed no long-term cognitive gains over children who did not go to Head Start.

PROJECT FOLLOW THROUGH

Not all the policy making in the 60s was naïve. The Office of Education and the Office of Equal Opportunity performed a landmark study that showed that one approach significantly outperformed others in grades K through 3. The study began in 1968 as the largest educational experiment ever conducted, although it is all but unknown among educators-Project Follow Through-which involved over 500,000 students in more than 180 communities. Originally conceived as part of President Lyndon Johnson's War on Poverty, Follow Through was intended to maintain the gains that were achieved in Head Start (although there were no real gains). It was designed as a "horserace" among various models of instruction and was billed as the definitive experiment of what works best in teaching disadvantaged children in the primary grades. Eighteen different sponsors of educational approaches were selected by the Office of Education. Local community parent groups each selected one of these models to be implemented in their neighborhood schools.

The evaluation of Follow Through occurred in 1976, after the various sponsors had enough time to implement their models in participating sites. The project was evaluated by two independent agencies, Stanford Research Institute and Abt Associates.

One model, Direct Instruction, was the overwhelming winner. It not only taught a larger number of students than any other model (over 100,000), it also served the largest number of communities (20). Of the 18 models, DI achieved the highest scores in all academic areas and resulted in children that had the most positive self-images. The DI model's third graders achieved first place in reading, math, spelling, and language. DI placed first in urban communities and first in rural areas, first with blacks, non-English speaking children, and Native Americans. DI was also first with non-poverty students that were included in Follow Through.

DATA SUPPRESSED

With such data support, the outcome of the "horserace" would seem to be unquestioned. But not in education, as Busing and Head Start illustrate. Policymakers applied the same data-be-dammed approach to the Follow Through results that they did to Head Start and Busing. They ignore or reject data that is not consistent with their prejudices.

In 1976 the final report on Follow Through was released. It contained no information about individual models. Instead, it concluded that Follow Through failed, and therefore that compensatory education failed. No winners were recognized and no losers were identified. The reason was that all the approaches that had been strongly endorsed by districts, foundations, and the educational press had failed.

The suppression of the Follow Through data on different models was spearheaded by the Ford Foundation. Follow Through models based on the Ford Foundation's philosophy performed below the level of the children who received no Follow Through. The foundation hired Ernest House and Gene Glass to critique the embarrassing results, which were scheduled to be disseminated by the National

Institute of Education (NIE). The NIE report showed performance by model, leaving little doubt about the poor performance of sponsors who focused on discovery learning, child-centered practices, and programs that followed Piaget's logic of lavishly using manipulatives to progress from the concrete to the abstract.

More Poor Reasoning

The Glass-House critique was published in 1978 in the Harvard Educational Review and was widely read. The main argument for discrediting the Office of Education evaluation was what amounted to a simple philosophical assertion that sponsors should not be compared. So in effect, the ultimate implication was that Follow Through should not have occurred because its goal was to provide comparative data about what works best.

In addition to the Glass-House critique of Follow Through, Gene Glass wrote an appeal to NIE, indicating why the results of Follow Through should not be disseminated. He actually argued against evaluations that presented empirical evidence. He urged NIE to replace such studies with "Those emphasizing an ethnographic, principally descriptive case-study approach to enable informed choice by those involved in the program."

NIE accepted the arguments for not presenting data by model and released no comparative data, simply a statement about the aggregate performance of the models. The aggregate performance was terrible; Follow Through failed. On the whole, Follow Through students did not perform better than (or in some cases, as well as) those who did not participate in Follow Through but went through traditional Title 1 programs.

In the end, all the Follow Through models were "validated," so the status quo was maintained. If policymakers wanted to believe that inducing positive self-images would make children feel more capable of learning, nothing could contradict this fantasy. In the same way, the policymakers could continue to believe in instruction based on student choice, extensive parent involvement, discovery learning, and reading through sight-word methods, they could do so with a clear conscience. The data barrier had been removed.

Chapter 22: Chapter One, Data Be Damned (2004)

Today's Myths

Thirty years later, models that were egregious failures in Follow Through are popular, particularly High/Scope[1], an early-childhood program that had achievement levels in reading, math, and language significantly lower than those of comparable children who did not participate in Follow Through. The average third grader in this program read at the first grade level.

The suppression of Follow Through data underscores the extent to which educators redefine problems and eschew data. Head Start, Title 1, and Follow Through were prompted by facts about performance in the form of empirical data. If empirical evidence is used to identify the problem, empirical evidence is needed to show the extent to which the problem has been solved. Also, if empirical data is used to determine that the aggregate of the Follow Through models failed, why wouldn't it be used to identify the performance of the individual sponsors that contributed to the overall failure? What happened in Follow Through provides evidence that when facts are pitted against educational prejudices about what should work, prejudices prevail. Political power proved to be a lot more powerful than black power. In 2002, an informal survey of school and district administrators disclosed that less than half of them had ever heard of the Direct Instruction model, and less than one tenth of them had ever heard of Project Follow Through.

College classes on public policy, such as that conducted by Gary Klass at Illinois State University, address American Education Policy and the history of attempts to identify what works with at-risk students. But history has been altered by educational policymakers. All the high-profile studies are there, but not Follow Through or Direct Instruction. For instance, Klass's unit provides a good synopsis of the Coleman Report, the failure of Busing and Head Start, and the other major developments that led to policy change. However, Follow Through is completely missing from the outline. The only thing it has to say about compensatory education (which is what Follow Through addressed) is:

---

1 Editor's note: The High/Scope program is discussed in chapter 20.

- "Compensatory education program show no effect" (lilt.ilstu.edu/gmklass/pos232 [class notes, American Education: "What Works"]).

Interestingly, the outline contains some information about what Klass believes works. It lists questionable correlates like wearing uniforms. It also identifies one study that followed up 66 students who went through a preschool program. The suggested benefit of this program is that it resulted in less crime and fewer special-education assignments. The preschool program was High/Scope, a complete failure in Follow Through. The follow-up study Klass cites was not rigorous in design and the claims have been extensively contradicted by more sophisticated studies. Even more outrageous is that the Follow Through study had over 500,000 students, which is 7576 times the number in the High/Scope study.

So political forces in education are able to change history and shape reality not only of the unsophisticated public, but of historians as well. These political forces distort both sides of the truth by discrediting success and making failure look like success. Rather than using data that addresses the problem, the political forces in education prefer what they call ethnographic, case-history data, which amounts to little more than anecdotal accounts, with no clear rules about how to use them. Do we judge a program to be better than another if it has more anecdotes or if it has "more convincing" anecdotes? Or do we simply count them? It certainly would not be very fair for a model that serves 100,000 children to be judged better than a model serving 5,000 children because the larger model has more "good anecdotes." And wouldn't it be reasonable to secure anecdotes from all the students? (How much do you like math? How good are you at math? Etc.)

Current Trends

The disregard for data provided by the history of compensatory education is the rule, not the exception, in education. The National Council of Teachers of Mathematics (NCTM) may hold the title of promoting the most paradoxical anti-scientific and anti-intellectual practices. The NCTM formally rejected empirical studies that showed the effects of different teaching methods. Its basis for this rejection: "The results were disappointing." Imagine an organization that is supposed to understand math, which includes statistics, asserts in effect that mathematical truth is falsity.

The NCTM has supported a long list of failed practices. At the top of the list is "discovery learning." It doesn't seem to matter how many times or how thoroughly empirical evidence shows that this practice is ineffective.

The NCTM is not the only professional organization of educators that promotes un-scientific notions. Its cousin, the National Council of Teachers of English, has staunchly supported failed practices such as the Whole Language approach to teaching reading, an unsystematic approach that liberally uses "literature" to teach reading in the beginning grades. These practices and others the NCTE has promoted have been shown to be ineffective, particularly with at-risk populations. Several Follow Through models used a version of Whole Language. They completely failed.

The International Reading Association (IRA) has an almost unblemished record of promoting approaches that have no evidential base. In general, the IRA supports the mottoes of progressive education, such as John Dewey's notion of "Learn by doing and do by doing," which disdain systematic preparation in subjects like reading and instead simply introduce reading, with the idea that children would learn to read if they read.

The IRA endorses Whole Language. It argues that language is learned naturally through interactions that are not highly structured. Reading is language. Therefore, reading should be learned through the same kind of casual interactions that succeed with language learning. It doesn't work.

Science Organizations Opposed to Science

Some of the more ironic rejections of data and science come from organizations that serve science teachers. An example is the National Science Teachers Association, which has a membership of 55,000 science professionals including science and math teachers. Although the association recognizes science in other fields, it does not apply scientific principles or logic to the teaching of science. This unusual prejudice was revealed in 2004 when California delivered a serious blow to one of the organization's sacred cows-teaching science through heavy doses of hands-on experiments. One of the criteria California proposed for evaluating K-6 science instructional materials limited the amount of "hands-on" activities... Comprising no more than 20 to 25 percent of science instructional time."

This limitation is reasonable because there is no empirical evidence that a heavy diet of hands-on activities is a worthwhile use of time, particularly for at-risk populations. The use of hands-on activities is based on problematic theories about how children learn. According to the theories, work with manipulative or hands-on material is supposed to be the basis for children internalizing the content and formulating concepts. The primary exponent of this philosophy was Jean Piaget. In Follow Through, four models applied Piaget's principles in their design. All of these models failed.

A curious response to the proposed California criteria came in the form of a letter to each state board member, with carbons to everyone from the Secretary of Education to Governor Arnold Schwarzenegger, pleading the case for hands-on material. The response was curious because it was signed not only by the executive director of the National Science Teachers Association, but also by the president of the National Academy of Sciences, Dr. Bruce Alberts. Understand that the Academy is among the most prestigious organizations in the world, composed exclusively of the most distinguished scientists in each field. A scientist doesn't simply "join" the academy. Membership is through invitation only.

So this response from such a prestigious group should carry the emphatic sanction of the science community and should be based on carefully reasoned research evidence and sound logic. In fact, the response was not only naïve, but was largely based on anti-scientific reasoning.

In response to the criterion that limited use of hands-on approaches, the petitioners stated, "teachers need to be able to make the decision about which instructional strategy will best teach a particular concept. If a teacher needs to present the concept through instruction that is 50 or 75 percent hands-on, the teacher must have the flexibility, and the resources to do so." The idea that teachers know which instructional strategy will best teach a particular concept is richly contradicted by research. It is scientifically illogical. If teachers make independent decisions about what's best, the effectiveness of the outcomes will tend to follow a normal distribution curve. On such a curve only a small but arbitrary percentage (possibly 5%) will identify or create what is best (based on performance of children). The rest will range from second best to Nth best. So the slogan and the assumption that the "average teacher" will identify what's best, is fanciful. Consider the un-addressed question. If a teacher fails to teach content that has been demonstrated to be teachable, how can the teacher "know best"?

The petitioners used the "teacher knows best" argument to discredit another California criterion. They wrote, "Teachers are the experts in how and when to teach particular materials, not textbook publishers. The criterion denigrates the ability of teachers to exercise their judgment about how best to meet the needs of their students." The rhetoric may be appealing but is quite antiscientific. Of the Follow Through models, the Direct Instruction model provided the greatest amount of control over what the teachers did and exactly how they did it. This model produced the best results. So the same teacher who would fail with "teacher-choice practices" would be able to succeed with the practices and sequences specified by Direct Instruction programs, even though the decisions about what to do or how to do it were dictated by the program, not the teacher's intuition.

The petitioners' final attack challenges whether Direct Instruction is superior to other approaches. "There is no research to suggest that Direct Instruction is superior to any other instructional strategies." According to this assessment, not only had Follow Through been erased from the record; so had more than 50 other studies involving Direct Instruction in a variety of content areas. For example, a school in Baltimore was the lowest and most notorious school in the district when it initiated the Direct Instruction model in 1997. The school was City Springs Elementary, and its ranking was 117th of 117 elementary schools. In 2003, City Springs ranked overall first in the district. A transformation of this magnitude has never been recorded by any other approach.

More relevant to science instruction was a comparison of middle school students who were taught the basic principles of chemistry and energy. One group was composed of failed students in a special class. The other group consisted of advanced-placement students. The students in a special class went through a Direct Instruction program. The advanced-placement students went through a more traditional, experimental approach. On a posttest that presented items and problems involving basic principles of chemistry and energy, the failed students performed as well as the AP students.

Although Alberts's motives in protesting hands-on instruction are not known, a possibility is that the National Science Teachers Association promotes a program that Alberts originated, City Science. The program is expressly designed for teaching science to "urban students" in elementary school and beyond, and the program is clearly based on the philosophy of hands-on manipulations. It is apparently well intentioned but presents no empirical data to suggest that this approach is successful in improving student performance, or that it would perform as well as a Direct Instruction approach.

CONVENTIONAL WISDOM PREVAILS

The fact that non-scientific reasoning and rejection of data extend to science organizations implies that education is fundamentally different from other enterprises, in which decisions are not circumscribed by data or shaped by logic. The fact that policymakers hold degrees, and show all the signs of being well educated and well intentioned provides absolutely no guarantee that what they recommend will be based on evidence of effectiveness or any knowledge of what works. Certainly not every decision maker in education is a bozo. The problem is that there are few clues from what they argue or how they argue that suggest whether what they embrace is ethereal or solid.

According to Grover Whitehurst, Director of the Institute of Education Sciences, Assistant Secretary of Education, only about

10% of current educational decisions are based on evidence of effectiveness. That means that the probability is about 10 to 1 that the opinions of randomly selected educational decision makers, whether they are in charitable foundations, schools, or state governments, are based on folk psychology and "traditional wisdom." Opinions of these people are not the stuff from which productive educational reform will emerge. If we are committed to serious educational reform, particularly for at-risk populations, the first step we must take is to recognize that educational decision makers lack the skill, knowledge, and respect for data that the task demands. They are probably uninformed about what actually occurs in classrooms of urban schools, and they probably hold strong antiscientific beliefs that lead to poor judgments about what is "best for the children." They are not the sole cause of the problems, but they certainly are not the hope for the solution, so long as they remain uninformed.

In summary, the problem is this:

> The educational system fails because it has a disregard for data. This disregard is nearly universal, even among those who cite data. The field's nonscientific stance pre-empts it from shaping educational practices by using the techniques that characterize scientific or systematic endeavors.

The solution is implied by the problem:

> Install people who respect and understand data.

In other words, put the kids first and use data on their performance as the ultimate yardstick of what actually works.

REFERENCES

Alberts, B. & Wheeler, G. (2004, March 4). Letter to California State Board of Education members. Retrieved January 14, 2005 from http://science.nsta.org/nstaexpress/letterto-califfromgerry.htm

Armor, D. J. (1972). The Evidence of Busing. *Public Interest*, 28, 90-128.

Coleman, J. (1966). *Equality of educational opportunity*. Washington, DC: United States Government Printing Office.

Dewey, J. (1916). *Democracy and education*. An introduction to the philosophy of education (1966 edn.), New York: Free Press.

Ed. gov *Education Innovator* (2003). City Springs Elementary School: Fulfilling the *No Child Left Behind* promise. Author. Aug. 18, 2003, Number 25.

Hart, B., & Risley, T. R. (1995). *Meaningful differences in the everyday experience of young American children.* Baltimore, MD: Brookes Publishing.

House, E. R., Glass, G. V., McLean, L. F., & Walker, D. F. (1978). No Simple Answer: Critique of the "Follow Through" evaluation. Harvard Educational Review, 28(2), 128-160.

Klass, G. M., Political Science 232 Course information. Retrieved December, 2004 from http://lilt.ilstu.edu/gmklass/pos232

Pettigrew, T. F. (1975). *Racial-discrimination in the United States.* New York: Harper & Row.

Research Advisory Committee of the National Council of Teachers of Mathematics (1995). Research and practice. *Journal for Research in Mathematics Education,* 26(4), 300-303.

Stallings, J. (1975). *Implementation and child effects of teaching practices in Follow Through classrooms.* Monographs of the Society for Research in Child Development, 40 (7-8, Serial No. 163).

Stebbins, L. B., St. Pierre, R. G., Proper, E. C., Anderson, R. B., & Cerva, T. R. (1977). *Education as experimentation: A planned variation model (Vol. IV-A: An evaluation of Follow Through).* Cambridge, MA: Abt Associates.

Westinghouse Learning Corporation (1969). *The impact of Head Start: An evaluation of the effects of Head Start on children's cognitive and affective development.* Athens, OH: Ohio University.

Whitehurst, G. J. (2002). Address given to the Council of Scientific Society Presidents December 9, 2002. Washington, DC.

CHAPTER 23

The state standards and policies that govern the adoption of curricular programs are not only affected by the recommendations of education researchers, but also by the professional standards for states and school districts. Engelmann addresses this issue by comparing the research protocol required for graduate students and the professional standards for states and school districts. He argues that all of these entities experiment on students and thus should be held to the same standards and legal requirements. Yet, there are no standards governing the experimentation of states and school districts. Engelmann discusses specific examples of failed experimentation by the state in education reform and its consequences. He explains how education reform would have been more carefully and strategically implemented if the state used the same ethical standards required of graduate students and how this would have led to the greater success of all children. Not only does Engelmann identify the problem with this element in the world of education, but, as in other areas, he supplies a blueprint to achieve real educational reform.

PROFESSIONAL STANDARDS IN EDUCATION (2004)*

Siegfried Engelmann

A graduate student who does a research study involving high-risk subjects who go through non-traditional untried methods for teaching beginning reading has to justify the proposal and follow established protocol for research on human subjects. The student is to provide a rationale that describes why he thinks the method will work. He also has to describe possible benefits for the subjects, a backup plan to be used if the subjects are experiencing stress or failure that may affect their later learning, and indicators that are to be used to determine if children are not progressing as anticipated. The student must make thorough disclosures to the parents of the subjects, explaining risks, and possible compensation, and indicating who will respond to questions or problems. Finally, the student must obtain parental permission.

Ironically, a state or a school district that adopts the same untested program the graduate student uses is not required to follow any of the protocol and rules of conduct that govern the graduate student's procedures. Yet, both are experimenting with children.

No, you say. The state adoption is not research. Yes it is.

If both the graduate student and the state experiment with children and both derive the same knowledge from the outcomes of the experiment, both are doing research. The state is simply doing it in a clandestine manner, calls it something other than research, and charges for it.

One *Webster's* definition of an experiment is, "any action or process undertaken to discover something not yet known or to demonstrate something known." According to this definition, the state adopts programs and teaching methods on the assumption that they will work well with children; however, at the time of the adoption, the state has no data that programs or practices will work well.

---

* Engelmann, S. (2004). Professional Standards in Education. Available from http://zigsite.com/Standards.htm. Reprinted with permission of Siegfried Engelmann.

If the state later receives data on the effectiveness of the approach, and if these data are generated by the students who went through the program or practice, the children were experimental subjects whose data generates knowledge of the approach's effectiveness. If the results are positive, confirming the decision-makers' expectations, the research was "a process undertaken to demonstrate something known." If the results are negative or null (which is nearly always the case) the research functioned as "a process undertaken to discover something not yet known." In either case, it was an experiment, even though it was labeled an advancement, a breakthrough, or a reform. Functionally, the name means little. If the "reform" was the basis for the field obtaining convincing documentation that the intervention was ineffective, the intervention served a research function. In fact, if it failed, the research function would be one of the few positive results of the intervention.

The problem of experimentation by states and districts is documented by an uninterrupted sequence of failed reforms, starting with the busing of inner city blacks and the new math in the 1960's, continuing through the open-school concept, the down-with-science humanism, the back to basics resolution, the teaching of reading through literature and whole language, and back to phonics. Whole language is a good example of failed reforms. The central argument that supports the approach holds that language is a whole. Reading is part of language. So reading should be governed by other facts we know about language. We see that language is effectively learned through situations in which language is *used*, not explicitly taught. Therefore, reading should be learned by actually reading, not being taught how to read. To many educators, this argument, although guilty of part-whole confusion, apparently seemed sound.

To support this argument, promoters of whole language presented what they assume is evidence. The evidence was often not of an experimental nature but consisted of analytical "research," possibly showing something about the structure of language, the structure of words, and obliquely relevant information, such as the fact that New Zealand is the most literate country in the world. The argument:

New Zealand is the most literate country in the world.

> New Zealand uses whole language.
> Therefore, our country will become as literate as New Zealand if we use whole language.

Of course, the conclusion doesn't follow from the evidence. We don't know whether whole language caused this remarkable performance, which means that there is no data about how students in New Zealand perform with a program known to produce superior results in the US.

Following the lead of Honig[1] in California, states and districts installed whole language wholesale. In California, schools were monitored to make sure they complied with the whole language mandates and discarded whatever reading programs were in use, without regard to the performance data of children. At least three districts in California that had exceptional results using Direct Instruction were forced to drop the DI and install whole language.

Within months after the implementation of whole language, even teachers who believed the hype and were trying to use whole language as it is specified observed that a large percentage of children were not learning to read. At the end of the first grade year, achievement test scores were significantly down.

In response to the performance of children, the states and districts issued caveats that had not been disclosed as part of the initial projections. The main assertion was that although children may be far behind at the end of kindergarten and first grade, they will catch up by the fourth grade. Exactly where the proponents of the reform got this information is not obvious. What is obvious is that many teachers told many parents, "Oh don't worry. He'll catch up by the fourth grade."

In the end, enough performance data was accumulated to discredit whole language completely. The data came in various forms, but mainly from achievement test performance of children in the early grades, and in Grade 4 (which revealed that the whole-language promise was a fabrication). Data also came from the

---

1 Editor's note: Bill Honig was the California State Superintendent of Public Instruction from 1983 to 1993.

rising number of referrals to special classes and from the number of retentions.

Perhaps as curious as the irresponsibility of state and district decision makers in installing and maintaining failed practices is what happens to them after the failed reform.

Following the disclosure of the reform's performance, decision makers do not say anything to the effect, "We screwed up. We are ashamed of ourselves for launching into a reform without sufficient data. We will never do it again." Instead, they presented a new reform based on their new insights about how children learn or about the structure of reading—as if science has just uncovered relevant data about the brain, learning, or human development; however, the new reform may have no more basis in data than the one it superseded. (After whole language, Honig became a phonics advocate, but without great contrition over the harm whole language did.) Furthermore, the administrators who engineer egregious failure do not have diminished status, but may actually go to a new district at a higher salary.

ETHICAL STANDARDS

Most states and districts abandoned whole language and placed serious restrictions on using "literature" as the primary vehicle for teaching reading in the early grades. However, the system has not been reformed so that it is consistent with our commitments both to science and children. Obviously, the research data could have been obtained far less painfully through smaller-scale studies conducted in accordance with the protocol the graduate student must follow.

This protocol is spelled out in detail in the American Psychological Association (APA) standards for "Ethical Principles of Psychologists and Code of Conduct." The Ethical Standards articulate proper precautions and requirements that are implied by the power that psychologists may use or misuse. Some standards are applicable to states and districts that conduct educational experiments that are billed as reforms. The Standards are not only easily adapted to the kind of experiments that states and districts perform;

they seem to be more necessary here than they are with small-scale experiments if we consider the "greater good."

Possibly, the key standard in the APA code is 3.04, which expresses the goal of "avoiding harm."

3.04 Avoiding Harm: *Psychologists take reasonable steps to avoid harming their clients/patients, students, supervisees, research participants, organizational clients, and others with whom they work, and to minimize harm where it is foreseeable and unavoidable.* (2002)

In the case of reforms, the harm is foreseeable and possibly unavoidable. To conduct research that provides evidence that whole language is not effective, some human subjects are required, and their failure must be documented. But the harm would be *minimized* by limiting the number of subjects and by terminating the treatment as soon as it became apparent that children were progressing below projections (which would mean long before the fourth grade or even the end of the first grade). The experiment would produce limited harm. Following clear signals of failure, the failing children could be placed in compensatory programs known to be effective. The state or district does not need to subject the entire school population to an experimental treatment for seven years (which is the period of adopting instructional programs in many states). The state or district does not need documentation of students who begin in K and go through the sixth grade before terminating the experiment. A much smaller sample of students and shorter experimental treatment would be able to generate data that is adequate.

A related issue is that if causing harm is unavoidable, is the "compensatory instruction" adequate compensation even for the minimized harm? A strong argument could be made that injured subjects should receive additional compensation. In any case there should be some form of disclosure to the subjects (or their parents) before the experiment. Section 8 of the APA Ethic's Code provides guidelines that address this issue and others.

Standard 8.01 is institutional approval. According to the standard, psychologists are to "conduct the research in accordance with the approved research protocol." Once states and districts acknowledge that their reforms function as research for some populations, the need for protocol logically follows.

Standard 8.02 presents guidelines for situations in which consent is required and outlines the features of the disclosers as well as the provisions for subjects to decline or withdraw from the research. The participants or their parents are to be informed of the purpose of the research and possible factors that may affect willingness to participate—potential risks, possible adverse effects, and possible positive benefits. Participants or parents also receive information about who will answer questions about details of the research or outcomes. Participants are to receive information about possible treatment alternatives and about compensation or costs.

Standard 8.05 describes conditions that do not require informed consent for research. One condition is "the study of normal educational practices, curricula or classroom management methods conducted in educational settings." This condition is prefaced by qualification that the "research would not reasonably be assumed to create distress or harm." That condition is not met by adoptions of significant reform measures or the adoption of new instructional material or practices that have no evidence of effectiveness. These are high-risk enterprises for at least the lower half of the school population.

Standard 8.07, Deception in Research, indicates that "psychologists do not deceive prospective participants about research that is reasonably expected to cause…severe emotional distress." For a small-scale educational experiment involving a discovery math program, the researcher may not know the extent to which distress is anticipated. For a larger population, however, the fact that there is no hard data on emotional distress presents a serious problem. In absence of data, we can assume that adverse consequences are probable if the failure rate is high. Failure in learning to read or do math causes strong emotional reactions in most students. So if a district were to install a new math program that featured discovery, the district would have to disclose that (a) it doesn't know the extent to which students will fail but (b) some who fail will have strong emotional reactions to the failure.

Standard 8.09 refers to humane care and use of animals in research. One provision is that "psychologists trained in research methods and experienced in the care of laboratory animals supervise all procedures involving animals and are responsible for ensuring appropriate consideration of their comfort, health, and humane treatment." Also, "psychologists make reasonable efforts to minimize the discomfort...of animal subjects...Psychologists use a procedure subjecting animals to pain, stress...only when an alternative procedure is unavailable."

Obviously, children are different from laboratory animals. For research purposes, however, it would seem reasonable to assume that the subjects' pain and stress would be monitored by an experienced person who supervises all procedures involving the experimental children, and who is responsible for ensuring appropriate consideration of their treatment.

Standard 10.09 refers to therapy; however, it is relevant to the kind of experimentation that school districts and states conduct:

Psychologists terminate therapy when it becomes reasonably clear that the client...is not likely to benefit, or is being harmed by continued service.

Because districts and states do not have counterparts for any of these requirements, they have no form of advocacy for the children who serve as subjects of their experimentation. The state or district does not provide disclosure of possible risks. It does not carefully monitor the installations of the approaches. It does not have anybody assigned to observe in the field and play devil's advocate. Nor does it terminate obviously poor approaches when it becomes reasonably clear that the children are being harmed.

TEXTBOOK ADOPTIONS

Textbook adoptions are prime exemplars of experimenting with children. Instructional products, particularly those for the primary grades, are extremely important because they account for a large part of the variance in student performance. A well-designed instructional program with demonstrated effectiveness may produce an effect size that is more than a standard deviation above that of a poorly designed instructional sequence. (Adams & Engelmann, 1996).

Textbooks for beginning reading, math and all other subjects in the elementary grades are virtually never evaluated on the basis of effectiveness with students before they are adopted. Furthermore, there are no standards of effectiveness, and worse, no requirements for publishers to first try out the material with children, secure data on effectiveness, and disclose the results, which means that publishers create programs for use in schools without any data on how they work. This would be like mass producing an automobile without ever testing the design before launching a sales campaign. The first time any children see the program for a new approach is *after it has been adopted.* And the first time any performance data is generated by the program is usually a year or more after it has been in use in classrooms.

The publishers' attitude about creating instructional material may seem cavalier, but they are not the villains. Their procedures are a consequence of the way adoptions are configured. The publishers' products are referenced to the adoption criteria formulated by the district or state. The agency sets up criteria for instructional programs; the publishers attempt to design the material so that it meets the criteria. The agency evaluates the program not by trying it out on a small scale, but by assembling committees to *inspect* the material and judge from inspection how well it seems to *meet the criteria.* Historically, nowhere in this procedure is the question of research data on effectiveness addressed.

At least one state—California—had statutes that called for publishers to field-test material, but during the whole-language era the California State Board openly rejected these statutes. The 1976 statutes (section 60226) specified that the publishers are to "develop plans to improve the quality and reliability of instructional materials through learner verification." The 1988 California adoption criteria even included a requirement that publishers were to provide a description of the field-testing process and an explanation of how the materials are to be improved "on the basis of the field-testing data collected."

Although this sounds as if the adoption process was aligned with the legislation, the following sentence in the 1988 Language Arts Framework declared, "This additional information is not to be considered as part of the criteria for recommending materials to the state board…"

A 1989 suit against the Board argued that the state had to comply with the legislation on learner verification. The state board argued that it had a self-executing authority to do as it chose in adopting textbooks and that the Board's actions were not subject to review by the legislature. The Board lost the lawsuit, and was ordered to require publishers to provide learner verification, but that ruling made little difference because the laws were repealed within a year, and the adoption process has gone on ever since without concern with learner verification. So California, like other states and districts, declared that it is not interested in assuring that programs that reach the classroom have a high probability of working.

Another practical reason for the publishers' inattention to data on effectiveness is that usually there is not sufficient time to conduct the kind of field-test research needed to shape effective instructional material. The timeline that the state presents allows the publisher possibly only two years to create a K-5 sequence that meets the state's new requirements; however, it would probably take 2-3 years to try out the material for one grade level, revise it to avoid the specific performance problems identified in the first tryout, and try out the material again. To test all the levels, at least some "continuing students" would start in K and go through at least the third-grade level. To do a responsible job on a K-5 sequence, therefore, would require four or five years with the most efficient design that had various groups on each grade level starting two to four months apart (so the group receiving the final revised version in the first grade would start possibly ten months after the group that received the first tryout version of the program).

Another problem is that states and districts have primitive rules for adopting programs. Every seven years many of the statewide adoptions are referenced to a new framework with new criteria; therefore, the accepted standard has become for publishers to revise or redesign their products every seven years. Many districts will not adopt any program for beginning reading that has a copyright older than 7 years. This practice assumes either that first graders change so much every seven years that they need new instructional approaches, or that the revised program will always produce better results than the earlier version. Given that the results of student performance are not used in any practical way by the state or district, the adoption practices for subjects in the primary grades are enigmatic.

Instructional materials, like the overall reforms, are experimental. *If the only basis that the publisher, state, and district has about the effectiveness of the product comes from field information obtained after the product had been adopted, the adoption process is functionally research.* The principle of avoiding harm applies here.

Just as there is a Food and Drug Administration, there should be an Educational Protection Administration that tests products to be used in schools with the same rigor that drugs, prosthetics, machines, and other health-care products are tested by the Food and Drug Administration.

Carnine points out that education is probably like the Food and Drug Administration from its formation in 1938 until the Thalidomide disaster in 1962 (2000). During this period, the administration relied partly on opinion from clinical experts. The Kefauver Bill of 1962 required research evidence that documented that products were effective before they could be marketed.

Education relies not partly, but almost exclusively on expert opinion. The committee that "reviews" a particular instructional program form opinions about how relatively effective the program will be. The committee's opinions are consistently wrong. Education needs a Kefauver Bill. The damage created by faulty instructional programs does not produce outcomes that parallel the physical deformities created by thalidomide, but a wealth of data shows that school failure is the most highly correlated factor with all of the teen problems—drugs, felonies, pregnancy, dropping out of school, emotional problems (NICHD, 1998).

If even some of this harm is corrected by using products and practices that lead to school success, there should be no reason for not testing and validating them in the same way drugs and related products are tested and validated. A bottle of aspirin has qualifications for its use with younger children. Some instructional programs that produce reasonable results with higher performers fail seriously with lower performers; however, there are no cautions for the use of these programs. The cost of an administration that provided such cautions should not be a barrier when the health of millions of children is at stake.

One of the most outrageous examples of states not avoiding harm occurred in California. In 1985 the Curriculum Commission of California had established criteria for evaluating programs submitted for teaching mathematics. A small publisher in California designed a program meeting all these criteria. It received a score of 96, 16 points higher than any other submission. The only field-testing that occurred before the program was published involved 18 students. Data on 7 of them were excluded from the final data analysis. Of the remaining 11 students, 61% made gains or had no change in score, while 39% experienced a loss. The average gain of the group was 19 percentile points. The average loss was 22 percentile points. This program captured 60 percent of sales in the state the first year. When questioned about these results, G. Thomas of the California Department of Education explained that the State Board of Education "has *never* asserted that any specific score correlates with the quality of potential success of a particular program."

RESEARCH IN EDUCATION

Researchers are providing additions to our knowledge of effective teaching practices, but research does not name specific products and rarely identifies them as exemplars. The research shuns specifics and attempts to derive general principles and general schemes. The aversion to specifics seems to be based on the assumption that if teachers are provided with general information about the various types of phonemic-awareness activities, or successful phonics techniques, they will be able to transduce this general information into effective, specific applications. (See National Reading Panel, April 2000.) There is no data that teachers have the ability (or the necessary training) to do this.

The irony of the research not identifying specific programs that are effective is circular. The only basis that the researchers have for knowing that phonological awareness and phonics are effective is through an analysis of superior programs. The consumer of educational material wants information about which programs work, just as the purchaser of an automobile wants information about which cars in a class are more "effective." Instead of providing the consumer with specific information, the researchers present general principles and often discussions that go far beyond the data. The logic they use is flawed. It is parallel to this:

All Dalmatians have spots.
Therefore, all dogs with spots are Dalmatians.

Here's the educational parallel:

All highly successful programs present explicit phonics.
Therefore, all programs that present explicit phonics are highly successful.

The logic is as flawed for the explicit phonics as it is for Dalmatians. There is no data that teachers are able to create highly successfully instruction from the kind of recommendations about phonological awareness or phonics provided by the 2000 Reading Panel. Furthermore, this excursion into general principles isn't needed. Just as the patient with serious heart problems requires a *specific* surgical procedure that has been demonstrated to be effective, the teacher needs *specific* products that have been demonstrated to be effective for teaching reading, math, and language. Just as the surgeon must be trained in specific procedures, teachers need training in how to use specific products so they are effective. If the researchers know which specific products work, the first responsibility of at least some of them should be to identify these products. Then the researchers have some kind of known base for developing what they believe to be the underlying principles that account for the success of these programs.

CONCLUSIONS

For a real educational reform to occur, the system must first recognize that it has done harm and continues to do harm. It must be institutionalized so that it follows standards for professional conduct that avoids unnecessary harm. Research should be conducted before the fact—before reform agendas are installed, before textbooks are adopted, before teachers enter the classroom or use a new procedure.

Next, educational agencies must identify all their practices that use teachers and children as the experimental subjects, from in-service formats to their textbook adoption practices and copyright requirements. Finally, the agencies need to apply a code of ethics to provide protocol for these experimental areas. States and districts need to find out information about effectiveness of proposed programs or practices through well-designed research that is governed by a strict code of conduct and strict guidelines of accountability. Concurrent with a sensible search for information about what works, adoption criteria and practices need to be scrapped. They have not worked in identifying programs that produce superior results. At best, they have generated indifferent practices in the publishing business and many products that range from mediocre to ineffective.

States need to work with major publishers to set up a new way to evaluate programs, a new way to adopt them, and a timeline that is appropriate for proper development of material that uses field tryouts and obtains data that the material works well with children.

Finally, researchers need to recognize that the basic-research model of deriving general "scientific principles" does not apply to education because education is an applied science. The procedures for reporting are parallel to medicine or automobile design, which recognizes that teachers need specific products and practices, not anything general or something they are supposed to invent. A start would be for researchers to evaluate how well teachers are actually able to apply general principles generated by research and use them to create highly successful applications.

The sum of the above would be a system that would be both scientific and would have the ethical code implied by the potential power of effective instruction.

BIBLIOGRAPHY

Adams, G. L., & Engelmann, S. (1996). *Research on Direct Instruction: 25 years beyond DIS-TAR*. Seattle, WA: Educational Achievement Systems.

American Psychological Association. (2002). *Ethical principles of psychologists and code of conduct*. Washington, DC: Author.

Carnine, D. (2000). *Why education experts resist effective practices (and what it would take to make education more like medicine)*. Washington, DC: Thomas B. Fordham Foundation.

Carnine, D. & Gersten, R. (2000). The nature and roles of research in improving achievement in mathematics. *Journal for Research in Mathematics Education*, (31) 2.

National Institute of Child Health and Human Development. (1998). *Overview of reading and literacy initiative*. Washington, DC: National Institute of Child Health and Human Development, National Institutes of Health.

National Reading Panel. (2000). Report of the National Reading Panel: *Teaching children to read: An evidence-based assessment of the scientific research literature on reading and its implications for reading instruction*. Washington, DC: National Institute of Child Health and Human Development, National Institutes of Health.

CHAPTER 24

The standards that govern education policy and program adoption are critical in the success of students. Like other variables influencing the education of children, Engelmann has identified the flaws in these standards, showing how they negatively impact the education and success of students. His understanding of how children learn allowed him to see how these standards may benefit some students, but fail others. In this article, Engelmann responds to the new Common Core Standards in education, describing them as distasteful, vague, and lacking understanding of how to teach young children. He reviews the seven mandates of mathematical practices for kindergarten and first grade, which were devised by the committee that created the Common Core Standards. Engelmann addresses the flaws in each of these mandates, specifically in relation to their use with at-risk students.

One of Engelmann's conclusions is that these mandates result from the committee's reliance on the Piagetian model of how children learn. Over four decades have passed since Engelmann demonstrated the flaws in Piaget's theories on child development, yet these theories are still considered accurate and valuable in the education of children. The problem with the Common Core Standards and similar standards is that they are not based on empirical evidence of what children learn and the technical details of how they learn, but instead on vague understandings and theoretical speculations. Through this article, as in other writings, Engelmann brings greater scrutiny to the world of education and the need to reevaluate its design and goals.

THE DREADED STANDARDS (2010)*
Siegfried Engelmann

Math Standards for the early grades, particularly K and 1, are distasteful, but the new Common Core Standards may have premier distasteful status.

What makes them distasteful? A subtle combination of vagueness, misplaced specificity, and a lack of understanding about teaching young children. But let the committee or braintrust that made up the descriptions about the standards speak for itself.

Below is a sidebar summary of seven mathematical practices for K and 1. They aren't practices for teachers, but presumably practices that are induced in children through instruction that complies with the standards. Think of at-risk kindergarten children as you read the list.

Mathematical Practices

1. Make sense of problems and persevere in solving them.

2. Reason abstractly and quantitatively.

3. Construct viable arguments and critique the reasoning of others.

4. Model with mathematics.

5. Use appropriate tools strategically.

6. Attend to precision.

7. Look for and make use of structure.

There is no doubt that these mandates are composed of English words and follow English syntax, but some of them don't seem to convey more than a suggestion of meaning or relate in an obvious

---

* Engelmann, S. (2010). The dreaded standards. Available from http://zigsite.com/PDFs/TheDreadedStandards.pdf. Reprinted with permission of Siegfried Engelmann.

manner to any specific standard or combination that would induce the mandate.

Mandate 1: Make sense of problems and persevere in solving them.

This item raises the question of whether the authors or committee who wrote it has a clear idea of what kindergartners are. They are little guys who are just getting their feet wet in the sea of formal instruction. Do we design material so it is easy for them? Not according to mandate one. Rather, it appears that we're going to make math "challenging" so kids have to frown and struggle as we remind them, "Persevere, damn it."

If this interpretation seems like a stretch, consider mandate one with the p word replaced by a Webster definition:

Make sense of problems and persist in the undertaking in spite of opposition or discouragement.

If children are going to persevere, we're going to have to do our part and provide them with opposition and discouragement. Why? Apparently so we can show them that they are to persevere, damn it.

Mandate 2: Reason abstractly and quantitatively.

This mandate is what seems to be a tautology, words that are strung together and say nothing more than what we would know if we said that the children are to learn math. In other words, if children learn anything relevant about math or even math applications, they have to learn to reason abstractly and quantitatively.

To confirm that the person on the street understands this interpretation I asked an unkempt person who was pushing a grocery cart down the sidewalk, "Can young children do math without reasoning abstractly and quantitatively?"

He looked at me and said, "No. Got any change?"

I think this response, particularly the reference to monetary application, is quite as thoughtful as mandate number 2, which is a good number for this tautology.

Mandate 3: Construct viable arguments and critique the reasoning of others.

If we're talking about kindergarteners, what mathematical arguments are they going to construct? And how are they going to determine their degree of "viability" without knowledge of facts?

For math applications nearly all relevant arguments will hinge on whether something is true or false. On the K level, we could expect the viable argument and critique might go something like this.

"I got more money than you do cause I got four dollars."
"Oh yeah? Show me."
"Those aren't dollars. They're pennies. You only got four pennies."

In a broader sense, exactly what are the properties of a viable argument? Is it one that's supported by or based on sound evidence? Is it unassailable or irrefutable in logical form? Or is viable some kind of slush word that refers to constructing, developing, and growing through the complexities of dynamic interaction? I forgot to ask the person with the grocery cart this question, so I remain unsure.

The ultimate question, however, is what central role would arguments or critiquing the reasoning of others have to do with kindergarten math? The children do not have extensive knowledge of the facts and relationships needed to formulate either arguments or critiques. And most relevant, where are the K standards that provide the instruction children receive to create these viable arguments and critiques?

Mandate 4: Model with mathematics.

No, Virginia, I don't know what this means. In this sentence, the word model is an intransitive verb; I have some idea of what mathematics is, but modeling with mathematics? I strike out. The dictionary doesn't help a lot. One meaning of model is: To design or imitate forms. I don't know what forms are being designed? Do kids design something out of mathematics? If they make a concrete model of anything it will be replete with mathematical details, but this isn't really modeling with math.

Another meaning of model is: to act as a fashion or art model. This possible meaning provokes some pretty strange images, like kids walking down the runway with numbers and geometric forms all over them. In this case, at least a kid would be able to answer the question, "What on earth are you doing?" "Modeling with mathematics."

Mandate 5: Use appropriate tools strategically.

This mandate seems to have redundant parts. If you use appropriate tools, it's given that you know that they're appropriate for particular "strategies." We could also express the same idea without reference to appropriate. "Use tools strategically." If we use them strategically, we must have selected the ones that are appropriate.

Even if we accept the mandate as being clear in form, however, the mandate does not suggest what kindergarten tools are related to math. Let's see: a calculator? Probably not, but certainly not as a central "tool." If we're talking about ruler, scissors, pencils and crayons, they are tools, all right, but for these, the best-phrased mandate would be something like, "Use tools appropriately." That mandate would imply both information about how to use the tools and also, what not to do with them. For instance, "Don't hit Daniel with your ruler; stop cutting Lynn's hair with your scissors, and don't ever write on the chalkboard with your crayons again, or stick pencils up your nose so you look like a walrus."

Mandate 6: Attend to precision.

Granted, these mandates are for math, not physics, but the committee who wrote the mandates should have some knowledge about the "scientific" relationship between precision and accuracy. The problem with attending to "precision" without reference to accuracy is that a little guy could give evidence of being very precise but dead wrong. For instance,

What's 5 + 1? *(Five.)*

What's 3 + 1? *(Three.)*

What's 9 + 1? *(Nine.)*

What's 1 plus 9? *(One.)*

The proof that the responses are precise is that we could make big bets on how the learner would respond to an item that was not tested, such as, "What's 18 plus one?"

We could even make sure that the learner is attending to precision by telling him to "Think carefully before you answer."

In the math arena we are concerned with accuracy, not only with the answers, but accuracy in the steps that the learner takes to arrive at the answers. Are the steps and answers correct? If so, the process is accurate. Note, however, that the students' accuracy is the result of the precision with which the process is designed and taught to the learner. So the precision is properly in the teacher's bailiwick, and we need to be very compulsive about precision, so the teacher will be able to accurately judge from the children's responses whether or not they are learning what is being taught.

Mandate 7: Look for and make use of structure.

Once more, Virginia, I am perplexed. Is this structure in the problems kiddies are working, in the surroundings, in the knowledge children have, or does structure lie in some intricate relation between hosts of the structural elements? Maybe nobody knows where the structure is and that's the reason the kids have to look for it. Or maybe the game is simply based on pragmatics. Find something—anything—you can make use of. That thing (whatever it is) has structure.

But once we've found the structure, how do we go about making use of it? Do we use it as a basis for performing mathematical operations? If so, the mandate is opaque and would be more clearly stated as, "Identify numerical relationships and express them in number operations."

In summary, singly or as a group, these sidebar mandates are an insult. Somebody might argue that they don't really reflect the actual standards for K. They are simply some kind of window dressing designed to call attention to … The words that follow are the ones that would make this justification an easy target to shoot down. What possible virtue would a document that is designed to change the lives of children through education have if it is cloaked in vagueness, with directives that have no obvious application to kindergarteners?

The sidebar is not the only problem. On the same page is an overview of what children are to learn more specifically in K. One item presents a very sophomoric analysis.

Number and Operations in base 10:

Work with numbers 11–19 to gain foundations for place value.

No, we're not going to carp over the fact that the heading refers to only one number, but focus on the assertion that the teen numbers (which should really start with 10 not 11 in base ten) provide a good foundation for place value. If you really thought about it and tried to come up with the most confused, screwed up, non- generalizable decade, 10–19 would win in a landslide. In other words, this decade, isolated from the other two-digit decades, teaches very little about place value.

Consider the relationship between the names and what the kindergartener is to write. One name is sixteen. For that name, you say the 6 first, but write it last. Hmmm. The same pattern holds for all the numbers that end with the word teen, 13 through 19. For some of these numbers the name for the second digit is a familiar counting number, 14, 16, 17, 18, 19. For 13 and 15, the name you say before saying "teen" is not really a counting number. You don't say threeteen or fiveteen, but you write a three or five as the second digit.

Then you have 10, 11,and 12, which have names that are totally independent of what you write. If they followed the pattern of 14, 16, and the others, the name for 10 would be zeroteen; 11 would be oneteen; 12 would be twoteen. Also, if all the teens were regular, 13 would be threeteen and 15 would be fiveteen.

Even though the pattern for the teen numbers is very lumpy, at best, let's say that we work on it until children are super firm in writing numbers from dictation and reading teen numbers.

Have they learned solid foundations for place value? Unless they work on other two-digit numbers, the answer has to be no. Here's the test. We tell them, "You're going to write a number you have written before. This number has two parts, but does not have a one in it. Write the number 75. Remember, write two parts—a part for 70 and a part for 5."

What are the odds of them writing it correctly? Given that the children don't know how to write 70, they wouldn't write 570 (the 5 before the 70.) They might write 57. They might forget the ban against using 1 and write 517 (thinking that the 10 in 70 is really 17). But they would have absolutely no basis for knowing that the 7 was the first digit.

Yet, the conventions that apply to 70–79, apply to 20–29, 30–39, 40–49, 50–59, and all the other decades through 99. So with respect to the relationship of name parts with what you write, which is more generalizable for place value, 70–79 or 10– 19? Clearly, 70–79. It doesn't have oddball irregular names for 70, 71, and 72 (compared to 10, 11, 12). The name for each digit to write is specified by the name, and they are written in the same order they occur in the name, not in reverse order.

Not only are there problems with the relationship of name to the order of digits. Children can't really learn much about place value for base ten numbers before they learn a range of two-digit numbers. If they become familiar with all numbers to 100, it is now possible to show them how the digits relate to place value. The rule we present is simply that the first digit tells the number of tens. The second digit tells the number of ones.

Now it's just a question of presenting examples like 56, 34, 81, 27, and 13, and asking the children:

How many tens?

How many ones?

If children can write and read the numbers correctly, this relationship is pretty easy to teach. But if the only numbers that children work with are 10–19, it doesn't make a lot of sense because the number of tens is no variable. There's always one ten. So this is a poor foundation because it doesn't show the relationship between the number of tens (the first digit) and the number of ones (the second digit). In other words, the only reasonable foundation for place value is the understanding that both digits of the numeral tell about groups. The first digit specifies the number of groups that have ten; the second digit specifies the number of groups that have one.

I haven't presented viable arguments and critiques about any of the actual standards for K, but I have pointed out enough slop to suggest why at least some of the actual standards would be distasteful. Most of this distastefulness results from the committee's strange notions of how children learn. The standards clearly follow the Piagetian myth that children first manipulate then internalize the manipulations, which slowly grows into "concrete operations," and later into "abstractions" or formal operations.

It does not work that way, and manipulatives are an instructional nightmare in K. The products—what children actually learn from manipulation activities—are trivial compared to what could be taught directly in the same amount of time. This fact implies the fundamental problem with these and other standards for the early grades. Committees keep writing standards that are not based on empirical evidence of what children are able to learn about math and the specific technical details of instruction that cause the learning.

Until those who create standards for the early grades let go of superstition and start looking at facts of performance, math standards continue to be a potpourri that includes standards that are perfectly reasonable both in terms of what is teachable and what is necessary for good math instruction, and nonsense standards that instructional programs have to incorporate if these programs are to be adopted by all the states that have bought into the latest distasteful standards.

APPENDIX A

DIRECT INSTRUCTION PROGRAMS AUTHORED BY ENGELMANN, 1969 TO 2014

READING

DISTAR Reading

Engelmann, S., & Bruner, E. C. (1969). *DISTAR Reading I*. Chicago: Science Research Associates.

Engelmann, S., & Bruner, E. C. (1969). *DISTAR Reading II*. Chicago: Science Research Associates.

Engelmann, S., & Bruner, E. C. (1969). *DISTAR Reading Fast Cycle*. Chicago: Science Research Associates.

Engelmann, S., & Hanner, S. (1969). *DISTAR Reading III*. Chicago: Science Research Associates.

Engelmann, S. (1975). *DISTAR Training Program for DISTAR Reading I*. Chicago: Science Research Associates.

Engelmann, S., & Bruner, E. C. (1977). *DISTAR Library Series*. Chicago: Science Research Associates.

Engelmann, S., Becker, W. C., & Carnine, L. (1978). *Continuous Tests for DISTAR Reading*. Eugene, OR: E-B Press.

Engelmann, S., & Bruner, E. C. (1978). *DISTAR Reading: An Instructional System*. Chicago: Science Research Associates.

Engelmann, S. (1979). *DISTAR Reading Activity Kit*. Chicago: Science Research Associates.

Reading Mastery

Engelmann, S. E., & Bruner, E. (1983). *Reading Mastery I*. Chicago: Science Research Associates.

Engelmann, S., & Bruner, E. C. (1988). *Reading Mastery: Fast Cycle (DISTAR)*. Chicago: Science Research Associates.

Engelmann, S., & Bruner, E. (1988). *Reading Mastery I: DISTAR Reading*. Chicago: Science Research Associates.

Engelmann, S., & Bruner, E. (1988). *Reading Mastery I: Teacher's Guide*. Chicago: Science Research Associates.

Engelmann, S., & Bruner, E. (1988). *Reading Mastery II: DISTAR Reading*. Chicago: Science Research Associates.

Reading Mastery Rainbow Edition

Engelmann, S., & Bruner, E. (1995). *Reading Mastery I* (Rainbow Ed.) (Teacher's Presentation Book, Student Material, Literature Guide, and Teacher's Guide). Columbus, OH: SRA/McGraw-Hill.

Engelmann, S., & Bruner, E. (1995). *Reading Mastery II* (Rainbow Ed.) (Teacher's Presentation Book, Student Material, Literature Guide, and Teacher's Guide). Columbus, OH: SRA/McGraw-Hill.

Reading Mastery Plus

Engelmann, S., Osborn, J., Bruner, E. C., & Seitz-Davis, K. L. (2002). *Reading Mastery Plus: Level K* (Teacher's Presentation Books, Student Material, and Teacher's Guide). Chicago: SRA/McGraw-Hill.

Engelmann, S., Bruner, E. C., Osborn, J., & Seitz-Davis, K. L. (2002). *Reading Mastery Plus: Level 1* (Teacher's Presentation Books, Student Material, and Teacher's Guide). Chicago: SRA/McGraw-Hill.

Engelmann, S., Bruner, E. C., Engelmann, O., Seitz-Davis, K. L., & Arbogast, A. (2002). *Reading Mastery Plus: Level 2* (Teacher's Presentation Books, Student Material, and Teacher's Guide). Chicago: SRA/McGraw-Hill.

Engelmann, S., & Hanner, S. (2002). *Reading Mastery Plus: Level 3* (Teacher's Presentation Book, Student Material, Literature Guide, and Teacher's Guide). Columbus, OH: SRA/McGraw-Hill. (Originally published 1969 as *DISTAR Reading III*, Chicago: Science Research Associates)

Engelmann, S., & Hanner, S. (2002). *Reading Mastery Plus: Level 4* (Teacher's Presentation Book, Student Material, Literature Guide, and Teacher's Guide). Columbus, OH: SRA/McGraw-Hill. (Originally published 1983.)

Engelmann, S., Osborn, J., Osborn, S., & Zoref, L. (2002). *Reading Mastery Plus: Level 5* (Teacher's Presentation Book, Student Material, Literature Guide, and Teacher's Guide). Columbus, OH: SRA/McGraw-Hill. (Originally published 1984.)

Engelmann, S., Osborn, J., Osborn, S., & Zoref, L. (2002). *Reading Mastery Plus: Level 6* (Teacher's Presentation Book, Student Material, Literature Guide, and Teacher's Guide). Columbus, OH: SRA/McGraw-Hill. (Originally published 1984.)

Reading Mastery Classic Edition

Engelmann, S., & Bruner, E. C. (2003). *Reading Mastery Level I* (Classic Ed.) (Teacher's Presentation Book, Student Material, Literature Guide, and Teacher's Guide). Columbus, OH: SRA/McGraw-Hill. (Originally published 1969 as *DISTAR Reading I*, Chicago: Science Research Associates.)

Engelmann, S., & Bruner, E. C. (2003). *Reading Mastery Level II* (Classic Ed.) (Teacher's Presentation Book, Student Material, Literature Guide, and Teacher's Guide). Columbus, OH: SRA/McGraw-Hill. (Originally published 1969 as *DISTAR Reading II*, Chicago: Science Research Associates.)

Engelmann, S., & Bruner, E. C. (2003). *Reading Mastery Levels I/II Fast Cycle* (Classic Ed.) (Teacher's Presentation Book, Student Material, and Teacher's Guide). Columbus, OH: SRA/McGraw-Hill. (Originally published 1969 as *DISTAR Reading Fast Cycle*, Chicago: Science Research Associates.)

Reading Mastery Signature Edition

Engelmann, S., & Bruner, E. C. (2008). *Reading Mastery Reading, Level K* (Signature Ed.) (Teacher's Presentation Book, Student Material, Literature Guide, and Teacher's Guide). Columbus, OH: SRA/McGraw-Hill.

Engelmann, S., & Bruner, E. C. (2008). *Reading Mastery Reading, Level 1* (Signature Ed.) (Teacher's Presentation Book, Student Material, Literature Guide, and Teacher's Guide). Columbus, OH: SRA/McGraw-Hill.

Engelmann, S., & Hanner, S. (2008). *Reading Mastery Reading, Level 2* (Signature Ed.) (Teacher's Presentation Book, Student Material, Literature Guide, and Teacher's Guide). Columbus, OH: SRA/McGraw-Hill.

Engelmann, S., & Hanner, S. (2008). *Reading Mastery Reading, Level 3* (Signature Ed.) (Teacher's Presentation Book, Student Material, Literature Guide, and Teacher's Guide). Columbus, OH: SRA/McGraw-Hill.

Engelmann, S., Osborn, J., Osborn, S., & Zoref, L. (2008). *Reading Mastery Reading, Level 4* (Signature Ed.) (Teacher's Presentation Book, Student Material, Literature Guide, and Teacher's Guide). Columbus, OH: SRA/McGraw-Hill.

Engelmann, S., Osborn, J., Osborn, S., & Zoref, L. (2008). *Reading Mastery Reading, Level 5* (Signature Ed.) (Teacher's Presentation Book, Student Material, Literature Guide, and Teacher's Guide). Columbus, OH: SRA/McGraw-Hill.

Engelmann, S., & Osborn, J. (2008). *Reading Mastery Language Arts Strand, Level K* (Signature Ed., Grade K) (Teacher's Presentation Book, Student Material, Literature Guide, and Teacher's Guide). Columbus, OH: SRA/McGraw-Hill.

Engelmann, Z., & Osborn, J. (2008). *Reading Mastery Language Arts Strand, Level K* (Signature Ed.) (Teacher's Presentation Book, Student Material, Literature Guide, and Teacher's Guide). Columbus, OH: SRA/McGraw-Hill.

Engelmann, Z., Osborn, J., & Davis, K. L. S. (2008). *Reading Mastery Language Arts Strand, Level 1* (Signature Ed.) (Teacher's Presentation Book, Student Material, Literature Guide, and Teacher's Guide). Columbus, OH: SRA/McGraw-Hill.

Engelmann, S., Davis, K. L. S., & Silbert, J. (2008). *Reading Mastery Language Arts Strand, Level 2* (Signature Ed.) (Teacher's Presentation Book, Student Material, Literature Guide, and Teacher's Guide). Columbus, OH: SRA/McGraw-Hill.

Engelmann, S., Silbert, J., & Hanner, S. (2008). *Reading Mastery Language Arts Strand, Level 3* (Signature Ed.) (Teacher's Presentation Book, Student Material, Literature Guide, and Teacher's Guide). Columbus, OH: SRA/McGraw-Hill.

Engelmann, S., Silbert, J., & Osborn, S. (2008). *Reading Mastery Language Arts Strand, Level 4* (Signature Ed.) (Teacher's Presentation Book, Student Material, Literature Guide, and Teacher's Guide). Columbus, OH: SRA/McGraw-Hill.

Engelmann, S., Grossen, B., & Osborn, S. (2008). *Reading Mastery Language Arts Strand, Level 5* (Signature Ed.) (Teacher's Presentation Book, Student Material, Literature Guide, and Teacher's Guide). Columbus, OH: SRA/McGraw-Hill.

Corrective Reading

Engelmann, S., Becker, W. C., Carnine, L., Meyer, L., Becker, J., & Johnson, G. (1975). *Corrective Reading Program.* Chicago: Science Research Associates.

Engelmann, S., & Haddox, P. (1978). *Corrective Reading Placement Test.* Chicago: Science Research Associates.

Engelmann, S., Hanner, S., & Johnson, G. (1978). *Corrective Reading: Series Guide.* Chicago: Science Research Associates.

Engelmann, S., Becker, W. C., Hanner, S., & Johnson, G. (1978). *Implementing the Corrective Reading Series.* Eugene, OR: E-B Press.

Engelmann, S., Meyer, L., Carnine, L., Becker, W., Eisele, J., & Johnson, G. (1988). *Corrective Reading: Decoding Strategies.* Chicago: Science Research Associates.

Engelmann, S. (1989). *Corrective Reading-Series Guide.* Chicago: Science Research Associates.

Engelmann, S., Osborn, S., & Hanner, S. (1989). *Corrective Reading: Comprehension Skills.* Chicago: Science Research Associates.

Engelmann, S., Haddox, P., Osborn, J., & Hanner, S. (2008). *Corrective Reading: Comprehension A* (Teacher's Presentation Book, Student Material, and Teacher's Guide). Columbus, OH: SRA/McGraw-Hill. (Originally published 1978, and revised 1998.)

Engelmann, S., Osborn, S., & Hanner, S. (2008). *Corrective Reading: Comprehension B1 and B2* (Teacher's Presentation Book, Student Material, and Teacher's Guide). Columbus, OH: SRA/McGraw-Hill. (Originally published 1978 as *Comprehension B*, and revised 1998 as *Comprehension B1 and B2*.)

Engelmann, S., Hanner, S., & Haddox, P. (2008). *Corrective Reading: Comprehension C* (Teacher's Presentation Book, Student Material, and Teacher's Guide). Columbus, OH: SRA/McGraw-Hill. (Originally published 1980, and revised 1998.)

Engelmann, S., Johnson, G., & Carnine, L. (2008). *Corrective Reading: Decoding A* (Teacher's Presentation Book, Student Material, and Teacher's Guide). Columbus, OH: SRA/McGraw-Hill. (Originally published 1978, and revised 1998.)

Engelmann, S., Meyer, L., Carnine, L., Becker, W., Eisele, J., & Johnson, G. (2008). *Corrective Reading: Decoding B1* (Teacher's Presentation Book, Student Material, and Teacher's Guide). Columbus, OH: SRA/McGraw-Hill. (Originally published 1978, and revised 1998.)

Engelmann, S., Meyer, L., Carnine, L., Becker, W., Eisele, J., & Johnson, G. (2008). *Corrective Reading: Decoding B2* (Teacher's Presentation Book, Student Material, and Teacher's Guide). Columbus, OH: SRA/McGraw-Hill. (Originally published 1978, and revised 1998.)

Engelmann, S., Meyer, L., Johnson, G., & Carnine, L. (2008). *Corrective Reading: Decoding C* (Teacher's Presentation Book, Student Material, and Teacher's Guide). Columbus, OH: SRA/McGraw-Hill. (Originally published 1978, and revised 1998.)

Horizons

Engelmann, S., Engelmann, O., & Seitz-Davis, K. L. (1997). *Horizons: Fast Track A-B* (Teacher's Presentation Book, Student Material, Literature Guide, and Teacher's Guide). Columbus, OH: SRA/McGraw-Hill.

Engelmann, S., & Hanner, S. (1998). *Horizons: Fast Track C-D* (Teacher's Presentation Book, Student Material, Literature Guide, and Teacher's Guide). Columbus, OH: SRA/McGraw-Hill.

Engelmann, S., Engelmann, O., & Seitz-Davis, K. L. (1998). *Horizons: Level A* (Teacher's Presentation Book, Student Material, Literature Guide, and Teacher's Guide). Columbus, OH: SRA/McGraw-Hill.

Engelmann, S., Engelmann, O., & Seitz-Davis, K. L. (2000). *Horizons: Level B* (Teacher's Presentation Book, Student Material, Literature Guide, and Teacher's Guide). Columbus, OH: SRA/McGraw-Hill.

Funnix

Engelmann, S., Engelmann, O., & Seitz-Davis, K. L. (2001). *Funnix, Beginning Reading*. Eugene, OR: Royal Limited Partnership.

Engelmann, S., & Engelmann, O. (2002). *Funnix Reading 2*. Eugene, OR: Royal Limited Partnership.

Journeys

Engelmann, S., Engelmann, O., & Seitz-Davis, K. L. (2000). *Journeys: Level K* (Teacher's Presentation Books, Student Material, and Teacher Guide). Columbus, OH: SRA/McGraw-Hill.

Engelmann, S., Engelmann, O., & Seitz-Davis, K. L. (2000). *Journeys: Level 1* (Teacher's Presentation Books, Student Material, and Teacher's Guide). Columbus, OH: SRA/McGraw-Hill.

Engelmann, S., Engelmann, O., Seitz-Davis, K. L., & Arbogast, A. (2000). *Journeys: Level 2* (Teacher's Presentation Books, Student Material, and Teacher's Guide). Columbus, OH: SRA/McGraw-Hill.

Engelmann, S., & Hanner, S. (2000). *Journeys: Level 3* (Teacher's Presentation Books, Student Material, and Teacher's Guide). Columbus, OH: SRA/McGraw-Hill.

Supplementary Reading Guide

Engelmann, S., & Jensen, J. (1982). *I Love Library Books*. Eugene, OR: E–B Press.

LANGUAGE

DISTAR Language

Engelmann, S., Osborn, J., & Lundeen, B. (1968). *Learning Language: Concept and Action Stories*. Urbana, IL: University of Illinois Press.

Engelmann, S., & Osborn, J. (1970). *DISTAR Language II* (Teacher's Presentation Book, Student Material, and Teacher's Guide). Chicago: Science Research Associates.

Engelmann, S., Olen, L., & Concillo, P. (1978). *Continuous Tests for DISTAR Language.* Eugene, OR: E-B Press.

Engelmann, S. (1979). *DISTAR Language Activity Kit.* Chicago: Science Research Associates.

Engelmann, S., & Osborn, J. (1986). *DISTAR Language I* (Teacher's Presentation Book, Student Material, and Teacher's Guide). Chicago: Science Research Associates. (Originally published 1969.)

Engelmann, S., & Osborn, J. (1986). *DISTAR Language I Mastery Test.* Chicago: Science Research Associates.

Engelmann, S., & Osborn, J. (1986). *DISTAR Language III* (Teacher's Presentation Book, Student Material, and Teacher's Guide). Chicago: Science Research Associates. (Originally published 1970.)

Engelmann, S., & Osborn, J. (1987). *DISTAR Language.* Chicago: Science Research Associates.

Language for Learning (DISTAR I)

Engelmann, S., & Osborn, J. (1998). *Language for Learning* (Teacher's Presentation Book, Student Material, and Teacher's Guide). Columbus, OH: SRA/McGraw-Hill.

Language for Thinking (DISTAR II)

Engelmann, S., & Osborn, J. (2002). *Language for Thinking* (Teacher's Presentation Book, Student Material, and Teacher's Guide). Columbus, OH: SRA/McGraw-Hill.

Language for Writing (DISTAR III)

Engelmann, S., & Osborn, J. (2006). *Language for Writing* (Teacher's Presentation Book, Student Material, and Teacher's Guide). Columbus, OH: SRA/McGraw-Hill.

Miscellaneous

Engelmann, S., & Gill, R. (1971). *Language Concepts Through Drawing.* St. Paul, MN: EMC.

Engelmann, S. (1971). *Language Concepts in Song.* St. Paul, MN: EMC.

Engelmann, S., Ross, D., & Bingham, V. (1982). *Basic Language Concepts Inventory.* Tigard, OR: C & C Publications, Inc.

English as a Second Language

Engelmann, S., Osborn, J., Garza, M., & Snyder, T. (2001). *Español to English* (Language for Learning) (Teacher's Presentation Book, Student Material, and Teacher's Guide). Columbus, OH: SRA/McGraw-Hill.

Engelmann, S., Johnston, D., Engelmann, O., & Silbert, J. (2010). *Direct Instruction Spoken English (DISE).* Dallas, TX: Sopris West.

Assessments

Engelmann, S. (1967). *Basic Concept Inventory.* Chicago: Follett Publishing Company.

Engelmann, S. (1967). *Manual for the Basic Concept Inventory.* Chicago: Follett Publishing Company.

Engelmann, S., Ross, D., & Bingham, V. (1982). *Basic Language Concepts Test, Manual.* Chicago: Science Research Associates.

Engelmann, S., Ross, D., & Bingham, V. (1982). *Basic Language Concepts Test.* Chicago: Science Research Associates.

MATHEMATICS

DISTAR

Engelmann, S., & Carnine, D. (1975). *DISTAR Arithmetic I* (2nd Ed.) (Teacher's Presentation Book, Student Material, and Teacher's Guide). Chicago: Science Research Associates. (Originally published 1970.)

Engelmann, S., & Carnine, D. (1976). *DISTAR Arithmetic II* (2nd Ed.) (Teacher's Presentation Book, Student Material, and Teacher's Guide). Chicago: Science Research Associates. (Originally published 1970.)

Engelmann, S., & Carnine, D. (1976). *DISTAR Arithmetic III* (2nd Ed.) (Teacher's Presentation Book, Student Material, and Teacher's Guide). Chicago: Science Research Associates. (Originally published 1972.)

Engelmann, S., Carnine, D., Becker, W. C., & Davis, G. (1978). *Mastery Tests for DISTAR Arithmetic I & II.* Eugene, OR: E-B Press.

Engelmann, S., & Carnine, D. (1990). *DISTAR Arithmetic.* Chicago: Science Research Associates.

Mathematics Modules

Engelmann, S., & Steely, D. (1978). *Mathematics Modules: Fractions, Decimals, Percents.* (Teacher's Presentation Book, and Student Material). Chicago: Science Research Associates.

Engelmann, S., & Steely, D. (1978). *Mathematics Modules: Basic Fractions.* (Teacher's Presentation Book, and Student Material). Chicago: Science Research Associates.

Engelmann, S., & Steely, D. (1981). *Mathematics Modules: Ratios and Equations* (Teacher's Presentation Book, and Student Material). Chicago: Science Research Associates.

Corrective Mathematics

Engelmann, S., & Carnine, D. (1981). *Corrective Mathematics Series Guide.* Chicago: Science Research Associates.

Engelmann, S., & Carnine, D. (1981). *Corrective Mathematics: Division* (Teacher's Presentation Book, and Student Material). Chicago: Science Research Associates.

Engelmann, S., & Carnine, D. (1981). *Corrective Mathematics: Multiplication* (Teacher's Presentation Book, and Student Material). Chicago: Science Research Associates.

Engelmann, S., & Carnine, D. (1981). *Corrective Mathematics: Subtraction* (Teacher's Presentation Book, and Student Material). Chicago: Science Research Associates.

Engelmann, S., & Carnine, D. (1981). *Corrective Mathematics: Addition* (Teacher's Presentation Book, and Student Material). Chicago: Science Research Associates.

Engelmann, S., & Steely, D. (1981). *Corrective Mathematics Comprehensive Placement Test*. Chicago: Science Research Associates.

Connecting Math Concepts

Engelmann, S., & Carnine, D. (2003). *Connecting Math Concepts: Level A* (Teacher's Presentation Book, Student Material, and Teacher's Guide). Chicago: Science Research Associates. (Originally published 1992, and revised 1997.)

Engelmann, S., & Carnine, D. (2003). *Connecting Math Concepts: Level B* (Teacher's Presentation Book, Student Material, and Teacher's Guide). Chicago: Science Research Associates. (Originally published 1992, and revised 1997.)

Engelmann, S., & Carnine, D. (2003). *Connecting Math Concepts: Level C* (Teacher's Presentation Book, Student Material, and Teacher's Guide). Chicago: Science Research Associates. (Originally published 1992, and revised 1997.)

Engelmann, S., Engelmann, O., & Carnine, D. (2003). *Connecting Math Concepts: Level D* (Teacher's Presentation Book, Student Material, and Teacher's Guide). Chicago: Science Research Associates. (Originally published 1992, and revised 1997.)

Engelmann, S., Kelly, B., & Carnine, D. (2003). *Connecting Math Concepts: Level E* (Teacher's Presentation Book, Student Material, and Teacher's Guide). Chicago: Science Research Associates. (Originally published 1992, and revised 1997.)

Engelmann, S., Engelmann, O., Kelly, B., & Carnine, D. (2003). *Bridge to Connecting Math Concepts* (Teacher's Presentation Book, Student Material, and Teacher's Guide). Chicago: Science Research Associates. (Originally published 1995, and revised 1997.)

Engelmann, S., Kelly, B., & Carnine, D. (2003). *Connecting Math Concepts: Level F* (Teacher's Presentation Book, Student Material, and Teacher's Guide). Chicago: Science Research Associates. (Originally published 1996, and revised 1997.)

Engelmann, S., & Engelmann, O. (2012). *Connecting Math Concepts: Level A* (Comprehensive Ed.) (Teacher's Presentation Book, Student Material, and Teacher's Guide). Columbus, OH: SRA/McGraw Hill.

Engelmann, S., Engelmann, O., & Carnine, D. (2012). *Connecting Math Concepts: Level B* (Comprehensive Ed.) (Teacher's Presentation Book, Student Material, and Teacher's Guide). Columbus, OH: SRA/McGraw Hill.

Engelmann, S., Kelly, B., & Carnine, D. (2012). *Connecting Math Concepts: Level C* (Comprehensive Ed.) (Teacher's Presentation Book, Student Material, and Teacher's Guide). Columbus, OH: SRA/McGraw Hill.

Engelmann, S., Silbert, J., Engelmann, O., & Carnine, D. (2012). *Connecting Math Concepts: Level D* (Comprehensive Ed.) (Teacher's Presentation Book, Student Material, and Teacher's Guide). Columbus, OH: SRA/McGraw Hill.

Engelmann, S., Engelmann, O., Kelly, B., & Carnine, D. (2012). *Connecting Math Concepts: Level E* (Comprehensive Ed.) (Teacher's Presentation Book, Student Material, and Teacher's Guide). Columbus, OH: SRA/McGraw Hill.

Engelmann, S., Kelly, B., Engelmann, O., & Carnine, D. (2012). *Connecting Math Concepts: Level F* (Comprehensive Ed.) (Teacher's Presentation Book, Student Material, and Teacher's Guide). Columbus, OH: SRA/McGraw Hill.

Funnix

Engelmann, S., & Engelmann, O. (2011). *Funnix Beginning Math.* Eugene, OR: Royal Limited Partnership.

Videodisc Programs

Engelmann, S., & Carnine, D. (1985). *Mastering Fractions.* Washington, DC: Systems Impact, Inc.

Engelmann, S., & Carnine, D. (1986). *Mastering Decimals & Percents.* Washington, DC: Systems Impact, Inc.

Engelmann, S., & Carnine, D. (1986). *Mastering Ratios.* Washington, DC: Systems Impact, Inc.

Engelmann, S., & Carnine, D. (1989). *Beginning Algebra.* Washington, DC: Systems Impact, Inc.

Engelmann, S., & Carnine, D. (1991). *Mastering Informal Geometry.* Washington, DC: Systems Impact, Inc.

Pre-Algebra

Engelmann, S., Kelly, B., & Engelmann, O. (2008). *Essentials for Algebra.* (Teacher's Guide, Textbook, and Workbook). Columbus, OH: SRA/McGraw Hill.

SPELLING

Dixon, R., & Engelmann, S. (1979). *Spelling Through Morphographs.* Columbus, OH: SRA/McGraw-Hill. (Originally published 1976.)

Dixon, R., & Engelmann, S. (1990). *Spelling Mastery Series Guide.* Chicago: Science Research Associate.

Dixon, R., Engelmann, S., & Meier, M. (1998). *Spelling Mastery A* (Teacher's Presentation Book, Student Material, and Teacher's Guide). Columbus, OH: SRA/McGraw-Hill. (Originally published 1980.)

Dixon, R., & Engelmann, S., & Meier, M. (1998). *Spelling Mastery B* (Teacher's Presentation Book, Student Material, and Teacher's Guide). Columbus, OH: SRA/McGraw-Hill. (Originally published 1980.)

Dixon, R., & Engelmann, S. (1998). *Spelling Mastery C* (Teacher's Presentation Book, Student Material, and Teacher's Guide). Columbus, OH: SRA/McGraw-Hill. (Originally published 1981.)

Dixon, R., & Engelmann, S. (1998). *Spelling Mastery D* (Teacher's Presentation Book, Student Material, and Teacher's Guide). Columbus, OH: SRA/McGraw-Hill. (Originally published 1981.)

Dixon, R., & Engelmann, S. (1998). *Spelling Mastery E* (Teacher's Presentation Book, Student Material, and Teacher's Guide). Columbus, OH: SRA/McGraw-Hill. (Originally published 1988.)

Dixon, R., Engelmann, S., Steely, D., & Wells, T. (1998). *Spelling Mastery F* (Teacher's Presentation Book, Student Material, and Teacher's Guide). Columbus, OH: SRA/McGraw-Hill. (Published in 1981 as *E* and in 1988 as *F*.)

WRITING

Cursive Writing

Miller, S., & Engelmann, S. (1980). *Cursive Writing* (Teacher's Presentation Book, Student Material, and Teacher's Guide). Chicago: Science Research Associates.

Expressive Writing

Engelmann, S., & Silbert, J. (1985). *Expressive Writing I* (Teacher's Presentation Book, Student Material, and Teacher's Guide). Chicago: Science Research Associates.

Engelmann, S., & Silbert, J. (1985). *Expressive Writing II* (Teacher's Presentation Book, Student Material, and Teacher's Guide). Chicago: Science Research Associates.

Engelmann, S., & Grossen, B. (2010). *Essentials for Writing*. Columbus, OH: SRA/McGraw-Hill.

Reasoning and Writing

Engelmann, S., & Seitz-Davis, K. L. (1991). *Reasoning & Writing: Level A* (Teacher's Presentation Book, Student Material, and Teacher's Guide). Chicago: Science Research Associates.

Engelmann, S., Brown-Arbogast, A., & Seitz-Davis, K. L. (1991). *Reasoning & Writing: Level B* (Teacher's Presentation Book, Student Material, and Teacher's Guide). Chicago: Science Research Associates.

Engelmann, S., & Silbert, J. (1991). *Reasoning & Writing: Level C* (Teacher's Presentation Book, Student Material, and Teacher's Guide). Chicago: Science Research Associates.

Engelmann, S., & Silbert, J. (1993). *Reasoning & Writing: Level D* (Teacher's Presentation Book, Student Material, and Teacher's Guide). Chicago: Science Research Associates.

Engelmann, S., & Grossen, B. (1994). *Reasoning & Writing: Level E* (Teacher's Presentation Book, Student Material, and Teacher's Guide). Chicago: Science Research Associates.

Engelmann, S., & Grossen, B. (1995). *Reasoning & Writing: Level F* (Teacher's Presentation Book, Student Material, and Teacher's Guide). Chicago: Science Research Associates.

SCIENCE AND SOCIAL STUDIES

Engelmann, S., Davis, K., & Davis, G. (1982). *Your World of Facts I* (Teacher's Presentation Book and Student Material). Chicago: Science Research Associates.

Engelmann, S., Davis, K., & Davis, G. (1982). *Your World of Facts II* (Teacher's Presentation Book and Student Material). Chicago: Science Research Associates.

Engelmann, S., & Carnine, D. (1987). *Understanding Chemistry and Energy*. Washington, DC: Systems Impact, Inc.

Engelmann, S., & Carnine, D. (1988). *Earth Science*. Washington, DC: Systems Impact, Inc.

MISCELLANEOUS

Engelmann, S. E., & Carnine, D. W. (1972). *DISTAR and Strategy Games*. Chicago: Science Research Associates.

Engelmann, S., Becker, W. C., Carnine, L., Meyer, L., Becker, J., & Johnson, G. (1975). *Management and Skills Manual*. Chicago: Science Research Associates.

Engelmann, S., & Colvin, G. (1983). *Generalized Compliance Training: A Direct-instruction Program for Managing Severe Behavior Problems*. Austin, TX: Pro-Ed Publishing.

COLLEGE LEVEL TEXTBOOKS

Becker, W. C., Engelmann, S., & Thomas, D. R. (1971). *Teaching: A Basic Course in Applied Psychology*. Chicago: Science Research Associates.

Becker, W. C., Engelmann, S., & Thomas, D. R. (1975). *Teaching 1: Classroom Management*. Chicago: Science Research Associates.

Becker, W. C., & Engelmann, S. (1976). *Teaching 2: Evaluation of Instruction*. Chicago: Science Research Associates.

Becker, W. C., & Engelmann, S. (1976). *Teaching 3: Evaluation of Instruction*. Chicago: Science Research Associates.

TRADE BOOKS-PARENTS

Engelmann, S., Haddox, P., & Bruner, E. (1983). *Teach Your Child to Read in 100 Easy Lessons*. New York: Simon & Schuster.

Engelmann, S., & Engelmann, T. (1981). *Give Your Child a Superior Mind*. New York: Simon and Schuster. (Originally published 1966. Published in 17 languages.)

APPENDIX B

ARTICLES, CHAPTERS, AND BOOKS AUTHORED BY ENGELMANN, 1966 TO MID-2014

1960s

Bereiter, C., & Engelmann, S. (1966). *Effectiveness of Direct Instruction on IQ performance and achievement in reading and arithmetic.* ERIC Documentation Reproduction Service No. ED030496.

Bereiter, C., & Engelmann, S. (1966). *Language learning activities for the disadvantaged child.* New York: Anti-Defamation League of B'nai B'rith.

Bereiter, C., & Engelmann, S. (1966). Observations on the use of Direct Instruction with young disadvantaged children. *Journal of School Psychology, 4*(3), 55–62.

Bereiter, C., & Engelmann, S. (1966). *Teaching disadvantaged children in the preschool.* Englewood Cliffs, NJ: Prentice-Hall.

Bereiter, C., Engelmann, S., Osborn, J., & Reidford, P. A. (1966). An academically oriented pre-school for culturally deprived children. In F. M. Hechinger (Ed.), *Pre-school education today: New approaches to teaching three-, four-, and five-year-olds* (pp. 105–135). Garden City, NY: Doubleday & Co.

Engelmann, S. (1966). The structuring of language processes as tool for thought. In D. Kestel (Ed.), *National Catholic Educational Association bulletin: Curriculum for renewal, 63*(1), 459–468.

Engelmann, S., & Engelmann, T. (1966). *Give your child a superior mind: A program for the preschool child.* New York: Simon and Schuster. (Published in 17 languages. Reprinted in 1981.)

Engelmann, S., & Gallagher, J. J. (1966). A study of how a child learns concepts about characteristics of liquid materials: Final report. ERIC Documentation Reproduction Service No. ED014428.

Engelmann, S. (1967). Cognitive structures related to the principle of conservation. In D. W. Brison & E. V. Sullivan (Eds.), *Recent research on the acquisition of conservation of substance* (pp. 25–51). Toronto, Ontario, Canada: Ontario Institute for Studies in Education.

Engelmann, S. (1967). Communications skills as an objective: Teaching communications skills to disadvantaged children. In *Education for the culturally disadvantaged: Proceedings of the National Conference on Educational Objectives for the Culturally Disadvantaged* (pp. 67–86). Little Rock, AR: South Central Region Educational Laboratory.

Engelmann, S. (1967). Relationship between psychological theories and the act of teaching. *Journal of School Psychology, 5*(2), 93–100.

Engelmann, S. (1967). Teaching formal operations to preschool advantaged and disadvantaged children. *Ontario Journal of Educational Research, 9*(3), 193–207.

Engelmann, S. (1967). Teaching reading to children with low mental ages. In F. E. McDowell (Ed.), *Education and training of the mentally retarded* (pp. 193-201). Washington, DC: Council for Exceptional Children.

Bereiter, C., & Engelmann, S. (1968). An academically oriented preschool for disadvantaged children: Results from the initial experimental group. In D. W. Brison & J. Hill (Eds.), *Psychology and early childhood education* (pp. 17–36). Toronto, Ontario, Canada: Ontario Institute for Studies in Education.

Engelmann, S. (1968). Priorities in preschool education. In D. W. Brison & J. Hill (Eds.), *Psychology and early childhood education* (pp. 51–60). Toronto, Ontario, Canada: Ontario Institute for Studies in Education.

Engelmann, S. (1968). Relating operant techniques to programming and teaching. *Journal of School Psychology, 6*(2), 89–96.

Engelmann, S. (1969). *Conceptual learning.* San Rafael, CA: Dimensions Publishing.

Engelmann, S. (1969). *Preventing failure in the primary grades.* Chicago: Science Research Associates. (Reprinted in 1997 by ADI Press.)

1970s

Engelmann, S. (1970). The effectiveness of Direct Instruction on IQ performance and achievement in reading and arithmetic. In J. Hellmuth (Ed.), *Disadvantaged Child, vol. 3. Compensatory education: A national debate* (pp. 339–361). New York: Brunner/Mazel.

Engelmann, S. (1970). How to construct effective language programs for the poverty child. In F. Williams (Ed.), *Language and poverty: Perspectives on a theme* (pp. 102–122). Chicago: Markham Publishing.

Engelmann, S. E. (1971). Does the Piagetian approach imply instruction? In D. R. Green, M. P. Ford, & G. B. Flamer (Eds.), *Measurement and Piaget* (pp. 118–126). New York: McGraw-Hill.

Engelmann, S. (1971). Failure prevention: A programming necessity. In J. G. Morrey (Ed.), *Learning and behavior management in teacher training: A BECRA symposium on essential components* (pp. 140–174). Pocatello, ID: Idaho State University.

Engelmann, S. (1971). The inadequacies of the linguistic approach in teaching situations. In Center for Applied Linguistics (Ed.), *Sociolinguistics: A crossdisciplinary perspective* (pp. 141–151). Washington, DC: Center for Applied Linguistics.

Becker, W. C., & Engelmann, S. (1973). *Program description and 1973 outcome data: Engelmann-Becker Follow Through model.* Washington, DC: Bureau of Elementary and Secondary Education, Div. of Compensatory Education. ERIC Documentation Reproduction Service No. ED096780.

Becker, W. C., & Engelmann, S. (1973). *Summary analysis of five-year data on achievement and teaching progress with 14,000 children in 20 projects,* Technical report 73-2, Preliminary Report. Washington, DC: Bureau of Elementary and Secondary Education, Div. of Compensatory Education. ERIC Documentation Reproduction Service No. ED096781.

Engelmann, S. (1974). Accountability. In M. Csapo & B. Poutt (Eds.), *Education for all children* (pp. 106–120). Vancouver, British Columbia, Canada: British Columbia Federation of the Council for Exceptional Children.

Engelmann, S. (1974). *Low performer's manual.* (Revised in 2005, available from: http://zigsite.com/PDFs/LowPerfManual.pdf)

Engelmann, S. (1974). A video-tape format for greatest control. *Instructional efficiency: A means for reducing formal classroom time* (pp. 13–17). Saigon, Vientam: SEAMEO Regional Center for Educational Innovation and Technology.

Engelmann, S., & Rosov, R. J. (1974). Tactual hearing experiment with deaf and hearing subjects. *ORI Research Bulletin, 14*(5), 1-43. ERIC Documentation Reproduction Service No. ED098770.

Engelmann, S. (1975). *Your child can succeed: How to get the most out of school for your child.* New York: Simon & Schuster.

Engelmann, S., & Rosov, R. (1975). Tactual hearing experiment with deaf and hearing subjects. *Exceptional Children, 41*(4), 243–253.

Becker, W. C., & Engelmann, S. (1976). *Analysis of achievement data on six cohorts of low-income children from 20 school districts in the University of Oregon Direct Instruction Follow Through model.* Technical report 76-1. Washington, DC: U.S. Office of Education, Bureau of School Systems, Division of Follow Through. ERIC Documentation Reproduction Service No. ED145922.

Engelmann, S., & Carnine, D. W. (1976). A structured program's effect on the attitudes and achievement of average and above average second graders. In W. C. Becker & S. Engelmann (Eds.), *Analysis of achievement data on six cohorts of low-income children from 20 school districts in the University of Oregon Direct Instruction Follow Through model: Technical report 76-1 Appendix B: Formative research studies* (pp. 102-117). Eugene, OR: University of Oregon, College of Education, Follow Through Project. ERIC Documentation Reproduction Service No. ED145922.

Engelmann, S. (1977). Sequencing cognitive and academic tasks. In R. D. Kneedler & S. G. Tarver (Eds.), *Changing perspectives in special education* (pp. 46–61). Columbus, OH: Charles E. Merrill Publishing.

Engelmann, S., & Granzin, A. (1977). Principles of Unfamiliar Learning. *Proceedings from the Conference on Speech-Analyzing Aids for the Deaf.* Washington, DC: Gallaudet College.

Engelmann, S., & Skillman, L. (1977). Developing a tactual hearing program for deaf children. *Proceedings from the Conference on Speech-Analyzing Aids for the Deaf.* Washington, DC: Gallaudet College.

Becker, W. C., & Engelmann, S. (1978). Systems for basic instruction: Theory and applications. In A. C. Catania & T. A. Brigham (Eds.), *Handbook of applied behavior analysis: Social and instructional processes* (pp. 325–377). New York: Irvington.

Engelmann, S., Granzin, A., & Severson, H. (1979). Diagnosing instruction. *The Journal of Special Education, 13*(4), 355–363.

Williams, P., Granzin, A., Engelmann, S., & Becker, W. C. (1979). Teaching language to the truly naïve learner: An analog study using a tactual vocoder. *Journal of Special Education Technology, 2,* 5–15.

1980s

Becker, W. C., Engelmann, S., & Carnine, D. W. (1980). Direct Instruction technology: Recent developments and research findings. In J. Ward & S. Bochner (Eds.), *Recent developments in special education*. Proceedings of the Professional Seminar in Special Education Held at Macquarie University in 1979 to Commemorate the International Year of the Child (pp. 4-91). Sydney, Australia: Macquarie University.

Engelmann, S. (1980). *The instructional design library series (Vol. 22): Direct Instruction*. Englewood Cliffs, NJ: Educational Technology Publications.

Engelmann, S. (1980). Toward the design of faultless instruction: The theoretical basis of concept analysis. *Educational Technology, 20*(2), 28-36.

Engelmann, S., & Granzin, A. (1980). Assessing labor cost of objectives. *Directions, 1*(4), 54-62.

Engelmann, S., & Steely, D. (1980). *Implementation of basal reading in grades 4-6: Final report*. Chicago: Science Research Associates.

Becker, W. C., Engelmann, S., Carnine, D. W., & Rhine, W. R. (1981). Direct Instruction model. In W. R. Rhine (Ed.), *Making schools more effective: New directions from Follow Through* (pp. 95-154). New York: Academic Press.

Becker, W. C., Engelmann, S., Carnine, D. W., & Maggs, A. (1982). Direct Instruction technology: Making learning happen. In P. Karoly & J. J. Steffen (Eds.), *Improving children's competence: Advances in child behavioral analysis and therapy*, (Vol. 1, pp. 151-206). Lexington, MA: D. C. Heath & Company.

Engelmann, S. (1982). *Advocacy for children*. (Available from: http://zigsite.com/AdvocacyChildren.html)

Engelmann, Z. (1982). On observing learning: An essay for the DI teacher. *ADI News, 1*(2), 1, 16. (Reprinted in 1988 in *ADI News, 7*(4), 3-5.)

Engelmann, S. (1982). Piaget and instruction. *ADI News, 2*(1), 1, 6-7.

Engelmann, Z. (1982). A study of 4th-6th grade basal reading series: How much do they teach? *ADI News, 1*(3), 1, 4-5, 19. (Reprinted in 1989 in *ADI News, 8*(4), 17-23.)

Engelmann, Z. (1982). Why attend the eighth annual DI conference? *ADI News, 1*(3), 1, 20.

Engelmann, S., & Carnine, D. (1982). Direct Instruction outcomes with middle-class second graders. *ADI News, 1*(2), 4-5. (Reprinted in 1989 in *ADI News, 8*(2), 2-5.)

Engelmann, S., & Carnine, D. (1982). *Theory of instruction: Principles and applications*. New York: Irvington Publishing. (Reprinted in 1991 as *Theory of instruction: Principles and applications* (Rev. ed.). Eugene, OR: ADI Press.)

Engelmann, S. (1983). Engelmann compares traditional basals with SRA's new *Reading Mastery 3 & 4*. *ADI News, 2*(3), 28-31.

Engelmann, S., Haddox, P., & Bruner, E. (1983). *Teach your child to read in 100 easy lessons*. New York: Simon & Schuster.

Engelmann, S., & Colvin, G. (1983). *Generalized compliance training: A Direct-instruction program for managing severe behavior problems*. Austin, TX: Pro-Ed Publishing.

Singer, G., Close, D., Colvin, G., & Engelmann, S. (1983). DI for severely handicapped learners. *ADI News, 2*(4), 3-4.

Carnine, D., & Engelmann, S. (1984). The Direct Instruction model. In S. C. Paine, G. T. Bellamy & B. Wilcox (Eds.), *Human services that work: From innovation to standard practice* (pp. 133-148). Baltimore, MD: Brookes Publishing.

Engelmann, S., & Meyer, L. A. (1984). *Reading comprehension instruction in grades 4, 5, and 6: Program characteristics; teacher perceptions; teacher behaviors; and student performance.* Paper presented at the 68th Annual Meeting of the American Educational Research Association (New Orleans, LA, April 23-27, 1984). Chicago: Science Research Associates.

Hanner, S., & Engelmann, S. (1984). Learner Verification for *Corrective Reading* Program. *Australian Association for Direct Instruction Newsletter,* May, 3-5.

Carnine, D., Engelmann, S., & Hofmeister, A. (1984-1985). Video disk instruction. *ADI News, 4*(2), 3, 5, 2.

Hofmeister, A. M., Engelmann, S., & Carnine, D. (1985). *Designing videodisc-based courseware for the high school.* Paper presented at the Annual Meeting of the American Educational Research Association (Chicago, IL, March 31-April 4, 1985).

Hofmeister, A. M., Engelmann, S., & Carnine, D. (1985). *Videodisc-based courseware for the high school mainstream.* Paper presented at the Third Annual Conference on Interactive Instruction Delivery in Education, Training, and Job Performance (February 13-15, 1985, Orlando, FL). Warrenton, VA: Society for Applied Learning Technology.

Hofmeister, A. M., Engelmann, S., & Carnine, D. (1986). The development and validation of an instructional videodisc program. In W. Sybouts & D. J. Stevens (Eds.), *National videodisc symposium for education: A national agenda* (pp. 25-33). Lincoln, NE: University of Nebraska-Lincoln.

Hofmeister, A. M., Engelmann, S., & Carnine, D. (1986). Observations from the development and field testing of an instructional videodisc program. *Journal of Special Education Technology, 7*(3), 42-46.

Hofmeister, A. M., Engelmann, S., & Carnine, D. (1986). Videodisc technology: Providing instructional alternatives. *Journal of Special Education Technology, 7*(3), 35-41.

Hofmeister, A. M., Engelmann, S., & Carnine, D. (1986). Videodisc technology: Providing the teacher with alternatives. In W. Sybouts & D. J. Stevens (Eds.), *National videodisc symposium for education: A national agenda* (pp. 34-39). Lincoln, NE: University of Nebraska-Lincoln.

Carnine, D., Engelmann, S., Hofmeister, A., & Kelly, B. (1987). Videodisc instruction in fractions. *Focus on Learning Problems in Mathematics, 9*(1), 31-52.

Engelmann, Z. (1987). Educational guidelines: Who is kidding whom? *ADI News, 6*(4), 2-3.

Woodward, J., Carnine, D., Gersten, R., Engelmann, S., & Gleason, M. (1987). Graduate training in special education: A focus on instructional leadership. *ADI News, 7*(1), 10-11.

Engelmann, S. (1988). The logic and facts of effective supervision. *Education and Treatment of Children, 11*(4), 328-340.

Engelmann, S. (1988). Theories, theories, theories: A critique of logic of whole language arguments. *ADI News, 7*(3), 5-6.

Engelmann, S., Becker, W. C., Carnine, D., & Gersten, R. (1988). The Direct Instruction Follow Through model: Design and outcomes. *Education and Treatment of Children, 11*(4), 303–317.

Engelmann, S., & Carnine, D. (1989). Supporting teachers and students in math and science education through videodisc courses. *Educational Technology, 29*(8), 46–50.

Hofmeister, A. M., Engelmann, S., & Carnine, D. (1989). Developing and validating science education videodiscs. *Journal of Research in Science Teaching, 26*(8), 665–677.

Williams, P., & Engelmann, S. (1989). Teaching absolute pitch. *ADI News, 9*(1), 23–26.

1990s

Carnine, D., & Engelmann, S. (1990). Making connections in third grade mathematics: Connecting Math Concepts. *ADI News, 10*(1), 17–27.

Engelmann, S. (1990). Teachers, schema, and instruction. *ADI News, 9*(3), 27–35. (Reprinted in 1991 as Teachers, schemata, and instruction. In M. Kennedy (Ed.), *Teaching academic subjects to diverse learners* (Rev. ed., pp. 218-233). New York: Teachers College Press.)

Steely, D., Carnine, D., & Engelmann, S. (1990). Teaching problem solving in mathematics. *ADI News, 10*(1), 28–39.

Engelmann, S. (1991). Change schools through revolution, not evolution. *Journal of Behavioral Education, 1*(3), 295–304.

Engelmann, S. (1991). How sensible is your reading program? A closer look at learner verification. *California Journal for Supervision and Curriculum Improvement, 4*(1), 16–22.

Engelmann, S. (1991). Why I sued California. *ADI News, 10*(2), 4–8.

Engelmann, S., Carnine, D., & Steely, D. G. (1991). Making connections in mathematics. *Journal of Learning Disabilities, 24*(5), 292–303. (Reprinted in 1992 in D. Carnine & E. J. Kameenui (Eds.), *Higher order thinking: Designing curriculum for mainstreamed students* (Rev. ed., pp. 75–106). Austin, TX: PRO-ED.)

Hofmeister, A. M., Engelmann, S., & Carnine, D. (1991). Technology and teacher enhancement: A videodisc alternative. *Technology in Education*. Alexandria, VA. Association for Supervision and Curriculum Development.

Engelmann, S. (1992). *War against the schools' academic child abuse*. Portland, OR: Halcyon House.

Engelmann, S. (1993). The curriculum as the cause of failure. *The Oregon Conference Monograph, 5*, 3–8. (Also available from http://zigsite.com/PDFs/Curriculumascauseoffailurepdffinal.pdf)

Adams, G. L., & Engelmann, S. (1996). *Research on Direct Instruction: 25 years beyond DISTAR*. Seattle, WA: Educational Achievement Systems.

Becker, W., & Engelmann, S. (1996). Sponsor findings from Project Follow Through. *Effective School Practices, 15*(1), 33–42.

Engelmann, S. (1997). Direct Instruction. In C. R. Dills & A. J. Romiszowski (Eds.), *Instructional development paradigms* (pp. 371-389). Englewood Cliffs, NJ: Educational Technology Publications.

Engelmann, S. (1997). Theory of mastery and acceleration. In J. W. Lloyd, E. J. Kameenui, & D. Chard (Eds.), *Issues in educating students with disabilities* (pp. 177-195). Mahwah, NJ: Lawrence Erlbaum.

Engelmann, S. (1999). The benefits of Direct Instruction: Affirmative action for at-risk students. *Educational Leadership, 57*(1), 77, 79.

Engelmann, S. (1999). Phonemic awareness in *Reading Mastery*. *Effective School Practices, 17*(3), 43-49.

Engelmann, S. (1999). A response: How sound is High/Scope research? *Educational Leadership, 56*(6), 83-84.

Engelmann, S. (1999). Response to "The High/Scope preschool curriculum comparison study through age 23." *Effective School Practices, 17*(3), 18-23.

Engelmann, S. (1999). Student-program alignment and teaching to mastery. Paper presented at the 25th National Direct Instruction Conference, Eugene, OR. (Reprinted in 2007 in the *Journal of Direct Instruction, 7*(1), 45-66.)

2000s

Engelmann, S. (2000). About reading: A comparison of *Reading Mastery* and *Horizons*. *Effective School Practices, 18*(3), 15-26.

Engelmann, S. (2001). Wesley Becker, the man. *Journal of Direct Instruction, 1*(1), 27-29.

Engelmann, S. (2002). *Models and expectations.* Eugene, OR: National Institute for Direct Instruction, 1-22.

Engelmann, S. (2002). *Prologue to Hirsch's cargo cults revisited.* Available from http://zigsite.com/HirschPro.htm

Engelmann, S. (2002). *Hirsch's cargo cults revisited.* Available from http://zigsite.com/Hirsch.htm

Engelmann, S. (2002). Response to Allington: Allington leveled serious allegations against Direct Instruction. *ADI News, 2*(2), 28-31.

Engelmann, S. (2002). *Summary of presentation to Council of Scientific Society Presidents, December 8, 2002.* (22 pp.). Available from http://zigsite.com/PDFs/CSSP_Acceptance.pdf

Engelmann, S. (2003). *Science versus basic educational research.* (19 pp.). Available from http://zigsite.com/PDFs/ScienceVersus.pdf. (Reprinted in 2008 in *Australasian Journal of Special Education, 32*(1), 139-157.)

Engelmann, S. (2004). About *Inferred functions of performance and learning.* Available from http://zigsite.com/InferredFunctions.htm

Engelmann, S. (2004). *At-risk reading naiveté.* Available from http://zigsite.com/EdWeek-Response.htm

Engelmann, S. (2004). Chapter one, *Data be damned*. Unpublished book. Available from http://zigsite.com/AtRisk.htm

Engelmann, S. (2004). Prologue comparative preschool study: High and low socioeconomic preschoolers learning advanced cognitive skills. Available from http://zigsite.com/CompPreschPro.htm

Engelmann, S. (2004). Comparative preschool study: High and low socioeconomic preschoolers learning advanced cognitive skills. (95 pp.). Available from http://zigsite.com/PDFs/CompPreschool.pdf

Engelmann, S. (2004). The dalmatian and its spots: Why research-based recommendations fail logic 101. *Education Week, 23*(20), 34-35, 48. (Reprint available at http://zigsite.com/Dalmatian.htm)

Engelmann, S. (2004). Prologue district-based teacher certification model. Available from http://zigsite.com/DistrictBasPro.htm

Engelmann, S. (2004). District-based teacher certification model. Available from http://zigsite.com/PDFs/DistBaseModel.pdf

Engelmann, S. (2004). Professional standards in education. Available from http://zigsite.com/Standards.htm

Engelmann, S. E., & Engelmann, K. E. (2004). Impediments to scaling up effective comprehensive school reform models. In T. K. Glennan Jr., S. J. Bodilly, J. R. Galegher, & K. A. Kerr (Eds.), *Expanding the reach of education reforms: Perspectives from leaders in the scale-up of educational interventions* (pp. 107-133). Santa Monica, CA: The RAND Corporation.

Engelmann, S., & Steely, D. (2004). *Inferred functions of performance and learning*. Mahwah, NJ: Lawrence Erlbaum.

Engelmann, S. (2005). Litmus test for urban school districts. Available from http://zigsite.com/LitmusTest.htm

Engelmann, S. (2005). Reading first = kids first. *Oregon's Future, 6*(1). (Reprint available from http://zigsite.com/OregonsFuture.htm)

Engelmann, S. (2005). Zig's commentary on Bersin's article "Making schools productive." Available from http://zigsite.com/bersinsArticle.htm

Engelmann, S., & Colvin, G. (2006). *Rubric for identifying authentic Direct Instruction programs*. Eugene, OR: Engelmann Foundation.

Engelmann, S. (2007). Improving reading rate of low performers (27 pp.). Available from http://zigsite.com/PDFs/readingrate.pdf

Engelmann, S. (2007). *Teaching needy kids in our backward system: 42 years of trying*. Eugene, OR: ADI Press.

Crawford, D., Engelmann, K. E., & Engelmann, S. (2008). Direct Instruction. In E. M. Anderman & L. H. Anderman (Eds.), *Psychology of classroom learning: An encyclopedia* (pp. 326-330). New York: Macmillan.

Engelmann, Z. (2008). Achieving a full-school, full-immersion implementation of Direct Instruction (10 pp.). Available from http://www.nifdi.org/pdfs/Dev_Guide.pdf

Engelmann, S. (2008). Prologue machinations of What Works Clearinghouse. Available from http://zigsite.com/prologue-wwc-10-7-08.htm

Engelmann, S. (2008). Machinations of What Works Clearinghouse (33 pp.). Available from http://www.zigsite.com/PDFs/MachinationsWWC%28V4%29.pdf

Engelmann, S. (2008). Socrates and education: Bussing. Available from http://zigsite.com/PDFs/SocratesAndBussing.pdf

Engelmann, S. (2009). Prologue to *low-performer's manual*. Available from http://www.zigsite.com/LowPerfomersPro.htm

Engelmann, S. (2009). Socrates on teacher training. Available from http://zigsite.com/PDFs/SocratesTeacherTraining.pdf

2010s

Engelmann, S. (2010). The dreaded standards. Available from http://zigsite.com/PDFs/TheDreadedStandards.pdf

Engelmann, S. (2010). Thank you, Josh Baker. Available from http://www.zigsite.com/PDFs/ThankYouJoshBaker.pdf

Engelmann, S., & Carnine, D. (2011). *Could John Stuart Mill have saved our schools?* Verona, WI: Full Court Press.

Engelmann. S. (2011). Critique and erasure: Responding to Eppley's *"Reading Mastery* as pedagogy of erasure." *Journal of Research in Rural Education, 26*(15), 1-4.

Engelmann, S. (2011). Socrates on AYP and social justice. Available from http://zigsite.com/PDFs/Socrates-on-AYP.pdf

Engelmann, S. (2011). Socrates on *Reading Mastery*. Available from http://www.zigsite.com/PDFs/SocratesOnReadingMastery.pdf

Engelmann, S. (2012). Homework is cruel in the primary grades. Available from http://zigsite.com/PDFs/HomeworkisCruelPrimaryGrades.pdf

Engelmann, S. (2012). Middle-class Follow Through students. Available from http://zigsite.com/PDFs/FTMiddleClass3.pdf

Engelmann, S. (2012). Socrates on Chicago's failure. Available from http://zigsite.com/PDFs/SocratesOnChicagoFailurev2.pdf

Engelmann, S. (2012). Socrates on program adoptions. Available from http://zigsite.com/PDFs/SocratesOnProgramAdoption.pdf

Engelmann, S. (2013). Socrates on gold standard experiments. Available from http://zigsite.com/PDFs/SocratesOnGoldStandards.pdf

Engelmann, S. (2014). Critique of lowercase d i (direct instruction). Available from http://zigsite.com/Critique_of_Lowercased_di%28direct_instruction.html

Engelmann, S. (2014). Research from the inside: The development and testing of DI programs. In J. Stockard (Ed.), *The science and success of Engelmann's Direct Instruction*, pp. 3-24. Eugene, OR: NIFDI Press.

Engelmann, S., & Stockard, J. (2014). Blinded to evidence: How educational researchers respond to empirical data. In J. Stockard (Ed.), *The science and success of Engelmann's Direct Instruction*, pp. 55-78. Eugene, OR: NIFDI Press.

Engelmann, S. (2014). Oregon's Matrix, The Emperor's Latest Clothes. Available from http://zigsite.com/PDFs/OregonMatrix_SEngelmann.pdf

Engelmann, S. (2014). *Successful and confident students with Direct Instruction*. Eugene, OR: NIFDI Press.

APPENDIX C

TRENDS IN ENGELMANN'S WRITING CAREER, 1966 TO 2014

The following graphs visually represent trends in Engelmann's writing career over 50 years. When possible, all of Engelmann's publications listed in Appendix B were placed into one of the four themes discussed in the body of the book. In some instances specific publications dealt with multiple themes; these were placed in the category that was their primary focus. Figure 1 shows the percentage of Engelmann's publications that fell into each of these four themes and demonstrates the focus and attention given to each topic over his entire career.

Figure 1: Engelmann Publications by Topic

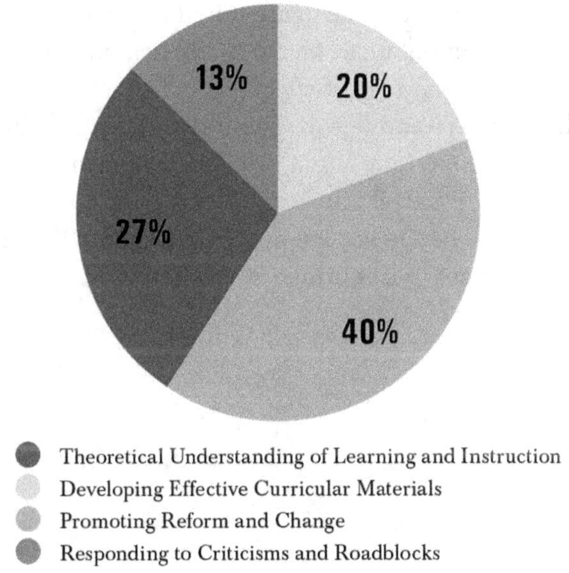

- Theoretical Understanding of Learning and Instruction
- Developing Effective Curricular Materials
- Promoting Reform and Change
- Responding to Criticisms and Roadblocks

Figure 2 reports the number of publications appearing during each decade. The peaks and valleys of Engelmann's publications over the decades no doubt correspond to the programs he was simultaneously developing and revising (listed in Appendix A and not included in this analysis).

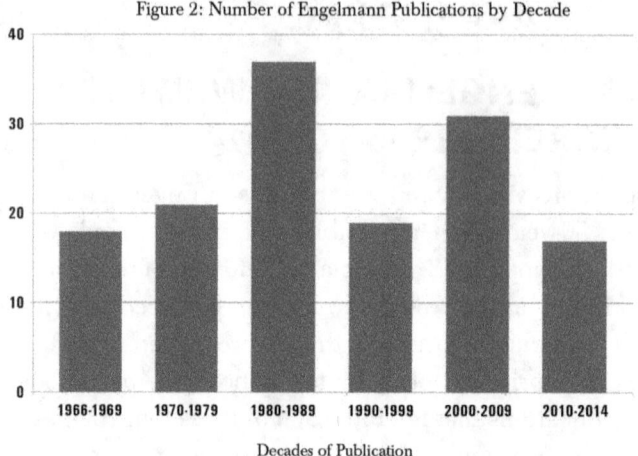

Figure 2: Number of Engelmann Publications by Decade

Figure 3 shows Engelmann's development and focus on specific themes over time. The lines in the figure represent the percentage of articles within a given decade that focused on each theme. They reveal Engelmann's initial focus on the theoretical understanding of learning and the development of effective curricular materials that embodied these understandings. Beginning in the late 1980s there was a shift in focus to writing about promoting reform and change in education as well as responding to criticisms and roadblocks. His focus on promoting change has intensified since the 2000s and the data suggests this focus will continue in the future.

Appendix C

Figure 3: Distribution of Themes in Engelmann's Writings by Decade

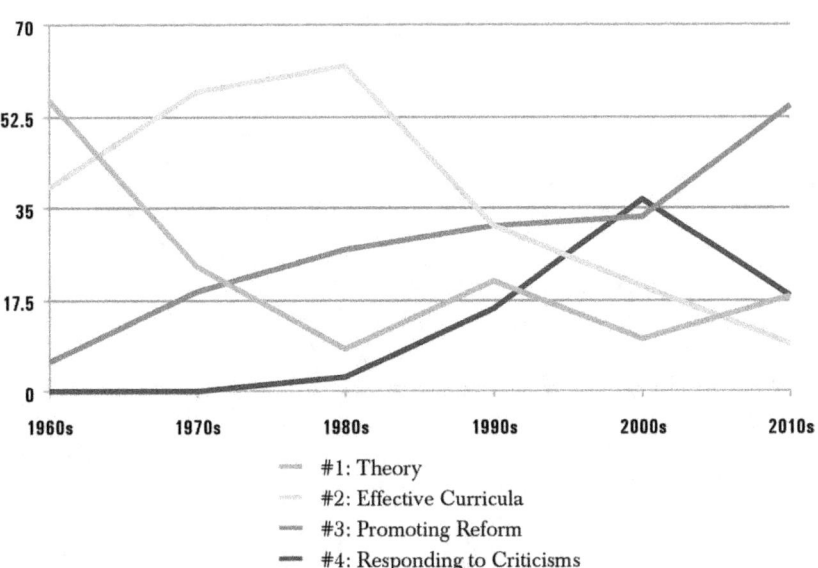

— #1: Theory
--- #2: Effective Curricula
— #3: Promoting Reform
— #4: Responding to Criticisms

APPENDIX D

A CHRONOLOGY OF ENGELMANN'S CAREER HIGHLIGHTS

1950s

1955: B.A. Philosophy with Class Honors, University of Illinois, Urbana.

1960s

1960–1964: Worked in different advertising agencies and began analyzing techniques for marketing to children in order to determine what type of input was necessary to induce retention.

1963: Filmed his teaching sessions with his twin sons in order to demonstrate the effectiveness of his techniques and theories of instruction to education departments in various universities.

1964–1966: Worked with Carl Bereiter as a research associate for the Institute for Research on Exceptional Children, University of Illinois, Champaign, Illinois.

1964: Creation of the Bereiter Engelmann preschool.

1966: *Give Your Child a Superior Mind* is published.

1966: Visiting Professor, Ontario Institute for Studies in Education, Toronto, Canada.

1966–1968: Senior education specialist, Downs Syndrome Project, Children's Research Center, University of Illinois.

1966–1970: Senior educational specialist, Institute on Exceptional Children and Bureau of Education Research, University of Illinois.

1967: First criticisms of Jean Piaget are published.

1968: Project Follow Through begins.

1968–present: President of Engelmann-Becker Corp., Eugene, Oregon.

1969: First *DISTAR* instructional programs are released. Initially *DISTAR Reading* and *Language*.

1970s

1970–1974: Associate Professor of Education, University of Oregon, Eugene, Oregon.

1970: *DISTAR Arithmetic I* instructional program is published.

1972–1975: Visiting Research Associate, Oregon Research Institute, Eugene, Oregon.

1974: Engelmann's first study using tactual vocoders with deaf subjects is published.

1974–2003: Professor of Special Education, University of Oregon, Eugene, Oregon.

1975–1981: Research Associate, Oregon Research Institute, Eugene, Oregon.

1975: *Your Child Can Succeed: How to Get the Most Out of School for Your Child* is published.

1975: *Corrective Reading* instructional program is published.

1975: First DI Conference is held, Eugene, Oregon.

1976: *Spelling Through Morphographs* instructional program is published.

1980s

1980: *Spelling Mastery* instructional program series is published.

1980: *The Instructional Design Library Series (Vol. 22): Direct Instruction* is published.

1981: *Corrective Mathematics* instructional program is published.

1982: *Theory of Instruction* is published.

1983: *Generalized Compliance Training: A Direct-instruction program for managing severe behavior problems* is published.

1983: *Reading Mastery* instructional program is published.

1983: *Teach Your Child to Read in 100 Easy Lessons* is published.

1984: Honorary doctorate degree from the Psychology Department of Western Michigan University.

1985: *Mastering Fractions* instructional program is published, the first in a series of videodisc programs.

1985: *Expressive Writing* instructional program is published.

1987: *Understanding Chemistry and Energy* instructional videodisc program is published.

1988: *Earth Science* instructional videodisc program is published.

1990s

1991: *Reasoning & Writing* instructional program is published.

1991: Engelmann sues the California State Board, Department of Education and Curriculum Commission.

1991: *Theory of Instruction* is revised and republished.

1992: *Connecting Math Concepts* instructional program is published.

1992: *War Against the Schools' Academic Child Abuse* is published.

1994: Engelmann receives American Psychological Association Fred Keller Award of Excellence.

1996: *Sponsor Findings from Project Follow Through* is published.

1996: *Research on Direct Instruction: 25 Years Beyond DISTAR* is published.

1997: National Institute for Direct Instruction (NIFDI) is established with Engelmann as the director.

1997: *Horizons Learning to Read* instructional program is published.

2000s

2000: Zigsite.com is launched.

2000: Engelmann is named one of the 54 "most influential people" in the history of special education by *Remedial and Special Education*.

2000: *Journeys Direct Instruction Reading* program is published.

2001: *Funnix Beginning Reading* instructional program is published.

2001: *Español to English (Language for Learning)* instructional program is published.

2002: Engelmann receives the Council of Scientific Society Presidents 2002 Educational Research Award (Award of Achievement in Education Research).

2002: *Funnix Reading 2* instructional program is published.

2003-present: Professor Emeritus of Special Education, University of Oregon, Eugene, Oregon.

2004: *Inferred Functions of Performance and Learning* is published.

2007: *Teaching Needy Kids in Our Backward System: 42 Years of Trying* is published.

2008: *Socrates and Education: Bussing* is published on zigsite.com (first in Socrates series).

2010s

2010: *Direct Instruction Spoken English (DISE)* instructional program is published.

2010: *Could John Stuart Mill Have Saved Our Schools?* is published.

2011: *Funnix Beginning Math* instructional program is published.

AUTHOR BIOGRAPHIES

Timothy W. Wood

Timothy W. Wood is a researcher for the National Institute for Direct Instruction. He received his B.A. in History from Lewis & Clark College with a focus on twentieth century U.S. history. He is also a graduate of Northwestern University's Museum Studies program.

Siegfried "Zig" Engelmann

Siegfried "Zig" Engelmann is professor emeritus of education at the University of Oregon and the primary architect of the Direct Instruction (DI) approach, an approach based on the principles originated in the Bereiter-Engelmann Preschool in the late 1960s. Engelmann is the senior author of more than 100 curricula using DI principles and numerous other articles and books. He has a bachelor's degree in philosophy from the University of Illinois and an honorary doctorate from the Psychology Department of Western Michigan University. He is the 1994 recipient of the Fred S. Keller Award from the American Psychological Association's Division of Experimental Analysis of Behavior. In 2000 the journal *Remedial and Special Education* named him as one of the 54 most influential people in the history of special education, and in 2002 the Council of Scientific Society Presidents awarded him the 2002 Award of Achievement in Education Research.

Carl Bereiter

At the time of publication (1966) Dr. Carl Bereiter was a member of the Institute for Research on Exceptional Children at the University of Illinois. He served as the Coordinator of Research for curriculum research and development for the preschool education of disadvantaged children, and as a consulting editor for the *Journal of Educational Measurement*. He received his Ph.D. in Educational Psychology from the University of Wisconsin.

Douglas Carnine

At the time of publication (1982, 1984-1985) Dr. Douglas Carnine had received his B.S. in Psychology from the University of Illinois in 1969, his M.A. in Special Education from the University of Oregon in 1971, and his Ph.D. in Educational Psychology from the University of Utah in 1974. He was an Associate Professor in the Department of Teacher Education, Mildly Handicapped Division at the University of Oregon and later a Professor of Education at the University of Oregon. He continued to collaborate with Siegfried Engelmann on publications and curriculum programs in the following decades, and has produced over 100 scholarly publications.

Dan Close

At the time of publication (1983) Dr. Dan Close had received his B.A. in Psychology from the Californian Lutheran College in 1971, his M.A. in Psychology from Idaho State University in 1973, and his Ph.D. in Special Education in 1977 from the University of Oregon.

Geoff Colvin

At the time of publication (1983) Dr. Geoff Colvin had received his Ph.D. in Special Education from the University of Oregon. His research has focused on behavioral interventions for students with behavior problems in general education settings. He has served as a teacher, school administrator, and research associate at the University of Oregon. Following this publication he continued to collaborate with Siegfried Engelmann and authored additional publications together.

Alex Granzin

At the time of publication (1979) Dr. Alex Granzin had received his B.S. at the University of New Orleans, and his Ph.D. at the University of Oregon. He participated in multiple research projects at the Oregon Research Institute and the University of Oregon before becoming a school psychologist.

Alan M. Hofmeister

At the time of publication (1985) Dr. Alan M. Hofmeister was the Director at the Artificial Intelligence Research and Development Unit, Utah State University, a position he still holds today (2014). He received his Ph.D. in Special Education with Honors from the University of Oregon in 1969.

Jean Osborn

At the time of publication (1966) Dr. Jean Osborn was a member of the Institute for Research on Exceptional Children at the University of Illinois. She continued to collaborate with Siegfried Engelmann on the development and revisions of multiple Direct Instruction reading, language, and writing programs, including the early *DISTAR Language* programs.

Philip A. Reidford

At the time of publication (1966) Dr. Philip A. Reidford was a member of the Institute for Research on Exceptional Children at the University of Illinois.

Robert Rosov

At the time of publication (1975) Dr. Robert Rosov was a Research Associate at the Oregon Research Institute.

Herbert Severson

At the time of publication (1979) Dr. Herbert Severson was a Research Scientist at the Oregon Research Institute, and served as Director from 1979-1986. He previously worked as an Assistant Professor of Psychology at the University of Northern Colorado, Greeley (1972-1975), University of North Colorado (1975-1980), and Assistant Professor of Educational Psychology and Director of the School Psychology Program at the University of Oregon (1975-1980).

George Singer

At the time of publication (1983) Dr. George Singer had received his Ph.D. in Special Education from the University of Oregon. While completing his doctorate, he worked as a researcher at the Oregon Research Institute, eventually becoming a Research Scientist.

Paul Williams

At the time of publication (1989) Dr. Williams had received his Ph.D. from the University of Oregon. He worked with Siegfried Engelmann on his doctorate and research on understanding the process of unfamiliar learning.

ACKNOWLEDGEMENTS

This publication honors the career of Siegfried Engelmann, his dedication to helping all children succeed, the vast number of his publications, and his impact on the field of education. His continued effort to help all children succeed is remarkable. His ability to recall the details of these publications to provide additional insight was invaluable. Jean Stockard must be recognized for her input and guidance throughout the process. Beth Wood revived the figures and graphs from the original publications to provide much greater clarity to help the reader better understand the impact of Siegfried Engelmann. Additionally, Christina Cox must be acknowledged for her design work and suggestions along the way. Ashly Cupit was an incredible aide throughout the process by transcribing the original articles and obtaining permissions to republish. The work of Jerry Silbert and Marge Mayo should also be recognized. Finally, this publication could not have been accomplished without the continuous support of my family and friends.

SUBJECT INDEX

A

absolute pitch, 3, 195-197, 199, 201, 203-206, 440

Abt Associates, 209-210, 222, 387, 396

academic child abuse, 225, 228, 440, 451

accelerated learning, 106

accountability, 79, 293, 410, 436

accreditation, 307-309

administrator(s), 193, 225, 227-228, 289, 293, 299, 302-304, 311, 335-336, 355, 389, 401, 405

aptitude, 29-31, 68, 117, 297, 344

arithmetic, 45, 65, 67-68, 115-116, 118-119, 121, 127, 131-135, 137, 142, 168-169, 172, 208, 223, 276, 429, 435-436, 450

assessment(s), 47, 90, 168, 200-201, 225-226, 273, 289, 304, 341, 393, 411, 428

attention deficit disorder (ADD), 200, 331

attitude(s), 31, 91-92, 105, 108, 121, 167-169, 172-173, 221, 252, 273-274, 284, 286, 316, 405, 437

autism, 113

B

Bank Street Early Childhood Education Model, 209, 211-217

behavior analysis, 208-209, 211-217, 222, 437

behavior(s), 12-13, 15, 17-18, 23-26, 31-33, 38, 45, 49-53, 57-64, 68-70, 81, 96, 101, 103, 122-123, 129, 153-154, 158, 174, 177-186, 221, 231-233, 238, 240, 243, 262, 264-266, 273-275, 278-288, 290, 294, 296, 357-358, 365, 436-439, 451, 454

belief(s), 2, 95, 100, 112, 137, 220, 315-316, 329, 353, 379-380, 395

Bereiter-Engelmann Preschool, 1, 3, 7, 11, 27, 31, 111, 115, 225, 449, 453

bias, 338-339

biology, 194

brain, 21-22, 119, 270, 304, 401

Brookings Institute, 340

busing, 383, 386-387, 389, 395, 399, 443, 452

C

chemistry, 394, 433, 451

City Springs Elementary, 393, 396

classroom(s), 3, 7-8, 32-33, 40, 58, 87, 94-97, 168-169, 171, 173, 189, 192-193, 197, 208-209, 219-220, 222, 229, 273-275, 278-280, 283-287, 289-290, 295, 298, 311, 314-320, 322-323, 329, 332, 340, 349, 354, 376, 383-384, 395-396, 403, 405-406, 410, 433, 437, 442

coaching, 48, 291, 323

Coalition for Educational Justice, 319-320

cognition, 123

cognitive-conceptual skills, 212

cognitively-oriented curriculum model, 209, 211-217; see also High Scope Preschool

Common Core, 413-414

compensatory education, 208, 222, 380, 385, 387, 389-390, 436

compliance training, 181, 184, 186, 433, 438, 451

comprehension, 29, 39, 171, 174, 212, 221, 249-250, 252-253, 257-259, 262-264, 426, 439

confidence, 3, 73, 96, 102, 105, 120, 143, 174, 330, 369

conspiracy, 343

consultants, 288-289

Coopersmith Self-Esteem Inventory, 210

Corrective Reading, 101, 426, 429-430, 439, 450

crime(s), 361-362, 364, 390

457

criticisms, 1, 4-5, 123, 353, 355, 357, 379, 445-447, 449

critics, 343, 353

critique(s), 4, 111, 167, 337, 355, 357, 387-388, 396, 414, 416, 421, 439, 443

curiosity, 170, 174

curriculum(a), 2, 8, 12, 31, 47, 76, 78-79, 92, 111-112, 117-118, 209, 211-217, 222, 226, 231, 251, 297, 299, 305, 319, 357-360, 361, 363, 365-369, 375, 403, 408, 435, 440-441, 447, 451, 453-454,

D

deaf, 18-19, 21, 71, 113, 145-151, 153-155, 157, 159-165, 437, 450; see also hard of hearing

decoding, 137-138, 168, 171, 174, 218, 249-252, 257, 426

deficiency(ies), 21-22, 59, 63, 65, 68-70, 117, 124, 296, 386

deficit(s), 8, 11, 22, 116, 135, 354, 382, 385

diagnosis(es), 13, 21-23, 57-61, 63, 68, 70, 305, 315

diagnostician(s), 21-22, 58-59, 70

Direct Instruction Spoken English (DISE), 428, 452

disability(ies), 9, 80, 305, 440-441

dissemination, 207, 218, 219

DISTAR, 2, 111, 167-170, 172-173, 208, 220, 369, 411, 423-424, 427-429, 433, 440, 450-451, 455

division, 117, 326, 429, 437, 453-454

Downs Syndrome, 179, 449

dyslexia, 40

E

educator(s), 15, 21, 23, 33, 57, 59, 122, 137, 168, 187-188, 241, 274, 296, 372, 385-386, 389, 391, 399

efficiency, 2, 27, 73, 86, 111, 113, 231, 437

endorsement(s), 287-288, 302, 369

energy, 147, 190-191, 394, 433, 451

enrichment, 116, 237

equality, 11, 228, 353, 395

error(s), 18, 36, 60, 83, 85, 90, 96-97, 99, 101, 193, 196, 238-239, 246, 253, 258, 357, 363

esteem, 210, 213, 222, 331

ethic(s), 402, 410

evaluation(s), 31, 43, 55, 175, 186, 207-209, 223, 242, 293, 297, 301, 305, 312, 386-388, 396, 433

evaluator(s), 103, 288, 341

exemplars, 404, 408

expert(s), 288, 296, 299-301, 307, 333, 337-338, 381, 393, 407, 411

F-G

field testing, 297, 329, 405, 408, 439

Follow Through, 3, 96, 112-113, 149, 168-169, 175, 207-8, 218-223, 277, 288, 322-323, 358, 386-393, 396, 436-438, 440, 443, 449, 451

Funnix, 427, 431, 452

game(s), 15, 28, 59, 64, 66-67, 69, 85, 105, 205, 418, 433

geometry, 431

gifted, 16, 32, 342

gold standard, 227, 337-338, 340, 344, 346, 349-350, 443

grammar, 13, 20-21, 23, 328

H

handicapped students, 179, 186

handicaps, 113, 177-178

handwriting, 107

hard of hearing, 113, 145 (see also deaf)

Hawthorne effect, 220, 344

High Scope preschool, 209, 357-359, 363, 365-367, 369, 389-390, 441 historians, 390

history, 2, 60, 76, 153, 313, 350, 376, 380, 382, 389-390, 452-453

homework, 100, 443

Horizons, 427, 441, 452

horserace, 386-387

humanism, 399

I

identity, 18, 25, 129, 133, 135, 137

idiom(s), 117, 297

Illinois Test of Psycholinguistic Abilities (ITPA), 120, 128

individualization, 81, 220, 377

induction(s), 43, 249, 264-265, 267

inequity(ies), 382

inference(s), 12-13, 45, 48, 105, 117, 131, 241, 251-252, 254, 257, 263-266, 271, 359

injustice, 317

innovation(s), 182, 290-291, 437, 439

innovator, 396

institutionalization, 186

integration, 189, 249, 251-253, 258, 383

integrity, 353

intellect, 137; see also intelligence and IQ

Intellectual Achievement Responsibility Scale (IARS), 210

intelligence, 29, 58, 76, 108, 116, 336, 454; see also IQ

interaction(s), 11, 180, 266, 279-280, 344, 391, 416

invention(s), 265-267

investigation(s), 23, 196, 323, 327, 373, 386

investigator(s), 17, 50, 146-148, 155, 169, 196-200, 289, 338-339, 373, 375, 385

IQ, 31-32, 55, 96-97, 207, 218, 223, 369, 385, 435-436

J-K

Journeys, 427, 452

justice, 310, 315, 317-321, 443

Keller Award of Excellence, 451, 453

kindergarten, 32, 47-48, 50-51, 80-81, 104, 173, 209, 218, 223, 331, 334, 382, 400, 413-414, 416-417

kindergartener(s), 415-416, 419

kinetic energy, 190-191

knowledge, 5, 7-8, 11, 23, 32, 45, 48-49, 61-69, 75-79, 91, 105, 107, 109, 134, 141, 190, 210-211, 221, 271, 296, 299, 309-311, 317, 319, 362, 375, 381-383, 394-395, 398-399, 408, 416-418

L

labeling, 25, 129, 265

laboratory(ies), 165, 209, 380, 404, 435

language(s), 2-3, 7-9, 11-16, 18, 21-26, 45, 55, 64, 70, 87, 94, 107-108, 111, 115, 117-124, 126, 128, 131-134, 136-138, 141-142, 157, 168, 180, 183, 206, 208-211, 213, 217, 221, 263, 289, 296-297, 301, 318, 322, 383-387, 389, 391, 399-402, 405-406, 409, 425, 427-429, 433, 435-437, 439, 450, 452, 455

Language Development (Bilingual) Model, 209, 211-217

Language for Learning, 428, 452

laws, 65, 406

lawsuit, 406

leaders, 289, 353, 442

leadership, 223, 289-291, 439, 441

learner(s), 1, 57-64, 66-70, 177-183, 185, 197, 205-206, 234, 252, 275-276, 287, 405-406, 418, 437, 439-440

learning, 1-5, 7-9, 11, 15-16, 23-25, 27-31, 33, 35-36, 39, 43-44, 46-48, 52-54, 57, 59, 68-71, 73-77, 79-80, 84-85, 87, 90, 92, 95-96, 98-100, 105-115, 117, 119, 121, 123, 125, 127-128, 136-138, 140, 142, 145, 167, 177, 179-180, 188-189, 192-197, 200, 205, 221-222, 226, 228, 231, 244, 271, 274, 277,

280, 282-283, 290, 298, 305, 318, 321, 325, 330-331, 342, 353-355, 379, 382, 384, 388, 391, 396, 398, 400-401, 403, 418, 421, 427-428, 435-442, 445-446, 452, 455

legislation, 406

linguist, 33

linguistics, 12, 436

liquid(s), 44, 48-50, 55-56, 435

literacy, 326, 331, 411

literature, 53, 99, 196-197, 205, 249, 274, 288-289, 332-333, 391, 399, 401, 411, 424-425, 427

litmus test, 442

logic, 49, 126, 296, 300, 368, 372-373, 375-376, 382-383, 388, 391-392, 394, 409, 439, 442

M

manipulations, 364, 368, 394, 421

manipulative(s), 295, 388, 392, 421

marketing, 7, 325-327, 449

mastery, 3, 9, 11, 73-84, 86-96, 98-101, 103-105, 107-110, 113-114, 117, 120-122, 128-129, 136, 153, 159, 163, 174, 187-189, 192-195, 220, 243, 246-247, 249-251, 253, 255-257, 259-263, 265-267, 269-271, 276, 278, 336, 373, 377, 423-425, 428-429, 431-432, 438, 441, 443, 450-451

mastery learning, 3, 107-108, 110, 188-189, 192-194

math (mathematics), 2, 7, 77, 87, 90, 93-94, 101-102, 107-108, 111, 131, 172, 189, 193, 207, 210-215, 218-219, 289, 294-295, 298, 303, 305, 309, 318, 322, 330-331, 334, 342, 384-385, 387, 389-391, 396, 399, 403, 405, 408-409, 411, 414-418, 421, 429-431, 439-440, 450-452

maturation, 46

maturity, 45

measure(s), 45, 63, 174, 204, 208-213, 218, 221-222, 298, 345, 347, 403

measurement, 44, 56, 436, 453

media, 51-52

medicine, 314-315, 339, 342, 410-411

memory, 83, 86, 205, 299, 331, 342

Metropolitan Achievement Test (MAT), 210, 213, 218, 221

misrule(s), 89-90

mistake(s), 14, 18, 69, 81, 83, 86, 94, 96-97, 100-101, 104, 135, 197, 238-240, 245-246, 258, 274, 276, 284, 286, 290

model(s), 1, 55, 66, 73, 87, 92, 109-113, 115, 131, 146, 167-168, 175, 177, 183, 186-187, 191, 193, 195, 205, 207-214, 217-219, 222, 239, 257-258, 277, 280, 283-284, 286-287, 290, 309-310, 322-323, 355, 358-359, 365, 368, 383, 386-393, 396, 410, 413-414, 416-417, 436-442

modeling, 97, 221, 238, 416-417

morality, 296

morphographs, 431, 450

movement(s), 93, 182, 191-192, 260, 296

multiplication, 429

music, 195, 198 (see also absolute pitch)

myth(s), 389, 421

N

naiveté, 300, 441

National Council of Teachers of English (NCTE), 296-297, 305, 391

National Council of Teachers of Mathematics (NCTM), 294-296, 305, 390-391

noncompliance, 181

norm(s), 70, 120, 168, 171-173, 183, 213, 342, 345, 349-350

normalization, 179-180

O

objectives, 30, 115, 117, 253, 257, 262, 271, 293-294, 435, 438 objects, 13-18, 23-25, 35, 45, 48-52, 54-56, 66, 120, 124, 127-129, 132, 154, 156, 178, 185

Occam's razor, 314

open classroom model, 209, 211-217

opinion(s), 53, 178, 207, 237, 241, 250-251, 294-295, 299, 308, 327, 395, 407

opportunity(ies), 47-48, 78, 86, 92, 102, 112, 115, 158, 193, 252, 297, 335, 383-386, 395

opposition, 415

oral reading, 171, 257-258

orientation(s), 23-24, 70, 80-81, 131

orthography, 34, 138

oscilloscope, 146

P

pace, 102, 104, 157, 321

pacing, 82, 97, 275, 278, 284, 289

paradigms, 441

parents, 130, 221, 298-301, 318-319, 398, 400, 402-403, 433

participation, 119, 160, 181, 197, 232

passion, 4-5

peer(s), 8, 11, 111-112, 208, 225, 291, 304

Perry preschool project, 366-367

philosopher, 227

philosophy(ies), 1-2, 5, 7-8, 90, 111-112, 221, 227-228, 298, 303-304, 325-326, 349-350, 355, 387, 392, 394-395, 449, 453

phoneme(s), 138, 146, 150, 373-374

phonemic awareness, 334, 372-375, 408, 441

phonic(s), 138, 142, 372-373, 376, 399, 401, 408-409

physics, 309, 417

placement(s), 2, 8, 73-74, 93, 97-99, 100-101, 109, 153, 185-186, 289, 384, 394, 426, 430

policy(ies), 3-5, 99, 223, 228, 300, 320, 354-355, 379, 386, 389, 397, 413

policymakers, 228, 320, 354-355, 379-383, 384-385, 387-389, 394

power, 3, 108, 188-193, 260, 303-305, 379-380, 384, 389, 401, 411

practicum (practica), 97, 169, 200, 287, 290

practitioners, 314

praise, 87, 184, 200, 238-239

precision, 103, 161, 235, 338, 414, 417-418

prejudice(s), 379-380, 383, 387, 389, 392

prepositions, 65, 126, 129

preschool(s), 1, 3, 7, 11, 27, 30-31, 56, 105, 111, 115, 223, 225, 353, 357-359, 361, 365-369, 385, 390, 435-436, 441-442, 449, 453

preschoolers, 7, 366, 385, 442

preteaching, 253

principal(s), 274, 319, 368, 384

principles, 2-3, 8, 43, 46-48, 53-54, 56-57, 73, 111, 113, 115, 129, 141, 145, 177, 179-180, 182, 186, 208-209, 227-228, 284, 341, 355, 391-392, 394, 401, 407-411, 435, 437-438, 453

priority(ies), 155, 284, 293, 303, 315, 317, 436

professional(s), 303, 305, 340-341, 391, 397, 410, 438, 442

protocol, 397-398, 401-403, 410

prototype, 291

psycholinguistic(s), 12, 18, 22, 120

psychologist(s), 59, 297, 401-404, 411, 454

psychology, 4, 12, 164, 305, 342, 349, 353, 395, 433, 435-436, 442, 451, 453-455

punctuation, 303

punishment, 68, 180

Q-R

qualification(s), 380, 403, 408

randomized assignment, 340, 341

ratio(s), 51, 67, 429, 431

rationale, 8, 101, 155, 157, 325, 362, 398

Raven's Coloured Progressive Matricies, 210, 212

readability, 244

reader(s), 173, 181, 251, 253-255, 257, 268, 276, 279, 297, 305, 372, 376, 382, 456

readiness, 29, 80

reading achievement, 169

reading comprehension, 212, 221, 426, 439

Reading Mastery, 78, 81, 91, 249-250, 253, 256-257, 259-260, 262-263, 265-267, 269-271, 336, 423-425, 438, 441, 443, 451

Reading rate, 442

reading skills, 8, 81, 304

reasoning, 112, 174, 314, 371-374, 388, 392, 394, 414-416, 432

Reasoning and Writing, 432

reform(s), 1, 223, 293-294, 296-297, 302-304, 372, 380, 382, 395, 397, 399-403, 407, 410, 442, 445-447

reinforcement, 46-47, 52-53, 82, 94, 155, 158, 181-182, 195, 205, 209, 220, 276-278, 293

reinforcers, 158, 185, 200

relearning, 69

reliability, 201, 287, 405

remediation, 2, 13, 21-23, 26

remedy(ies), 21-22, 58-60, 66-70, 240, 274, 276-277, 317, 319, 382

researcher(s), 3, 225, 227-228, 337, 354-355, 371-372, 374, 397, 403, 408-410, 444, 453, 455

responsive education model, 209, 211-217

retardation, 179, 296, 299

reteaching, 84, 102, 108-109

retention(s), 7, 11, 77, 87, 99, 192-193, 218, 222, 258, 401, 449

retesting, 120

revolution, 227, 440

reward(s), 155, 157, 180, 182, 186

rhyme(s), 28, 34, 40, 139, 141, 157

rhyming, 28, 34, 40, 141, 150, 157, 373

Ritalin, 331

ritual, 313, 350

RNA chain, 189

roadblocks, 1, 353, 355, 445-446

robot(s), 336, 353

routine(s), 87, 91-92

rubric, 442

rule(s), 13-15, 18-25, 33-35, 50, 53, 55-56, 61, 64, 66, 87, 89, 93-99, 100, 103, 117, 128, 135, 137-142, 155-156, 172, 180, 182, 210, 234, 251, 253, 258-261, 262-268, 278, 285, 300, 318, 330, 334, 390, 398, 406, 420

S

salary(ies), 380, 401

schedule(s), 38, 75-76, 80-81, 93-94, 109, 150, 158, 280, 282-283, 286, 328, 333

schema (schemata), 91, 440

science(s), 2, 113, 169, 172, 187, 189-190, 193, 208, 222, 260, 271, 313, 349, 391-392, 394-396, 399, 401, 410, 423-424, 426-433, 436, 438-441, 443-444, 451

scientist(s), 392, 455

sensitivity, 153, 316

signal(s), 28, 78, 104, 147, 201, 285, 289, 402

signaling, 280

simulations, 187-188

skeptic, 363

skepticism, 315, 323-324

sociolinguists, 385, 436

Index

sociology, 123

song(s), 198-200

special education, 289, 437-439, 441, 450, 452, 453-455

speech(es), 71, 113, 130, 137, 145, 147-149, 152-155, 163-165, 179, 184, 257, 261, 263, 266, 437

spelling, 37, 100, 107, 210-211, 213, 216-217, 281-282, 387, 431-432, 450

spontaneity, 49

stairway, 75-77, 79-80, 82, 109

standardized test, 246

standards, 2-3, 12, 15-16, 103, 121, 180, 227, 294-296, 301-305, 309, 312-313, 315, 328, 330-331, 333-334, 337, 343, 349, 354, 374-375, 384, 397, 401, 405, 410, 413-414, 416, 418, 421, 442-443

Stanford Achievement Test (SAT), 169, 171-174, 330

Stanford-Binet IQ scores, 31, 120

Stanford Research Institute, 387

STAR study, Tennessee, 340

stereotype(s), 188-189

stimulus(i), 14, 276-277, 279, 281

strategy(ies), 11-12, 65, 67, 74, 87, 92, 96, 102, 107-109, 121, 185, 195, 197, 199, 208, 220, 252, 255, 258-259, 310, 381, 392-393, 417, 426, 433

subtraction, 429

superintendent(s), 303, 375, 400

supervision, 4, 226-227, 273-277, 280, 283, 286-288, 291, 439-440

supervisor(s), 169, 226, 273, 275-290

symbol(s), 33-35, 39, 133-136

T

tactic(s), 380-381

tactual, 3, 113, 145-150, 154, 159-160, 162-165, 206, 437, 450

tantrum(s), 180, 183-184

teacher training, 4, 208, 227-228, 288-289, 307-310, 312, 320, 324, 436, 443

technology(ies), 113, 165, 178-179, 186-189, 206, 212, 290, 437-441

text(s), 37, 89, 172, 248, 252, 254, 258, 260, 262, 268, 277, 373

textbook(s), 89-90, 189, 334, 393, 404-406, 410, 431, 433

theory(ies), 3-4, 8-9, 43-48, 54-56, 111, 113, 115, 177, 186, 190, 194, 198, 209, 212, 231, 290, 302, 317, 343, 353-354, 392, 413, 435, 437-439, 441, 447, 449, 451

traditionalist(s), 80, 302

trainee(s), 168-169, 173, 287

trainer(s), 149-150, 152, 156-159, 161, 163, 286-287, 300, 322-323, 329, 381

training, 4, 21-22, 28-29, 49, 52, 74, 97, 117-121, 123, 148-164, 169, 179, 181-186, 196-197, 200, 205, 208, 219, 222, 227-228, 276, 278-279, 283, 286-291, 298-299, 303, 307-315, 317, 319-321, 323-324, 339, 376-377, 381, 409, 423, 433, 436, 438-439, 443, 451

transformation(s), 20, 48-49, 51, 88, 108, 219, 383, 394

Tucson Early Education Model (TEEM), 209, 211-217

U-V

unfamiliar learning, 71, 113, 145, 197, 437, 455

universities, 308-309, 314, 449

validity, 7, 43, 111-112, 307, 312, 340-341, 343-346, 348-349

variable(s), 2, 8, 27, 54, 58, 61, 73, 112, 114, 135, 153, 227, 275, 278, 291, 341, 345, 350, 368, 375, 413, 421

verbs, 117

vibration(s), 113, 147, 150

vibrators, 147-148, 153, 154

video, 187-189, 191, 193, 233, 439

videodisc(s), 194, 431, 439-440, 451

463

vocabulary(ies), 15, 18, 21, 76, 79, 89-91, 122, 124, 126-128, 139, 150, 154, 156, 158-163, 249, 251-254, 257, 260, 262, 271

vocoder(s), 3, 113, 145, 147-149, 152-155, 160-161, 163, 165, 206, 437, 450

volunteers, 198, 318

vouchers, 300

W

waivers, 318

war, 386, 440, 451

waves, 191-192, 256, 336

Wavetek Signal Generator, 201

weaknesses, 29, 112, 226, 249

wealth, 5, 207, 407

What Works Clearinghouse (WWC), 338, 343, 443

whole language, 296-297, 301, 391, 399-402, 405, 439,

Wide Range Achievement Test (WRAT), 171, 173, 218

wisdom, 95, 98, 109, 394-395

NAME INDEX

A

Adams, M., 333

Adams, G., 369, 405, 411, 440

Addams, J., 254-256

Adler, E., 275, 290

Alberts, B., 392, 394-395

Alessi, G., 297, 305

Anderman, E. M., 442

Anderman, L. H., 442

Anderson, R. B., 396

Arbogast, A., 424, 427, 432

Armor, D. J., 395

Ausubel, D. P., 123

B

Bachem, A., 196, 206

Baillio, B., 188, 194

Baker, J., 443

Beck, I. L., 250, 271, 333

Becker, W., 149, 168, 175, 197, 206-208, 218, 221-223, 232, 277, 290, 323, 423, 426, 429, 433, 436-438, 440-441, 450

Bellamy, G. T., 439

Bereiter, C., 116, 223, 435-436, 449, 453

Berman, P., 289-290

Bernstein, B., 123

Bersin, A., 442

Bingham, V., 428-429

Bishop, A. J., 295, 305

Block, J. H., 188, 194

Bochner, S., 438

Bodilly, S. J., 442

Brady, P. T., 196-197, 206

Brigham, T. A., 437

Brison, D. W., 56, 435-436

Brophy, J. E., 277, 290

Brown-Arbogast, A., 432

Bruner, E. C., 190, 223, 423-425, 433, 438

Bunderson, C. V., 188, 194

C

Carnine, D., 168, 179, 186, 188, 219, 275, 277, 288, 290-291, 407, 411, 429-431, 433, 437-440, 443, 454

Carnine, L., 423, 426, 433

Cerva, T. R., 396

Chall, J., 250, 271

Chard, D., 441

Clark, D. L., 289-290, 454

Close, D., 178, 182-183, 186, 439, 454

Coleman, J., 380, 382, 389, 395

Coles, G., 305

Colvin, G., 178, 181-182, 186, 433, 438-439, 442, 454

Concillo, P., 428

Crane, G. W., 147, 164

Crawford, D., 442

Cronin, D. P., 219-220, 223, 290

Csapo, M., 436

Cuddy, L. L., 197, 206

D

Davis, G., 283, 289-291, 429, 432-433

Davis, K., 425, 432-433

Derman, L., 56

Deutsch, M., 123

Dills, C. R., 441

Dixon, R., 431-432

E

Edmonds, R., 289-290

Eisele, J., 426

Engelmann, K., 442

Engelmann, O., 424, 427-428, 430-431

Engelmann, T., 146, 433, 435

Englert, C. S., 277, 290

F

Fabre, T., 277, 290

Feynman, R., 334

Flamer, G. B., 44, 56, 436

Flanagan, J. L., 148, 164

Ford, M. P., 44, 56, 387, 436

G

Galegher, J. R., 442

Gallagher, J. J., 435

Garza, M., 428

Gates, M., 169, 171

Gault, R. H., 147, 164

Gersten, R., 218-219, 223, 277, 280, 283, 288-291, 411, 439-440

Gill, R., 428

Glang, A., 280, 291

Glass, G., 155, 387-388, 396

Gleason, M., 218, 223, 439

Glennan, T. K., 442

Granzin, A., 58, 70-71, 197, 206, 437-438, 454

Green, D. R., 44, 56

Green, W., 283, 289-291, 436

Grossen, B., 425, 432

Guelke, R. W., 148, 164

H

Haddox, P., 426, 433, 438

Halle, M., 148, 165

Halpern, A., 182, 186

Hanner, S., 271, 423-427, 439

Hart, B., 385, 396

Hechinger, F. M., 116, 435

Heinz, J. M., 148, 165

Heiry, T., 218, 223

Hellmuth, J., 223, 436

Hirsh, J. D., 331

Hofmeister, A., 188, 439-440, 454

Honig, B., 400-401

House, E. R., 338, 387-388, 396, 440

Huberman, A. M., 289, 291

Hughes, G. W., 148, 165
Hughes, M., 209
Huyssen, R. M. J., 148, 164

J
Jensen, J., 427
Johnson, G., 426, 433
Johnston, D., 428
Joyce, B., 280, 291

K
Kameenui, E. J., 440-441
Kamii, C., 49, 56
Kaplan, A., 350
Karoly, P., 290, 438
Keating, T., 218, 223
Kelly, B., 430-431, 439
Kennedy, M., 440
Kerr, K. A., 442
Kestel, D., 12, 435
Kirk, S. A., 116
Klass, G., 389-390, 396
Kneedler, R. D., 437
Kringlebotn, M., 148, 165

L
Levine, L., 147, 165
Lloyd, J. W., 441
Loucks, S., 289, 291
Lundeen, B., 427

M
Maggs, A., 277, 290, 438
Markel, G., 283
McCarthy, M. M., 289-290
McCaslin, E. S., 250, 271
McDowell, F. E., 28, 436

McLaughlin, M. W., 223, 289-290
McLean, L. F., 396
Meier, M., 431
Meyer, L., 426, 433, 439
Mill, J. S., 443, 452
Miller, B., 432
Miller, S., 283, 289-290

N-O
Nadler, R., 369
Nimnict, G., 209
Olen, L., 428
O'Loughlin, 188
Olsen, J. B., 188, 194
Orwell, G., 336
Osborn, J., 116, 424-428, 435, 455
Osborn, S., 424-426

P
Paine, S., 439
Peterson, H., 254
Pettigrew, T., 382, 396
Piaget, J., 3, 9, 43-44, 46, 56, 209, 221, 353, 388, 392, 413, 436, 438, 449
Pickett, J., 71, 148, 165
Plato, 227, 307
Polsgrove, L., 277, 291
Poutt, B., 436

R
Reidford, P. A., 116, 435, 455
Reith, H. L., 277, 291
Rhine, W. R., 438
Risberg, A., 71
Risley, T. R., 385, 396
Romiszowski, A. J., 441

Rosov, R., 145-146, 437, 455

S

St. Pierre, R. G., 396

Schrader, M., 146

Schwarzenegger, A., 392

Schweinhart, L. J., 357-359, 361, 364, 366, 368-369

Seitz-Davis, K., 424-425, 427, 432

Semmel, I., 277, 291

Severson, H., 58, 437, 455

Showers, B., 280, 291

Silbert, J., 425, 428, 430, 432, 456

Singer, G., 178, 180, 182-183, 186, 439, 455

Skillman, L., 146, 437

Slentz, K., 182, 186

Snyder, T., 428

Socrates, 227-228, 307-351, 443, 452

Stallings, J., 396

Stebbins, L. B., 396

Steely, D., 232, 429-430, 432, 438, 440, 442

Steffen, J. J., 290, 438

Stevens, D. J., 165, 439

Stevens, K. N., 142, 148

Stockard, J., 443-444

Sullivan, E. V., 56, 435

Sybouts, W., 439

T

Tallmadge, G. K., 349

Tarver, S., 437

Taylor, V., 182, 186

Thomas, D. R., 208, 222, 382, 408, 411, 433

Tuddenham, R. D., 44, 56

W-Z

Walker, D. F., 396

Ward, J., 438

Weikart, D. P., 357-359, 361, 364, 366, 368-369

Weisberg, H. I., 223

Wells, T., 432

Wheeler, G., 395

White, W. A. T., 218, 223

Whitehurst, G., 394, 396

Wiener, N., 147, 165

Wiesner, D., 147, 165

Wilcox, B., 439

Williams, F., 436

Williams, P., 195-197, 206, 437, 440, 455

Witcher, C., 146

Wittrock, M. C., 290

Woodward, J., 439

Wynn, 196, 206

Youngmayr, L., 146

Zoref, L., 219, 275, 288-289, 291, 424-425